more pressing issue to the world of theological education than it is today. In *Character and Virtue in Theological Education*, Oxenham brings fresh insight to the conversation that honors the past, present, and future of theological education from a global context. And because virtue is both caught and taught, I especially appreciate the manner by which he puts out his insight in this book – that is, not only through thorough research and academic discourse, but also through visions (of what seminaries might become), dreams, and story. My hope is that more would catch on to this vision – for the sake of Christian witness and the global kingdom of God.

David C. Wang, PhD
Editor, *Journal of Psychology and Theology*
Associate Professor, Biola University, La Mirada, California, USA

Dr Marvin Oxenham is ideally suited to be published in this area of character and virtue studies in theological education. He is course leader in a masters course on theological education at London School of Theology and has written course material on the subject. He is supervising PhD students in the area and recently arranged a Europe-wide conference on the subject. This area of study in theological education is relatively new and growing. I saw some of the contents of this book when it was still just a manuscript and consider it a very useful and innovative contribution to the overall literature on theological education.

Graham Cheesman, PhD
Honorary Lecturer, Queens University Belfast, UK
Former Director, Centre for the Study of Theological Education, Belfast, UK

Character and Virtue in Theological Education by Marvin Oxenham is a breath of fresh air in theological education for our generation. The mission and vision of theological education was the formation of those who obeyed the call of the Lord for ministry and mission. This was through academic excellence, character, and spiritual formation. Today we have an overemphasis on academics with only lip service given to character and spiritual formation. This book brings us back to the centrality of character and virtue. Without this re-envisioning we are headed for fossilization. Look at Paul as he deals with Timothy and Titus. In ministry, what matters is who they are in Christ, while the study of God's word is for all followers of Christ. The Bible is the transforming Word and it is the need of the hour if theological education is to impact the church to be salt and light. A must-read for all theological educators if we want to see impact and not status quo.

Ashish Chrispal, PhD
Regional Director for Asia, Overseas Council

I strongly endorse Marvin Oxenham's *Character and Virtue in Theological Education*. Marvin's characteristically creative contribution to this topic flows from his long engagement and deep well of international theological educational research, observation, collaboration and influence. He is an avid conversation leader and effective advocate of learning and dialogue at the institutional, regional, and international levels in theological education.

Ralph E. Enlow, Jr., EdD
President, Association for Biblical Higher Education

In his letter to the Colossians, the Apostle Paul writes that Christians are to be "hidden with Christ in God. When Christ, who is your life, appears, then you also will appear with him in glory" (Col 3:3–4). In the media, marketing, and celebrity-frenzy cultures which affect even theological educators, there is a tendency to jump quickly to the glory part of the Pauline text and not take too seriously the idea of hiddenness. This book displays in creative and engaging ways why we are called back to life in Christ, even that hidden life. Christian virtues are not only fundamental for educators and those who call themselves followers of Christ, they are fundamental for the church and for our participation in God's mission. This is a must-read for educators all around the globe.

Rosalee Velloso Ewell, PhD
Executive Director,
Theological Commission World Evangelical Alliance

At a time when the purpose and focus of theological education is being widely questioned – in both Western and Majority World contexts – there is a need to hear a voice advocating for a neglected aspect of the discourse: an emphasis on character and virtue. Marvin Oxenham, with his roles in, and contribution to, a global network of theological educators, is very well placed to be able to explore this theme in a clear, relevant and nuanced manner.

Allan Harkness, PhD
Founding Dean and Advisory Director,
Asia Graduate School of Theology Alliance

It would appear that the most fundamental goal of a good theological education should be to facilitate our students' growth in Christlike character, virtue and integrity. Yet, oddly, much current evangelical theological education appears to devote minimal attention to character and virtue. I suspect there are multiple reasons for this. Some may see this as solely the task of the local church. Others may balk at the challenges of teaching and assessing affective educational objectives – the more so in an era of online learning. And furthermore, government accreditation rules do not permit much attention to the character of students. Those who fulfil the academic requirements must be passed. Personally, I have long been concerned about the marginalization of character education in much contemporary theological education, as well as about the way that, in earlier Bible colleges, such education was often trivialized as a set of rigid rules. Therefore I find it particularly heartening that a theological educator of the caliber of Dr Marvin Oxenham has written and been published in this area. As other endorsements testify, he has an ideal background for this task and I am confident this book will make a valuable contribution to a critically important cause.

Patricia Harrison, PhD
Graduate Research Supervisor,
London School of Theology, UK, and Asia Graduate School of Theology Alliance
Senior Advisor, Theological Education by Extension

Character and virtue are the highest attributes we expect from a deep and consistent study on theological education, not only for teachers and students but extended to our local church and our vast circle of influence. Dr Marvin Oxenham, in a brilliant and biblically based way, describes the means and conditions by which we will achieve this goal – a commitment to the Word and a humble heart.

Marcio Matta
President, Associação Evangélica de Educação Teológica na América Latina

Today in evangelical circles, a lack of an integrated focus on character transformation may be because of the spiritual impatience in the long journey of transformation, a tendency made worse by the pressures of a culture of relentless hyperactivity. This activist impulse, when blended with our culture's thoroughgoing pragmatism, can devolve into a handful of pre-packaged simple steps to spiritual success. Yet, the preparation of religious leadership is particularly concerned with meaning, purpose and identity. This novel on character and virtue is a useful resource for theological educators as they reflect on the central place of moral formation in preparing authentic leaders.

Marilyn Naidoo, DTh
Professor, Practical Theology,
University of South Africa, Pretoria, South Africa

Emphasis on character development has been a "missing person" in evangelical theological education. Recent efforts to balance cognitive learning outcomes with an emphasis on ministry competency development have been a necessary corrective, but ancient education's striving for imbricating virtues and character into learning have now become conspicuous by their absence. Dr Marvin Oxenham noticed this and has begun leading an effort to re-integrate character education into our evangelical theological curricula. His longstanding experience in quality assurance and evaluation in theological schools, in addition to the more recent emphasis of his doctoral studies, have enabled him to bring character education into the spotlight. This emphasis constitutes yet another necessary balancing factor in our efforts to train men and women for ministry vocations across the world.

Paul Sanders, PhD
Director Emeritus,
International Council for Evangelical Theological Education

The issue of character and virtue education has become increasingly pressing in the contemporary world. This is seen starkly in the increased emphasis on character and ethical decision-making in accreditation standards across the world. In theological education the issue is of prime importance as character and virtue are make-or-break in the success of those seeking to serve others. With his strong background in the classics, in theological reflection, and in contemporary higher education, Marvin Oxenham is ideally placed to address the topic of character and virtue in creative and meaningful ways.

Perry Shaw, EdD
Professor of Education,
Arab Baptist Theological Seminary, Beirut, Lebanon
Author, *Transforming Theological Education*

Public perception and trust towards religion and religious leadership has been waning for many decades, shaped at least in part by the unfolding of stories of sexual misconduct, abuse of minors, and the failure to report such abuses. Indeed, in many contexts around the world, the future of religion as a viable social institution is at risk due to significant (and now increasingly public) failures in character and virtue on the part of its leadership. There has never been a time when the cultivation of character and virtue has been a

ICETE Series

Character and Virtue in Theological Education

Character and Virtue in Theological Education

An Academic Epistolary Novel

Marvin Oxenham

© 2019 Marvin Oxenham

Published 2019 by Langham Global Library
An imprint of Langham Publishing

www.langhampublishing.org

Langham Publishing and its imprints are a ministry of Langham Partnership

Langham Partnership
PO Box 296, Carlisle, Cumbria, CA3 9WZ, UK
www.langham.org

ISBNs:
978-1-78368-697-1 Print
978-1-78368-698-8 ePub
978-1-78368-700-8 PDF

Marvin Oxenham has asserted his right under the Copyright, Designs and Patents Act, 1988 to be identified as the Author of this work.

All rights reserved. No part of this publication may be reproduced, stored in a retrieval system or transmitted, in any form or by any means, electronic, mechanical, photocopying, recording or otherwise, without the prior written permission of the publisher or the Copyright Licensing Agency.

Requests to reuse content from Langham Publishing are processed through PLSclear. Please visit www.plsclear.com to complete your request.

Scriptures taken from the Holy Bible, New International Version®, NIV®. Copyright © 1973, 1978, 1984, 2011 by Biblica, Inc.™ Used by permission of Zondervan.

British Library Cataloguing-in-Publication Data
A catalogue record for this book is available from the British Library

ISBN: 978-178368-697-1

Cover & Book Design: projectluz.com

Artwork featured on cover is "David with the Head of Goliath" by Caravaggio. Original artwork found in the Galleria Borghese. The reproduction used here is in the Public Domain, uploaded to Wikimedia Commons by Masur, 2011.

Langham Partnership actively supports theological dialogue and an author's right to publish but does not necessarily endorse the views and opinions set forth here or in works referenced within this publication, nor can we guarantee technical and grammatical correctness. Langham Partnership does not accept any responsibility or liability to persons or property as a consequence of the reading, use or interpretation of its published content.

CONTENTS

Preface xiii
Introduction 1

Part I: The Vision

1 A New Start 7
2 When Crisis Strikes 9
3 The Vision in a Nutshell 15
4 Three Key Definitions 21
5 Why Not Spiritual Formation 27
6 Character and Virtue in Higher Education 35
7 Character and Virtue in Theological Education 43
8 Virtue for Social Impact 57
9 Virtue for Political Impact 67
10 Discipleship as Virtue 75
11 What Churches Want 83
12 A Fresh Expression 91
13 An Aristotelian Framework? 101
14 Justifying Aristotle 113
15 A Global Heritage 121
16 A Manifesto for Character and Virtue in Theological Education . . . 131
17 Considering Objections 141
18 Whose Character? Which Virtue? 151

Part II: The Tradition

19 A Theology of Character and Virtue – with Method 161
20 Virtue in Ancient Cultures 169
21 Character and Virtue in the Old Testament 175

22	Virtue in the Classical Era	185
23	Virtue in the New Testament	193
24	The Roman Road to Virtue	209
25	Virtue from Cassian to the *Carmina Burana*	217
26	The American Case Study	233
27	Historical Fragments	241
28	Virtue after Postmodernity	251

Part III: The Practice

29	A Question of Practice	261
30	Taxonomies of Virtue	269
31	Virtues Described	279
32	Character as Sought	293
33	Character as Caught	301
34	A Venue for Virtue?	311
35	Virtuous Curriculum	317
36	Character as Taught	327
37	Andragogy of Virtue	337
38	The Assessment Dilemma	351
39	Assuring Quality	363
40	Ten Years Later	371
	Select Bibliography	377
	Index	391

> The virtues of this life are certainly its best and most useful possessions.
> AUGUSTINE

> Good theology is *aretegenic*, productive of virtue.
> GUNTON

> Of those who graduate from seminary, very few fail in ministry because of inability to study, think, teach, or preach – the skills and content we focus on in seminary. Failure in ministry is linked to difficulties in character.
> TENELSHOF

> Virtue, to put it bluntly, is a revolutionary idea in today's world and today's church. We've had enough of pragmatists and self-seeking risk-takers. We need people of character.
> N. T. WRIGHT

> We strongly encourage seminaries, and all those who deliver leadership training programs, to focus more on spiritual and character formation, not only on imparting knowledge or grading performance, and we heartily rejoice in those that already do so.
> CAPE TOWN COMMITMENT

> What constitutes the good for man is a complete human life lived at its best, and the exercise of the virtues is a necessary and central part of such a life.
> MACINTYRE

> In Africa, we have many teachers who possess impressive diplomas, but what we need are models that Christians can imitate.
> FERDINANDO

> An educated but immoral humanity goes backward rather than forward, degenerating.
> COMENIUS

Preface

It was 1020 BC, and the people of Israel were under the domination of the Philistines. They were outnumbered, raided and hiding in caves and cisterns. Their leaders were floundering, and they could not make their own swords. Despite occasional forays of courage and brief seasons of victory, the pressure was relentless and there was continual bitter war. To make things worse, the Philistines brought forth Goliath, who defied the Israelites at Sokoh and incurred further dismay. It was the shepherd David who brought down the giant, refusing to fight with conventional weapons and using Goliath's own sword to cut off his head. In humility and grace, he inaugurated a new season of flourishing for his people.

It was AD 1610, and Michelangelo Merisi, also known as Caravaggio, was on the run after having killed a man in Rome. As part of his plea for mercy to Paul V, he offered a painting of *David and Goliath*. This was probably his last painting, for he died of a fever shortly thereafter on his return voyage to Rome. He had painted this story before, but this time it was different, for he produced an autobiographical work that signalled a deep change in his character. The image of Goliath's head, with its eyes still open and mouth gaping, is, in fact, a self-portrait. This is how Caravaggio saw himself, condemned and hopeless after a life of vice. On the blade of Goliath's sword in David's hand, one can distinguish the inscription "HASOS" which is an acronym of the Augustinian motto *humilitas occidit superbiam*: "humility conquers pride." As Caravaggio's final painting, this was his final message to the world. After a life of vice, virtue has won.

It is AD 2019, and theological education is suffering from Philistine domination. As we face the giants that occupy the land of contemporary education, we often feel outnumbered, forced into conformity and unable to fully deploy our own weapons. We struggle under the predominance of critical thinking, the supremacy of measurement paradigms, the captivity of secular accreditation, the pressures of efficiency, the prioritization of academics, the demands of professional competences and the strains of achievement and ranking. In all this, we strive to keep alive that which is at our heart: the holistic formation of kingdom humans. This book argues that it is time to arm our slings with the stones of virtue and character and reclaim portions of lost territory that are rightfully ours. It is time to revise our tactics and revisit our calling. It is time to inaugurate a new season of flourishing for the church and society as we recover the central place of character and virtue in global theological education.

Introduction

Stories are powerful tools of inspiration, and I have written this book on character and virtue in theological education as an academic epistolary novel. To be clear, I am not a novel writer, so please do not expect great drama, but as you read through this collection of forty short letters, I hope that your imagination will be stirred by the honest story of two friends who struggle with their challenges and dreams as theological educators. Do not let the nimbler style mislead you, however, for this is also a substantial piece of academic research, as can be seen in the nearly 1,200 references. Although practitioners are my primary audience, I have also written for scholars, postgraduate students and doctoral researchers, and the extensive bibliography at the end of the book is my main gift to them.

In terms of content, the letters have been organized into three sets. The first set presents a vision of character and virtue in theological education. Here you will explore some of the trends related to character and virtue education in society, church, higher education and theological education. You will also understand some key definitions, engage with some foreseeable objections and be presented with a theoretical framework that is rooted in Aristotelian thought and virtue ethics.

The second set of letters works out a theology of character and virtue education through the use of historical and biblical sources. The historical quest covers premodernity, modernity and postmodernity and the biblical quest focuses on both the Old and New Testaments, with a special feature on the letter to the Romans. The purpose of this section is to anchor the educational practices related to character and virtue within a theological framework.

The final set of letters deals with practice. Here, a number of functional issues are dealt with, such as how to achieve virtue literacy, how to deal with organizational and strategic practicalities (character being *sought*), the role of community (character as being *caught*), the kind of curriculum and andragogy that should be in place (character as *taught*) and some of the specific challenges of assessment, certification and quality assurance. These letters are very down-to-earth and provide tangible instructions for any theological school that wishes to place character and virtue education at its core.

The letters have been written in sequence and each set is important for the next. The initial set tells us what we are talking about and why it is important, the second tells us of where it all comes from, and the third set tells us what we might do about it in practice. I encourage the visionary readers, who might be tempted to read just the first part, to consider the other two parts. The same goes for the theologians and historians, who may be attracted by the second part. But I think that the greatest temptation will be for the practitioners, who may want to skip directly to the final chapters to see "how to do" character and virtue education. My plea is that you will avoid this shortcut and give due consideration to the theoretical foundations that will cement your practice.

There are many topics covered in the letters and their tone will vary accordingly. Some will expand on familiar themes such as discipleship or deal with practical suggestions for learning and teaching. These topics can be easily digested and implemented. Other topics will be more philosophical and explore underlying frameworks, political nuances or the objections to character and virtue education. The issues involved in character and virtue education are, in fact, complex, and call for various levels of scholarly engagement. As we speak of character formation, we will also touch on some huge theological and ethical debates, such as the discussions around moral theology, the interplay between sanctification and the will, or the growing field of virtue ethics. The breadth of topics has meant that I have not been able to dig into many issues as deeply as they deserve. I have chosen to acknowledge them but to remain focused on the educational issues. The footnotes will be useful here in pointing to further research.

I am also aware that theological educators will tend to read this book through the lens of their particular specialism. Sadly, this means that no one will be fully content. For systematic theologians, my work will not be theological enough. For biblical scholars, it will not be biblical enough. For theological philosophers, it will not be philosophical enough. For missiologists, it will not be global enough. For church historians, it will not be historical enough. For practitioners, it will not be practical enough. Experts in Augustine will be appalled that so little has been said about him. Aquinas scholars will be offended that more space has not been afforded to the *Summa*. Lutherans will feel that Luther's dissent over Aristotle should have set the tone of the book. Asian colleagues will wish for more critical engagement with Confucius, and Latin American friends will wonder why Freire is barely mentioned. Bonhoeffer lovers will want an entire chapter on *Discipleship*, and Hauerwas fans will be disappointed that, though his critiques are regularly acknowledged, he is never engaged with systematically. I apologize for all this in advance. I have dreaded the closing publication deadline, for there is no day that passes when I do not come across one more resource and one more area that I know so little about.

Indeed, I feel like a miner who is sitting at the entrance of a deep shaft and is pointing the way.

If I have one regret, it is that I have not been able to give a broader global scope to my topic. I am Italian, and, although I have considered traditions from other parts of the world, and have imagined my two characters as corresponding between the Minority and Majority worlds, my embeddedness in classical culture is evident. I am convinced that much of what I have written is globally transferrable, but I do wish that I had had more time and space to thoroughly investigate the rich traditions of character and virtue in other cultures. If there are scholars who wish to cooperate in future projects of this kind, do not hesitate to contact me.

A final word about my expectations. I hope that some of our traditional ways of doing theological education will be challenged by what I have written and that those who are already innovating in character and virtue education will be encouraged, inspired and further equipped. In dreaming up the vision that is expressed in these letters, I have purposely gone overboard, and I do not imagine that anyone will actually try to imitate the project of the academy that Siméon ends up realizing. This is a story of fiction and I am not sure that it could actually work out in reality. But it might. If anyone does try such a radical experiment, I would love to hear from you and learn from you.

Part I

The Vision

1

A New Start

What wonderful news, Siméon! You are greatly honoured and rightly petrified by the vastness of what is being asked of you. I was saddened to hear of the closure of the school, because it was the only place where theological education was taking place in your region. To hear, however, that the faith communities have now met across denominations, focused on education, and agreed on a new start is a good sign. Actually, as I look at the breadth of the mandate that you have been given, I can see a prophetic opportunity that, if used well, can provide inspiration to theological educators in many parts of the world. You have been handed a blank sheet and you can rethink things from the core. And this is not an opportunity given to many.

Your situation is unique, but at the same time it is commonplace. We know that Christian theological education has been critically looking at itself for the last century or so. Some attribute the beginning of the debate to the American theologian Niebuhr, who critiqued theological education for being outdated in terms of contemporary thought and religious temper.[1] And you may also recall Farley, who picked this up thirty years later and made the shaking claim that theological education was fragmented and pursuing distorted professional and academic traditions. These rips in the fabric have slowly expanded and they seem to have reached your region. The ashes on which you are called to build are intellectual and professional ashes. They are, to use the "Kelsey model" that we have often discussed, Berlin ashes.[2] Ashes of a school that for over thirty years had excelled in academic teaching and research and in the professional training of ministers.

As you move forward, you've sought me out as a kindred mind. In this first letter, let me simply encourage you. There is a multitude of theological

---

1. Niebuhr, *Purpose of the Church and Its Ministry*.
2. Kelsey, *Between Athens and Berlin*.

educators who are struggling with these same issues. From some of the textbooks on my shelves, it is evident that there is a growing conversation shared by Catholics, Protestants, Evangelicals and Orthodox on the nature and purpose of theological education (you will recall our participation in those remarkable consultations in Germany and Crete). We are becoming more self-reflective and, while we may not all fully subscribe to the same catalogue of ailments, we do admit to a degree of dereliction of duty.[3]

Much of this you already know, for we have studied it together over the years. Now it is time to dream of a new model of theological education that places character and virtue at the centre. By God's grace, this is what we will do.

May you find company in our loyal friendship as we journey together.

---

3. Gustafson, "Reflections," 19.

2

When Crisis Strikes

Thank you for your detailed diagnosis of what has happened. Understanding the past is important as we consider the future. I found it especially helpful to read more about the history of the school and what led to its closure, and about the relationship of the school with faith communities and the broader society. Allow me to comment on the main points that you have raised.

The Loss of Accreditation

The changes in your government's legislation led to the loss of accreditation, and this decreed the end of the school. But you're right that the school was probably already inevitably declining by the time this happened. The successes in obtaining university status in the previous decade had seemed like a good thing at the time. But, as you've pointed out, the excessive tightening of academic identity ended up being a Philistine captivity. The school was so caught up with observing standards, raising academic profiles and producing compliance documents that it lost the ability to see the bigger picture. As you know, I am in favour of quality assurance and accreditation, but here is a case where standards, policies and procedures have become a straightjacket that have hampered a school from the transformation that might have saved it.

Academic Pride

You mention excessive academic emphasis. We are both scholars, and the phrase "excessive academics" sounds like an oxymoron. How is it possible that there can be too much critical, intelligent study? And yet you are probably right. The drive for excellence in academic standards contributed to slaying the school. As you've pointed out, the professors were publishing in renowned journals. The lectures and academic conferences were well attended and academic ranking was up. But academic excellence had become an idol, and the extreme obsession with propositional truth, critical thought and hermeneutical accuracy had drained the transformational vigour such that no other good was being produced in the lives of graduates. Theology, in brief, was not nourishing holiness.[1]

But there was something else as well. You were on the leadership team there for many years, and you say that something felt terribly wrong. If I may sum it up in one word, it was a feeling of pride. The school had an unhealthy vanity of its status. It arrogantly handled Scripture and tradition.[2] It was a community where pecking orders, competition and tense relationships were commonplace. Its publicity was inflated.[3] Most significantly, pride was perceived in the attitude of the graduates who returned to leadership positions in their churches. They carried with them an air of superiority, even of cynicism, which, together with a disdain for non-academic work, smelled of a rotting corpse. Failure in the virtue of humility fabricated the feet of clay that caused the fall.[4]

Disconnection from Faith Communities

The complex relationship between faith communities and theological schools has been long discussed. We've argued many times whether the academy exists to prophetically lead the church or whether the church should provide the direction for the theological academy. I think we agree that the academy can *both* serve the church *and* be an instrument of change and reform. What you are describing, however, is the tragedy of a theological school that became self-referential and completely lost the confidence of the faith communities. The highly educated, professionalized clergy that the school produced did not match the real needs of the communities it claimed to serve. Graduates were seen as "spiritually cold," as having "lost the fire" and as being overly

---

1. "The more a man is educated, whether in theology or in secular science, the holier he needs to be if he would be saved" (quoted in W. Ward, *Life of John Henry Cardinal Newman*, Vol. 1 [London, 1912], 516). According to Gunton, "Good theology is *aretegenic*, productive of virtue" (Gunton, "Church as a School of Virtue?," 223).

2. "We theologians have sought to recast our discipline so as to acquire a legitimate home in the great edifice of science, but instead we have 'dug a hole and pitched [ourselves] to its bottom'" (Volf, 4).

3. "Are we not much too prone to be proud of our achievements in theological seminary life? Is it not true that sometimes our promotional effort suggests that we are thanking God that we are not as other schools are?" (Taylor, "Sources of Renewal," 320).

4. "The failure of organizations is the failure of moral virtues" (Singh and Botha, in Stückelberger, *Global Ethics*, 339).

polished and critical. Their preaching and teaching was lofty and irrelevant, and anecdotes of graduates who discussed authorship theories with new converts were sadly commonplace.

Your point about misaligned expectations is well stated. Whereas the academy was training graduates to be scholars and professional ministers who would be ordained in a traditional church setting, many faith communities were looking for lay leaders who could creatively steer new forms of church in a changing society. In addition, graduates were simply not fit for ministry,[5] and the vast amount of learning that was meticulously administered was seen as mostly irrelevant by the faith communities. The school might have been saved if it had recognized that, perhaps, less might have been more.

Societal Disconnection

Interdisciplinary programmes might also have been a saving factor, if only they had been implemented. As it was, theology was the only discipline in the school, and there was no dialogue with other "secular" disciplines. The professors were trained theologians who focused on their specific academic careers and had little or no involvement in society. The demands of publication robbed their schedules of other pursuits and of any form of involvement in politics, volunteering, social service or even discipleship and church life. Most of them did not have genuine friends outside the walls of their theological community. And this made the school an island of theological irrelevance.[6]

In the eyes of society, it was an odd place where orthodoxy was established around issues that no one cared about and that made little difference anyway. The graduate employment statistics indicated that only 2 percent pursued a career in local society, and that over 65 percent of those graduating wanted to progress in academic theology. It seems that the study of theology had become an ingrown world of its own. The deep social unrest and the street demonstrations that took place in your country during your last term in the

---

5. In 2016 the Francis Shaeffer Institute of Church Leadership Development (FCICLD) surveyed over 8,000 ministers and produced the *Statistics on Pastors*. According to this research, 53 percent of pastors claim that seminary does not adequately prepare them for ministry. "Most seminary courses are seen as irrelevant to the type of ministry the students, who are in the ministry now, face. Many good, conservative seminaries are graduating aspiring Christian ministers and leaders who have little faith or practical tools on how to pastor and lead" (Krekcir, *Statistics on Pastors*, 6). Likewise, research in the UK reveals that 41 percent of church leaders consider their theological education "too detached from the church and the world and too theoretical" (Kinnaman and Hempell, "Perceptions," 24).

6. In listing the external and internal crises of theology, Volf represents theologians today as stuttering to reply to the basic question: "What does theology have to offer?" (Volf, 45).

school were a golden chance to speak with theological relevance into a badly torn society. But sadly, you seemed to be the only one who saw this, and your voice was ignored.

Responding to Change

The final point you've raised about responding to change is perhaps the most significant, as it encapsulates several problems. I guess the simplest way of saying this is that, as the world in your region changed very quickly, the school stayed the same. Although stability can be a good thing, there are also cases where fossilization can mean death.[7]

What exactly changed? The school was founded at the beginning of the twentieth century in a time when students were looking for full-time, residential training as a passport into adult life and professional ministry. Those were times when theological resources were relatively scarce, and the library in the school, together with course syllabi and the taught courses, represented one of the few ways in your region to access any kind of theological knowledge. Churches were also sending students to "trustworthy" places that had traditional curricula that would lead to degree certification and ordination. The university at the time was also in the throes of the scientific revolution, and theology was struggling to establish itself as a respectable academic discipline. All this contributed to the birth of this institution and to the design of programmes that were fit for purpose in those times.

But those times have changed. Students have changed, and many now come to theological training as adults, either looking to enhance their lay vocations or simply desiring personal development. Information technology has also radically changed, and in a digital age, students are no longer looking to educational institutions as the sole repositories of knowledge. Churches also are no longer the same. They work more closely together with each other and interdenominational boundaries are less sharp, meaning that there is less interest in perpetuating particular intellectual or theological traditions. Faith communities are increasingly led by teams of lay leaders, rather than by one main pastor or priest, and this means that theological training is needed at

---

7. "Educational stability is a great thing, but on its own it may not be a good sign . . . educational ideals are often extremely stable in the epoch of senile conservatism which marks the end of a civilization . . . If education is a vital response to the deep changes of society, it needs to respond with great courage and innovation in proportion to the changes in place. As Dewey stated: 'It is radical conditions which have changed, and only an equally radical change in education suffices'" (Dill, "Challenge of Contemporary Moral Education," 223).

different levels and not just for ordinands. Theology students will normally have jobs, families and ministries, and theological schools need to make room for new delivery arrangements, for lifelong learning patterns and for vocational education training opportunities.

Postmodernity has also meant that higher education is embracing diversity, questioning rationality, exploring interconnected knowledge and renewing its interest in linking humanities and the scientific disciplines. This cultural shift makes it difficult for the new generations to relate to the rigid, rational approach to the study of theology that has characterized a previous generation of scholars, among whom are many of their teachers and the authors of their textbooks. Existential forces have also increased the awareness of the importance of formation in the lives of adult students, which is mismatched by the relegation of formation to the voluntary and extra-curricular realm.

The school should have done more research into these trends. But it did not, and it probably never fully engaged with the fact that theological education is called to continually revise its mission and adapt to changing contexts. The school did not ask the hard questions about the mutable nature and purpose of theological education and, in so doing, it missed the opportunity to remodel its *missio Dei*.

As you say, the closure of the school was a gradual unravelling. There was disconnection at multiple layers, failure to adapt to change, reduction in numbers and, finally, the forfeit of its educational status and financial viability.

—

This has turned out to be a rather dismal letter, so thank you for your final words on the goodness of your colleagues and of the students with whom you've journeyed. There are indeed many good people involved in this turn of events and God is at work in their lives. But there is no denying that something has gone wrong. You now have a chance for a new start, and I believe that an emphasis on character and virtue represents a prophetic opportunity for theological education in your region.

May the accuracy of our analysis not infect our souls with the same pride that we condemn.

3

The Vision in a Nutshell

You are impatient, my dear Siméon, and are asking me to share my conclusions before I have even drafted my preambles! But you are right. All good articles begin with an abstract, and I am not in the business of writing a suspense novel. I will burn my fire and reveal my hand, summarizing my conclusions and outlining what I see as a way forward for theological education in your region.

A Radical Aim

My main thesis is that Christian theological education should reclaim character and virtue education. Although it should not be sought to the exclusion of the traditional aims of academic engagement, professional training and spiritual formation, it should be redeemed to a place of prominence.

You will note that I am referring to the so-called "four-fold model" of theological education that includes academics, ministerial training, spiritual formation and character education.[1] I argue that, although all these aspects are important, the one that receives less explicit attention and intentional work is character education. And yet, if we imagine four horses pulling the chariot of theological education, the horse of character and virtue should be a winning champion. The vision I am setting forth is not purely cosmetic. To the contrary, it reaffirms that character and virtue are central to theological education and calls us to radically re-envision our educational schemes. That is why your situation is most promising, for you have been given a fresh start.

You will ask me, what then are the aims of this new educational vision? We know how to design and deliver theology programmes whose learning

---

1. An example of the four-fold model is found in *Pastores Dabo Vobis* which lays out four areas of priestly formation: human formation, spiritual formation, intellectual formation and pastoral formation (John Paul II, *Pastores Dabo Vobis*, 26–36).

outcomes relate to knowledge, understanding and competences, but what does this look like when it comes to character and virtue? How do we design outcomes that relate to virtue in the lives of individuals? What kind of learning will transform character? How can we structure education so that *being* rises to a place of prominence alongside *doing* and *knowing*? These questions, and more, will be the object of our correspondence.

What Is Needed Most?

I am an academic, and I recognize the value of academic theology. My observation, however, is that the problems of society and faith communities are not usually in direct connection to poor theology. Nor are the main troubles related to skills and competences. Important as academic knowledge and ministry competences may be, it seems to me that what really counts is character. In the letters that follow, I will argue that crises in leadership, democracy, morality, legality, fraternity, inequality and corruption are calling for the same thing: citizens and leaders of virtue. The roots of these crises are found in the vices of selfishness, pride, violence and envy, and they will be addressed by the virtues of women and men of justice, generosity, temperance and courage. If asked to choose between a leader, citizen, colleague, spouse or neighbour who is academically sharp and tremendously competent or one who is well formed in her or his character, most would choose the latter. Surely, this is true in ministry, and we've seen the havoc generated by the untamed character of many theology graduates. Should this not shape our priorities in theological education as we design our graduate profiles?

Beyond these practical considerations, however, we do well to also think through the lens of our *missio Dei*, and consider how character and virtue education can bring glory to God and fulfil his purposes. I have thought of three such purposes.

God Wishes to Bless Students

The first group who will be blessed by focusing on character and virtue are students. As these individuals who pursue a vocation to study theology are formed in character and virtue, they will be the first to benefit.[2] They will

---

2. In the UK, 72 percent of prospective students indicated that personal development was the main reason for pursuing theological education; this was followed by 57 percent ministerial training and 36 percent academic training (Kinnaman and Hempel, "Perceptions," 26). This is also true in secular studies where students are "interested in topics that are pressing to them,

benefit in becoming better people, better spouses, better parents, better citizens, better friends and better members of a community. Surely, this fulfils God's purposes. In my next letters, I will argue that we are created for virtue and that we flourish as we are educated for virtuous action.[3] Character and virtue education will contribute to such flourishing.

I will also argue that to be virtuous is to be happy and, although this should not be mistaken for the ultimate goal in the Christian life, it certainly should influence our *missio Dei*.[4] Today's generations are suffering the effects of excessive individualization.[5] They are plagued by the anxiety that comes with liberty[6] and feel the weight of disempowerment that accompanies the lack of universal values.[7] As they are liberated from vice and are formed in virtue, they will benefit from happiness that comes with the freedom to do what is right, to feel what is noble and to be what is good. This is not moral indoctrination, but a vision of "liberal" education that frees us to be what we are meant to be.[8]

Character and virtue education also readdresses a distorted view of leadership that we perpetuate through our theological education programmes. For reasons I will not examine here, we have assumed that the *missio Dei* of theological education is to train leaders.[9] But many of our students will never

---

like how happiness can be found, the true nature of love and friendship, the purpose of the good life" (Pavela, "Renewed Focus," 735).

3. "Education . . . is the means by which humans are trained to be able to properly evaluate diverse situations and act in such a way as to benefit themselves and their society. This can be understood as being educated in virtuous action" (Spears and Loomis, *Education for Human Flourishing*, 42).

4. "There is something deeply wrong with any attempt to give an account of the moral life that avoids happiness . . . it may be that happiness is wrongly thought to be the end of moral life, but it is quite another matter to think it has no relevance to living well" (Hauerwas, "Happiness," 6).

5. "There is . . . a nasty fly of impotence in the tasty ointment of freedom cooked in the cauldron of individualization" (Bauman, *Liquid Modernity*, 35).

6. Oxenham, *Liquid Modernity*, 176–182.

7. "My generation [student voice] grew up into a world in which there has been no universal version of a 'good' . . . instead we have been taught that even thinking these terms must necessarily lead to the imposition of someone's hegemony over someone else, and that there's nothing but particularistic identities shattering all universals. I don't think you realize how disempowering this has become" (Pavela, "Renewed Focus," 734).

8. "Christian ethics can unveil the wisdom of biblical virtues without pushing it into legalism" (Stückelberger, "Integrity," 326).

9. The leadership training paradigm is historically linked to Schleiermacher's justification of theological education as the production of leadership necessary for "the social ordering and survival of a specific religious community" (Farley, *Theologia*, 86–87). This clerical paradigm leads to the professionalization of learning. However, it was not always this way, and Farley reports that there have been periods of pious learning, specialized learning and a return, today, to formational learning (Farley, 12).

be leaders. Despite a growing assumption of many discipleship programmes, we are not all called to be leaders. Placing character and virtue at the core of theological education makes our mission universal, for everyone is called to be a person of virtue, regardless of their calling or position in ministry.

God Wishes to Bless Faith Communities

The second group that will benefit from a greater emphasis on character and virtue education are the faith communities. You will notice, Siméon, that I have chosen the term "faith communities" instead of "churches" to reflect a broader spectrum of traditions and to avoid some of the structural connotations that have determined ecclesial divisions. Faith communities benefit from an emphasis on character and virtue in many ways. The most obvious way is through receiving theology graduates who have been shaped in character.

As I write, I'm thinking of our friends with whom we have stood in difficult church situations in recent years. Thiago in Argentina. Woo-jin in Korea. Ivan and Yulia in Ukraine. Or Abioye, with whom I am corresponding now as he manages the disastrous split in his African denomination. Indeed, we might even recall your own sad situation seven years ago that nearly ended your own ministry. What were the causes of breakdown and failure in these communities? Clearly, they had very little to do with poor theological preparation or with inadequate skills, but, in every case, the core problems were related to character. Faith communities suffer because of distrust and irascibility. They split because of pride. They get flogged by the media because of lust and greed. On the other hand, they flourish because of humility, chastity, temperance, generosity and passion.

The *missio Dei* of theological education is to contribute graduates who will bless their faith communities by their character, by their virtuous example and by their commitment to disciple others in character.

God Wishes to Bless Society

There is a final group that will benefit from the education of character and virtue, and that is society. This is an important point and we will dialogue further on it. Here I simply wish to state that a programme of theological education can bless society by producing virtuous citizens. This can bring nothing but good. More virtue in society will strengthen the social bonds of solidarity. It will reduce crime rates and delinquency. It will combat corruption and increase productivity. It will increase justice and reduce the need for punishment. It will improve democracy and contribute to better laws and better politicians.

Theological education is strategically positioned across the planet to provide a robust injection of virtuous citizens into society. Theological education can bring change and make a difference. This is not only a good in itself but it can be a powerful apologetic for the relevance of the Christian faith.

—

There you have my vision in a nutshell. I trust that you will understand that, in comparing academic and ministry training with character and virtue education, I am not setting up a false dichotomy. I am persuaded that the different foci of theological education are complementary and are not in competition. Good character and virtue education cannot happen without solid academic work and practical training. I will say even more: character and virtue arise *from* good theology, so academic work is of the outmost importance. My point in this letter is that knowledge and competence that do not operate holistically within formational objectives are missing the main point of theological education.

Clearly, such a brief statement about so much cannot but raise many questions. I eagerly wait to hear from you. May you be granted a courageous heart as you face uncharted waters.

4

Three Key Definitions

I have received your questions and they are sharp, as I expected. You are clearly preparing to justify your case with your stakeholders, and I pray that their minds will be open. It is great to hear that you are going on a trip to observe a number of theological schools in different parts of the world. I look forward to reading your report, especially as it relates to our growing vision of character and virtue education. You have asked me to be more precise about what I mean by "theological education," "character and virtue education" and "virtue." And I am happy to share my initial research on these terms with you.

What Is Theological Education?

At first, I was surprised that you asked me to define theological education. It seems such an obvious thing, but, on further reflection, the answers are far from granted. The classical definition is that theological education is the tertiary study of theology for vocational or academic purposes within an institutional context and leading to degree certification. In brief, it is education in the discipline of theology at university level. One would also normally specify that theological education is distinct from religious studies: the former being rooted within theological traditions and the latter being generally characterized by interdisciplinary study of religions and of religion itself.

But here all simplification ends, for the definition of theological education greatly depends on the theological persuasion of those who are defining it. As we think of Christian theological education, we need to distinguish between mainline Protestant, Evangelical, Roman Catholic and Eastern Orthodox traditions, each of which has a distinct vision of theological education.[1] Theology counts, and different convictions in the areas of ecclesiology,

---

1. Gustafson, "Reflections," 21.

missiology and Christology will have a deep impact on how the nature and purpose of theological education are defined. I realize that, for you, this issue is particularly forceful, because you have been commissioned by a wide range of faith traditions to develop a common model in your region. Given your circumstances, a first step might be to understand how different traditions relate to thinking of theological education in terms of character and virtue education. I have made a note of this and will write a letter later on to explore it further.

But let me come back to defining theological education. As I look at my starting definition, I wonder if, in light of what I wrote in my previous letter, it is really fitting at all. As we consider the failure of theological education in your region, could it not be that the very definition of traditional theological education is problematic? If, for example, faith communities are tired of polished academic graduates and are looking for lay leaders, why should theological education be restricted to "tertiary level"? Is it really even necessary to produce "degrees"? Furthermore, if students are mobile and are looking to be trained in a quick-paced society, why do we need to continue to operate in traditional "institutional" contexts? Might we not break down this church–academy dichotomy and explore shared educational spaces? And again, if the "Berlin" model is too limited in its "academic and vocational purposes," should we not investigate other purposes?

Dear Siméon, the more I write, the more I realize that I have more questions than answers. I probably do not have a comprehensive definition of theological education, and I am starting to wonder if we should even be looking for one.

What Is Character and Virtue Education?

Your second question is central to our correspondence. In defining character and virtue education, I hope to do better than in my previous answer, for I have done enough research to provide a good initial approximation of what I am talking about. In fact, I have a rather clear object in mind when I speak of "character and virtue education" and I am carefully using language that latches onto a specific tradition.

Although it might have been sufficient to use the phrase "character education," I have chosen to add the term "virtue" to make the connection between character and virtue explicit and to dispel confusion over some other uses of the term. The term "character," in fact, can be found in association with many things, such as personality traits, leadership styles and learning styles. I mean none of these. We will not be talking about education that deals with being introverted or extroverted or with being a visual or an auditory learner. These are good things, but they do not have moral weight, for there is no morality attached to being a lateral thinker or to being creative rather than conservative. When, instead, we speak of character and virtue, we are talking about universal categories that merit praise or blame, such as being cowardly, unfair or intemperate.[2] When I use the term "character and virtue education," therefore, I am explicitly linking character to that which is morally valuable.

I think we can agree that, in the context of Christian theology, "there is no escaping the concept of virtue."[3] Christianity is a religion of redemption from evil to good, and a life of virtue tallies with God's creational intent. If this is true, theological education should include the moral formation of students and we should use terminology of "character and virtue education" to identify outcomes in theological education that go beyond the realms of cognition, competence and the spirit, to include the moral disposition of the individual.

One common error, which has turned many people off the subject, is the association of character and virtue with rules and prescription.[4] One friend wrote to me about growing up force-fed character and virtue by a patriotic, dutiful and mindlessly loyal father. This did not have a positive impact on him, and, to this day, he still feels a sense of discomfort every time character and virtue are mentioned. When hearing about my research, another friend candidly asked me if I was writing to serve the Catholic preoccupation with celibacy and sexual rules in the seminary or if I was going to revive rules that specified cold showers, twenty-five minutes of quiet time and silence at meals while sitting only with those of your own gender. These approaches were popular in the past and functioned as socialization devices. British and American educational efforts in the 1800s were, in part, conceived to raise up generations of gentlemen who, thanks to their theological education, would not cut their fingernails, pick their teeth, comb their hair or spit in public.[5] I will not assess these approaches here, nor am I against rules or appropriate manners, but they are not what character and virtue education is about.

---

2. Whereas a personality-centred viewpoint elicits understanding, a character-centred viewpoint considers the individual "as an agent who can be held responsible for his actions and for the traits in question" (Vasalou, "Educating Virtue," 74).

3. Gunton, "Church as a School of Virtue?," 211.

4. Socrates himself was not satisfied simply with a long list of virtuous acts in his search for virtue (Plato, *Meno* 72d, quoted in Spears and Loomis, *Education for Human Flourishing*, 60).

5. Neuhaus, *Theological Education*, 61.

Character education is more than adherence to rules.[6] We are not aiming at mere external conformity to moral rules but at a deep, permanent and informed transformation of character.

Much more of this in our next letters.

What Is Virtue?

You now ask me to define virtue. Just like Socrates, you desire "to seek out . . . what virtue is."[7] This may be the most difficult question to answer briefly and I will select only a few basic aspects. In doing so, I will be dipping into the Aristotelian tradition of which I will give a thorough treatment later on. Here is a good starting definition that I would like to unpack:

> Virtues constitute stable dispositional clusters concerned with praiseworthy functioning in a number of significant and distinctive spheres of human life.[8]

Notice, first of all, that the virtues have to do with "praiseworthy functioning." It is difficult to identify what virtues are, but we gain a clearer vision when we describe how they function. I like to think of virtues as being like electrons. They are too small to be seen, but we know that they exist by the traces they leave and the effects they produce. So it is with the virtues. Virtue is seen in how we function emotionally, in how our reason elaborates, in what we desire, in how our will determines courses of action, in how our perception picks up situations and in how others perceive us.[9] This praiseworthiness assumes a standard of good and evil and, when it is seen, virtue is immediately recognized as that which is appropriate.

Virtues are also "dispositions," which means that they dispose our person to function in a certain way. Others have successfully spoken of virtues as traits or as strengths which make us what we are. Once a particular virtue has become a part of our character, it functions across our being, making us do, feel, think, want, perceive and be perceived in ways that are praiseworthy.

---

6. "Character – the transforming, shaping, and marking of a life and its habits – will generate the sort of behaviour that rules might have pointed toward but which a 'rule keeping' mentality can never achieve" (Wright, *After You Believe*, 7). See more about the interplay between rules and character in Wright, 43–49.

7. Plato, *Meno* 81e.

8. Arthur et al., *Teaching*, 28.

9. Arthur et al., 28.

Aristotle further claims that these dispositions are "settled," meaning that, once they are part of our character, it becomes natural to perform virtuous actions.[10]

Notice that the definition speaks about "clusters" of virtues. We will describe individual virtues later on, but here let me note that virtues have been classified and organized in different ways. We have, for example, the cardinal virtues of prudence, justice, fortitude and temperance. We have the Christian virtues of faith, hope and love. We also have moral virtues like kindness, compassion and generosity, civic virtues like decency, loyalty and diligence, and intellectual virtues like attentiveness, open-mindedness and curiosity. We then have some virtues which are foundational, such as prudence, constancy and love, and specific lists of virtues and vices like the seven capital vices of pride, envy, wrath, sloth/acedia, avarice, gluttony and lust and the corresponding seven capital virtues of humility, kindness, abstinence, chastity, patience, liberality and diligence. None of these lists is exhaustive and there is overlap between them, but these clusters help us see that the virtues function in a number of "significant and distinctive spheres" of human life. They are both private and public. They have to do with the mind and with moral action. They have to do with material and immaterial goods. They can be God-related, self-related, neighbour-related or object-related and they are always interrelated.[11]

And finally, virtues are "stable" dispositions. Aristotle famously said that "one swallow does not make spring,"[12] meaning that one instance of virtue does not constitute a virtuous character.[13] A greedy person can occasionally give alms, but that does not make the person generous, any more than an occasional act of goodness will make a tyrant merciful. In order for virtue to exist in an individual, it must be a relatively enduring component of character.[14] Thankfully, the opposite is also true as one act of vice does not destroy a virtuous character. Such departures are incidental, and those who are generous remain virtuous even if they occasionally do not help those who are in need.

---

10. For Aristotle, "Excellence is . . . the complete absence of contrary passions to the point where acting other than virtuously becomes a kind of impossibility . . . The truly virtuous person is a friend to 'himself'" (Mahn, "Kierkegaard after Hauerwas," 175).

11. Hauerwas reminds us that "all the virtues are interrelated. So, for example, we can't be appropriately courageous if we lack kindness" (Hauerwas, *Letters to a Godson*, loc. 991).

12. Aristotle, *Nicomachean Ethics* 1, 7.

13. "Character of the relevant kind can only be exhibited in a succession of incidents and the succession itself must exhibit certain patterns" (MacIntyre, *After Virtue*, 125).

14. Aquinas argues that "the moral virtues are the enduring traits of character that persons must possess if they are to be able to sustain a course of activity" (Porter, *Recovery of Virtue*, 70).

Character and virtue work together, with character functioning as the whole and the virtues as the components.[15]

Virtue is not easy to define,[16] and philosophers and theologians alike have written much in this regard,[17] so please take these few pages as no more than a conversation starter.

—

I trust this letter will reach you before you leave. I am especially thinking of your wife and daughter as they will be alone during your weeks of travel. Truly, little of what we accomplish would be possible without their generous spirits.

May we be grateful for the quiet virtues of those around us.

---

15. Racelis, "Developing a Virtue Ethics Scale," 21.

16. Meno confesses to Socrates, "I have given myriad long speeches about *arête* to many people, entirely well spoken, or so it had seemed to me. But now I am not even able to say at all what it is" (Plato, *Meno* 80b).

17. Aquinas defines virtue as "A good quality of the mind, by which we live righteously, of which no one can make bad use, which God brings about in us, without us" (*Summa* 1–2.55.4, quoted in Porter, *Recovery of Virtue*, 110). Gunton looks to God's attributes to define virtue: "God's 'virtues' are God in the perfect coincidence of being and act. This, we might say, is God's character, the settled shape of what he is and does" (Gunton, "Church as a School of Virtue?," 217–218). MacIntyre notes that "there are just too many different and incompatible conceptions of a virtue for there to be any real unity to the concept or indeed to the history" (MacIntyre, *After Virtue*, 181).

5

Why Not Spiritual Formation

I was a little concerned to hear that you fainted in the airport but am relieved that you found good assistance and have been given a clean bill of health. As you say, it was probably a combination of fatigue and of some food that you were not used to eating while abroad. In any case, take care and get some rest now. I can't say that I'm a good example in this, as I've also spent more than five months travelling this year. We need to be wise stewards, learn to say no, and allow some good things to remain undone, lest we become undone ourselves.

Typicality in Spiritual Formation

It's taken me a few days to work through your long letter describing the schools you have visited. I've paid particular attention to the areas of spiritual formation and how it relates to character and virtue education and I would like to write this letter about that. This is, in fact, a pivotal issue around which many other things revolve, so here are some thoughts.

It seems that the schools that you've visited are fairly typical. Their curricula feature a standard blend of academic and practical courses, with good placement programmes and a variety of extra-curricular activities. When you asked about their holistic vision of education, schools generally claimed that they value spiritual formation and that they have extra-curricular structures in place to support it. Students attend chapel, are involved in worship, belong to small prayer groups and occasionally receive spiritual direction. One school had morning prayers and organized a day of prayer and fasting twice a year. Mentoring is also happening in many schools, and students are assigned to either an older student or a member of staff for regular meetings to discuss problems, pray together and be accountable in their personal goals. The smaller schools mentioned the importance of personal relationships between students and faculty, with "open-door" policies that encouraged relational dynamics.

I checked the websites of some of these schools, and their programme outcomes explicitly mention that their programmes "aim to facilitate spiritual growth and maturity." I also noted that there are some cases where spiritual formation activities are taking place in the classroom, both through structured courses in spiritual theology that teach about spiritual disciplines, spiritual gifts, discernment practices and discipleship, and across the entire curriculum, where spiritual topics are blended with academic and practical topics. This is a growing trend and reflects a desire for spiritual formation.[1]

The conversation became more intriguing, however, when you asked schools to provide a definition of spiritual formation. The answers included: "a set of practices that shape the spirit and the soul," "cultivation of one's relationship with God," "soul nurture," "individual growth and maturity" and "developing our innermost being in relation to God."[2] You did not press further, but it would have been interesting to explore the theological frameworks that underlie these definitions and shape the related educational practices. My impression is that many schools have not worked on this in detail and that issues related to theological anthropology, the definition of "maturity," the deep meaning of "being spiritual" and the educational tools that should be used to help an individual become "more spiritual" are largely unaddressed. Needless to say, this is important, especially given the significance of this area in the lives of those in ministry.[3]

An Unfamiliar Category

Spiritual formation, however, is not my main topic. I am most interested in your question on the relationship between spiritual formation and character and virtue education. Here, to use your own words, you felt that you were entering uncharted waters. Your interviewees expressed intrigue and curiosity, as if the association of words was unfamiliar and they were being invited to explore

---

1. The *Statistics on Pastors 2016* report indicates that, compared with twenty years before, 75 percent of pastors claimed that they "are better at their spiritual formation." The report does not specify, however, if this improvement is linked in any way to seminary training (Krekcir, 2). In the UK, 65 percent of church leaders indicated that the spiritual climate and emphasis of spirituality in a theological school was the most important factor in considering or recommending a theological college (58 percent prioritized mission and purpose and 48 percent prioritized academic rigour) (Kinnaman and Hempell, "Perceptions," 70).

2. For an overview of the efforts at defining "spirituality," see Steibel, "Christian Education and Spiritual Formation," 341–347.

3. One of the three biggest problems reported about pastors today is their lack of spiritual growth (Krekcir, *Statistics on Pastors*, 19, 20). In the UK, 86 percent of prospective theology students expect to be spiritually transformed (Kinnaman and Hempell, "Perceptions," 20).

something new. Character and virtue education appeared as a relatively new term, especially in relation to spiritual formation.

It is remarkable that no one reacted against the assumption in your question, which is that character and virtue are important in theological education.[4] No one said: "Ah yes. Character and virtue. Sorry, we are not interested." The response was actually the opposite, and school leaders tried to convince you that their schools were committed to this area. Although they listed many good things that they are doing, their language was imprecise and there did not seem to be an explicit plan in place. Notably, the conversations gravitated back to the same extra-curricular activities that they had just described for spiritual formation, mainly, chapel, prayer and relationships. The overarching assumption was that spiritual formation and character and virtue education were pretty much synonymous.[5]

There was one school, however, that was reticent to relate character and virtue to spiritual formation. For them, character and virtue smacked of moralization and they preferred to think of spiritual formation in terms of "growth in Christ." They had thought this through and claimed that spirituality should be restricted to subjective and mystical experiences and should not make any reference to our moral lives. They argued that Christianity is not about ethical behaviour but about a relationship with Christ, and that an excessive focus on being good can distract us from grace, breed self-righteousness and negatively impact our spiritual growth.[6] I will not present counter-arguments here, but I admit my struggle in conceiving genuine growth in Christ that is unrelated to moral formation.[7]

---

4. "In recent years there has been an explosion of interest in spiritual formation . . . much of the literature focuses on specific practices, such as meditation, fasting, service, and solitude. We believe that a sustained attention to Christian virtue is a crucial aspect of this process" (Austin and Geivett, "Being Good," 10).

5. Hull, for example, defines spiritual formation as "a process through which individuals who have received new life take on the character of Jesus Christ by a combination of effort and grace" (Hull, *Complete Book of Discipleship*, 19).

6. "In some segments of the church it is now routinely suggested that Christianity is not about ethics; rather it is about a relationship with Christ. While we applaud any resistance to reducing Christianity to an ethical system, we are concerned that Christian antipathy toward ethical theory is itself unchristian. Christianity is not merely about ethics, but it does essentially include ethics" (Austin and Geivett, "Being Good," 1).

7. "The vital linkage between our experiential knowledge of Christ and growth in moral formation [should be] understood as the inculcation of character traits, or virtues" (Austin and Geivett, 296).

Why Not Spiritual Formation: A Scholarly Discussion on Spirituality and Character

My main argument in this letter is that we should keep the language of spiritual formation and character education separate. Although there may be some overlap in some of the practices, when it comes to educational effects, spiritual formation and character education are not the same thing. There are many people, for example, whom we might consider spiritual and pious but whose characters are far from being well developed.[8] I am convinced that assimilating character education into the realm of spiritual formation has a negative effect and that the specificity of both terms is potentially lost. Unless we move away from this imprecision, I see little hope for a new vision. I am advocating that we move away from a common "three-category model" of theological education that includes academic engagement, ministerial training and spiritual formation and embrace a "four-fold model" that adds character and virtue education as a fourth, distinct, category.[9] This will not only focus our efforts in character and virtue education but will also contribute to a sharper definition of spiritual formation itself.

A scholarly discussion on the distinction between character education and spiritual formation took place in 1987 when twenty-three scholars from a variety of Christian traditions gathered at an Association of Theological Schools (ATS)-sponsored "Issues Research Seminar." David Kelsey provided a nice summary of this discussion, and what follows is my summary of his summary.[10]

For completeness' sake, I need to first report that the seminar agreed to use the term "formation" rather than "education" – which I actually disagree with. While I agree that we need a term that carries the notion of shaping and moulding, I think the term "education" is better, mostly because it is the

---

8. "At first glance, it may seem that character development is a part of spirituality. We must, however, add what Paul Tournier once remarked, that especially among pious people, there would seem to be only a few who have a fully developed character. It is not a given, apparently, that pious people are also mature people" (Ott, *Understanding and Developing*, 225). Lindbeck reminds us that "neurotics can be saints" (Lindbeck, "Spiritual Formation and Theological Education," 13).

9. "The four-category model arises from a further subdivision of the third category of the three-category model. Spiritual formation is thus divided into two parts – spiritual development and personal or character development, which form categories in their own right. Students, often coming into college at a crucial age, usually need significant personal and social development and the connection between personal and spiritual development is mentioned often in the literature" (Cheesman, "Perspectives in Theological Education").

10. Kelsey, "Reflections on a Discussion."

term that is normally used in the discipline. Rather than abandon the term "education" just because it has been associated with academic and professional training, I'm convinced that we should reinstate its broader holistic meaning. While the term "formation" might serve theological education on the short run, on the long run its religious overtones might break down an otherwise fruitful dialogue with the broader educational tradition.

The main debate in the seminar focused on three competing terms that might be used to describe the object of formation: the "soul," that which is "spiritual" and "character." The term "soul" did not gain much traction because of a long and complicated set of philosophical traditions that did not seem helpful. The two competing terms that remained were thus "spiritual" and "character." Here is how the debate went.

It was acknowledged that the term "spiritual" takes on many different meanings, including a "pre-theological" meaning (not tied to any worldview), a "theologically generic" meaning (representing all religious traditions and looking for broad common denominators) and a "theologically specific" meaning (tied particularly to the Christian tradition). The last meaning is the one that is most pertinent, and Kelsey outlines a set of further distinctions that define spirituality in Trinitarian terms. We can thus think of (1) theocentric spirituality, which is God-focused and includes mystical traditions and practices that deepen our relationship with God; (2) pneumatically centred spirituality, which is Spirit-focused and includes, for example, charismatic experiences that draw us nearer to God; and (3) Christocentric spirituality, which is mostly focused on discipleship and on following Jesus.

Of the three, theocentric spirituality is probably the one that is commonly associated with spiritual formation, and when the schools you visited used the term "spirituality" they were probably thinking of helping their students cultivate their relationship with God. In educational terms, this kind of spiritual formation involves a set of practices that nurture and deepen our relationship with God. In the Catholic tradition, *Pastores Dabo Vobis* lays out the fundamental values of spiritual formation as active participation in the Church's holy mysteries, service of our needy neighbour and union with Christ. The last is found and developed in communion and in mystery, in the Eucharist, in developing friendship with Jesus and in faithful meditation on the Word of God (*lectio divina*). Although the schools you visited were not Catholic, their understanding of spirituality was similar, as they associated their practices of spiritual formation with "God-related" activities like prayer, worship and spiritual disciplines.

The seminar then considered the term "character." This term, again, was seen as having many uses, but the one that emerged as the most useful is the philosophical usage linked to Aristotle, Aquinas and a number of contemporary philosophers. Formation in this tradition means helping students understand the virtues, act in certain ways, develop settled dispositions and become more mature in the art of reflective practice as they wisely relate virtue to their lives. This is distinct from the kind of theocentric spirituality that we have just seen and reflects Aquinas's distinction between supernatural and natural happiness. The former is found in the contemplation of God and the latter in developing virtue.[11]

The seminar concluded without a consensus but with a preference for the term "character" as best fitting the formational objectives of theological education. Those who preferred the term "spiritual" argued that "character" was generic and too far removed from the religious concerns of theological education. I would frankly argue just the opposite, claiming that theological education can greatly benefit from engaging the rich tradition of character and virtue education and should be cautious of exclusive jargon. Choosing the terminology of character and virtue education preserves us from religious parochiality and plugs us into a larger conversation where we can think theologically about human flourishing and build bridges into many fruitful debates with contemporary social sciences.

Mapping Terms

So what does this mean for you? As you think of your new educational project, should you speak about spiritual formation or about character and virtue education? I suggest that you use both terms, but that you privilege the latter as your distinctive focus. I have scribbled a little diagram below that might help summarize Kelsey's Trinitarian distinction and visualize where character education might fit in.

As you can see, spiritual formation and character education are kept distinct, but there is an overlap between Christ centred-discipleship and character education. My suggestion is that you reserve the term "spiritual formation" to describe the theocentric and Spirit-centred activities that are aimed at cultivating a relationship with God. These activities will typically include worship, chapel, prayer and the spiritual disciplines. Use the term "character education" instead to speak of that which overlaps with a Christ-

---

11. Porter, *Recovery of Virtue*, 63–68.

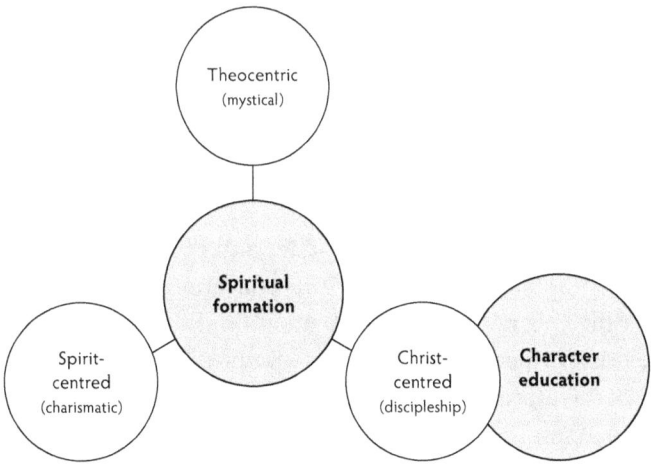

centred, discipleship-oriented focus. Here you will place an emphasis, for example, on the imitation of Christ as the ideal life, on fulfilling the innate purposes of human-ness, on becoming "authentic" and on responding virtuously to the world because of the work of Christ.

My diagram is nice and simple, but reality is less clear cut and you need to keep your distinctions movable. One can argue, for example, that practices of prayer are beneficial to growth in character, that the fruit of the Spirit has to do with practising virtues and that spiritual disciplines like fasting are similar to temperance habituation practices. One could also argue that everything is spiritual, but I do not find that educationally helpful. I suggest that, while allowing shaded borders, you use the language of spiritual formation for God-related formation and the language of character and virtue education for nourishing character dispositions.

Using Discipleship Language?

A final note on discipleship. In my chart you can see that character education overlaps with discipleship, and one of the research papers presented at the ATS seminar argued that the biblical language of discipleship should be used to absorb the language of character education. Surely, to speak of discipleship as growing in virtue because of our relationship to Christ is a solid proposal.[12] But I would advise against making the two coincide and insist that the terminology of character and virtue education stands best on its own. The terminology

---

12. Hall, "Theological Education As Character Formation," 64, 65.

of discipleship is, in fact, too indeterminate and it can easily slip back into the familiar arena of spiritual formation practices or catechetical activities. Likewise, the language of discipleship can be too broad and include prayer life, worship and missional mandates which are not, strictly speaking, within the remit of character and virtue education.

—

I've argued about terminology in this letter and I've tried to make a case for the distinctiveness of character and virtue education with respect to spiritual formation. Still, it is not an either–or situation. Both are necessary, and we need to be transformed spiritually through our relationship with God as we actively work on improving our character. I will be very interested to see how this all percolates in your mind and is transformed into educational practice.

May we be careful in the distinctions that we seek to make but remain holistic in the lives that we seek to live.

6

Character and Virtue in Higher Education

I commend you for meeting the rector of the local university and I trust that you have collected some useful perspectives. It stands to your credit that the leader of such a large institution would meet with you over lunch. Your suggestions about theological dialogue with other disciplines seems to have met with a favourable response, and the insights the rector gave you into their lifelong learning plans seem very useful. Your conversation over character and virtue education, admittedly, did not go very well. His strong reaction against what he described as moral paternalism reflects the common feeling that character education has no place in the university. But allow me to interject that it also betrays unfamiliarity with some of the broader trends that are taking place in global education. Let me fill you in on some of these, both for your own encouragement and for the sake of future conversations. This letter is thick with references that make it a little more scholarly but, given the potential audience that you might be using it with, I think it is appropriate.

A Renewed Tradition

While character education may seem like a novelty, it is both an ancient tradition and a significant trend in contemporary education.[1] Let me write a little more about this second point. There are those, in fact, who are claiming that the late twentieth and early twenty-first centuries constitute a revival phase

---

1. "From its beginnings, whether we trace these to Socrates or to the founding of modern universities in the Middle Ages, and throughout most of it history up to the mid-twentieth century, higher education has centered on the question of the meaningful life, true life'"(Volf, 30).

for character and virtue education.² My data is mostly limited to European and North American contexts, but I suspect that similar data can be found in other regions.³

To start with, we can look at the impressive literature around the subject. If you play around with the Google Ngram Viewer, you can map the word frequency in over 5 million books that have been published in the last two hundred years. The Viewer suggests that, after a dramatic decline in interest between the 1930s and the 1980s, the publications in the last thirty years containing the word "character education" have grown seven-fold.⁴ If you try a similar keyword search in EBSCO, you will find over 26,000 entries on character education, of which more than 16,000 related to journal articles. The *Journal of Moral Education* confirms these statistics, revealing that articles on moral education in higher education have doubled in the last forty years.⁵

There is also a growing body of empirical research⁶ in character education, and, in recent decades, several specific journals have given attention to this area, such as the *Journal of Moral Education*, the *Journal of Character Education* and the *Journal of College and Character*. Prestigious academic publishers like Routledge have inaugurated series in this field⁷ and there are plenty of institutes, centres and associations that have sprung up, such as the Association for Moral Education, the VIA Institute on Character, the Jubilee Centre for Character and Virtues, and the Character Education Partnership. UNESCO also supports a values education programme called Living Values that is active in eighty-four countries.⁸ The reputability of moral discourse and moral education has further been enhanced through the work of a number of scholars⁹ and thanks to the

---

2. Kiss lists twelve trends that characterize the return to moral education (Kiss and Euben, "Debating Moral Education: An Introduction," 10).

3. Martin Buber, considered to be one of the prominent educationalists in the foundation of the Jewish nation, claims that "Education worthy of the name, is essentially education of character" (Buber, *Between Man and Man*, 104).

4. See https://books.google.com/ngrams/graph?content=character+education&year_start=1900&year_end=2008&corpus=15&smoothing=3&share=&direct_url=t1%3B%2Ccharacter%20education%3B%2Cc0.

5. Lee and Taylor, "Moral Education Trends," 413.

6. The "Learning for Life" Project in the UK involved over 70,000 respondents in a research project around character education (Kristjánsson, *Ten Myths*, 274).

7. Routledge series on Citizenship, Character and Values Education.

8. See http://www.livingvalues.net/.

9. These include Rawls, Kohlberg, Williams, MacIntyre, Gillgan and "a growing number of educators (e.g. Bok, Colby and Ehrlich) who have argued that questions about right and wrong, justice and injustice, virtue and vice are essential elements for good education" (Kiss and Euben, "Debating Moral Education: An Introduction," 9).

emergence of new pedagogical constructs that focus on the recognition and development of human abilities and virtues.[10]

Governments are increasingly supportive of character and virtue education. In 1944, for example, England passed its new Education Act, meant to develop the "most abiding assets and richest resources – the character and competence of a great people."[11] The National Curriculum that is currently in place in the UK makes a specific point of developing the "moral child," of cultivating "ethical" perspectives and of making provisions for healthy citizenship.[12] In the USA, the Character Education Partnership[13] (CEP) reports that character education is mandated by state legislation in twenty-three states and encouraged in eighteen, with only eight states without any legislation. An Australian example is found in the Australian Values Education[14] initiative that was introduced by the government to actively encourage value education projects. Character education projects are also internationally supported by foundations, such as the John Templeton Foundation that has donated over $50 million in the last six years to projects in the area of Character Virtue Development.[15]

Trends in Higher Education

Although the strongest inroads into character education are in primary and secondary school education, there is also a growing trend in adult education. In my reading I have found character education in the university being referred to as "of utmost importance,"[16] as "the most challenging and important goal in higher education,"[17] as the "inclusive meta-objective,"[18] as "a central issue in

---

10. See, for example, the Positive Education movement (Bott et al., "State of Positive Education").

11. Birdwell et al., *Character Nation*, 9.

12. Demos, Britain's leading cross-party think-tank, is making recommendations for change in policy across England to "Create a statement of intent and a character education framework, assess character development and reform Ofsted, embed character into school practice, support and incentivize character education and support teachers to develop character" (Birdwell et al.). This trend is not without its contradictions and the UK National Curriculum suggests that schools should be pluralistic and not teach objective values of right and wrong (see David Charter, "Schools Told It's No Longer Necessary to Teach Right from Wrong," TimesOnline, 31 July 2006).

13. See http://character.org.

14. See http://www.curriculum.edu.au/values/values_homepage,8655.html.

15. https://www.templeton.org/funding-areas/character-virtue-development.

16. Gretchen and Firmin, "Character Education," 184.

17. Larson, "Examination of the Effectiveness," 4.

18. Walker et al., *Towards a New Era*, 81.

the advancement of education,"[19] as a "fundamental goal"[20] and as an "essential element."[21] Prestigious foundations are suggesting that doctoral studies should be conducted with a view to character formation,[22] and non-formal and lifelong learning programmes for adults are also advocating the centrality of character.[23] Universities are beginning to offer courses and degrees in character education, such as the Moral and Character Education course at Stanford or the MA in Character Education offered at Birmingham University. In curricular design, the shortfalls in programmes that have focused exclusively on *knowing* and *doing* are motivating scholars to reconsider the sphere of *being* as a legitimate outcome in higher education.[24] The importance of the character-shaping role of the university is clearly perceived at a global level, as illustrated by the 1988 UNESCO "Report on the World Conference on Higher Education" that claims that current global emergencies such as population growth, pollution, global warming and energy supplies are best addressed by developing a greater moral framework in higher education.[25]

---

19. Gretchen and Firmin, "Character Education," 184.

20. Berkowitz and Fekula, "Educating for Character," 17.

21. Kiss and Euben, "Debating Moral Education: An Introduction," 9.

22. A study of doctoral education by the Carnegie Foundation suggests that scholars must be formed, not just trained: "The idea of formation, borrowed from religious educators, refers to the kind of education that leads to an integration of mind and moral virtue that we often call character or integrity . . . The doctorate carries with it both a sense of intellectual mastery and of moral responsibility. That the entire process concludes with all members of the community dressed in religious robes and engaged in an act of ordination of the novice by the master with a priestly hood is no accident" (Walker, *Formation of Scholars*, Foreword).

23. The "primary purpose of learning and education" (in lifelong learning) includes the development of one's own character, "a character that becomes reality as a result of growing experience" (Tuschling and Engemann, "From Education to Lifelong Learning," 454).

24. Barnett and Coate (*Engaging*) have tried to analyze what curriculum means in an age of uncertainty. "The authors suggest an 'engaging' model that integrates the realms of knowing, acting and being. The treatment of being in higher education curricula is, in their opinion, probably the most problematic and must be spoken of *sotto voce*, as out of line with the dominant discourse of an age preoccupied with performance and productivity" (Oxenham, *Liquid Modernity*, 194). The idea of students as persons rarely shows up in benchmarks, module descriptors or learning outcomes. This occurs despite an urgent need to rediscover the personal dimension, especially in an age of uncertainty and change, where even employers are increasingly looking for personal qualities of being.

25. "Higher education itself is confronted therefore with formidable challenges and must proceed to the most radical change and renewal it has ever been required to undertake, so that our society, which is currently undergoing a profound crisis of values, can transcend mere economic considerations and incorporate deeper dimensions of morality and spirituality" (in Arthur, Wilson and Godfrey, *Graduates of Character*, 13).

The Reasons for the Revival

So why is this revival taking place? Different explanations are suggested, starting from the claim that this is not new, and that the university has always been engaged in character education.[26] Contextual explanations are also suggested, the most popular of which is that character education is growing in response to the moral decline of society.[27] A significant body of literature[28] suggests that violence, bullying and antisocial behaviour are rooted in the crisis in character education. In places like Korea, character education is considered as violence prevention,[29] and in China the return to Confucian morality is associated with the moral vacuum left by the country's modernization policies.[30] The response to the counter-culture of the 1960s is also a good illustration. In this period, the established *in loco parentis* structures of the university were challenged, and restrictions such as dress codes, restrictions on food, disciplinary systems and curfews were removed.[31] Although students did not obtain more power, they did obtain more freedom, but with this freedom came a diminished level of moral behaviour. This, according to analysts, led to a moral crisis in the university,[32] which in turn has bred a renewed interest in character education.

But it is not only moral crises that are calling for character education; global crises are also begging for solutions. According to UNESCO, the "formidable challenges" of today's societies should be met with greater "morality and spirituality."[33] If the world is going to change and improve, we need to educate citizens to be good people. The supporters of civil rights movements, the environmentalists, the marginalized groups and those who are disillusioned with utopian visions of science – all recognize that it is the responsibility of

---

26. Universities are involved in moral education, whether they take it up as an "explicit topic of reflection or make it an object of deliberate inculcation" or not (Kiss and Euben, *Debating Moral Education*, 187).

27. Lickona, *Educating for Character*, 1; White and Murray, *Evidence-Based Approaches*, 127; Berkowitz, "Educating for Character," 17.

28. Dill, "Challenge of Contemporary Moral Education," 223; White and Murray, *Evidence-Based Approaches*, 127.

29. Nucci et al., *Handbook*, 328.

30. To, Yang and Helwig, "Democratic Moral Education in China," 405.

31. Kiss and Euben, *Debating Moral Education*, 45.

32. "Most college educators are well aware [that] there are significant moral problems prevalent on college and university campuses – alcohol abuse, date rape, academic dishonesty, vandalism, and assault, to name a few" (Berkowitz, "Educating for Character," 17). See also B. Seaman, *Binge*.

33. Arthur and Godfrey, *Graduates of Character*, 13.

higher education to prepare students for democratic citizenship.[34] Political crises, terrorism prevention and financial crises are likewise demonstrating that policy and regulation can only go so far, and they are turning the attention of public opinion back to issues of character and virtue.[35] As the familial and religious structures that have traditionally shaped the character of youth are eroded,[36] societies are looking to schools to educate their youths' character,[37] and higher education is seen by some as the most powerful defence against the erosion of the cultural and moral tenets of a society.[38]

On a very practical level, interest in character is also linked to graduate employability. I recently chatted with a friend who is a high-ranking officer leading a UN project. He candidly told me that, for him, curriculum, degrees and experience count for very little in interviewing candidates. Most of his potential employees need specific on-the-job training in any case. In offering a job, the thing that really counts for him is character.[39]

David and Goliath

I think that it is safe to say that, while it might be too early to speak of genuine revival of character education in the university, there certainly is a renewed interest. There are also voices, however, that are altogether sceptical and suspicious of this resurgence,[40] and we would be foolish to believe that the university has fully opened its arms to character and virtue education – as you

---

34. Kiss and Euben, *Debating Moral Education*, 35–38.

35. "The corporate and financial crises of the past decade, and the looming political crisis of today, have revived in the public's mind the ancient truth that character matters" (Koons, "Three Humanisms," 207).

36. The American Council of Civil Society indicates that higher education is one of the most hopeful sources for character and citizenship development: "Especially in our era, when the social authority of religious belief has weakened, and when more young people than ever go on to some form of higher education, the modern university may be our truest cultural barometer, our most accurate indicator of who we are becoming" (Elshtain, "Call to Civil Society," 10).

37. "For many students, character and virtues will be acquired in school – or not at all" (Gretchen and Firmin, "Character Education," 194).

38. Smilie, "Humanitarian and Humanistic Ideals," 63. The time that young adults spend in university education is one of the "last large-scale opportunities to shape the character of tomorrow's leaders" (Berkowitz and Fekula, "Educating for Character," 17).

39. "As technical skills become increasingly specialized, it is likely that more employers will view training in 'hard skills' as a process most effectively done in-house, so that new hires learn how to do things 'our way.' The soft skills associated with strong character, however, are much harder to teach in a two-week crash course (Kinnaman, *What's Next?*, 34).

40. "While we are sceptical of the sceptics, we respect the significance of the questions they pose. For example, why are we seeing a new preoccupation with ethics? . . . What cultural anxieties or economic forces does it address or respond to, and what social ideals or political

have seen in your conversation with the university rector. The Goliath of the university is surely not the home of the David of character education.

The evidence that I have quoted above is admittedly relatively small and unfocused.[41] Moral development is generally not treated as a responsibility of the university and morality is normally not nourished intentionally and systematically. In many cases, morality is not even a proper university subject. Whereas, in the past, university presidents used to deliver compulsory seminars in moral philosophy to all graduating seniors, in many universities such moral education is not available even when students explicitly look for it.[42]

Many voices want to keep character education out of the university and most higher education communities seem to function under the eleventh commandment: "Thou shalt not tell thy neighbour what to do."[43] Students interviewed in the *Graduates of Character* project indicated that, during their university studies, they had never sensed any sort of intentional project aimed at the formation of their character. Although their education had given them judgment tools and had helped them to avoid bias and sensationalism, they claimed that if there had been any influence on their values during their university years, it came from relational sources such as their mothers, peers or a handful of teachers. For them, discourse around character and virtue was mostly unrelated to their university experience.[44]

This reflects some of the broader trends around the nature and purpose of higher education which I have written about elsewhere.[45] We operate in

---

agendas does it promote, either explicitly or implicitly?" (Kiss and Euben, "Debating Moral Education: An Introduction," 15).

41. Pavela, "Renewed Focus," 734.

42. "You can scan a hundred syllabi for introductory courses in philosophy and religion without finding one whose stated goals include the teaching of ethics and the improvement of students' moral character. Universities today teach about morality, but they do not presume to teach morality . . . Hardly any academic or co-curricular programs set as a goal to enhance students' moral maturity and foster a stronger sense of personal integrity" (Hoekma, in Kiss and Euben, *Debating Moral Education*, 250, 263).

43. Kiss and Euben, 262.

44. The *Graduates of Character* report concludes that (1) the tradition of virtue language has been eroded, and as a result an impoverished discourse on character has contributed to a lack of coherence in the rationale of the educational system; (2) there is a lack of clarity in the moral objectives that schools set themselves, especially in the area of personal responsibility; (3) practice in this area is rarely evaluated; (4) government initiatives to enhance character education remain patchy, narrowly focused and marginal rather than brought into mainstream provision; (5) there is little support or training in this regard for teachers; (6) while employers repeatedly draw attention to the lack of skills and relevant knowledge in their new employees, they also point to the missing dimension of personal character (Arthur and Godfrey, *Graduates of Character*, 10–12).

45. Oxenham, *Liquid Modernity*.

a knowledge economy, where learning is commodified, and in which the university's main purpose is to contribute to domestic economic wealth and to career advancement. As Lyotard suggested, performativity is the essential aim of education, and the cultivation of skills and competences prevails over the cultivation of ideals and human growth.[46] This is statistically proven in America, where nearly 70 percent of the population are convinced that the purpose of going to college is to prepare for a specific job or career, compared to 14 percent who believe that it should contribute to developing moral character.[47]

Overall, the place of character and virtue education in the university is hazy at best, and the process of bringing character education to a level of appropriate engagement is laborious.[48] Virtue is not a priority,[49] and in some universities character education is considered anti-liberal, sectarian and anti-intellectual. In others, it is applauded in theory but is nowhere seen in practice. In a few universities, character education is affirmed but generally relegated to the extra-curricular realm.

—

So, dear Siméon, as you can see, although we are part of a growing global movement, we are still a minority. The project you are undertaking will be misunderstood and criticised, but optimism is on our side.

May you find hope in your innermost man as you struggle with adversity and incomprehension.

---

46. J. Lyotard, *The Postmodern Condition: A Report on Knowledge* (Manchester: Manchester University Press, 1979), 4–5.

47. Kinnaman, *What's Next?*, 8, 9.

48. Gretchen and Firmon, "Character Education," 183.

49. "Overall . . . students' moral and civic development is not a high priority in US higher education today. We have been struck again and again by the many lost opportunities for moral and civic growth in curricular and extracurricular programs on most campuses" (Colby et al., *Educating Citizens*, 277).

7

Character and Virtue in Theological Education

This letter comes on the back of the previous one, because I realized that you might also benefit from a more detailed perspective on what is happening within theological education. Although the signals are timid, there are some hopeful manifestations. These are being fuelled by trends in the broader culture, by the voice of faith communities and by a renewed discourse within theological education itself.

Change Is in the Air

In my first letter I mentioned the climate of enquiry and change in theological education. From our global travels, this is evident to both of us. Theological schools all over the world are reshaping their curricula, innovating in teaching and learning, broadening their horizons, considering new issues, enhancing quality assurance protocols, finding new ways to deal with financial pressures and engaging with new delivery technologies. We are seeing an unprecedented volume of work at the theoretical level that includes discussions around the kinds of leaders that should be trained, reflection on the fragmentation and integration of curricula and explorations of appropriate andragogy. In two of the main journals related to theological education there has been a regular flow of articles on change, the future and purpose.[1] A very helpful overview is found

---

1. In the last two decades, *Theological Education* has featured articles on change (5, no. 4 [1969]; 34, no. 2 [1998]; 50, no. 2 [2015]); on the future (5, no. 1 [1968]; 21, no. 1 [1984]; 28, no. 1 [1991]; 44, no. 1 [2008]; 46, no. 2 [2011]); and on the purpose of theological education (2, no. 2 [1966]; 7, no. 3 [1971]; 14, no. 2 [1978]). In *The Journal of Adult Theological Education* the keyword search for "change" yields seventy results, "future" yields sixty-three results and "purpose" yields fifty-four.

in *Reflections on the Literature on Theological Education Published between 1855 and 1985* by Gustafson, and I encourage you to browse this substantial piece of research. Gustafson concludes that, in general, theological educators have become more change-oriented, more sensitive to various contexts and more attentive to societal turns as they impact educational reforms.[2]

Golden Threads in the Literature

This bodes well for a renewed discourse around character and virtue, but we should not get too excited. Despite the positive climate of enquiry and change, it is still rare to find sustained discourse around character and virtue in theological education. In the literature we find no more than occasional articles and brief book sections.[3] Character education is sometimes mentioned in discussing the importance of "being" or as a sub-topic of other practical subjects, such as leadership and mentoring. Most often, character education appears in connection with spiritual formation but, as we've seen, this is imprecise and not always helpful. Some theologians,[4] such as Stanley Hauerwas,[5] Alasdair MacIntyre, N. T. Wright, Miroslav Volf,[6] Volker Rabens and Christoph Stückelberger, are producing brilliant work in the areas of character and virtue, but this is usually not applied specifically to theological education.

A quick survey of two of the main journals that are dedicated to theological education confirms this picture. Browsing *Theological Education* from 1964 to 2017, I found a good stock of writing around spiritual formation, but only one article and one special supplement dealing specifically with character or moral education.[7] Likewise, a combined keyword search in *The Journal of Adult Theological Education* for "character education" and "virtue" produced only seven articles, of which only one is really pertinent.[8] The "Reflections" report by Gustafson reveals that, until 1985, there was no mention of character education in the literature, and references to spiritual formation were made only

---

2. Gustafson, "Reflections," 1988.

3. Ott, *Understanding and Developing*, 224–228.

4. For a review of the literature dealing with the Christian discourse on virtues and character, see Moisés Mayordomo, "Möglichkeiten und Grenzen einer neutestamentlich orientierten Tugendethik," *Theologische Zeitschrift* 64, no. 3 (2008): 213–257.

5. "The virtues do in fact express central aspects of the Christian life" (Hauerwas, "Christian Virtues Exemplified," 335).

6. Yale Center for Faith and Culture, https://faith.yale.edu.

7. Kelsey, "Reflections on Theological Education," 62–75; and *Theological Education* 21, Supplement 1 (1988).

8. *The Journal of Adult Theological Education* 10, no. 1 (2013).

in listing the ailments of theological education. Moral issues are mentioned, but they are marginal, and framed either in terms of moral and social reform, as a defence of the moral order or as solutions to moral problems, but never in terms of personal growth in character and virtue.[9]

We can find some attention to character and virtue in some of the recent monographs on theological education. The work of Farley and Kelsey, for example, proposes a modified version of *paideia*. But, although their so-called "Athens" model is promising in contrast with the "Berlin" *Wissenschaft* model, their focus is mostly on the *habitus* of the intellectual virtues, and they do not provide a full-blown vision of character and virtue education that includes moral and public virtues.[10] Reading their work, it feels like a promising start that has been cut short.

Overall, I think we can safely conclude that, in the last century or so, character and virtue education has not been an object of sustained attention in the literature on theological education.

Golden Threads in Practice

When it comes to practice, there is a similar scenario. On the positive side, an increasing number of theologians and church leaders have begun to employ practices of moral and virtue formation within a vision of communal discipleship, and some have announced that the virtues are back.[11] In theological schools, these inroads typically include extra-curricular activities, but we can find schools that intentionally design character-focused learning outcomes[12] and offer specific courses.[13] Further evidence is seen in international consultations,[14] in research that is being done in the measurement of character

---

9. Gustafson, "Reflections," 37, 39, 42.

10. Farley and Kelsey align with a number of contemporary philosophers in the virtue-epistemology tradition who claim that the primary aim of education should be "the acquisition and development of intellectual character virtues" (Kotzee, Carter and Siegel, "Educating for Intellectual Virtue," 2).

11. Mahn, "Kierkegaard after Hauerwas," 172.

12. For example, the European Nazarene College.

13. For example, the Spiritual Formation and Character Education course at London School of Theology.

14. For example, the 2013 conference at Calvin College on the topic "Virtues, Vices and Teaching" or the 2017 General Assembly of the European Evangelical Accrediting Association on "Character Education in Theological Education."

development[15] and in conversations that are beginning around the accreditation of character education.[16]

The situation varies as we look at different Christian traditions. Many evangelical schools, for example, are solidly anchored in a pietistic moral tradition and tend to encourage communities of virtue, moral instruction and the importance of positive example.[17] The Church of England also offers some encouraging signs, and the Initial Ministerial Education and Common Awards schemes place a renewed emphasis on character, recognizing that general culture is failing to positively shape character and that the leadership and clergy in contemporary Anglicanism need to be shaped in virtue.[18]

Some very hopeful signals come from Catholic seminary training. Catholic literature has a long-standing interest in formation[19] as it reflects the sensitivities of the Jesuit objective of *eloquentia perfetta*, which included character formation.[20] Vatican II also ushered in a resurgence of interest in moral theology and a renewed attention to the virtues.[21] Faithful to this tradition, Catholic educators are responding to the invitation of *Lumen Gentium* to train seminarians for a life of holiness. Other documents confirm this overall support of formation in virtues,[22] most notably *Pastores Dabo*

---

15. "The Spiritual, Character, and Virtue Formation of Seminarians," February 2016–July 2017, John Templeton Foundation, https://www.templeton.org/grant/the-spiritual-character-and-virtue-formation-of-seminarians.

16. The ICETE "Standards and Guidelines for Global Evangelical Theological Education" includes a commitment to "Integrating principles, quality measures and assessment of character education into our global indicators, within our vision of holistic theological education" (https://icete.info/resources/sggete/). In its definition of "Biblical Higher Education" as "transformational," the Association for Biblical Higher Education foresees education that will "appropriate and collaborate with the work of God's Holy Spirit in the process of developing personal values and virtues worthy of His adopted children" (see "Accreditation FAQs," https://www.abhe.org/accreditation/faqs/).

17. Fundamentalist Protestants tend to "enforce a strong religious orientation among their faculty and vigorous oversight of their students' behaviour and beliefs" (Kiss and Euben, *Debating Moral Education*, 46).

18. Heywood, "Educating Ministers of Character," 7.

19. Taylor, "Sources of Renewal," 321.

20. González, *History of Theological Education*, 84.

21. "The Second Vatican Council saw a call for renewal in moral theology . . . It is safe to say today, as exemplified by the theme of this volume, that virtue once again plays a prominent role in Catholic moral theology" (Cloutier and Mattison, "Resurgence of Virtue," 228).

22. The "National Certification Standards for Lay Ecclesial Ministers" includes the "demonstration of basic human virtues" as one of its standards (Alliance for the Certification of Lay Ecclesial Ministers, 4). The *Ratio Fundamentalis Institutionis Sacerdotalis* (Sacred Congregation for Catholic Education, "Gift of the Priestly Vocation") also makes an urgent call for the formation of priests to include the "acquisition of those virtues which support the Christian soul" (4). The *Program of Priestly Formation* also has many references to virtue,

Vobis[23] that repeatedly points to the virtues as decisive for the pastoral and spiritual life of the priest.[24] Although this is auspicious, Catholic formational practices tend to dovetail human virtue with spiritual formation and devotion to God. In *Optatam totius*, for example, character formation is mentioned, but the major emphasis is on the practices that shape the spiritual lives of priests.[25] Although we've seen that there can be a profitable overlap between spiritual formation and character education, the weight of practice in current Catholic theological education seems to favour a theocentric vision of spiritual formation rather than an Aristotelian-type approach to character education.

In mainline Protestant schools it is more difficult to find practices in character education, for they have frequently embarked on secularization processes that share the views of the secular university around moral formation. In many Protestant seminaries, ethics courses are historical and comparative and do not prescribe any behavioural change. Moral instruction is not meant to be formational, but informational and critical.[26] This is not to say that theological divinity schools and inner-university Christian movements are indifferent to virtue and character; examples like the Yale Center for Faith and Culture[27] and the Oxford Character Project[28] by the Oxford Pastorate indicate the contrary. But even in these cases, the focus tends to remain on the extra-curricular realm.

---

prescribing, for example, that the human formation of candidates must lead to growth into a "person of solid moral character with a finely developed moral conscience, a man open to and capable of conversion: a man who demonstrates the human virtues of prudence, fortitude, temperance, justice, humility, constancy, sincerity, patience, good manners, truthfulness, and keeping his word, and who also manifests growth in the practice of these virtues" (Committee on Priestly Formation of the United States Conference of Catholic Bishops, 30).

23. John Paul II, *Pastores Dabo Vobis*, 16.

24. *Pastores Dabo Vobis* is a fundamental document for the training of priests, featuring repeated references to obedience, charity, faith, humility, mercy, prudence, chastity, honesty, justice, loyalty, truthfulness, compassion, integrity, generosity, self-control, altruism and constancy.

25. Neuhaus, *Theological Education*, 98.

26. "When we look closely at the content of the curriculum, we find very little that directly addresses the questions of how to discern right and wrong . . . if we interrogate the instructors about whether the goals for these courses include the cultivation of virtue, we will receive a quick and emphatic denial" (Kiss and Euben, *Debating Moral Education*, 252).

27. See https://faith.yale.edu.

28. https://oxfordcharacter.org.

The Death of Character and Virtue

The signals are thus mixed. Some good things are happening, but we are far from witnessing an explicit and sustained focus on character and virtue education in theological schools. Actually, I fear that the opposite is true.

I recently held a seminar at a conference entitled "The Death of Character and Virtue in Theological Education." I will forward the full paper, but here is a summary of the twelve factors that I suggested are contributing to the death of character and virtue. The first four are cultural, the next two are educational and the final six are specific to theological education.

1. *A culture of rationalism and research.* The Enlightenment claimed that what really counted was the search for the truth and that the key to human progress was found in rational research. Consequently, theological education has been pressured to prioritize rationality, the transmission of cognitive truth and research.[29]

2. *The ethics of authenticity.* This phrase, used by Charles Taylor,[30] captures the notion that what counts in ethics today is to "be ourselves." External moral standards, such as those that are implied in character and virtue education, are judged as paternalistic and rejected.

3. *The therapeuticalization of society.* This word describes a society whose self-perception is linked to trauma and therapy. Identity is modelled around psychological wounds, lack of self-esteem and damaged memories. This means that students often come to theological education as victims needy of love and healing rather than with a sense of responsibility to develop their own character.

4. *Managerialism and measurability.* The Scientific and Industrial Revolutions introduced the concept of total quality management in education and set off conversations around effectiveness and measurability in quality assurance. The assumption that effective education can be measured makes things very difficult for formational activities such as character education.

---

29. For a detailed treatment of the shift of theology from *sapientia* to *scientia*, see Treier, *Virtue and the Voice of God*.

30. Taylor, *Ethics of Authenticity*.

5. *The captivity of accreditation.* A lot of good can be done through secular accreditation, but the scrutiny of this kind of quality assurance usually does not include the formational dimension.

6. *The loss of the uni-versity.* I have argued elsewhere that postmodernity has shaken the vision of unity in the university and replaced it with fragmentation.[31] In this kind of university, the virtues become rootless, isolated and easily susceptible to being "plucked off."

7. *The changing purpose of higher education.* When the university is considered mainly as a place to prepare for a specific career,[32] the purpose of theological education can be seen in terms of preparation for professional ministry.[33] If theological education is motivated by an increase in earning potential, this makes it difficult to prioritize character formation.[34]

8. *The occupation of standard curricula.* Many curricula in theological education are dominated by Schleiermacher's classification of theology (systematics, biblical studies, dogmatics/history and practical theology). In this arrangement, formational outcomes are left homeless.

9. *Discipline replacing character education.* Disciplinary codes are necessary in regulating learning communities, but they do little to shape character. Schools that have many rules may be very far from character and virtue education.

---

31. "Foucault's archaeology redefines what were considered sure foundations ... Knowledge is fragmented and there is no unifying or overarching canopy that holds knowledge together" (Oxenham, *Liquid Modernity*, 140).

32. This opinion seems to be held equally by those with no faith convictions and practising Christians (Kinnaman, *What's Next?*, 11).

33. 71 percent of church leaders interviewed in the UK indicated that theological education is "mostly about ministry training," against 29 percent who believed it was "mostly about personal development" (Kinnaman and Hempell, "Perceptions," 21).

34. Increasing earning potential, together with gaining practical skills and determining a career path, appears as the most popular reason for American students considering Bible college. Growing spiritually and learning about the Bible ranked last (Kinnaman, *What's Next?*, 19). "By and large [prospective students] are not primarily seeking spiritual formation or biblical training; they want transactional, not transformational, education" (Kinnaman, 41).

10. *Theological reasons.* I will write about these elsewhere, but there are some theological traditions that are particularly averse to Aristotelian character education.[35]

11. *The safety of academics.* Critical thinking and good academic practice generate a sense of competence. The sterilized, tidy environment of critical debate can, however, kill the beneficial bacteria of character education.

12. *The figure of the professor.* In many contexts the professor is called the "lecturer," reinforcing the notion that the profession entails teaching, doing research and supervising (this is also what most standard job descriptions look like). Fostering character education is an optional activity that can be done in one's spare time, as long as it does not detract from the "main" tasks.

These are a handful of cultural and educational factors that I think have contributed to the death of character and virtue education in theological education. Other reasons can be imagined as well, and we are facing a remarkable challenge.

Diagnosing Health and Death

Perhaps my generalizations are unfair. That's why I've developed a little diagnostic tool that uses three parameters to assess the health of a school when it comes to character and virtue education. The test uses the parameters of *clarity*, *centrality* and *intentionality*.

First of all, for character and virtue education to be alive and well in a theological school, its practices should be *clear*. Evidence of this would include specific references in mission statements, recognizable programme learning outcomes and explicit conceptual and theological frameworks that undergird character and virtue education. Definitions of key character and virtue terminology should also be clear and should not be confused with spiritual formation. An explicit language of virtue and character education should be used in the learning community, in spoken language, visual language (art) and reflective language. By reflective language, I mean the choice of words that we

---

35. Luther, in coherence with his vision of the dramatic consequences of the fall, "thumbed his nose at the long medieval tradition of virtue" (Wright, *After You Believe*, 58), considering it mere pretence and prideful human effort. He considered Aristotle's book on ethics the "worst of all books because it flatly opposes divine grace and all Christian virtues" (Herdt, "Virtue's Semblance," 150).

make to describe what is happening. For example, in laying out regulations regarding drunkenness, a school that is clear about character education will explicitly link drunkenness to the vices of gluttony and lack of self-control, and propose remedial virtues like moderation. This may seem like a minor point, but it is this kind of reflective vocabulary of virtue that makes a virtue-shaping community come alive.

Clarity should also be seen in the practicalities of shaping character. Theological schools are institutions where the "how"-related questions of pedagogy demand a response. It is not enough to give lectures and sermons on the importance of moral uprightness in Christian discipleship; such teaching must also "tell us how."[36] The specific practices of character and virtue education need to be spelled out, but these can be very easily confused with other good practices. I came across a school recently that had announced a new character formation programme. Although the programme promised to encourage students towards virtuous moral identity, the content was focused on exploring family dynamics, defining personal histories, taking personality tests, undertaking clinical interviews and reading counselling textbooks. There is nothing wrong with that but, while promising a character formation programme, the school had not clearly worked it out and was actually offering a programme in Christian counselling and psychotherapy.[37]

The second parameter is that character and virtue education must be *central* to the life of a theological school. By this, I mean that character and virtue education should be moved from the periphery of extra-curricular activities to the centre of accredited and certified educational delivery. Character outcomes should be a core feature of the curriculum and they should be carefully assessed and included in the certification requirements. It should not be possible to graduate from a theological school while maintaining a vicious character.[38] Excellent grades and a certification of ministry skills and competences should never suffice.

I have a sad example of this engraved on my memory. I had a third-year undergraduate theology student who was simply awful in terms of his character. He was selfish, unfriendly in the community, arrogant, indiscreet

---

36. Kiss and Euben, *Debating Moral Education*, 252.

37. Tenelshof, "Encouraging the Character Formation," 85–87.

38. "If students can sit for years at a time studying the Bible and Christian theology, and there is no consequence in terms of transformation – and indeed, if there may even be change for the worse – then there are serious problems, perhaps with the programme, or the teaching, or the students, or even maybe the teachers themselves" (Ferdinando, "Theological Education and Character," 50).

with female students, disrespectful of authority, uninterested in spiritual things and regularly drunk over the weekends. And yet he had an excellent mind and outstanding abilities, and was shrewd enough to never blatantly break major disciplinary rules. Needless to say, he graduated with a first-class degree in theology. I do not know where he is today, but unless God's grace has intervened dramatically, he is probably doing damage somewhere.[39]

Unless character education becomes central to theological education, I fear that this kind of disaster will continue to be possible. Quality assurance agencies can play a part here, and they should require schools to have monitored practices of character and virtue education. If it is not central for accreditation, in fact, it will likely not be central for schools. We need to reclaim the centrality of these practices and be accountable for them.

Third, we can measure the health of character education practices by their *intentionality*. In other words, a school should be purposeful in achieving outcomes in character and virtue education. Being eloquent should not take the place of being deliberative, and we need to guard against the aspirations of well-meaning catalogues.[40] Most theological educators know that character is important, but they are not always able to describe their intended action plans. Intentionality in character and virtue education requires a high level of focus, planning and implementation.

We recognize that character education often happens spontaneously in theological schools and not because of specific, well-articulated and monitored educational plans. Good things are being done by good people and these generate a positive impact on character. But this is random at best and it misses some great opportunities. Let me give you an example. Many schools have mentoring programmes in which students are personally supported by a more mature student or member of staff. Mentoring is a great educational device and it could powerfully serve the purposes of character and virtue education, but it rarely does so explicitly. Research indicates that the most common functions of

---

39. "It is entirely possible to be a seminary graduate who, while possessing vast amounts of religious information, possesses neither the character that Jesus sought to instil in his followers, nor the competency to lead in the most basic aspect of Kingdom mission, making disciples . . . we might suggest that the passing on of Christian knowledge to those who lack the character and competency out of which it might be put to use is akin to passing along car keys to someone who is clearly drunk – they may be able to use the tool, but if nothing horrible comes to pass, it will be by sheer grace" (Rozko, "Missiological Future," 7).

40. Lofty rhetoric about character education is often unmatched in practice (Hoekma, in Kiss and Euben, *Debating Moral Education*, 251).

mentoring are to provide friendship, support and encouragement.[41] How much better might we serve our students if the existing mentoring structures were intentionally arranged to support the formation of character and virtue? Sadly, it is assumed that students engaged in the study of theology will somehow become better people on their own.[42] But the study of theology itself will never create godliness.[43]

I hope that this three-fold diagnostic tool will be useful as you make plans for a new school where character and virtue education will be clear, central and intentional. I'm guessing that you might be frowning at my critical spirit as I imply that character education is dead in theological education. I confess that I had produced a gentler version of this letter, but I've chosen to send you the original draft, with the recognition that we are not dealing with an all-or-nothing scenario but with degrees of health. I find comfort in the fact that global theological education is searching for its future. Change is in the air, and I hope that by using words that are strong we will begin a reversal and not set off reactions.

A Strategic Poise

Let me end on a hopeful note. Theological education is strategically poised to offer a unique contribution to character and virtue education. There are several reasons for this. First, theological education is an expression of higher education, and I have already illustrated how the university is a place of particular hope.[44] There is much promise when young adults gather together over extended periods of time to be formed, especially as they engage with

---

41. A study conducted in the Christian College Coalition revealed thirty-five mentoring functions of which the most commonly experienced were "providing friendship," "belief in capabilities" and "emotional support." Character issues do not appear on the list, although they might be seen within the categories of "constructive criticism" and "role modelling" (Cunningham, in Pazdan, "Wisdom Communities," 46).

42. "Responsible action motivated by a virtuous moral identity, namely, character, is taken for granted. As Christians, we tend to assume . . . that our students have a responsible moral identity" (Tenelshof, "Encouraging the Character Formation," 83).

43. "It does not quite follow that . . . everything is right with [a student's] religious life if he does study" (Warfield, "Religious Life," 185).

44. "The space that it [the university] once occupied in the moral formation of students has not been filled with equivalent sources of ethical guidance" (Kiss and Euben, *Debating Moral Education*, 263).

humanistic disciplines that shape them to be an educated public that thinks carefully about itself and about its role in society.[45]

Second, the discipline of theology is particularly conducive to moral formation. Although the revival in moral education is being led today by the disciplines of psychology and philosophy,[46] theology should also play a leading role. Religion, in fact, is considered the main source of ethical values,[47] and society expects institutions that are training religious leaders to take the lead in shaping citizens of character.[48]

Third, theology provides a robust metaphysical context that is needed for character education. A metanarrative is necessary to avoid difficulties in character education,[49] and lofty secular ideals, such as those of Durkheim and Dewey, do not provide this.[50] We will see later on how theologians like Aquinas[51] can be of great help in providing the kind of integrated vision of human selfhood that is badly needed today.[52]

And finally, theological education provides a unique context for character education. It not only features the necessary theoretical commitments in the areas of ontology, epistemology and anthropology, but also provides the practical structures for formation, including a strong commitment to community. Theological education has a long-standing history of good

---

45. "Christians, for all their shortcomings, still represent an ongoing educated public" (Hauerwas, in Kiss and Euben, 106).

46. Of 945 articles published in the *Journal of Moral Education* between 1971 and 2011, psychology was foundational for 54.8 percent and philosophy for 49.4 percent (Lee and Taylor, "Moral Education Trends," 420).

47. A major source of core ethical values is religion and that teaching character outside of a religious context can be "hollow and misleading" (Roso, "Culture and Character Education," 33).

48. One of the trends in the revival of moral education is the "growing acknowledgement of the need for spiritual exploration as a part of moral education since it is the realm of religion and spirituality, in its less doctrinaire forms, that engages many of the students' deepest questions and strongest convictions about how to live an ethical life. But this renewed interest in spirituality and its links to moral education makes many in the academy deeply uneasy" (Kiss and Euben, "Debating Moral Education: An Introduction," 12).

49. "The 'extreme difficulty' of the task of character education . . . is no longer merely a conflict between two generations, but between a world which for several millennia has believed in a truth superior to man, and an age which does not believe in it any longer" (Buber, *Between Man and Man*, 110).

50. "Without the religious undergirding, the secular educational systems of France and the USA failed to deliver the grounds of shared morality that Durkheim and Dewey were looking for. They have ended up with a colourless and impoverished morality" (Dill, "Challenge of Contemporary Moral Education," 233).

51. See MacIntyre, *After Virtue*, 177–180.

52. "The contemporary discussion about virtues . . . would benefit from taking Aquinas more seriously . . . virtue ethics could be strengthened by the notion of God" (Tjeltveit, "Foundations of Moral Selfhood," 74).

practices in character and virtue education and a growing desire to integrate academic and professional education with formation. Faculty and leaders in theological schools are especially sensitive to moral outcomes and theology students are particularly pliable to formational input. Stakeholders, as well, are typically concerned with character issues. Overall, there are few contexts that have more potential for character and virtue education to flourish than a theological school.

—

If I may generalize the message of this letter, I fear that we have slipped off the shoulders of giants. Theological education could do much more than what it is currently doing. There is a desire to change and an unprecedented window of opportunity. But there is also a slowness in making the aims of character and virtue education clear, intentional and central.

May we be discerning in our zeal, avoiding the rashness of youth and the resignation of age.

8

Virtue for Social Impact

Funny things happen when you near sixty. You start to look back at your life and wonder about the significance of what you've accomplished, and then you look at yourself and laugh at your silly speculations. I am in that season now, and all of this thinking about virtue is teaching me to re-examine the legacy I am leaving as a person rather than as a performer. In his book, *The Road to Character*, *New Yorker* columnist David Brooks contrasts résumé virtues with eulogy virtues.[1] Whereas the former have to do with our professional accomplishments, the latter relate to the aspects of our character that others will praise when we're no longer around. So, while you and I are currently intent on performing well to achieve a project of significance, let us not forget what really counts.

The Scope of the *Missio Dei*

Speaking of significance, I recall sharing a room with you during the 2010 Lausanne Movement congress. Do you recall the conversation we had that evening in the coffee lounge over the social impact of the gospel? I don't know if I ever told you, but that particular conversation allowed me to crystallize some of my own thinking around the mission of the church, seeing it as more than just personal evangelism and church planting. Following Cape Town, I re-read Bebbington's analysis of evangelicalism[2] and reconsidered how my horizon had been occupied by a particular "evangelical" culture that had emphasized conversionism, activism, biblicism and crucicentrism. While I still hold to much of that, my vision of the *missio Dei* has enlarged to include

---

1. Rebecca Mead, "David Brooks's Search for Meaning," *The New Yorker*, 27 May 2015, https://www.newyorker.com/culture/cultural-comment/david-brookss-search-for-meaning.

2. Bebbington, *Evangelicalism in Modern Britain*, 7.

other priorities, such as cultural discipleship,[3] a theological vision of work, a re-appreciation of beauty alongside truth and goodness, a commitment to social improvement and a vision of impacting the world of ideas as well as the personal lives of individuals.

So, while personal evangelism remains important to me, I now believe that other activities also have intrinsic value. In addition to a great mandate, I also see a cultural mandate. While I believe in my ministry as a teacher in the theology department of my university, I also have a God-given "secular" calling in the educational department where I teach and do research. While I continue to wish to proclaim the truth of the cross, I also feel it is important to move truth forward in all spheres of life. I believe we should pray for "spiritual" things, but also that we should be giving thanks for the benefits of common grace that include beautiful art, good food and great books. I love my neighbour and work for his salvation, but I also love my neighbourhood and I work for its improvement (which is why, for example, I recently ran for local elections).

Much of this was between the lines in Cape Town. We were challenged to bear witness to Jesus Christ "in every sphere of society and into the realm of ideas."[4] We were also reminded that an integral mission is not only about proclaiming the gospel, but also about discerning its truths as they impact the worlds in which we live. We were challenged to think of the good news as not only for individuals but also for society that is broken and included per se in the mission of God.[5] I know that for many Christians this is "old school," but for me it has been a gradual journey of realization.

A Gift to Society

So, you may ask me, what does this have to do with our conversation over character and virtue in theological education? Very much, and in every way. What I see, in fact, is that the formation of women and men of character and virtue is one of the greatest gifts that the church can give society. We are not just training pastors and church leaders to build the church, we are contributing to the formation of citizens who will bless the world.

This vision shifts our thinking considerably. It complements knowledge with an attitude of virtue and presence. It brings together the proclamation of the gospel from the mountaintop with the shining of the gospel into the

---

3. See Mouw, *Challenges of Cultural Discipleship*.
4. Lausanne Movement, "Cape Town Commitment," Foreword.
5. "Cape Town Commitment," 17.

valleys of the world. It means not only leading earthly individuals to heaven but bringing heavenly goodness to earth. In educational terms, this vision bursts into our learning outcomes and revitalizes the dimension of *being* alongside *knowing* and *doing*, and enriches our theological curricula beyond academic achievement and practical competences.

To say that society is positively impacted by virtue resembles a tautology. But it deserves thought. Imagine a society where everyone is just, compared to a society where everyone is unjust. Or greedy. Or proud. Or intemperate. More virtue simply makes the world a better place. Dante, in the *Divine Comedy*, imagines paradise in terms of layers of virtue, whereas hell is represented by layers of vice. This is the history of the world. Good history was made by good people. Prosperous societies were marked by virtue. The best friendships are those grounded in the shared good. The history of Israel was one where kings of good character brought blessings and where bad kings brought disaster. Plato's *The Republic* suggested that society would be ruined when the guardians of the state lost virtue, and Montesquieu made it clear that virtue was the essential ingredient for justice and order in a democratic society.[6]

Society does not need more rules or better structures, it needs better people. The Swiss professor Christoph Stückelberger elaborates on this point from his own experience.[7] After a lifetime devoted to developing structural ethics that were meant to help international companies, non-governmental organizations and governments to act and legislate in a way that is ethically responsible,[8] Stückelberger concludes that the real problems of the world are not the structures, but the people. If we want virtue, he claims, the solutions are found not in virtuous institutions, but in virtuous people.[9]

Good ideas are also insufficient, and even the greatest ideologies fall short if they are not matched by the character of the people they arouse. The French Revolution, for example, offered wonderful slogans of liberty, equality and fraternity, but the key to the real revolution, or lack thereof, was in the character of the French. Liberty was not possible without the virtues of love, civility and faithfulness. Equality was not possible without the virtues of justice

---

6. "When virtue ceases, ambition enters those hearts that can admit it and avarice enters them all" (*L'Esprit des lois*, in Hunter, *Death of Character*, 4–6).

7. In Stückelberger, Fust and Ike, *Global Ethics for Leadership*, https://www.globethics.net/documents/4289936/13403236/GE_Global_13_web.pdf/.

8. See https://www.globethics.net/.

9. "There are no virtuous institutions, there are only virtuous people" (C. Stückelberger, "Integrität: Die Tugend der Tugenden – Der christliche Beitrag zu einer globalen Tugend für Wirtschaft und Politik," Farewell lecture at the University of Basel, Department of Theology, 2 November 2016 (unpublished manuscript).

and generosity. Fraternity was impossible without humility, benevolence and patience.

Every time the virtues are missing, we see society that is doomed to war, poverty and decadence. I am thinking of the failure of communism in your neighbouring countries. Whatever one thinks of Marxist ideology, the collapse of these regimes was due not primarily to faulty ideas, but to the character of the communist leaders who abandoned their drive for justice, equality and compassion and fell prey to greed, pride and violence. After two terrible wars driven by great ideologies, Europeans have acknowledged that character-shaped social communities are the basis for peaceful coexistence. "The Charter of Fundamental Rights of the European Union," in fact, sets the foundations of closer union and a peaceful future in Europe not on ideology, but on a spiritual and moral heritage found in the six fundamental rights of "The Charter": dignity, freedom, equality, solidarity, citizens' rights and justice.[10] A careful reading of these rights points to a virtuous citizenry as the hope for social peace and unity.

The Cry for Virtue

The cry for virtue is not a niche topic for educators; nor is it a private issue.[11] It is a high priority in today's societies and the Nobel Peace Prize is awarded every year to an individual or organization that has demonstrated the virtues of justice, generosity, compassion and peace.[12] Character is the barometer that sets social temperatures and nourishes social prosperity and happiness.[13] Character diminishes crime rates, reduces herd behaviour, curtails materialism and nihilism,[14] increases mental well-being, produces beneficial health effects and enhances the labour market.[15]

---

10. At EUR-LEX: Access to European Union Law, https://eur-lex.europa.eu/legal-content/EN/TXT/?uri=CELEX:12012P/TXT.

11. "The development of a person's character is not entirely a private matter for individuals and their families. It is accepted that character is intimately linked to the ethos of society itself and shaped by public forces" (Arthur et al., *Teaching*, 26).

12. "According to leading analysts, the citizens of our nation [America] have reached two conclusions about our current direction. First, we suffer from growing inequality. And second, we suffer from moral depletion . . . public distress about the state of our social morality has reached nearly universal proportions: 87 percent of the public fear that something is fundamentally wrong with America's moral condition" (Elshtain, "Call to Civil Society," 4).

13. "Character matters . . . because without it, trust, justice, freedom, community and stability are probably impossible" (Hunter, *Death of Character*, 6).

14. See Kierkegaard, *The Present Age*.

15. Birdwell, Scott and Reynolds, *Character Nation*, 9.

Let me give you a few examples from the world of work, where studies are emerging on the place of virtue ethics in enhancing the professional paradigms of law,[16] health, media[17] and business. Virtue ethics scales are being devised to identify virtuous qualities of professionals, to improve evaluations of ethical behaviour and to enhance organizational deontology.[18] Similar conclusions link character and the quality of work produced by craftsmen[19] and professional workers.[20] Organizations in general are paying more attention to issues of personal character,[21] and emotional intelligence is progressively being seen as impacting teamwork productivity.[22] There is a widespread recognition that the corporate world has come under pressure because of its unethical behaviour, and that this has contributed to the crisis of investor confidence,[23] to the stock market decline[24] and to the 2008 global financial crash.[25] It is increasingly accepted that non-virtuous business practices lead to increasing entropy, disorder and inefficiency,[26] and that, in corporate management, the qualities

---

16. In *The Lost Lawyer*, A. Kronman makes the case that the key to the law profession is not knowledge and competence, but the virtue of prudence. "Prudence is the lawyer's central virtue" (Kronman, 5). A legal education, therefore, "must do more than impart information and technical skills. It must inculcate the character virtues of prudence and public spiritedness" (Kronman, 154).

17. Magali do Nascimento Cunha, "Global Values in Media," in Stückelberger, Fust and Ike, *Global Ethics for Leadership*, 393–400.

18. "The *Virtue Ethics Scale* developed by Shanahan and Hyman (2003) . . . identifies managers' beliefs about the virtuous qualities of businesspeople; the *Multidimensional Scale* developed by Reidenbach and Robin (1990) . . . can be used to improve evaluations of business ethics; and the *Virtue Ethical Character Scale* (VECS) of Chun (2005) . . . is a scale of organizational virtues that seeks to validate the traditional virtue dimensions mentioned in the virtue ethics literature" (Racelis, "Developing a Virtue Ethics Scale," 16).

19. Sennet, in Arthur, Wilson and Godfrey, *Graduates of Character*, 13.

20. Carr, *Educating the Virtues*, 115.

21. Joan Elise Dubinksy, "Global Values in International Organisations," in Stückelberger, Fust and Ike, *Global Ethics for Leadership*, 407–428.

22. Pavela, "Renewed Focus," 735.

23. Sir Mark Moody-Stuart, "Global Values in Business," in Stückelberger, Fust and Ike, *Global Ethics for Leadership*, 369–391.

24. Racelis, "Developing a Virtue Ethics Scale," 16.

25. Wright, *After You Believe*, 10.

26. Racelis, "Developing a Virtue Ethics Scale," 23.

of efficient and successful managers (such as respect, generosity, friendliness, tenacity and courage[27]) should align with the categories of the virtues.[28]

Discussions around virtue are also emerging in the sciences. In cultural anthropology, for example, ethical behaviour is considered to be the product of evolution that has helped man to survive. Darwin first suggested this in *The Descent of Man*, claiming that "the development of moral qualities in human beings lies in social instincts that can be strengthened by exercise or habit."[29] Edward O. Wilson, Professor in Entomology at Harvard, raises the stakes, claiming that "Ethics is everything ... We are adults who have discovered which covenants are necessary for survival, and we have accepted the necessity of securing them by sacred oath."[30]

We have already seen some of the educational data, so here I will just note that good character improves educational performance,[31] school engagement[32] and the development of cognitive skills.[33] Concerning higher education, an important study was conducted within the Bologna Process called Tuning 2000.[34] This study consisted of a large-scale consultation among graduates, employers and academics to identify general skills and competences required of all university graduates. A careful look at the thirty competences confirms that they are impossible without the virtues. For example, critical and self-critical abilities need humility. The skill to work autonomously requires temperance and self-control. The will to succeed requires constancy and courage. Interpersonal skills require patience and compassion. Ability to work in teams requires

---

27. "Business virtues in the Philippines setting revolve chiefly around, on the one hand, Care and Respect which is characterized by sympathy, respect, generosity, support, and friendliness; and, on the other hand, a rather peculiar Courage-related characteristic involving a certain degree of ambition, pride, superiority, and aggressiveness" (Racelis 30).

28. "In the numerous and almost endless bibliography on corporate management, the qualities of an efficient manager are enumerated more or less repeatedly. The terms used in those books may at times appear to be new, but the concepts, as expected, do not go beyond the sphere of virtues" (Racelis, 23).

29. Pavela, "Renewed Focus," 734.

30. Pavela, 744.

31. In *Why Johnny Can't Tell Right from Wrong*, Kilpatrick claims that "academic reform depends on putting character first" (Lickona, *Educating for Character*, 1). See also Birdwell, Scott and Reynolds, *Character Nation*, 19.

32. "Recent empirical evidence ... indicates that ... Aristotelian character education has instrumental benefits, for instance in the form of higher grades in traditional school subjects" (Kristjánsson, *Aristotelian Character Education*, 55).

33. Habl, "Character Formation," 145.

34. The Tuning 2000 project was supported by the European Commission and by the European University Association, involving over 100 higher education institutions, 15,000 graduates, 3,000 employers and 1,500 academics (http://www.unideusto.org/tuningeu/).

loyalty, faith and magnanimity, and appreciation of diversity requires love and open-mindedness. And so on. Even if no mention was made of character and virtue in the Tuning project, we can see that genuine graduate competences are achievable only through character and virtue. Whereas *technè* has sought to replace *arête*, a closer look tells us that genuine *technè* prospers only in the presence of *arête*. As the competences agenda is increasingly dominating higher education, it is important to see that the underlying strength of competences is found in the education of character and virtue.

Theological Education and Society

As theological educators we should be taking the lead in this renewal. If the greatest hopes for moral improvement in society are found in faith communities and in higher education,[35] we, as theological educators, are uniquely positioned in both of these groups. We represent faith communities but we also operate in higher education and, from this exclusive vantage point, we can contribute to the fitness of the world,[36] be active in the improvement of society and speak responsibly as its conscience.[37]

I fear that too often we either tiptoe around with an inferiority complex or arrogantly proselytize with a superiority complex. Society does not respond well to either, but more readily accepts, expects and even welcomes the engagement of faith communities in character and virtue education. David Hume, who was an avowed enemy of religion, defended religion for its ability to strengthen society and improve morality.[38] Solzhenitsyn famously stated that "the line between good and evil runs through the human heart," and faith communities are in the business of educating the heart.[39] If religion is accepted as a positive moral force, we who engage in theological education should promote human flourishing through the cultivation of personal responsibility, respect of law and solidarity with ones neighbours.[40]

---

35. Elshtain, "Call to Civil Society," 9, 10.
36. Maskell and Robinson, *New Idea of the University*, 27.
37. "Men of character are the conscience of the society to which they belong" (Emerson, *Complete Works*, 1454).
38. W. Jordan, "Religion in the Public Square: A Reconsideration of David Hume and Religious Establishment," *The Review of Politics* 64, no. 4 (2002): 687–714.
39. Koons, "Three Humanisms," 205.
40. "By elevating our sights toward others and toward ultimate concerns, religious institutions help us turn away from self-centeredness, or what Tocqueville terms 'egotism,' democracy's most dangerous temptation, through which 'citizens have no sympathy for any but

Sadly, Christians are sometimes slow to see this. A survey conducted in the UK a few years ago indicated that 57 percent of practising Christians did not believe that theological education had any significant influence on culture.[41] This is an example of a ghetto mentality that relegates theological education to inward-looking contexts. Although some theological schools are including social issues in their curricula, I'm not sure that this corresponds to the kind of intentional impact that we have been discussing.[42] The renewed interest in fields such as social justice is a good start, but we need to do more than just raise awareness and educate the mind.[43] As we teach social justice, we should intentionally shape our graduates to be just. As we do theological work on peace-making, so we need to nourish peace-makers. As we teach a theology of culture, we need to raise up a generation of Christians who love and pursue beauty, harmony, creativity and order. As we teach a theology of work, we must plan to shape our graduates to be positive components in the workforce.[44]

An Apologetic of Virtue

I went out for a nice run before finishing this letter and, as often happens, I've come back with some fresh thoughts. This might come as a rather unexpected twist, but I'd like to shift your thoughts briefly to apologetics. Those of us who teach apologetics know that the bite of postmodernity has weakened the effectiveness of classical and propositional apologetics. As heirs of modernity, we've composed our apologetics songs to the tune of rationalism and the rhythm of the Enlightenment, but now we are no longer sure what to sing. Having explored what apologetics might look like in postmodernity and after postmodernity, we are left wondering if there is still a place for this discipline.

Why not think of character and virtue education as a fresh line of apologetics strategy – a strategy that is no longer made of rational words, but of virtuous deeds? In a sense, it would be a return to the work of early apologists who had to defend the place of Christians in the Roman Empire. My growing conviction is that the contribution to society of women and men of

---

themselves." At their best, then, our houses of worship foster values that are essential to human flourishing and to democratic civil society" (Elshtain, "Call to Civil Society," 9).

41. Kinnaman, "Perceptions," 22.

42. See Mouw and Lovin, "Public Character in Action," v–xi.

43. Roosevelt claimed that to educate a person in mind and not in morals was to educate a menace to society (Lickona, *Educating for Character*, 1).

44. In America, employers are just as likely to hire Bible college graduates as any other candidate (Kinnaman, *What's Next?*, 33).

character and virtue can be an apologetics statement testifying to the relevance of Christianity. In Lewis's words, we must have "men with chests"[45] who deploy virtue. And theological schools are a starting place.

—

So, a toast to significance. Although our pursuit of virtue is not primarily utilitarian,[46] we have good reason to consider it useful. Thank you for letting me know that you are organizing a consultation with the faith communities in your region. You are very wise in listening carefully and seeking the prophetic voice of the community. I am sorry to hear that you still are not well – do get some rest.

May we grow out of parochiality and be magnanimous to all those we call neighbours.

---

45. "In a sort of ghastly simplicity, we remove the organ and demand the function. We make men without chests and expect of them virtue and enterprise. We laugh at honour and are shocked to find traitors in our midst. We castrate, and bid the geldings be fruitful" (C. S. Lewis, *Abolition of Man*, 26).

46. Hauerwas raises a theological objection to this strategy on the grounds that it makes civic republicanism into an idol: "Widespread enthusiasm for virtue may provide the churches, who have become increasingly irrelevant to the public discussion of the issues before the American polity, a way to contribute to that polity by producing people of virtue . . . even if enticing, this is a false hope" (Hauerwas and Pinches, *Christians among the Virtues*, 149). See also Herdt, "Hauerwas among the Virtues," 214.

9

Virtue for Political Impact

I've seen news about the elections in your country and the signals of a democratic crisis are evident. Your leaders are powerful but, despite their respect for the written law and the intricate administrative machinery, they appear to be ignorant, blind and incapable of wise governance. It seems that competition for power is the real agenda behind their skilled words. They are, sadly, the kinds of leaders that our soft-bellied and aimless societies produce. If we have embraced the values of individualism, subjectivism and hedonism, is it really a surprise that the political classes do little better?

These political scenarios can easily make us feel cynical, discouraged and powerless. But history is rife with similarities, and I find particular comfort in looking to Socrates and Plato,[1] for, even if the crisis of democracy in fourth-century Athens was very similar to what I have just described, they did not give up, but acted on the conviction that education was the key to political health. This brings me to the topic of this letter, in which I will argue that character and virtue education are a powerful remedy for today's political decadence and democratic crises.

The Effects of Virtuous Government

As you know, I travel often to Italy and last week I visited Siena. I spent the afternoon in the Palazzo Pubblico where I admired the frescoes completed by Ambrogio Lorenzetti between 1338 and 1339. The frescoes are entitled *Allegoria del Buono e Cattivo Governo e I loro Effetti in Città e in Campagna* (translated: "An Allegory of Good and Bad Government and the Effects Thereof in the City and in the Countryside"). The frescoes were commissioned by the Government of the Nine in Siena to provide inspiration to those who met in

---

1. Jaeger, *Paideia*, 238.

these rooms to govern the city. The frescoes are remarkable in many ways, not only because they are among the first examples of secular art in an epoch in which religious themes prevailed, but also because of their rich reference to historical events, literary works and the traditions of virtue and vice. There are four frescoes in all, two depicting good government and its effects in the city and countryside, and two depicting bad government and its effects. Let me try to describe them to you (you may wish to do a quick Google image search so you can actually see them).

The *Allegory of Good Government* is an explosion of virtue metaphors, starting with *Justice* that is represented as Divine Wisdom and is holding a book and a set of scales that are administered by two angels. The angels are performing acts of commutative justice (we see one man being decapitated and another one crowned) and distributive justice (the angel is providing two merchants with measuring instruments). *Concord* sits beside *Justice* with a shaving plane in her hand, as a symbol of equality and of the need to level out civil conflicts. A rope links *Concord* and *Justice* to each other and to twenty-four citizens representing the various components of the Sienese community. The rope also joins the Commune, representing the city government with the symbols of Siena. Hovering over the Commune we see the three theological virtues; *Faith*, *Hope* and *Charity*. Sitting at the side of the Commune, we find the four cardinal virtues, each holding symbolic objects: a sword and crown for *Justice*, an hourglass for *Temperance*, a club and shield for *Fortitude* and a mirror for *Prudence*. We also find *Peace*, lying gently over a heap of weapons with an olive branch in her hand, and *Magnanimity* who is dispensing crowns and coins.

The marvellous effects of good government are shown in the next fresco, where we see luxurious city squares, stores full of goods, lovely ornaments and flowers on the terraces. The citizens are industrious and busy with many occupations, including studying and teaching. There are also scenes of leisure, as a maiden with a crown on her head rides to her wedding, and a group of youths hold hands and dance. In the countryside, we find citizens and farmers travelling safely on the roads, hunting in the forests and cultivating vines and olive groves. The virtue of *Security* hovers over the countryside, holding the gallows of punishment in one hand and an inscription with the invitation to walk and work without fear in the other. It is notable that Lorenzetti shows us both noblemen riding on horses and beggars on the side of the road, indicating that good government does not necessarily flatten out all social inequalities, but allows them to cohabit in peace and security.

By contrast, the opposing fresco shows the effects of bad government in the city and in the countryside. The city is in ruins. Citizens are pulling down its buildings. There are killings in the streets and innocent people are arrested. There is hardly any sign of economic activity. The countryside is on fire and armies are marching towards the city, while *Fear* flies in the sky. All this is the result of government that is in the hands of vice. At the centre of the *Allegory of Bad Government*, we find *Tyranny*, depicted as a cross-eyed monster with diabolic fangs and horns. There are no ropes linking *Tyranny* to citizens and a black devilish goat sits at his feet. The three-winged vices of *Avarice*, *Pride* and *Vainglory* hover over him and at his side we find *Cruelty*, *Betrayal*, *Corruption*, *Fury*, *Division* and *War*. We also see *Avarice* with a long hook intent on snaring two purses. The other vices that dominate in bad government are: *Pride* with a sword and yoke; *Vainglory* holding a dry branch as a symbol of volubility; *Cruelty* showing a snake to an infant; *Betrayal* holding a lamb who is becoming a scorpion; *Corruption* with wings and claws; *Furore* with the head of a boar, the torso of a man, the body of a horse and the tail of a dog; *Division* with a saw (in opposition to the shaving plane held by *Concord*); and *War*, poised with a sword, a shield and a black robe. In all this, *Justice* lies dethroned and is bound and despoiled with her scales overthrown.

I find these paintings exceptionally pertinent to contemporary politics. But I also find myself thinking about theological education. What is the link between theology, theological education, a virtuous citizenry and government? Lorenzetti's frescoes make it clear that the virtues in government rely on divine intervention. In the Good Government fresco, the middle strata of the scene depict the classical virtues of human institutions, but the top level shows that Divine Wisdom is the only source that is able to hold true justice and impart the essential benefits of the theological virtues (the opposite holds true in the fresco of bad government, where there is a clear connection between satanic agency and human vice). This is a theological vision of politics that links spiritual realities with virtue and vice. But it is also a source of inspiration for our theological schools as they endeavour to make every effort to form citizens who will contribute to the political health of our societies. This is what I would like to explore in this letter.

Virtue and Social Welfare

Neither you nor I are political philosophers, but we have done enough reading in the field to know that virtue and social welfare are frequently linked. One of the dominating ideas in Aristotle's *Politics* is that the quality of a constitution is directly related to the character of its citizens.² Aristotle claims that "A city can be virtuous only when the citizens who have a share in the government are virtuous; and in our state all the citizens share in the government. Let us then inquire how a man becomes virtuous."³

For Aristotle, moral education is not a niche subject for intellectuals or religiously inclined individuals but is constituent of the fabric of all political societies. In his view, the only real problems of democracy are problems of character.⁴

Of course, Aristotle is not alone. Many contemporary political philosophers concur that character education is the bedrock of democracy and that character development goes hand in hand with democratic development.⁵ In America, for example, as the founding fathers sought a government for the people, they placed a prime value on the character of the people. Jefferson, Madison and Tocqueville all believed that virtue was the key to providing safety, vigour and happiness to the rising American democracy.⁶ Tocqueville, in particular, was convinced that morality was essential to a vibrant democracy and that, without virtue, society would be bound for destruction and disaster.⁷ These founders of American democracy reasoned that, if people rule themselves to ensure a good, free and just society, the people themselves must be good and love justice.⁸

---

2. Aristotle, *Politics* 1337a11–19. "The character of citizens matters to preserving constitutions and also to their quality. The better the character of the citizens, the better the constitution" (Curren, "Aristotle's Educational Politics," 552).

3. Aristotle, *Politics* 7.13, quoted in Boyd and King, *History of Western Education*, 37.

4. Jaeger, *Paideia*, 287.

5. "Democracy [is] . . . unworkable without an educated and morally responsible populace" (Gretchen and Firmin, "Character Education," 184). "Democracy is the government of the people; the people themselves are responsible for ensuring a free and just society. That means that people must, at least in some minimal sense, be good" (Lickona, *Educating for Character*, 6). "It only seems sensible that the possibility of a just society over time requires that most of its citizens are, to some degree, virtuous. This means that citizens themselves must endorse and embody certain virtues central to social cooperation. Such virtues are what political theorists call 'civic virtues'" (Timpe and Boyd, *Virtues and Their Vices*, 416). See also Adler, *The Paideia Proposal*.

6. "[T]he steady character of our countrymen is the rock to which we may safely moor" (Jefferson); "Is there no virtue among us? If there be not, we are in a wretched situation . . . to suppose that any form of government will secure liberty and happiness without any form of virtue in the people is a chimerical idea" (Madison); "How could society escape destruction if . . . moral ties are not tightened?" (Tocqueville), (all in Hunter, *Death of Character*, 4–6).

7. "Liberty cannot be established without morality, nor morality without faith" (Tocqueville, in Kiss and Euben, *Debating Moral Education*, 208).

8. See the Declaration of Independence, Washington's Farewell Address, Lincoln's Gettysburg Address and Second Inaugural Address, and King's Letter from the Birmingham Jail (Elshtain, "Call to Civil Society," 12).

The links between good character and good government can be seen in many parts of the world. In Israel, for example, Martin Buber believed that the establishment of the Jewish nation should not be ultimately built on the possession of land, the ideas of a nation or political structures, but on the formation of character.[9] His vision was deeply influential in establishing the Israeli educational system. I'm sure that it would not take much to unearth many other similar examples from all over the world.

Virtue in Liberal Democracy

Let me share a few thoughts about liberal democracy, for it is a popular form of government that presents a particular challenge when it comes to moral education. Liberal democracies value freedom and autonomy and believe that the state exists to guarantee the freedom of each individual to pursue his or her own values. But how can this be reconciled with the call to educate citizens in virtue and character? Does one not exclude the other? Can a state guarantee freedom and educate about character at the same time? Although there is a general agreement that freedom in a liberal democracy does not mean freedom from all values[10] and that there is a need for shared civic virtues,[11] there is plenty of debate over how these civic virtues are decided.

On one end of the spectrum, we find communitarian visions of democracy that try to identify shared patterns of virtue in a society.[12] These so-called "perfectionist" accounts of liberalism claim that there is an objectively good human life, and that the state needs to recognize it and promote it.[13] The civic humanism of Aristotle, Cicero, Machiavelli, Milton, Montesquieu and Jefferson are examples of this. In these accounts it is quite easy to find the place of character and virtue education, for civic virtues normally align with classical views of virtue.

---

9. B. Ott, "Martin Buber on Character Formation."

10. "Democracy is not a values-free form of government" (Gretchen and Firmin, "Character Education," 184).

11. "Civic virtues are excellences of character that promote or, in part, constitute the purpose of the state" (Timpe and Boyd, *Virtues and Their Vices*, 416).

12. "The best type of human life, that in which the tradition of the virtues is most adequately embodied, is lived by those engaged in constructing and sustaining forms of community directed towards the shared achievement of those common goods without which the ultimate human good cannot be achieved" (MacIntyre, *After Virtue*, xii).

13. In communitarianism, civic virtues are "those virtues of persons as citizens that promote or constitute a particular community's ends of the objectively good human life" (Timpe and Boyd, *Virtues and Their Vices*, 417).

By contrast, anti-perfectionist visions of liberalism are more problematic, because they claim that the state should be neutral when it comes to views of the good life. As I was thinking about this, I recalled examining the doctoral thesis of one of your students who did some theological work around Rawls's *A Theory of Justice*. That was, by the way, a fantastic example of your ability to engage with an important thinker on the topic of moral development in liberal democracies.[14] I could not find my copy of the thesis, so I will rely on memory.

I recall that Rawls does some helpful work around the conundrum that we have just mentioned, carving out a place for civic virtue under the label of "political virtues." He does not suggest a grand, all-encompassing picture such as what we have seen in Lorenzetti's frescoes, but argues for a minimalist provision that will help us maintain a just and stable regime.[15] Rawls encourages political virtues that are acceptable to all free and equal citizens[16] such as non-domination, respectfulness, autonomy, civility, tolerance, reasonableness[17] and fairness. Although Rawls does not use the terminology of the classical virtues, we can see that his theory of justice relies on them, even if indirectly. Respectfulness, in fact, needs *humility*; freedom and fairness need *equity*; respectfulness calls for *open-mindedness*; public reason needs the *intellectual virtues*;[18] and toleration requires the virtues of *patience, generosity* and *love*.

To achieve all this, education is paramount, and Rawls argues for the existence of educational sources that will promote civic virtue and help us achieve the ideals of political justice.[19] I would claim that theological schools

---

14. "In Part III of *A Theory of Justice*, Rawls provided a picture of how individuals might be brought up in a just state to develop the virtues expected of good citizens. Although his interest was not in moral education per se, his discussion of how individuals acquire a sense of justice and of how they develop what he called self-respect stimulated other philosophers to explore the psychological foundations of virtue and the contributions made by friendship, family, community, and meaningful work to good moral character" (Leif Wenar, "John Rawls," *The Stanford Encyclopedia of Philosophy* [Spring 2017 Edition], ed Edward N. Zalta, https://plato.stanford.edu/archives/spr2017/entries/rawls/).

15. Rawls, *Theory of Justice*, 195. "Civic virtues are not defined as part of a view of human flourishing or human excellence in general, but, rather, as a set of features of character that are necessary to maintain a just and democratic society. In this way, civic virtue is identified and justified by the need to have citizens possess certain features of character in order to maintain a just and stable regime" (Timpe and Boyd, *Virtues and Their Vices*, 422).

16. "Even though political liberalism seeks common ground and is neutral in aim, it is important to emphasize that it may still affirm the superiority of certain forms of moral character and encourage certain moral virtues" (Rawls, *Theory of Justice*, 194).

17. Rawls, *Theory of Justice*, 54–58.

18. "A variety of intellectual virtues are of central importance to political liberalism that include attentive listening, patience with fellow participants and sharing of social space" (Timpe and Boyd, *Virtues and Their Vices*, 428).

19. Rawls, *Theory of Justice*, 56.

can be one of these sources of civic virtue that serve to enhance political virtues in liberal democracies.[20] Theological education might even be more effective than the sources that Rawls envisions to create a just society because it aims at changing individuals and not just institutions.[21]

Morality, Religion and Theological Education

This leads me to my final point, which is the one closest to us. The general public does not naturally associate theological schools with the promotion of liberalism. Just the opposite. They are often depicted as the seedbeds of intolerance, indoctrination and coercion. I'm not saying that we must embrace everything that political liberalism stands for, but we should reclaim higher ground and point out that the Christian religion has much to contribute when it comes to political virtue.

There are certainly many bad examples of the mixing of religion and politics, but there are also many good examples of religion contributing to good government.[22] Tocqueville wrote extensively about the links between religion and democracy and had a high view of the benefits of religion to politics.[23] It was religion, according to him, that taught people how to use freedom well, how to distinguish liberty and licence, how to justify self-regulation, how to live in communities and how to combat the materialistic and nihilistic tendencies

---

20. A case for the education of civic virtue can be made in both perfectionist and anti-perfectionist visions of liberal democracy. A perfectionist vision will "concern instilling in a citizen those traits of character that will, at once, make for a good citizen and an objectively good life" (Timpe and Boyd, *Virtues and Their Vices*, 429). An anti-perfectionist vision will include knowledge of constitutional and civic rights and "encourage the political virtues so that they will want to honour the fair terms of social cooperation in their relations with the rest of society" (Rawls, *Theory of Justice*, 199).

21. "It has been the project of liberal political and ethical theory to create societies that could be just without people that constitute those societies being just . . . Rawls does not exclude considerations of virtue, but he assumes, like most modern political and ethical theorists, that any account of virtue is secondary to principles and institutions that are more determinative than virtue itself" (Hauerwas, "Difference of Virtue," 249).

22. The New Hampshire Constitution (1784) stated that "morality and piety, rightly grounded on evangelical principles, will give the best and greatest security to government" (Hunter, *Death of Character*, 41).

23. "Religion is no less the companion of liberty in all its battles and its triumphs; the cradle of its infancy, and the divine source of its claims. The safeguard of morality is religion, and morality is the best security of law and the surest pledge of freedom" (Tocqueville, *Democracy in America*, 60).

associated with democracy.²⁴ Since democracy removed authoritarian bonds, it desperately needed to strengthen moral bonds if society was to be held together. The best way to do this was, according to Tocqueville, submission to God.²⁵

You can see where I am going with this. Buber has said it well: "Genuine education of character is genuine education for community."²⁶ We, as theological educators, should be energized at the prospect of contributing to our political communities through the education of character. This is not a return to Constantinian thinking nor a revival of some of the failing "Christendom" political models. It is an alternative vision of Christian political engagement that contributes to nourishing citizens and leaders of virtue.²⁷

—

I trust that I have not fatigued you with this complex letter. I have a delightful little booklet on my shelf by Graham Cray entitled *Disciples and Citizens*. The title says it all. If we trained disciples to be better citizens, would that not make a statement about the relevance of the Christian faith to a world that is otherwise sceptical and uninterested?

As you come under the authority of your newly elected government, may you beat the sword of political cynicism into a ploughshare of action.

---

24. Tocqueville claims that religion is one of the elements that can successfully combat destructive and anti-democratic tendencies, safeguard morality, and preserve the security of the law and the duration of freedom (Kiss and Euben, *Debating Moral Education*, 209–210).

25. "How is it possible that society should escape destruction if the moral tie be not strengthened in proportion as the political tie is relaxed? And what can be done with a people which is its own master, if it be not submissive to the Divinity?" (Tocqueville, *Democracy in America*, 338).

26. Buber, *Between Man and Man*, 116.

27. "Where instruction is less general, and where the principles of morality, of religion, and of liberty are less happily combined, we perceive that the talents and the virtues of those who are in authority become more and more rare" (Tocqueville, *Democracy in America*, 27).

10

Discipleship as Virtue

Dear Siméon, I welcome your disagreement with me over the use of the term "discipleship." A few letters ago, I argued that our current use of the term "discipleship" is too imprecise and religiously slanted to be useful for character and virtue education. In your return letter, you have argued that it is important to keep the term and that we should not discard it, but rather enrich it with a greater understanding of character and virtue. Your main point is that discipleship is the essence of the Christian life and that all formational activities should be framed within its objectives. You are even considering including the word "discipleship" in the name of your school. This is a semantic discussion, but it merits a full reply.

The "Discipleship" Word

Let me first back up and look at the history of the term "discipleship." This is not my particular area of expertise but, from what I've gleaned, the revival of the term is relatively recent.[1] Discipleship has largely built on the successes of evangelism, and organizations like The Navigators and Campus Crusade for Christ have done much to provide "follow-up" programmes intended to build the long-term faith of the converted. But there is more. Discipleship is also considered a key to church growth and a cure for lukewarm churches.[2]

This revival of discipleship has come with a deeper reading of the Great Commission in Matthew 28, and has benefited from the rediscovery of top-quality theological literature, such as Bonhoeffer's *Discipleship*, Thomas à Kempis's *The Imitation of Christ* or the writings of A. W. Tozer. Generally

---

1. Porter, *Recovery of Virtue*, 5. The Ngram Viewer indicates that the term "discipleship" has increased in publication frequency by over 300 percent since 1940.

2. R. Bodner, *The American Discipleship Problem: The Lukewarm Christian Epidemic* (self-published, 2015).

speaking, the discipleship movement has brought a constructive awareness that the "Christian thing" entails a walk of sanctification and growth and not just an experience of salvation, the supernatural or the sacramental.[3]

Discipleship Paradigms

But what exactly is meant by the term "discipleship" today? I admit that I nourish a love–hate relationship with the term, because it says so much and so little at the same time.[4] Sometimes the word "discipleship" is lightly used to provide a false sense of depth and gravity, and churches advertise "world-changing discipleship programmes" that in reality are only slightly enhanced adult Sunday school programmes. Other times, the so-called call to "discipleship" simply demands that folk give more, sing more loudly and show up at meetings.

There are also many thoughtful uses of the term "discipleship," and these vary greatly. An overview of some of the key concepts that emerge from the indexes of recent books[5] published on discipleship suggests that the term "discipleship" is used to talk about "replication," "orientation to others," "consecration and submission," being "more than just a believer," "counting the cost" and "being crucified," "service and ministry," "prayer and purity," "leadership training," "mentoring" and "Bible study."

In addition to these concepts, different paradigms also sprout up from a variety of historical, cultural and theological roots and define different aims of discipleship. We have, for example, a *service and performance paradigm*,[6] in which the main objective of discipleship is active service such as evangelism, church planting, social work, cultural and political involvement or more disciple-making. There is then a *teaching paradigm*, in which the main aim of discipleship is to enhance knowledge and understanding of theology and

---

3. Porter, *Recovery of Virtue*, 4.

4. "In the Christian world, the word discipleship is discussed by many, but fully comprehended by few" (Beagles, "Growing Disciples in Community," 81).

5. The indexes of the following book were consulted: Kilpatrick, *The Mystery of Discipleship* (2006); Bodner, *The American Discipleship Problem: The Lukewarm Christian Epidemic* (2015); Dever, *Discipling: How to Help Others Follow Jesus* (2016); Willard, *The Great Omission* (2006); Eims, *The Lost Art of Disciplemaking* (1978); Putman, *Real-Life Discipleship* (2010); Ogden, *Discipleship Essentials* (1988); Chan, *Multiply: Disciples Making Disciples* (2012); Geiger, *Transformational Discipleship* (2012).

6. Hull, *Complete Book of Discipleship*, 18.

of the Bible in order to experience personal transformation[7] and be able to better teach the Bible to others.[8] We also have *membership paradigms*, where discipleship entails enculturation to a particular denomination or faith community, and *mystical and devotional paradigms*,[9] where discipleship has to do with encountering God, experiencing his presence and witnessing supernatural intervention.

The list goes on. We have *consecration paradigms*, where disciples are defined as those who are "completely devoted" to God, meaning that individuals prioritize faith-related activities over secular work and are actively involved in missions. There are *enchantment paradigms*, that aim at walking wisely in the world with a sense of mystery. There are *leadership paradigms*, where to be a disciple means acquiring the characteristics and abilities of a leader. There are *relational paradigms* that define a successful disciple in terms of healthy interpersonal relationships, usually within small-group contexts.[10] These often dovetail with *therapeutic paradigms*, which define a disciple as one who has found inner healing and health.

Sometimes one or more of these paradigms prevail, but most frequently they are blended into an integrated approach.[11] Each paradigm normally points to Jesus as the prime example, depicting him alternately as the master servant, the great teacher, the spiritual man, the great healer or the leader of all leaders. Each paradigm also has a different idea of what "maturity" is, ranging from "being active" to "having critical knowledge and understanding" or to "knowing how to be effective." And, finally, each paradigm normally contemplates some form of replication, where those who are discipled reach out to disciple others.

Although there is reason to rejoice in this richness, it does make it extremely difficult to know what is being said when one uses the word "discipleship." In such a heterogeneous panorama, I wonder if we should be looking for a comprehensive definition at all.

---

7. "The goal is to understand what the Bible is saying and allow the truth to transform your thought process and lifestyle" (Chan, *Multiply*, 11).

8. "Bible teaching is the paramount means of disciple-making and the most serious deficiency in contemporary Church leaders" (Lausanne Movement, "Cape Town Commitment," IID, 3).

9. Ogden, *Discipleship Essentials*.

10. Some might call this third-stream psychological discipleship or relational discipleship. In essence, this movement encompasses the ways people get along. See, for example, Crabb, *The Safest Place on Earth*; Wilhoit, *Spiritual Formation as If the Church Mattered*; Gorman, *Community That Is Christian*; and Drurey, *Relational Discipleship*.

11. Gallati, *Rediscovering Discipleship*, 12.

Character, Virtue and Discipleship

I trust that you are beginning to see my point about the difficulties in associating such a broadly understood term with the specific vision of character and virtue education. What can we conclude? Does character and virtue education have no place whatsoever in the broad landscape of discipleship? Is there no overlap at all? To the contrary, I believe that character and virtue education has a vital place in discipleship, in at least three ways.

First, whether it is acknowledged or not, virtue represents an underlying force in all the discipleship paradigms. Although explicit references to character and virtue are rare, none of the proposed discipleship paradigms could function without specific character traits. However we define the mission of God, character is important.[12] The service paradigm, for example, operates through the virtues of *compassion* and *love*. The teaching paradigm requires *intellectual virtues*. The devotional paradigm presupposes *humility* and *temperance*. The enchantment paradigm is grounded in the virtue of *wisdom*, and the leadership paradigm calls on the virtues of *courage*, *magnanimity* and *temperance*. There are also general virtues at work in all the paradigms, such as *constancy*, *love* and *faith*. Perhaps thinking of discipleship more explicitly in terms of the virtues could provide a unifying theme across the different paradigms.

Second, virtue reasoning can be very helpful in diagnosing the excesses and the defects of the various discipleship paradigms. Aristotle has reminded us that virtue is found in the middle (*in medio stat virtus*) and that both excesses and defects of virtue will result in vice. Understanding how discipleship can be defective in virtue is relatively easy, but there is just as much danger in placing an excessive emphasis on good things. Let me give you a couple of examples.

The therapeutic paradigm builds on the virtuous habit of introspective knowledge, and it rightly reminds us that *not enough* of this virtue can hinder a healthy growth in character. But *too much* introspection is not a good thing either, for it can generate the vices of irresponsibility, victimization and passivity, and can induce individuals to shift liability for their current character onto their past experiences and relationships.

Another example can be found in the leadership paradigm as it relates to humility. Once again, the defects of humility are easily seen in pride. But the excesses are more difficult to spot. It seems odd, in fact, to speak of "excessive humility," especially given the recent emphasis on servant leadership. In this case, the language of character and virtue education is helpful because it allows

---

12. Ferdinando, "Theological Education and Character," 49.

us to see that too much humility can become self-effacement. This is a vice that will detract from the effectiveness of a leader.[13]

There is a third place for character and virtue in current understandings of discipleship. This is more explicit and introduces a further paradigm that I have not yet mentioned, which is the *moral paradigm*. In this paradigm, the main aim of discipleship is to correct the moral life of the believer and to cultivate righteousness.[14] This paradigm can be recognized when discipleship texts speak about being the "salt of the earth," "deeds that accompany faith," the "fruit of the Spirit," the "transformation of the affections" and "holiness."[15] This is not a prevalent paradigm, but I have found a few successful discipleship programmes that make specific reference to virtue and morals[16] and a handful of authors who speak of discipleship as character.[17]

One of the most popular books on discipleship today is surely Bonhoeffer's *Discipleship*, and it seems to fit best into this kind of moral paradigm. The context in which Bonhoeffer wrote was one of acute vice where, in Nazi Germany, Christians had been lulled into slumber by the doctrine of justification and had become immune to the appeal to virtue.[18] Bonhoeffer uses the Sermon on the Mount to speak about becoming like Jesus through conformity to his ethical patterns of life.[19] Although he does not specifically refer to the categories of the virtues, Bonhoeffer writes forcefully about truthfulness,[20] loving[21] our enemies, humility that accompanies hidden righteousness,[22] and the vices of wrath, pride and avarice.[23]

---

13. This was the point made by Machiavelli in *The Prince*.

14. "Since there is no biblical mission without biblical living, we urgently re-commit ourselves, and challenge all those who profess the name of Christ, to live in radical distinctiveness from the ways of the world, to 'put on the new humanity, created to be like God in true righteousness and holiness'" (Lausanne Movement, "Cape Town Commitment," IIIE – 1B).

15. See Kilpatrick, *The Mystery of Discipleship* (2006); Tozer, *Discipleship* (2008); Ogden, *Discipleship Essentials* (1998); Geiger, *Transformational Discipleship* (2012).

16. The Pantego Bible Church in Dallas has ten core virtues in its "becoming" model (https://www.pantego.org/core-competencies).

17. "Discipleship is the relationship I stand into Jesus Christ in order that I might take on his character" (Dallas Willard, notes taken at his speech at the Spiritual Formation Forum, Los Angeles, May 2004). See also O'Connell, *Making Disciples*.

18. Bonhoeffer, *Discipleship*, 4–5.

19. Bonhoeffer, 21.

20. Bonhoeffer, 128.

21. Bonhoeffer, 137.

22. Bonhoeffer, 146.

23. Bonhoeffer, 121.

Sadly, the moral discipleship paradigm seems to be the least popular today. Maybe it is because moral constraints are unpopular in postmodern, liberal contexts[24] or perhaps it reflects the rejection of moral discourse in faith communities that have suffered from legalistic abuse.[25] Or maybe it is because moral paradigms are associated with efforts to inculcate goodness as if it were a matter of technique and of continual bending of the will in obedience to given rules.[26] This is a fundamental mistake that we need to correct and there is much to learn from the focus in virtue ethics on becoming a good person (rather than on continually choosing to obey rules). Character education aims at making us good people who will naturally do what is good, without having to constantly make conscious choices. The aspiration is that moral actions will eventually be performed spontaneously as an expression of consolidated character.[27] As Aquinas reminds us, it is possible to "make a journey without thinking of one's destination at every step."[28] Becoming a disciple in this sense is not like learning to bake a cake through scrupulous obedience to the guidelines in the recipe book, but more like writing a book as an expression of who we are. This can never be replaced by technique or by discipline.

Pathways of Enquiry

That was a bit of an overview of discipleship trends. As you can see, the term "discipleship" is normally not associated with character and virtue. Although I agree with you that it *should* be associated, and that the link between moral character and discipleship is obvious, for the moment it is not. That is why I hesitate to use the term "discipleship" for your new school.

---

24. "Sometimes the questions of personal morality are denigrated as bourgeois" (Neuhaus, *Theological Education*, viii).

25. "Catholic approaches to character education have often seemed to be legalistic: post-Reformation Catholic moral theology tended to concentrate on precepts rather than on the virtues" (Arthur, *Education with Character*, 50).

26. "Hauerwas draws an important distinction between morality as rule based and virtue based. In his view moral rules are precisely defined, rigid and apply most to quandaries, whereas virtues are not precisely defined, are flexible and apply to the whole life. For this reason, he proposes a theory of virtue as an alternative to rule-oriented accounts of the moral life, although he admits that moral rules do have a subordinate place to play in the moral life" (Porter, *Recovery of Virtue*, 105).

27. "The moral virtues . . . shape the human agent as a desiring creature in such a way that he spontaneously desires and seeks what is in accordance with the truly good life that he is trying to lead" (Aquinas, *Summa* 1–2.55.4). "The truly virtuous person does not require constant conscious deliberation on his final end in order to act in accordance with it" (Porter, *Recovery of Virtue*, 103).

28. Porter, 103.

Let me conclude by mentioning possible pathways of theological enquiry to strengthen the links between character and virtue education and God-honouring, Christ-centred and Spirit-empowered discipleship. One pathway is found in the *imitation principle*, which looks to figures like Jesus and Paul as models of virtue. We have specific texts in the New Testament that talk about imitation and plenty of biblical stories through which we can cultivate *mimesis* in discipleship programmes. Extra-biblical texts featuring heroes of virtue and villains of vice, such as the Greek and Roman classics, can also be used as helpful discipleship aids.[29]

Another theological pathway is found in the *recapitulation theory* of the atonement that claims that the good news of the gospel is not just that we can be saved from eternal punishment through penal substitution, but that we can be transformed into flourishing human beings through the power of the resurrection. If this is the effect of the atonement, then following Jesus as disciples means becoming virtuous like him because he has re-set humanity on the path of virtue. This kind of christologically centred discipleship keeps character and virtue education from becoming a self-centred, self-developmental pursuit and orients us to serve others as we are conformed to the image of God in Christ.[30]

A final pathway links the New Testament understanding of discipleship with classical culture. Let us remember that Plato, Aristotle and Seneca lived roughly in the same epoch as Jesus, Peter and Paul. This encourages us to look for overlaps in the classical approaches to character and virtue education and Christian discipleship. The very term "disciple" (*mathetes*) is a term that the Greeks used before the Christians did to denote someone who was committed to following a master teacher through a life of apprenticeship and training in virtue.[31] We might therefore be surprised to find deeper meanings of discipleship as we explore these original contexts.

—

So we began in disagreement. Where are we now? On the one hand, you are right: it is possible to think of discipleship in terms of virtue. On the other, I

---

29. "These philosophical, rhetorical, and literary works often advocated the merits of restraint and balance, exemplified best by Aristotle's tenet of the Golden Mean. These works encouraged and celebrated the ability to check desires and inclinations that naturally ran to excess (such as the desires for fame, material possessions, and even knowledge). Too, these works provided examples of those characters who could not restrain themselves, those characters who over-stepped their bounds and were consequently punished (often by the gods)" (Smilie, "Humanitarian and Humanistic Ideals," 64).

30. Gunton, "Church as a School of Virtue?," 228.

31. Hull, *Complete Book of Discipleship*, 53–54.

still feel that the current use of the term is too indeterminate. Everybody seems to be taking up a particular vision of discipleship and if you were to apply the "discipleship" label to your new school, it would be associated with much more and with much less than what you have in mind.

May you cultivate attentiveness in the words you choose, realizing their power in shaping principles, practices and persons.

11

What Churches Want

My compliments, Siméon. You have read the Cape Town Commitment better than I have, responding to its dual call to consult with the church[1] and to focus on character formation.[2] You have pulled off a momentous consultation with a variety of faith communities, churches and denominations in your region around the topic of character and virtue education and how it might relate to theological education. If it had not been for the monsoon that kept you indoors the entire time, the event would have been perfect!

Shared Concerns

As I read through the list of participants, I was struck by the diversity of the gathering. You had mainline Protestants, Catholics, Evangelicals, Orthodox, Pentecostals and a strong representation of new faith expressions and cell-church networks. The interests ranged from those of the structured churches, who were looking for ordination training, to those of informal house groups, who were mainly interested in lifelong development. You had charismatics who were concerned about the gap between theology and spirituality,[3] and reformed Calvinists who were worried about the balance between divine grace

---

1. "We urge that institutions and programs of theological education conduct a 'missional audit' of their curricula, structures and ethos, to ensure that they truly serve the needs and opportunities facing the Church in their cultures" (Lausanne Movement, "Cape Town Commitment," IIF – 4C).

2. "We strongly encourage seminaries, and all those who deliver leadership training programs, to focus more on spiritual and character formation, not only on imparting knowledge or grading performance, and we heartily rejoice in those that already do so as part of comprehensive 'whole person' leadership development" ("Cape Town Commitment," IID – 3D).

3. "Theology and spirituality have for long been so thoroughly separated that spiritual formation . . . is in danger of being an orphan, an erratic block, within the seminary" (Lindbeck, "Spiritual Formation and Theological Education," 22).

and human effort.⁴ Around the same tables, you had senior pastors with PhDs, young unschooled leaders, critical scholars and bloggers. You had some who were proudly pietistic and others who were loftily un-pietistic.⁵ You had the entire spectrum of attitudes towards culture described by Niebuhr, from those who fully embrace culture, to those who believe that the Christian life can be lived fully only as a separated community in the desert.⁶ Frankly, just having this group together for a consultation bordered on the miraculous. So well done!

Despite these differences, a set of common themes emerged around character and virtue in theological education. The first was the concern over mismatched priorities in leadership training.⁷ This is not new, and we know that, whereas theological schools have traditionally placed a premium on academic engagement, churches have tended to have higher expectations around practical training and formational issues.⁸ This was restated clearly during the consultation.

Second, there was agreement on the priority of character formation for those in church leadership.⁹ It was recognized that moral expectations of ecclesial leadership are higher than in other professions, mostly because church leadership is intrinsically moral and has to do with the promotion of character and with moral formation of others.¹⁰ In the job of a pastor, priest or spiritual director, godliness is not an option.¹¹ This point stirred an unexpected measure

---

4. "Can a theological tradition which is centred in grace, not works . . . be . . . linked with an educational model which aims at character formation?" (Hall, "Theological Education As Character Formation?," 56).

5. Neuhaus, *Theological Education*, 154.

6. See Dreher, *Benedict Option*.

7. "Some leadership training programs focus on packaged knowledge, techniques and skills to the neglect of godly character. By contrast, authentic Christian leaders must be like Christ in having a servant heart, humility, integrity, purity, lack of greed, prayerfulness, dependence on God's Spirit, and a deep love for people" (Lausanne Movement, "Cape Town Commitment," IID, 3).

8. "The call and education of men and women to become ministers in God's church requires them to recognize, develop, inhabit, teach and model qualities of Christian character" (Heywood, "Educating Ministers of Character," 6).

9. Lindbeck, "Spiritual Formation and Theological Education," 16.

10. "Much professional dereliction and public ill has often been traceable to such failures of personal character as greed, vanity, egotism, intemperance, prejudice, discrimination, weakness of will, cowardice, and so on" (Carr, *Educating the Virtues*, 121).

11. "Ministry is a learned profession, but before and above being learned, a minister must be godly" (Warfield, "Religious Life," 182).

of passion and some used the strong language of "impending doom" in the church unless the crisis of character in Christian leaders is solved.[12]

This point was supported by the survey you conducted on the concerns and expectations that churches have of their ministers. The highest concerns across denominational lines gravitated around positive and negative marks of character. Other preoccupations included undisciplined living, self-protection in ministry, and professional immaturity. Among the top positive expectations, participants indicated that leaders need to serve without regard for acclaim, demonstrate responsibility and Christian example, and be ready to acknowledge personal limitations. When asked to rank their expectations around theological education, participants voted most for the option suggesting that it should "sanctify the habits of the heart."[13] This was true across the board, including those coming from the mainline Protestant tradition who, while admitting their suspicion about moral formation as a typically "Catholic thing,"[14] confirmed that their communities shared an increasing interest around formational practices.[15] They also noted a growing hunger for a lived-out faith in Protestant circles and a diminished confidence in the powers of sheer intellectual pursuit.[16]

After a session in which you asked participants to share stories about moral fallout, the third consensus that emerged from the consultation was that character issues do more damage than theological ones. Moral fallout of Christian leaders produces deeper damage in the community than the damage

---

12. "Nkoma . . . a Zhosa Christian leader from South Africa, speaks of a crisis in character: 'unless we can get an incorruptible type of leader who will not be bought with money, with position, with success and with the promise of other things, then Africa will be doomed'" (Kohls, "Church Leadership in Africa," 116).

13. These results reflect the study conducted by *Ministry in America*, which is probably the most exhaustive study of ministry in North America (Schuller, Strommen, and Brekke, *Ministry in America*). "The very highest positive concern and the most emphatic negation on the part of over 5,000 randomly selected respondents focused respectively on positive or negative marks of character . . . The highest expectations of the ministry are associated with the character of the minister" (Meye, "Theological Education," 96, 113).

14. "For some Protestants, the language of moral formation has a suspiciously Catholic flavour" (Neuhaus, *Theological Education*, viii).

15. "Mainline Protestant churchgoers have taken interest in shaping their habits through concrete practices, illustrated, for example, in the ongoing popularity of the book *Practicing Our Faith* among adult Sunday schools and Christian discussion groups. While they haven't yet followed Benedict into the desert, many Christians now take a more active approach in schooling their desires" (Mahn, "Kierkegaard after Hauerwas," 173).

16. "Protestants have tended to think that all problems can be solved at the intellectual level. The men who come to us now to be trained for Christian ministry do not begin in faith . . . they hunger for it" (Association of Theological Schools, "Standards," 195).

done by poor theological preparation or by practical incompetence.[17] The media are also generally uninterested in bad theology or bad preaching, but they will make a big deal about bad character. Without setting up false dichotomies between theory and practice, it is evident that missions, denominations, churches and dioceses are more likely to be ripped apart because of lack of virtue than because of theological mistakes. When asked to choose between a pastor or priest with sharp critical thinking skills, deep knowledge and understanding, professional competences and abilities to counsel and administer, or a pastor or priest who is humble, courageous, temperate, prudent, just and wise, the choice of participants unanimously fell on the latter.[18] Everyone agreed that the time is ripe for a greater focus on virtue in theological education.[19] For many, this was an invigorating conclusion.[20]

Finally, several participants voiced the concern that, in embracing a new emphasis on character and virtue education, theological education should not lose its academic vocation.[21] Academic theology should not be abandoned in favour of formation, and everyone agreed that there should be ongoing intellectual engagement with the content of their faith. Someone jokingly indicated that this was necessary if for no other reason than to be able to maintain, articulate and argue their differences with each other.

---

17. "Although this anxiety concerning 'character' flaws in spiritual leaders is quite instructive in itself, the concern for character is not limited to an ecclesiastical venue. There is scarcely a sector of national life – political, commercial, educational, entertainment – which has not suffered the blight of 'character' scandal in high places – and in all places. But the churches and their ministers can take scant comfort from shared pain and scandal! This common distress simply accentuates the task of ministry and the challenge to institutions to prepare ministers of authentically spiritual character" (Meye, "Theological Education," 97).

18. "Of those who graduate [from seminary], very few fail in ministry because of inability to study, think, teach, or preach – the skills and content we focus on in seminary. Failure in ministry is linked to difficulties in character, relationships, emotions, spiritual maturity, and other character problems" (Tenelshof, "Encouraging the Character Formation," 83).

19. "We are diminished by wave upon wave of moral failure. No time has been riper for a Christian treatment of specific virtues that are largely ignored or misunderstood" (Austin and Geivett, "Being Good," 1).

20. "Virtue, to put it bluntly, is a revolutionary idea in today's world and today's church. But the revolution is one we badly need . . . After you believe, you need to develop Christian character by practicing the specifically Christian virtues . . . To give wise leadership in our wider society and in the confusing and dangerous times we live in, we urgently need people whose characters have been formed in the same way. We've had enough of pragmatists and self-seeking risk-takers. We need people of character" (Wright, *After You Believe*, 25).

21. 70 percent of prospective theology students indicate that academic rigour is extremely or very important in choosing a theological school. 70 percent of church leaders likewise believe that academic rigour enhances faith (Kinnaman and Hempell, "Perceptions").

Five Church Models

Beyond these shared concerns, the consultation brought out many differences. The Orthodox, for example, liked to think of virtue as the evidence of participation in divine life, while the Catholics more easily accommodated character education into their vision of defending the moral order of society. The Lutherans tended to see the virtues as the activation of their faith under the impulse of grace, whereas the Calvinists were excited at the prospect of working out right beliefs about virtue in order to achieve an ordered life in obedience to the law of God. The Pentecostal representatives were quick to see virtue as the fruit of the Holy Spirit, whereas some of the conservative Evangelicals applauded virtue as a staying force against moral relativism.

I found your summary very helpful, and in particular the taxonomy you've produced of why different churches might be attracted to character and virtue education. I agree that ecclesiology is an important starting point, because what is understood about the nature and purpose of the church will influence the nature and purpose of theological education. So well done on arranging this taxonomy around the question of the purpose of the church. Correct me if my summary of your five models is inaccurate.[22]

The first church model you've identified is one in which the main purpose is to *love God and neighbour*. In this kind of church, leaders express love in all its dimensions, ranging from pastoral care to the transformation of culture. Leadership training for this kind of church aims at comprehensive maturity and includes intellectual, moral, spiritual and relational dimensions. This model aligns well with character and virtue education, for love is the queen of the theological virtues, and virtues like justice, moderation, self-control and altruism will advantage this kind of church.

A second model claims that *liberating persons and societies from oppression* is the main purpose of the church. This vision embraces moral and social reform and those in leadership serve as agents of change, freeing both individuals and collectives from bondage. The training of this kind of leader takes place by engaging with the narratives of oppression and liberation within biblical theology and by providing training in the social sciences that will help recognize, unmask and confront repressive circumstances and ideologies. Character education sits well within this model, especially when it comes to education in public virtues. Much repression can be directly linked, in fact, to shortfalls in the virtues of justice, temperance and prudence and to the

---

22. Gustafson, "Reflections," 32–43.

proliferation of the vices of avarice, pride and vainglory. Graduates who deeply understand and live out public virtue and who are eloquent around issues of liberation and oppression through the lenses of virtue and vice are very attractive to this kind of church.

The third model claims that the purpose of the church is seen mostly in *creating and sustaining Christian identity*. For this tradition, maintaining identity is considered an urgent and important task in the midst of a quickly changing, pluralistic and syncretistic world, and the role of the minister is to revive and redefine the distinctive identity of the church. She or he does this through teaching, through perpetuating traditions, through the orchestration of church life and through the provision of an example of clear and coherent Christian identity. Theological education that serves this kind of church requires historical and exegetical work around "the Christian tradition" and the cultivation of the ability to communicate Christian identity in different cultural milieus. Character and virtue education also harmonizes well with this kind of training, especially given the emphasis on the historical roots of character education and the reappropriation of the Christian features of the virtue tradition. Graduates will be appreciated as they sustain and replicate Christian character identity and as they articulate the broad moral tradition of Christianity.

The fourth model focuses on the *pursuit of an evangelical mission*. Here, the church is mostly seen as an agent of salvation that rescues the world from sin through the gospel and builds the personal lives of believers according to biblical discipleship patterns. The leaders in these churches are evangelists, pastors and disciple-makers and their theological training typically features strong views of Scripture and an emphasis on the doctrine of the atonement. Theological education for them also features a strong emphasis on practical theology and on field experiences that relate to evangelism, church planting, communication, pastoral care and discipleship. Character education also finds fertile ground in this tradition through association with a walk of repentance and the call to sanctification. Furthermore, the pietistic literature that is popular in this tradition has much in common with character education.

The final, *pastoral care* model is a good example of a model that blends with several others. In this model, the purpose of the church is to help people find their spiritual and mental health. It is, in a way, a vocation to human fullness. Leaders in this kind of church are trained to administer "salvation" in broad terms, including mental, spiritual, physical and relational recovery.[23] In their training, they will first be brought to be "healed" themselves,[24] and then they will be supervised, trained in reflective practice and sent out to do field service in a variety of recovery contexts. Character education in this context has a different appeal, mainly due to its vision of human flourishing in which virtue is cultivated as the road to a good, full, happy and healed life.[25] There are interesting parallels with the positive psychology movement that seeks to enhance the potential for good and virtue in each of us.

—

It has been impossible for me to capture the richness of your consultation in this brief letter, and I wish that I could have been there with you. It is clear that, across the theological distinctions and denominational boundaries, there is a common concern over the dramatic shortage of living models of virtue and character in church leadership.[26] Your consultation has confirmed that character and virtue should be taught by those of us involved in leadership training.[27] Although theological education varies greatly in other regards, there seems to be agreement on this point.

You are bringing together many different voices. May you be an agent of harmony in the apparent cacophony of sounds.

---

23. Desirable leadership qualifications in Africa place pastoral experience as the most important qualification, followed by the requirement to be highly educated and married (Kohls, "Church Leadership in Africa," 121).

24. "The formation process is its own kind of psychotherapy . . . [for] to be part of the healing ministry requires that the student be healed to some extent as well" (Gustafson, "Reflections," 36).

25. Volf argues that the current crisis of theology is due to the fact that it fails to wrestle with the most important question of the flourishing life (Volf, 8, 29, 34).

26. "There is an abundance of Christian leaders, charismatic figures who create an impressive wake with their gifts and scholarship. There are Christian celebrities aplenty. But living models of unequivocal virtue are in short supply" (Austin and Geivett, "Being Good," 1).

27. "We have heard the overwhelming call of our biblical heritage and current understanding of ministry toward depth of Christian character as a prime mark of the minister. Should not a program which takes up several years of a person's life have an educational goal commensurate with the shape of their future ministry? If virtue cannot be taught, where do its mediators reside?" (Meye, "Theological Education," 118).

12

A Fresh Expression

One of the interesting outcomes of your consultation was the discussion around the name of the proposed school. So far, we have spoken vaguely about "school," "educational project" and "vision," so it is nice now to have a proposed name that will help focus our imagination. Several proposals were made by the participants and, in the end, the consensus was found for the Theological Academy for Character and Virtue. I like it! You will call yourself an "academy," which of course is reminiscent of the olive grove dedicated to wisdom where Plato held his lessons in Athens. The name also leaves your options open in terms of certification and accreditation, and you have astutely inserted the reference to theology while keeping the place of character and virtue prominent. From now on, in my letters I will simply refer to the "academy."

The topic of this letter builds on the last. My apologies for having overlooked the important post scriptum in your report. You made a note about your lengthy conversation over coffee with the couple who lead a cell-church network. These emerging movements are changing the face of the church in many parts of the world, and we do well to include them in our conversation and planning.

Emerging Features

The couple with whom you spoke are typical of the kinds of Christians who gravitate towards emerging church networks. Both are second-generation Christians coming out of conservative church contexts. They are highly educated professionals in their early forties. Although they are leaders in their churches, neither of them receives a salary for their "church" work, nor have they had any formal theological education. They have more non-believing friends than Christian friends and they struggle to see the connection between structured church services and the realities of "seekers" who wish to explore faith issues in a more relational context. Their faith story is one that has grown weary of "absolute certainties" and of the unconvincing, pat answers to their honest questions and to those of their friends.[1] This, together with a growing unease about the moral shallowness of those who go through the motions of the Christian faith, has contributed to a vision of "church" that privileges orthopraxy over orthodoxy. For them, "good faith" is humble, teachable, integrated, curious, appreciative, communal, active and tough, and it pursues truth, beauty and goodness wherever it is found. Conversely, "bad faith" is arrogant, unwise, dishonest, exclusive, selfish, unteachable, coercive, needy and lacking in integrity, and it is based on unquestionable authority.

After a season of personal crisis, they made the painful decision to leave their family churches and eventually banded together in their homes with other, like-minded seekers. This spontaneous movement is now loosely organized into a cell-church network, counting hundreds of homes and lay leaders across the region.

These small house churches offer us much to reflect on and there are several aspects that set them apart from many traditional churches. They typically emphasize the values of family where no one is left out, of mission where all are involved, of training where everyone is equipped locally, and of gathering informally rather than in structured venues with well-crafted programmes.[2] They prefer messy to tidy, informal to formal and relational to professional. Everyone belongs to a small group that is committed to identifying with the life of Jesus, to transforming the secular realm and to living a communal life. This causes them to welcome the stranger, serve with generosity, participate as producers, create as created beings, lead as a body and take part in spiritual activities.[3] They also typically seek out different forms of worship, are open to innovation and are advocates of communal forms of ecclesiology in which shared lay leadership is preferred to ordained ministry.[4]

Of the five church models we discussed in my last letter, I'm not sure where this kind of church fits in, but I'm not surprised to hear that they are attracted to educational plans that focus on character and virtue. The "good faith" vs. "bad faith" list that I have just enumerated above is unambiguously linked to virtues and vices. The same can be said about their ideas on discipleship. Rather

---

1. The features that follow retrace the biography of emerging church leader Brian McClaren (appreciation to S. Burson, "Apologetics and the New Kind of Christian" [PhD diss., 2015], 5–10).
2. Chan, We Are Church, http://wearechurch.com/values-1.
3. E. Gibbs and R. Bolger, *Emerging Churches* (Grand Rapids: Baker, 2005), 45.
4. T. Sine, *The New Conspirators* (Downers Grove, IL: InterVarsity Press, 2008), 61.

than focus on models that are based on the transmission of knowledge or on the development of ministry skills, this kind of church pursues virtue-based discipleship in a close-knit community.

Beyond Organ Reject

So where does this take us when we think of serving these kinds of churches? First of all, it is easy to anticipate that they will reject traditional theological education as a genetically incompatible transplanted organ. I have a cousin who is leading a similar movement and he once told me that they would never give leadership roles to graduates from theological colleges unless they could properly deconstruct them.

Several points of tension are easy to see. Traditional theological education is typically analytical, organized, individualistic, tied to Enlightenment rationalism, orthodoxy-oriented and committed to truth narratives.[5] By contrast, these new churches are interested in that which is narrative, informal, communal, postmodern, praxis-oriented, committed to inclusivity and hermeneutically open. The kind of theological education that might interest them is one that offers a deeper reflection on issues of authority, certainty and biblical inerrancy, that works on political and global visions, that focuses on a rediscovery of Jesus, that cultivates greater sensitivity to pluralism and inclusion and that features more critical engagement with how language influences life and hermeneutics.[6] These churches are also exploring meaningful spirituality and are enquiring about a kind of formational space that most theological education programmes simply do not consider.[7]

These new church movements are quick to criticize systems of theological education that have been shaped by Christendom presuppositions, because they perceive them as having lost their missiological bearings and as being inadequate in preparing contemporary kingdom leaders.[8] Churches in postmodernity are simply not the same as churches in modernity. I remember a professor who, during my own seminary training thirty years ago, told me that I should spend one hour of sermon preparation for every minute that I would spend preaching.[9] For him, the Sunday homily was the crucial element

---

5. Belcher, *Deep Church*, 40–42; and McClaren, *New Kind of Christian*, 18.
6. McKnight, "Ironic Faith of Emergents," 62–63.
7. McLaren, *Finding Our Way Again* (2008) and *Naked Spirituality* (2011).
8. Rozko, "Missiological Future," 4.
9. Currently, 45 percent of pastors spend 10–15 hours a week in sermon preparation (Krekcir, *Statistics on Pastors*, 15).

of church life, and the job of a pastor was to sit in a study thirty-five hours a week and emerge for a thirty-five-minute sermon. That might have been fine a hundred years ago, when the professional-vocational model of the minister was fulfilled in the pulpit,[10] but it does not work with this new kind of church.

Lifelong Growth

In terms of structure, these new churches are not drawn to theological education that is defined in terms of teachers and students who pursue higher learning in a set of buildings, under the same authority and according to the same rules.[11] They prefer a form of education that deconstructs previous learning and pursues temporary, tentative and unarranged bits of knowledge and helps to develop useful competences. In contrast with the traditional authoritative approaches to teaching and learning, they prefer un-authoritative learning that is free from preconceived purposes and rational frameworks and that operates outside the bounds of structure in the service of the kingdom.[12]

The education they are looking for resembles a constructivist, lifelong learning approach[13] that is student-centred, affordable and accessible. This new kind of church will welcome learning programmes that are longer rather than shorter, and which will allow participants to receive ongoing opportunities for reflection, mentoring and accountability within the context of ministry.[14] For them, those who teach should not be academics so much as successful practitioners. Theological education should be culturally and contextually situated,[15] have a strong emphasis on immersive learning environments that engages in reflective praxis, and be based on the dynamics of a learning community rather than on individual achievement.

---

10. Rozko, "Missiological Future," 4.

11. Bauman, "Universities," 17.

12. Oxenham, *Liquid Modernity*, 39.

13. Interest among potential theology students for non-formal or informal education (90%) is three times higher than the interest in gaining university or college credit (30%) (Kinnaman and Hempell, "Perceptions").

14. "We believe that students should actually read more, write more, discuss more, reflect more, and do ministry a lot more often. We need to give them the time and the space to do all of these things well. If the end goal is not the conferral of a degree but actually becoming a certain kind of person, there simply are no shortcuts to be taken" (Rozko, "Missiological Future," 10).

15. In-service training that does not require leaving church or ministry and that allows for opportunities to study while reflecting on practical experience represents the highest demand (65%) when it comes to gaining experience (Kinnaman and Hempell, "Perceptions").

These kinds of churches are also likely open to new approaches to certification that operate in portfolios of spiritual maturity, Christ-like character or the competencies needed for a holistic ministry.[16] As a lay-oriented movement, they are not quite sure what to do with advanced degree programmes for ministry professionals.[17] They generally do not mind very much if their leaders have accredited degrees in theology, but what they care about deeply is that leaders be trained for kingdom leadership.

I need to be careful here in setting up a false dichotomy that sets these new kinds of churches on one side and traditional theological education on the other. Many of these emerging churches have a huge appreciation of traditional academic theology and many of their leaders hold conventional theology degrees. Conversely, many traditional theological colleges are sensitive to the issues that these churches are raising and are incredibly creative and proactive in finding solutions. It is generally true, however, that these new churches are less interested in a higher education degree in theology and are much more focused on developing kingdom individuals.[18]

I think there are great hopes for character and virtue education in these churches. They are prophetic and provocative,[19] and are open to innovative, informal, ongoing models of formation that attempt to work out and equip lay leaders for what it means to live virtuously in the complexity of postmodern contexts.

Helping to Stay in Church

Let me conclude this letter in a bit of an odd way, by sharing with you a few quotes from a biographical novel entitled *Leaving Church* by Barbara Brown Taylor. This story is an honest and refreshing view of church ministry that should make us think deeply. Here are a few annotated quotes from this book.

Doctrine That Alienates

> Doctrines are works of genius, but like books they tend to draw people's attention away from the living human neighbours that

---

16. Rozko, "Missiological Future," 4.
17. Among practising Christians, 83 percent are convinced that theological colleges exist mainly to train ministry professionals (Kinnaman and Hempell, "Perceptions," 21).
18. Rozko, "Missiological Future," 4.
19. McKnight, "Five Streams of the Emerging Church," 36–39.

> are standing right in front of them. I watched those living human beings wince at the vitriol they heard from those with whom they worshiped God.[20]

Theological education sharpens the critical abilities of our students to sort out false doctrines, but good grades in doctrine can mistakenly be equated with success in church ministry. The problem with doctrine is not only false doctrine, but also true doctrine that alienates us from our neighbours and that makes us break the great commandment. There is nothing more horrific than orthodoxy without compassion.

Sadly, compassion is not a mandatory element of most graduate profiles. We work hard to fashion sharp women and men who bring sharpness into the church, and then we wonder at churches that are all cut up. We need love.

Being Dumbfounded

> If it is true that God exceeds all our efforts to contain God, then is it too big a stretch to declare that dumbfoundedness is what all Christians have most in common? Or that coming together to confess all that we do not know is at least as sacred an activity as declaring what we do know?[21]

Most theological education focuses on what we can know and gives the impression that knowledge trumps mystery. Or that mystery is a temporary state that we can put up with until we get more education. Or even further, that mystery is a fall-back for those who have failed to acquire knowledge. Surely we do not believe that. Our vision of God, our anthropology, our interpretation of creation and the fall, our pneumatology, our eschatology and much of our biblical scholarship point to the mystery of the human condition.

The problem is that we cannot assess dumbfoundedness nor include it on a curricular map. Our students will not pass exam papers that are left blank in the name of mystery. We struggle to articulate apophatic theology. We do not graduate students who excel in not knowing, nor will we impress our accreditors by championing our schools as the places that stand back in the face of the unknown. Hence, we substitute assurance and knowledge for wonder and mystery.

---

20. Taylor, *Leaving Church*, 108.
21. Taylor, 111.

But in doing so, we remove mystery from theological education, from the experience of those training for ministry and from the life of the church. No wonder society perceives us as arrogant and as having all the answers, rather than being communities of those who are overwhelmed in awe and dumbfounded as we walk in a faith that is bigger than life. We need humility.

Holy and Lonely?

> Few of us [clergy] spoke openly of the toxic effects of being identified as the holiest person in the congregation.[22]

> Before I knew it, I was in the water, fully immersed and swimming in the light. I never found who my saviour was, but when I broke the surface, I looked around at all of those shining people with makeup running down their cheeks, with hair plastered to their heads and I was happy to be one of them. If being ordained meant being set apart from them, then I did not want to be ordained anymore. I wanted to be human.[23]

The author of the book narrates the thrill that, at the start of her ministry, came with her being set apart in her role, of being special even in the way she dressed and through the collar she wore. As her ministry continued, however, she felt the increasing burden of being in a "special" category. She tells the story of an evening pool party with the church community after she had resigned from ministry, during which she was thrown into the pool fully dressed. She calls this her "second baptism," in which she found great relief from the distance that she had created with the community around her.

Regardless of our theological convictions on ordination, power and distancing, we need to engage with the reality that the ordinands, missionaries and pastors we train are unlikely to be thrown into a pool fully dressed.[24] We've known the loneliness that comes with holiness. We need friendship.

---

22. Taylor, 149.
23. Taylor, 119–120.
24. "Who wants a clergyman leaning on the bar at a bacchanalia? Especially a clergy person who has heard your confession?" (Taylor, 144).

Gaining the Sabbath

> If my first loss upon leaving church was my regular Sunday job, then my first gain was the Sabbath.[25]

Theological educators preach the Sabbath rest, but amidst the pressures of compliance with quality assurance, pressure to publish or perish, the locusts that devour our budgets, increasing workloads and thinning staff, the urgent pastoral demands of fragile students and the new technologies that need to be mastered, we must confess that the Sabbath remains a hazy mirage. Sabbath and rest are associated with sloth, lack of productivity and guilt. Those who are honoured are the ones who work most, who answer emails at 11:00 p.m., who grade papers on Saturdays, travel to speak on Sundays and arrive exhausted on Monday.

As our graduates imitate our examples, the Sabbath is lost to the church. And sometimes we fall to illness and stress. We need order.

Too Much Sunshine

> In my role I could act out my best nature for hours at a time. I could produce kindness when all I felt was fatigue. I could present patience when circumstances warranted irritation. I could shine like the sun until long after dark when I needed to, but my soul did not operate on a solar calendar. My soul operated on a lunar calendar: coming up at a different time every night and never looking the same way two nights in a row. Where my role called for a steady circle of bright light, my soul waxed and waned. There were days when I was as full as a harvest moon and others when not so much as a sliver appeared in the sky. My soul's health depended on the regular cycle of these phases. I needed the black nights that gave the starts their full brilliance as much as I needed the nights when the moon shone so brightly that I could make shadow puppets with my hands. The problem with the collar was that it did not allow for such variations. It advertised the steady circle of light, not the cycles, so that it sometimes scorched my

---

25. Taylor, 137.

neck. I do not think I was the only one who suffered from too much sun in the church.[26]

I know that I've often suffered from "too much sun." Theological education, like many churches, operates on a solar calendar of planned brightness. Classes are scheduled, chapels offer good worship, administrators must be smilingly available, the corridors are swept and polished, burned-out light bulbs are changed, meetings have orderly agendas, essays are returned within agreed deadlines and graduation is a gloriously orchestrated spectacle. If imperfections are found, they are addressed, and action is taken. Processes are refined and respected. The machine is tuned to hum along efficiently. Schools are effective, and quality is assured.

But we suffer from too much sun. Staff, faculty and students live in the normal phases of a soul-lunar calendar, and too much efficiency will lead to feigning and burn-out. We need temperance.

Feeding on the Fed

Feeding others was my food.[27]

Whether we are in leadership in a church or in a teaching position in a theological college, others come to us to be fed. We know nutrition. We set diets. We cook the food. We make arrangements for the tables. We serve the meals, clean up and show the way to the exercise room. We are the seers. The *magistri*. The doctors. The ones in the gap. The feeders.

But we are also those who feed ourselves by what we are and what we do. This leaves us vulnerable. Especially when we encounter the shadows of un-success, when our food is shunned, when we see contamination and wastage, and when our recruits march out on us singing that they have found a new David who has slain 9,000 more than we have. We need benevolence.

—

Siméon, may the vision of these fresh communities refresh your vision and your person. May you be loving in your doctrine, humble in your knowledge, a good friend with all, well ordered in your resting, temperate in your planning and benevolent in your prescriptions. May I be the same. And may we together help shape leaders for such churches.

---

26. Taylor, 147–148.
27. Taylor, 75.

13

An Aristotelian Framework?

I've not heard from you in the last few weeks, but I know you are busy with the follow-up of the consultation. Your travel schedule to meet church leaders and speak at the two regional youth rallies looks quite daunting, especially during the hot and humid months. I hope you achieve one of your objectives, which is to assemble a competent and supportive board. Let me know how it goes and try to get some vacation time with your family.

As I wait to hear from you, I will deal with your request for further clarifications on the Aristotelian framework which I am setting forth as the underlying theoretical foundation for character and virtue education in theological schools. At the outset, I apologize for the philosophical nature of this letter and recommend that you serve yourself a cup of your good local coffee as you read.

Why a Framework?

First of all, why do we need a theoretical framework? Can we not simply look for inspiration, good ideas and specific practices that will help us achieve our desired aims for character and virtue education? Unfortunately, that is not a good idea. MacIntyre writes about this as he introduces his landmark work *After Virtue*. He suggests a thought experiment: what would happen if scientific practice were done outside of a theoretical framework with no more than fragments of detached knowledge?[1] Clearly, there would be chaos. MacIntyre claims the same is true in moral philosophy, where detached fragments of

---

1. MacIntyre, *After Virtue*, 1, 2.

ethical practice cannot be left to float about without a coherent theoretical framework to hold them together.[2]

When it comes to the practices of character and virtue education, we are thus wise to look for a theoretical framework that will help us structure our practice and avoid pastiches of incoherence, and will assist us as we navigate the semantic minefields of moral education.[3] Like the man in the parable who needed to sit down before he built his tower, we need to consider a foundation for our edifice.

The Contours of a Framework

What might such a foundation look like? This is not a simple question, because we are looking for a framework that is reasonably coherent and structured, that addresses the basic metaphysical questions of human nature and the ultimate good, that has an ethical structure (defining what is good and how to pursue it) and that is explicitly linked to education. Furthermore, since we are looking at theological education, we also need a framework that is theologically congruent. As we survey the field of educational philosophy, there is really only one great framework that satisfies these requirements, and that is Aristotle's. He writes as a philosopher, a moral ethicist and an educator who has been an unsurpassable source of inspiration across generations.[4] Also, as we will see, the links between Aristotle's thought and Christian theology run deep and wide.

What, then, does Aristotle's educational framework look like? I have volumes of notes on Aristotle, whose work, as you can appreciate, is vast and complex. I have drafted a simplified version for this letter, but I will also send you a separate set of files with a more comprehensive exposition and set of references. If you are going to lead innovation in the practice of character and virtue education in theological schools, this is something you will need to

---

2. "Increasingly educators at colleges and universities are recognizing the importance of educating for that elusive thing called character. But their efforts are often piecemeal – a service-learning program here, a residential contract there. Here's what a comprehensive approach to character education might look like" (Berkowitz and Fekula, "Educating for Character," 17).

3. Arthur, *Teaching Character and Virtue in Schools*, 22.

4. In a survey of moral education trends, Aristotle regularly ranks in the highest positions in terms of research topics and disciplinary approaches (Lee and Taylor, "Moral Education Trends," 408, 410, 426). According to Kristjánsson, "Aristotle's pioneering work continues to serve as an unsurpassable source of inspiration for contemporary moral educators" (Kristjánsson, *Aristotelian Character Education*, 59).

dig into. I will also abstain from historical references to keep the framework uncluttered and easier to see.

My outline will follow the philosophical structure I've mentioned above, looking at Aristotle's theoretical framework for character and virtue education through the categories of metaphysics, ethics and education.

The Metaphysics of Character and Virtue

Let's start with metaphysics and in particular with Aristotle's vision of human nature and of the ultimate good. There are three connected words that can help us in this essential summary: purpose, happiness and virtue.

The question of *purpose* is the one with which Aristotle begins. The emphasis on purpose is the reason why Aristotle's framework is sometimes called a *teleological* framework, as it seeks to recover the *telos* of humanity.[5] If we want to know what the purpose of all human action is, Aristotle argues that we must discover what the good for mankind is.[6] It is, in fact, our nature that determines our purpose. Aristotle's claim in response to this query is that we are designed to be agents of goodness and virtue and that, consequently, we fulfil our purpose in being good.[7]

This leads us to the second keyword: *happiness*. Aristotle argues that when the *telos* of human life is fulfilled, we achieve happiness and human flourishing. Just as the acorn grows to be an oak tree, so human beings flourish by means of virtue in what Aristotle calls *eudaemonia*. The term itself is not easy to translate, but it may be summarized as the state of being well and doing well. *Eudaemonia* is an ultimate good that is not subordinated to any other good[8] and denotes the kind of happiness that comes with being well favoured in relation to oneself and to the divine.[9]

---

5. "Centuries later, Aquinas formulated a similar teleological theory of goodness, claiming that 'what is good for a thing' is directly correlated to 'what that thing is.' There is in Aquinas' theory no gap to be bridged between 'is' and 'ought.' If we know what something is, we know what it ought to be" (Porter, *Recovery of Virtue*, 43–44).

6. Aristotle, *Nicomachean Ethics* 1.7.

7. "The natural perfection of the human person consists in acting in accordance to virtue" (Aquinas, *Summa* 1–2.5.5, quoted in Porter, *Recovery of Virtue*, 70).

8. "Aristotle suggests that the only other good not subordinated to other goods is happiness . . . No one seeks happiness so that something else happens, indeed, obtaining happiness eliminates all other needs" (Spears and Loomis, *Education for Human Flourishing*, 62). See also *Nicomachean Ethics* 1095a 1–27.

9. "What does the good for man turn out to be? . . . Aristotle . . . gives to it the name of *eudaemonia* – as so often there is a difficulty in translation: blessedness, happiness, prosperity. It is the start of being well and doing well in being well, of a man's being well-favoured himself

The third word, *virtue*, occupies a central place in Aristotle's metaphysics. For Aristotle, purpose, happiness and virtue coincide and are necessary for each other. The virtues, in fact, lead to human flourishing and contribute to meeting man's highest purpose.[10] Just as a knife finds its purpose in having a sharp edge and cutting, so man's nature is fulfilled in virtue. The framework thus finds its metaphysical anchor in the statement that "human happiness is the activity of the soul in accordance with virtue."[11]

The Ethics of Character and Virtue

Let me now discuss the properly "ethical" component of Aristotle's theoretical framework. When I began my journey into Aristotle, I must confess that I had some wrong expectations. I was looking for a nice, exhaustive list of virtues that I could neatly abide by. But there is no "bag of virtues" in Aristotle's framework. What we have, instead, is a flexible and open-ended description of virtue. With the exception of some virtues, like the cardinal virtues, which are prototypical and persist pretty much universally with slight variations, most of the virtues vary according to context.[12] Virtue is not rigid but living, and the virtues in the Aristotelian framework are organically and unpredictably regulated by wisdom as the realities of life unfold (more of this below when we speak of *phronesis*). Virtue, for Aristotle, is the best balance available given the circumstances and options. As a (penitent) modernist, I admit that this was disappointing, but I have found that this aspect of Aristotle's framework is actually one of the greatest points of attraction.

I will not say more on Aristotle's views on ethics, for most of our correspondence will be focusing on it. In one of my first letters, I shared the definition of the virtues as "stable dispositional clusters concerned with praiseworthy functioning in a number of significant and distinctive spheres of human life."[13] I will not comment on this again, but keep it in mind as we progress. This might be a good place to note my reliance on Alasdair MacIntyre

---

and in relation to the divine" (MacIntyre, *After Virtue*, 148).

10. "The virtues are precisely those qualities the possession of which will enable an individual to achieve *eudaemonia* and the lack of which will frustrate his movement toward that telos . . . What constitutes the good for man is a complete human life lived at its best, and the exercise of the virtues is a necessary and central part of such a life . . . within an Aristotelian framework the suggestion therefore that there might be some means to achieve the good for man without the exercise of the virtues makes no sense" (MacIntyre, *After Virtue*, 148, 149).

11. Aristotle, *Nicomachean Ethics* 1.7.

12. Arthur, *Teaching Character and Virtue in Schools*, 37.

13. Arthur, 28.

as a contemporary "Aristotelian" author. His book *After Virtue* has become a landmark in contemporary ethical discourse, and we will be frequently looking to it to provide a coherent metaphysical and moral framework for virtue ethics to undergird our efforts in character and virtue education.[14]

The Education of Character and Virtue

What about Aristotle's educational framework? Although Aristotle does not write extensively and explicitly about education,[15] both of his major works (*Nicomachean Ethics* and *Politics*) are based on the double assumption that education is a vital activity in the community and that its primary concern should be the cultivation of character.[16] For Aristotle, the soul is always developing, either towards vice or towards virtue, and education is the force that will make the difference.[17]

---

14. Chronologically, it was Elisabeth Anscombe who, in 1958 with the paper "Modern Moral Philosophy," broke new ground in normative ethics, proposing an alternative to Mill's utilitarianism and Kant's deontology and returning to Aristotle's proposals around character, virtue and human flourishing (E. Anscombe, "Modern Moral Philosophy," *Philosophy* 33, no. 124 [Jan 1958]: 1–16).

15. "The only extended discussion of education in the Aristotelian corpus is in Book VIII of the *Politics*, where Aristotle advocates that schooling should be publicly provided and 'one and the same for all' (VIII.1 1337a23). Isolated remarks about education appear in earlier books of the Politics, and a few can be found in the *Nicomachean Ethics* and elsewhere . . . A central claim about happiness in the *Nicomachean Ethics* is that it requires the possession and exercise of intellectual and moral virtues, and a central related feature of the *Politics* is its identification of education that cultivates these virtues as the primary tool of statesmanship (*Politics*, VIII.1)" (Curren, "Aristotle's Educational Politics," 543).

16. A dominating idea in the opening of Book 8 of *Politics* is "that education is a prerequisite for the practice of virtue and is thus a matter of public concern (1337a20–21). The foregoing makes this easy enough to understand: the proper aim of politics is to enable citizens to live the best kind of life. In order to live such a life, a person must be virtuous. The development of virtue depends on a variety of things beyond a person's control. To educate someone is to train and teach him so he acquires the moral and intellectual virtues, develops the good judgment needed for prudent self-governance and participation in political rule, and learns to take pleasure in the excellent activities with which a good life is occupied" (Curren, 551).

17. "Adequate, systematic training in the virtues is central to Aristotle's project, although it could happen that individuals without this training might, by natural traits, talents or internal dispositions, do on occasion what virtue requires. But this happy gift of fortune is not to be confused with the possession of the corresponding virtue" (MacIntyre, *After Virtue*, 149). Gutek, *Western Educational Experience*, 42.

Aristotle's approach to education is holistic. It includes reason,[18] but it is not exclusively rationalistic. It includes knowledge[19] and the transformation of the mind, but this is only one step in a complex process. It includes emotion,[20] but it cannot be accused of emotivism.[21] It includes the will, but it goes beyond ingenuous adherence to rules of the law.[22] It includes practice and action, but it is much more than just doing the right thing at the right time. Aristotle's educational framework places a high premium on intellectual virtues but never does so to the detriment of the moral virtues, and the two work hand in hand to nourish both practical intelligence and goodness.[23]

We will come back later to the practicalities of all this, but for now I've selected two further key words to navigate the vast topic of Aristotelian education: *phronesis* (wisdom) and habituation.

---

18. "The genuinely virtuous agent . . . acts on the basis of a true and rational judgment" (MacIntyre, *After Virtue*, 150).

19. There is a need "to recognize a certain set of qualities as virtues and the corresponding set of defects as vices" (MacIntyre, 151).

20. "Because Aristotle thinks that virtue is a unified, unconflicted state where emotional responses and rational assessments speak with the same voice, he, like Plato, thinks that the education of our emotional responses is crucial for the development of virtuous character. If our emotional responses are educated properly, we will learn to take pleasure or pain in the right things. Like Plato, Aristotle thinks that we can take a person's pleasures and pains to be a sign of his state of character" (Marcia, "Moral Character"). "Virtues are dispositions to act in particular ways and to feel in particular ways . . . To act virtuously is not, as Kant was later to think, to act against inclination; it is to act from inclination formed by the cultivation of the virtues. Moral virtue is an '*éducation sentimentale*' . . . What I particularly enjoy will of course depend upon what sort of person I am, and what sort of person I am is of course a matter of my virtues and vices" (MacIntyre, *After Virtue*, 149, 160).

21. For Aristotle, the virtuous man is the one who most fully uses his rational ability (Gutek, *Western Educational Experience*, 41).

22. "The exercise of the virtues requires . . . a capacity to judge and to do the right thing in the right place at the right time and in the right way. The exercise of such judgment is not a routinizable application of rules. Hence perhaps the most obvious and astonishing absence from Aristotle's thought for any modern reader: there is relatively little mention of rules anywhere in the *Ethics*" (MacIntyre, *After Virtue*, 150).

23. "Aristotle contrasts the ways that the two kinds of virtues can be acquired: intellectual virtues are acquired through teaching, the virtues of character from habitual exercise. We become just or courageous by performing just and courageous acts; we become theoretically and practically wise as a result of systematic instruction. Nonetheless these two kinds of moral education are intimately related . . . The exercise of intelligence is what makes the crucial difference between a natural disposition of a certain kind and the corresponding virtue. Conversely the exercise of practical intelligence requires the presence of the virtues of character; otherwise it degenerates into or remains from the outset merely a certain cunning capacity for linking means to an end rather than those ends which are genuine goods for man. According to Aristotle then, excellence of character and intelligence cannot be separated . . . 'It is clear that a man cannot have practical intelligence unless he is good' (1144a37)" (MacIntyre, *After Virtue*, 154, 155).

Phronesis

One of richest terms in Aristotle's educational framework for character and virtue is *phronesis*. This is probably best translated by the word "wisdom," but it is also referred to as the cardinal virtue of prudence. In Aristotle's framework, *phronesis* plays a fundamental role as the guardian and regulator of the entire spectrum of the virtues.[24] It is by *phronesis*, in fact, that we are able to perform two fundamental operations that relate to character. The first is to help us understand what the virtues are, and the second is to help us deploy them in the specific circumstances of life. Let us look at these in turn.

When it comes to understanding the virtues, Aristotle claims that every virtue has both excesses and defects and that virtue is found in the moderation of the golden mean (*in medio stat virtus*[25]). So, for example, too much justice can become tyranny, while not enough will degenerate into submissiveness and passivity. Courage in excess is recklessness, and courage in defect is cowardice. Generosity in excess is prodigality and generosity in defect is avarice. And so on. Each virtue, if not moderated, can easily slip to the left or to the right and become a vice. How do we walk the balanced path of virtue? Circumstances alone will not provide sufficient guidance, and Aristotle claims that it is the exercise of *phronesis* that will inform our judgment and help us understand what virtue is.

The second function of *phronesis* is to help us deploy the appropriate virtue at the appropriate time. Let me illustrate. There will be times when a given virtue is required, and other times when the same virtue is entirely inappropriate. A solider in the heat of battle, for example, will need courage to press forward despite his or her fears. But in different circumstances, such as a long time of inactivity during a siege, the same soldier must deploy the virtue of patience. So the virtue that is required in one circumstance becomes inappropriate in another.

Let me further illustrate through two examples from our own lives. I recall, decades ago, when I interviewed you to be my doctoral student. We had known each other for years and you had always spoken softly about your achievements. I was a little surprised, therefore, by your boldness during the interview. On

---

24. MacIntyre, 154.

25. "Virtue is destroyed by excess and defect" (*Nicomachean Ethics* 2.2). See also *Nicomachean Ethics* 1106a 26–1106b 35. "The key for Aristotle is moderation. Courage, for example, is the moderation of cowardice and extreme self-protection on one hand and fool-hardiness and rash irresponsibility on the other. For each virtue therefore, there are two corresponding vices. And what it is to fall into a vice cannot be adequately specified independently of circumstances" (MacIntyre, *After Virtue*, 154).

reflection, however, I understood that your behaviour was entirely appropriate for the circumstance. You did not lose the virtue of humility on that occasion, but wisely chose to deploy the virtue of assertiveness. I am having a similar experience in my local church at the moment with the virtue of mercy. As you know, I tend to always cover the faults of others, but as a leader of my local church I am now grappling with a case of an abusive husband. And this is requiring unrelenting justice. I am learning that I cannot always be uncritically merciful and that there are circumstances in which the most appropriate response is severity. As Ecclesiastes reminds us, there is a time for everything, and we must know the difference.

How then do we know the difference? That is what *phronesis* does. It is the exercise of reason that helps us discern which virtue to deploy in the varied circumstances of life.[26] It is the perception of the salient features of a situation that suggests the most appropriate action and indicates which virtue will yield the best outcome.[27] *Phronesis* keeps us from flat legalism, blind rules[28] and rigid moral codes and makes us discerning and responsible as we choose to do the right thing, at the right time, for the right motives and for the best possible result.[29] If we imagine the virtues as being like a tool belt, *phronesis* tells us which tool we should use for the job at hand.

We will return several times to *phronesis* in our correspondence for it is a fundamental component of Aristotle's educational framework. Character education is not so much about teaching people what to do or what not to do, but about nourishing them to become wise and good so they will recognize and do what is good. *Phronesis* is the rational rudder that steers us off the rocks of vice, helps us see what virtue truly is and makes us wise in using the appropriate virtues in our everyday life.

---

26. "Aquinas would later argue that humans do not automatically choose that which promotes their healthy functioning, hence reason must be engaged to help select those virtuous actions that will set me on the pathway to flourishing" (Porter, *Recovery of Virtue*, 70–71).

27. Nucci et al., *Handbook*, 17.

28. "Aristotle thinks rules inadequate to capturing the widely varying requirements of different situations and relies, instead, on the sensitivity – some have likened it to connoisseurship – of the virtuous individual to moral distinctions and nuance" (Slote, "Virtue Ethics," 326).

29. "Not everyone can find the middle of a circle, but only a man who has the proper knowledge. Similarly, anyone can get angry – that is easy – or can give away money or spend it; but to do all this to the right person, to the right extent, at the right time, for the right reason, and in the right way is no longer something easy that anyone can do. It is for this reason that good conduct is rare, praiseworthy, and noble" (Aristotle, *Nicomachean Ethics* 1109a25–30).

Habituation

As we come nearer to the implementation phase of the academy, we will discuss the practical ways in which the Aristotelian framework for character and virtue works out. Here, I need to at least make mention of one major device, which is *habituation*. Indeed, together with the development of *phronesis*, this may be the key educational device in Aristotelian character education.

Habituation is easily understood by answering the question of how we get to be good at something. Let me again use a personal example. I recall that you are very good at playing the piano.[30] How did you get to be good at it? Although you may have had a natural disposition, your real secret has been in your countless hours practising, learning from mistakes and repetition. You have repeated your scales so many times that finding the right notes on the keyboard is now a built-in habit. Technically speaking, you have been "habituated into a practice." Ability, harmony, rhythm and a musical ear are a part of you and have become natural because of repetition.

Aristotle claims that the same is true for virtue. It becomes a natural part of us in the same way that we get to be good at any *technè*: by constant repetition and habituation.[31] Virtue becomes a part of us by repetition of good acts, which become "second nature" and shape the habits of the soul.[32] The virtues, claims Aristotle, are made perfect by habit.[33] So, by practising actions of justice, we become more just. As we face our fears, we become more courageous. As we give, we become more generous, and as we abstain from excesses, we become more temperate. Although reason plays an important role in the process,[34] Aristotle claims that habits precede reason, and through habituation we

---

30. "Music conduces to virtue" (Aristotle, *Politics* 8.5).
31. "Moral excellence comes as a result of habit" (Aristotle, *Nicomachean Ethics* 2.1103a16–17; *Works* 2.1742). "Education serves to produce *abito*. Constancy in exercise of the virtues is fundamental, and this can be obtained through teaching and repetition" (Trombino, *La Filosofia Greca Arcaica e Classica*, 180). Aristotle is concerned with a complete life: "For one swallow does not make a summer, nor does one day; and so too one day, or a short time, does not make a man blessed and happy" (*Nicomachean Ethics* 1.7).
32. Nucci et al., *Handbook*, 18; Robinson et al., "Humanistic Education," 4.
33. "Neither by nature, then, nor contrary to nature do virtues arise in us; rather we are adapted by nature to receive them and are made perfect by habit" (*Nicomachean Ethics* 2.11103a).
34. "There are different theories on whether this is a cognitive process, but there is agreement that habituation is 'reasoned' habituation (especially in adults) and not just blind repetition" (Nucci et al., *Handbook*, 18).

evade our instinctive appetite of avoiding pain and pursuing pleasure and are consciously formed into virtue.[35]

There is, admittedly, some circular reasoning in the Aristotelian framework and, more generally, in the virtue ethics approach. On the one hand, a theory of virtue claims that we will act in good ways once we become women and men of virtue. On the other hand, the same theory claims that we become virtuous as we habituate good actions. So which comes first? Although this makes for a rich debate, I do not really wish to disentangle being and doing and, for our purposes, we can agree to keep them interdependent.[36]

Summary

Let me bring it all together by sharing the following summary of the distinctive elements of an Aristotelian framework: "Firstly, the focus in virtue ethics is on the person and his/her character traits, not on a particular decision or principle. Secondly, virtues are good habits and are learned by practicing. Thirdly, appropriate virtues are discovered by witnessing and imitating behaviour; to become virtuous, one must see others practicing good habits. Fourthly, persons seek the 'ethic of the mean.' Fifthly, virtues should be examined within a 'community' setting. Sixthly, aspirations are key motivators in virtue ethics."[37]

Another good summary is found in the four traits of what Aristotle called *hexis*,[38] which includes: the definition of virtue as an appropriate emotional response to moral circumstances;[39] the prevision of certain kinds of conduct that follow emotional response; the independence of virtuous conduct from

---

35. "Goodness of character has to do with pleasures and pains . . . we require to be trained from our earliest youth, as Plato puts it, to feel pleasure and pain at the right things. True education is just that" (*Nicomachean Ethics* 2.3, in Boyd and King, *History of Western Education*, 39).

36. "Do our acts flow from our being . . . or is the act more important, so that we form our persons from what we do? . . . The two are so interdependent that it scarcely seems possible to disentangle them" (Gunton, "Church as a School of Virtue?," 212).

37. Murphy, in Racelis, "Developing a Virtue Ethics Scale," 18.

38. *Hexis* are "the things in virtue of which we stand well or badly with reference to the passions" (Aristotle, in Ellingsen, "Privation Theory of the Vices," 12).

39. "Cowardice and bravery, for example, are distinct. The emotion – fear – is the same, but the relation is different: Cowardice involves feeling too much of it, while bravery involves feeling the right amount of it. On the traditional account, a virtue is a *hexis* that involves feeling the right amount of a certain emotion, while a vice is a *hexis* that involves feeling it in some other amount (i.e., feeling it either too much or too little)" (Ellingsen, 12).

contextual factors;[40] and the stability of virtues that are acquired through long habituation.

In looking to Aristotle we are not alone, for most of the recent popular approaches to moral education are Aristotelian[41] and the interest in Aristotle in the field of moral education is such that some have heralded an Aristotelian renaissance.[42] Although the uses of Aristotle are many, varied and controversial, the overall perception is that, when it comes to a theoretical framework in the budding field of character and virtue education, there is only one major player.

—

Although not a philosopher in your training, you have always enjoyed a hard thinking session and I trust that this summary of Aristotle has enriched you. I also hope that you have had a sufficient supply of coffee to uphold you. I imagine this letter will reach you between travels. Keep safe.

May you find the golden mean of wisdom between the excesses of ostentation and the defects of simplicity.

---

40. "A *hexis* will tend to issue in its typical conduct in all situations where that conduct is called for, and not merely some: being brave only under certain circumstances is not the same thing as being brave, full stop" (Ellingsen, 13).

41. "US-style character education, social and emotional learning (AKA emotional-intelligence theory), communitarian brands of citizenship education and positive psychology's virtue theory – all claim to be informed by and seek inspiration from the thoughts of the ancient philosopher Aristotle" (Kristjánsson, *Aristotelian Character Education*, 49).

42. See Carr, *Educating the Virtues*, 109; Walker et al., *Towards a New Era*, 81; Curren, "Aristotle's Educational Politics," 544; MacIntyre, *After Virtue*, 147. In British political circles the order of the day seems to be that "we are all Aristotelians now" (Kristjánsson, *Aristotelian Character Education*, 279).

14

Justifying Aristotle

I have taken a brief holiday at the end of this long summer and while walking along the seaside I was thinking of the questions you might ask me about Aristotle. I know, what a terrible waste of a good walk! I did, however, quickly jot down a few thoughts before they slipped away, so this letter will be short.

Since you have not responded yet to my previous letter, I am second-guessing your possible objections, but I'm quite sure that you will want to know why we, as Christian theological educators, should ground our work in the educational theories of a non-Christian philosopher like Aristotle. Was Luther right in claiming that Aristotle was a misleading buffoon?[1] Should we not rather just refer to the Bible? To quote Tertullian once again, what has Athens to do with Jerusalem?

Let me say a couple of things at the outset. First, I am not suggesting an exclusive and uncritical reading of neo-Aristotelian education. There is much in Aristotle, in fact, that we disagree with. For example, he uncritically accepted slavery, believed that women were inferior to men and excluded the virtues of charity, humility and forgiveness, which are foundational in Christianity. The Aristotelian framework also makes questionable links between metaphysical biology and teleology and takes for granted the structure of the *polis* which today no longer exists.[2] We can also list other critiques, such as his potential narcissism in seeking happiness as a primary goal,[3] the presentation of character as a settled state rather than an ongoing struggle,[4] and the war-like

---

1. MacIntyre, *After Virtue*, 165.
2. MacIntyre, 162–163.
3. Gunton, "Church as a School of Virtue?," 226.
4. Kierkegaard and Hauerwas claim that the road to excellence is not increasingly "settled" but increasingly characterized by struggle: "Formation is not to make opposing possibilities progressively impossible, but rather to initiate the very self-conflict or inner struggle" (Mahn, "Kierkegaard after Hauerwas," 176).

orientation of his virtues that are in contrast with the Christian peace-oriented virtues.[5] Although we need to take a critical distance from these items, I still believe that we can learn a lot from Aristotle.[6]

I am also making some underlying assumptions about theological method. I will write more about this in a separate letter, but here I just want to note that the Bible was not written to provide an educational framework and that the doctrine of common grace encourages us to search for wisdom in many sources. There is plenty of theological work that defends the use of pagan sources. Abelard, for example, claimed that philosophers can be authorities in matters of faith and argued that ancient philosophers were able to write so effectively about the virtues because they were virtuous people themselves.[7] As he points out, there is a long tradition of Christian writers, including Augustine, Alcuin and Ambrose, who engaged fruitfully with the classical writings on the virtues.[8] So we are in good company.

Why Aristotle?

I come now to justify why I have chosen the neo-Aristotelian framework as my starting point in character and virtue education. There are several reasons for choosing Aristotle, some of which I have already mentioned. I have three lists to answer the question. The first list is mine and the next two are from contemporary Aristotelian educationalists whom I happen to be reading while on holiday.

Here are my eight reasons for choosing Aristotle (forgive the numbered list):

1. As we have seen, Aristotle is the most prominent thinker around moral education and the practices of character and virtue education. In choosing Aristotle we have chosen the best and most popular source. As someone has written: "Aristotle is hot."[9]

---

5. Hauerwas, *The Difference of Virtue*, 251.

6. "As we believe Saint Paul and Saint Thomas meant to teach us, Greek accounts of the virtues are there to be used by Christians, not built upon, an entirely different thing. Before proper use can occur, differences must be made clear" (Hauerwas, 303).

7. Abelard's second book, *Theologia Christiana*, was written to answer this charge (Marenbon, *Philosophy of Peter Abelard*, 281).

8. Marenbon, 282.

9. "If Aristotle is hot in moral and educational circles... contemporary virtue ethics is even hotter... Reviving and restoring old concepts is not necessarily old-fashioned" (Kristjánsson, *Aristotelian Character Education*, 274).

2. In Aristotle, the virtues are central, making his framework the most suitable for our purpose.

3. Aristotle's framework involves all spheres of human life, including the will, emotions and reason.

4. Aristotle is an educationalist. Although it is not upfront in his writings, education is the underlying force of much that he writes.

5. Aristotle puts an emphasis on being and not just on obeying rules, and this is an important safeguard against religious legalism.

6. Aristotle places a high premium on the community, and this provides a strong antidote to contemporary individualism.

7. Aristotle provides a flexible framework that calls us to exercise human wisdom that accommodates some of the situationists' arguments on the importance of context.

8. Aristotle's flexible framework is not culturally confined and welcomes global expressions of virtue and character education.

Here, now, is a second list by James Arthur, who has developed some brilliant materials on Aristotelian character and virtue education through the Jubilee Centre for Character and Virtues.[10] He provides five reasons for choosing Aristotle:[11]

1. Aristotle does not present an instrumentalist vision in which character leads to greater success, employability or social benefit, but provides a vision rooted in a clear conception of human flourishing.

2. There are a number of functions in the Aristotelian framework, such as acquisition and habit and the golden mean structure, that work well in practice.

3. The positive role of emotions[12] that Aristotle provides sits well with some current therapeutic trends that have identified the importance of going beyond bare behavioural modification.

4. There is attention to the adjudication between conflicts in virtue practice, to the acknowledgement of the dilemmas of conflicting

---

10. https://www.jubileecentre.ac.uk.

11. Arthur et al., *Teaching*, 26–31.

12. For Aristotle, emotions are a positive force, not a problem. They are "reason-responsive and educable, not just ungovernable passion" (Arthur et al., 29).

virtues and to the outlook where conduct is virtuous if chosen for the right reason, motivated by right emotions and judged by wisdom.

5. As we have already mentioned, Aristotle does not conceive of education as an addition to moral philosophy, but as the starting point without which the study of morality is fruitless.

My final list comes from another key contemporary advocate of Aristotelian education, Kristján Kristjánsson.[13] He has explored why an ancient author like Aristotle is seen today as the principal authority in education, more so than Plato, Locke, Rousseau, Kant or Dewey. In his view, the answers are found in Aristotle's geniality of explanation, in his common-sense approach and in the analogies between Athenian society and ours. Kristjánsson claims that several of these reasons work together to make Aristotle more appealing to contemporary educators than any other candidate.[14] Kristjánsson provides an extensive list of the pros of Aristotelianism, and I list them here for you (some repeat my previous points):[15]

1. Aristotle focuses on an ontological basis.

2. Aristotle finds ultimate justification in a theory of universal human flourishing and not in cultural relativity.

3. Aristotle provides an idea of value that is intrinsic rather than merely instrumental.

4. Aristotelianism has the ability to counter situationism.

5. Aristotle has respect for ordinary moral language.

6. Aristotle is not other-worldly or abstract but deals with the nature and open-ended specification of moral virtues.

7. Aristotle provides a unique and central role of emotions.

8. Aristotle provides a framework of moral holism that is well integrated with intellectual virtues and that allows us to navigate ethical conundrums.

---

13. Kristjánsson, *Aristotelian Character Education*.

14. "There is simply a variety of distinct features of the Aristotelian position that commend themselves to contemporary educators, and they do commend themselves in that way because they accommodate – better than other candidates in the field – certain powerful and prevailing assumptions in current moral philosophy and moral psychology" (Kristjánsson, "There Is Something about Aristotle," 52).

15. Kristjánsson, 53–57.

9. Aristotle stays away from an individualist approach, integrating ethics and politics and claiming that virtue happens in, for and because of community.
10. Aristotle provides an educational emphasis that is often not found in moral philosophy.

There are many other authors who might also be cited[16] in justifying the choice of Aristotle, but I think that these three lists have more than achieved my purpose.

Theological Congruence

In my last letter, I mentioned the importance of having a framework that was theologically congruent. Clearly this is a very important point, and I will here give you some initial thoughts on how we might be thinking theologically about an Aristotelian framework. We will be testing this claim at several stages as our correspondence develops, so please consider these as preliminary comments.

For starters, there is congruence between Aristotle's notion of the stability of the virtues and the Christian view of good and evil. Before the time of Aristotle, virtues were conceptualized as being random, incoherent and subject to the intervention of capricious gods. This was typical of Greek tragedy and of the so-called "heroic age." Aristotle changed this and suggested the existence of a cosmic order that made the virtues stable and in harmony with each other.[17] Surely this bears a strong resemblance to the Christian vision of cosmic order and stable moral truth.[18]

We also considered *phronesis* in my last letter. This is the exercise of reason to understand what virtues are and how to be wise in deploying the virtues that are most fitting to the circumstances of life. I find this vision to be coherent with a Christian vision both of creation and of spiritual discernment. It fits well with a vision of creation because it depicts humankind as thinking beings who are able to understand good and evil and are responsible for their choices. It also fits well with our understanding of spiritual discernment, seen as the

---

16. Curren argues for a return to Aristotelian frameworks to restore plausibility to the philosophy of moral education (Curren, "Aristotle's Educational Politics," 533).

17. "The presupposition . . . is that there exists a cosmic order which dictates the place of each virtue in a total harmonious scheme of human life" (MacIntyre, *After Virtue*, 142).

18. The notion of stable virtues is one that Aquinas builds upon as he founds his ethical theology on Aristotle.

practice of listening to the voice of God and responding to the call of wisdom in the varied circumstances of life.

Another point of resemblance can be found in the conception of happiness. We have seen that, in Aristotle's framework, happiness and virtue coincide, and this is something that Aquinas also pursues in the *Summa*. He agrees with Aristotle that natural happiness is found in acting out and habituating virtue,[19] and that character education is the application of our efforts to achieve natural happiness through human virtue.[20]

A full treatise could be developed on Christian theology and Aristotelian education, but we do not have space to do so. Let me simply list a few other areas of analogy between Aristotle and Christian theology:

- the importance of community;
- the vision of man as a social being;
- the role of reason in shaping character;
- the notion of virtues as settled dispositions of character;
- the indication of human flourishing as an appropriate pursuit;
- the connection between purpose and goodness;
- the connection between happiness and virtue;
- the importance of virtue in human development;
- the role of human agency;
- the place of the will and the conscience in acquiring virtue;
- the identification of core virtues;
- the derivation of morality from a basic conception of human nature;
- the claim that individuals have goals outside the confines of the self;
- the notion that virtue can be taught.[21]

In my effort to appraise the work of Aristotle, we must, however, remain critical.[22] As mentioned before, many of the Christian virtues were never considered by Aristotle and, as Hauerwas would argue, even the definitions of some basic virtues, like courage, meant different things in Ancient Greece and

---

19. Porter, *Recovery of Virtue*, 63.

20. "Even though Aquinas affirms that the true end of human life is supernatural, he takes the natural end of human life as the proximate norm for moral reflection... Elsewhere, Aquinas simply says that the happiness proper of this life consists in the operation of virtue, without mentioning contemplation at all" (Porter, 83, 84).

21. Arthur, *Education with Character*, 48, 49, 56, 57.

22. "There are clear lines of division separating the secular and religious ideas of character... Christianity seeks to explain aspects of human development and human character differences by reference to God" (Arthur, *Education with Character*, 45).

Christianity should reject them.[23] One might also be rightfully suspicious of a project that starts with human happiness and could well end up in narcissism.[24]

It would be equally grave to imply that nothing is missing in Aristotle. Indeed, Aristotle has not said it all. Perhaps you have read the little booklet by N. T. Wright entitled *After You Believe*? I think I've already quoted it in a previous letter, but one of the great passages in this booklet is where Wright argues that Christianity has taken Aristotle to a new level.[25] He compares Aristotle's framework to a two-dimensional model that sits beside the three-dimensional model of Christian theology. So, for example, whereas both Aristotle, Jesus and Paul shared a vision of human flourishing, the Christian vision is much richer, for it promises not only individual realization in the here and now, but also the status of being priests and rulers in God's coming kingdom. Or, concerning Aristotle's *eudaemonia*, we've seen that Aquinas agreed with Aristotle on the attainment of natural happiness through virtue. But Aquinas takes it further and conceives of a supernatural or perfect happiness that is found only in God and in the contemplation thereof.[26] There is a double, complementary, view of Christian happiness that is both natural and supernatural[27] and that corresponds to our efforts in spiritual formation and character education respectively.

The Christian vision goes deeper than the self-serving classical world as it includes the virtues of love, kindness, forgiveness and humility. Furthermore, although there is agreement between Aristotle and the New Testament writers on the need to grow in virtuous character, Christianity can rely on the transforming power of the Holy Spirit and not just on human willpower and

---

23. Hauerwas, "Difference of Virtue."

24. "The weakness of an ethic of virtue is that, unless its Aristotelianism is transcended, it contains a danger of ethical narcissism inasmuch as the subject's intentionality is directed towards itself and its own self-realization" (Gunton, "Church as a School of Virtue?," 226).

25. Wright, *After You Believe*, 35–36 and chapters 2 and 3.

26. This distinction between human happiness and celestial happiness is beautifully illustrated by Giotto's frescoes in the Cappella degli Scrovegni in Padova: human happiness is shown as overcoming vice, whereas celestial happiness is depicted as requiring divine revelation and the theological virtues of faith, hope and charity.

27. The two kinds of happiness are complementary: "The natural end of human life is not rendered otiose or irrelevant by the fact that we are actually directed toward a supernatural end . . . the specific ideal of humanity, as he [Aquinas] sees it, is not a life spent in contemplation alone (as if that were possible), but a life that incorporates other sorts of activities as well" (Porter, *Recovery of Virtue*, 67).

determination.[28] As Wright puts it, Aristotle is a signpost that points in the right direction, but Christianity provides the road home.[29]

As you can see, there is much theological reflection to be done, but, at the same time, in choosing Aristotle we have chosen the Rolls-Royce of theoretical frameworks for character and virtue education. Whereas other frameworks may be possible[30] and Aristotle is not perfect, we are setting our project on solid ground.

—

Please respond when it is convenient. I feel a twinge of guilt as I enjoy the Mediterranean Sea and you are so busy. Thank you for the short email telling me that you have successfully assembled a very competent board. I look forward to hearing more about that.

As we consider Aristotle, may we emulate his intellectual thoroughness, his explanatory diligence and his commitment to improving his world.

---

28. "Only by the grace of God and the atoning work of his Son Jesus Christ on the cross are we able to come to an accurate understanding of what it means to flourish as a human being. This is not something we can learn from Plato and Aristotle" (Spears and Loomis, *Education for Human Flourishing*, 65).

29. Wright, *After You Believe*, 36. "When you go for the Christian goal you get everything that was worthwhile in Aristotle's scheme thrown in as well, whereas it does not work the other way around" (Wright, 70).

30. An alternative framework might be the Vygotskian approach, but this applies mostly to children who are maturing in adolescence (Crawford, "Educating for Moral Ability," 118). Kohlberg's developmental psychology is also popular and proposes a number of stages in moral development of individuals (see the "Character Development Ladder" in Arthur, *Education with Character*, 55). The limit of Kohlberg's proposal is that it only emphasizes moral reasoning and not moral awareness, feeling or action. His theory fails to provide a complete framework for moral education because being able to reason well on morals does not necessarily entail being moral.

15

A Global Heritage

I have returned from my holiday, and since I've still not heard from you, I've continued to muse about your possible responses to my letters on Aristotle. Forgive me for putting questions in your mouth, but I can anticipate another critical point in proposing an Aristotelian framework as the basis for your academy. This question is geographical and cultural: why should a Greek like Aristotle have global relevance? While Aristotelian thinking has made a significant contribution to cultures in the Majority World, this is not necessarily true in the Minority World, and regions like yours draw on their own rich tradition of thinkers. Indeed, many cultures struggle with Aristotle's linear-logical kind of thinking, so why should global theological educators embrace Aristotle's framework for character and virtue education? Is this not the kind of cultural imperialism that we have been battling for years?

Cultural Colonialism?

Let me start by saying something about cultural colonialism. It goes without saying that there is no excuse for the ugly pages of colonial history during which Western and Christian cultures arrogantly imposed themselves on the richness of local traditions, cultures and thinkers. As C. S. Lewis said, there is "poison from the Western lands that has spread its dark shadow over the earth"[1] (by the way, while on holiday, I read *The Poisonwood Bible* that you had recommended[2]).

The disciplines of education and theological education are not immune from this imperial levelling, and we have seen innumerable schools, universities

---

1. "The poison has brewed in these West lands, but is has spat itself everywhere by now... The shadow of one dark wing is over all Tellus" (Lewis, *That Hideous Strength*, 180).

2. B. Kingsolver, *The Poisonwood Bible* (New York: Harper Perennial Modern Classics, 2005).

and seminaries cloned from Western counterparts. I don't think that this was completely wrong, and the missionary influence also brought many good things. But hopefully the times of homologizing are behind us and as we design theological education, we should embed curricula in local cultures, follow local styles of teaching and learning and shape learning communities in line with their own roots. Character should also be nourished in locally recognizable ways and the virtues should be in dialogue with age-old traditions.

And yet, while applauding diversity and contextuality, I struggle with those who claim that *nothing* can be accepted beyond the local and the traditional. In our desire to recommend the indigenous, we run the risk of parochialism, and in reacting to abuses of domination, we are in danger of forfeiting the blessings of sharing. I have thought about this theologically, and I think that within a vision of common grace we can say that God has blessed the world with many good things that *come from many places*. We can also say that, in his sovereign grace, God had used some cultures as "gateways" of blessings to the rest of the world. The mechanical clock, for example, was created in China, mathematics was devised in Mesopotamia, fire was first controlled and used in Kenya and "margherita" pizza was invented in Naples. But these are gifts for the entire world. Just because the source is not ours and the place is not ours, it does not mean that we should consider everything that is foreign as a cultural imposition. We can apply the same line of reasoning to education and conceive that there are bits of educational theory and practice that God has chosen to bless the world with through different cultural channels.

There is no doubt that the scars of a colonial past are still fresh. But should we hesitate to accept the goodness of the scientific method of research, degree classifications or the invention of the university itself, just because they have originated in the West? Might we not rather help the next generation to appreciate and embrace everything that is good wherever they see it and whatever its source? You know the saying about throwing out the baby with the dirty bathwater. As we throw out the filthy bathwater of colonial abuse, let us discern the God-given babies.

Aristotle As Global Heritage?

You can see where I am going with this in relation to Aristotle's framework for character and virtue. Might it be considered a gift of providence? Could it be that God shed some light into a remote corner of a small Mediterranean peninsula to allow an obscure philosopher to formulate universal truths about what it means to flourish as human beings? Might we consider Aristotelian educational theory as a generalizable good without it becoming an issue of power?

Let me qualify this better. First of all, I am not launching a defence of Aristotle's *entire* philosophy. In particular, I do not wish to defend his linear-logical way of thinking, for I know that cultures like yours thrive on lateral thinking. I am focusing only on the *educational components* of Aristotelian thought, and in particular on his framework for character and virtue education. Of the vast legacy Aristotle has left, this is the only piece I am interested in at the moment. Although there might be many connections with Aristotle's broader thinking, I will leave it to others to argue about these.

I am also keen to clarify that Aristotle is *not the only voice* that has spoken about character and virtue education. What I am suggesting, however, is that he is *an important voice* and that what he says might be universally relevant. To be sure, the call to rediscover an Aristotelian framework of character and virtue education is not an invitation to succumb to Greek thought, but an appeal to recognize a universal truth about human growth. Aristotle did not say it all, nor did he perhaps even say it first, but he did say it well.

The rest of this letter will contain some examples of how other global traditions around character and virtue education are in harmony with Aristotle. I have selected three. The first is the ancient tradition of Confucianism, the second is the tradition that is embedded in Islam and the third is a contemporary example about education for democratic citizenship. In seeing these, I hope to reinforce my point about the universality of the proposals that bear Aristotle's name.

Aristotle and Chinese Traditions

Let me start out with the ancient traditions of China, mainly Confucianism, as one that is content-rich in terms of character and virtue.[3] Four questions can be asked to illustrate how Confucius and Aristotle share many ideas on character and virtue.

First, how important is character and virtue in Confucianism? This is easily answered, because the essence of Confucianism is found in becoming *ren*, which is best understood as loving people through virtuous qualities. Becoming such a moral entity is, according to Confucius's successor Mencius,

---

3. Confucianism is not easily separated from Daoism and Buddhism. "There's a saying in China: 'The three teachings of Confucianism, Daoism and Buddhism are like the legs of a tripod; you cannot lack even one'" (Chen and Yu, "Traditional Chinese Philosophies," 30).

the defining characteristic of mankind.[4] It is easy here to see the confluence with Aristotle's thinking on human flourishing.

Second, why should character and virtue be developed? From what I have seen, Confucianism makes a strong link between virtue and utility. *Ren* is not only the highest moral achievement that leads to spiritual fulfilment,[5] but it is also what is needed for a healthy society. It is interesting that, just as Aristotle was responding educationally to a crisis in Athenian democracy, so Confucius was addressing the tumultuous times in Chinese history.[6] For Confucius, virtue brings order and peace in a time of war and social disruption.[7]

A third question is about what the virtues are. Here, again, we find a remarkable similarity to many of the virtues listed by Aristotle and by the Christian tradition. *Ren*, first of all, is love, expressed in selflessness, compassion and acceptance of others. The main properties of *ren* are found in *li* as propriety, *xiao* as filial piety, *ti* as brotherly love, *zhong* as loyalty, *shu* as tolerance, *yi* as righteousness, *zhi* as wisdom and *xin* as integrity.[8]

And finally, how are character and virtue shaped in Confucianism? Once again, there is agreement on placing the burden on education. The Confucian philosopher Xunzi makes it clear that human nature can be changed for the better through proper education.[9] Confucius outlined a "curriculum" that began with the aspiration to become *ren* and was followed by an educational plan that included instruction, active thinking, review, empathy-preceding-action and self-reflection.[10] Just as Aristotle did, Confucius placed great importance on the influence of the community both in promoting and in hindering goodness. Buddhism, similarly, believes that through education everyone can become a moral person in an awakened state.[11]

---

4. "Mencius pointed out that everyone had the potential of becoming a person of *ren*, and that one cannot be considered human without the four propensities of compassion, righteousness, propriety and wisdom . . . Here Daoism also stakes its highest moral principle that to be moral corresponds with being natural" (Chen and Yu, 34, 37).

5. "The spiritual emphasis on morality is perhaps most strongly expressed in Buddhism that claims that the aim of moral education is nirvana" (Chen and Yu, 40).

6. "This milieu led to a troubling collapse in etiquette and good manners in society. In an attempt to offer a solution to this crisis in manners, Confucius developed the philosophy which we today refer to as Confucianism" (Chen and Yu, 31).

7. "Through learning and self-cultivation, people can better manage the family, make the country orderly and bring peace to the world" (Chen and Yu, 31).

8. Chen and Yu, 31.

9. Chen and Yu, 35.

10. Chen and Yu, 33.

11. Chen and Yu, 40.

Korea is an example of how Confucianism has influenced education, and its history is dominated by the notion that the only kind of education is moral education.[12] This was also seen in China, at least until the communist revolution, when it was replaced by socialist ideology and by the thinking of Mao Zedong, who believed that moral education should serve the revolution by means of indoctrination into the virtues of patriotism, obedience and collectivism.[13] With the opening up of China, moral education changed tone, and the virtues of independence, self-motivation and creativity were encouraged as those that would contribute to the modernization of Chinese society and its economy. At present, there seems to be an ideological vacuum and a decline in morality, and some observers indicate a return to traditional values and to Confucian moral traditions.[14]

Just as the West is returning to Aristotelian character education, so Chinese culture seems to be looking to a Confucian past to reshape its present moral identity.

Aristotle and the Islamic Tradition

In my effort to acquit Aristotle of Western imperialism, let me write briefly about a tradition of character and virtue that is embedded in a non-Western religious tradition. Aristotelian thinking, in fact, can also be found in Islam. I begin by pleading guilty, as I am not a scholar of Islam, nor have I engaged in sustained studies in this regard. I realize that we are dealing with a diversified world and that generalizations are difficult, so I look to my friends and colleagues who live in Islamic contexts to develop my thinking. The small point I wish to make here is that Aristotle is not a foreigner in Islamic moral theology. Indeed, Aristotelianism might have had an important part in early Islamic philosophy, with notable Islamic scholars like Avicenna and Averroes translating Aristotle into Arabic and developing Aristotelian dialogue with Islam. We should not forget that it was, indeed, Averroes who revitalized Aristotle and, indirectly, returned him to the West in the twelfth century.

---

12. J. Lee, "Moral and Character Education in Korea," 328.

13. To, Yang and Helwig, "Democratic Moral Education in China," 404.

14. "At the same time as the modernization and marketisation of the country was underway, there appears an ideological vacuum and a decline in morality. Contemporary problems of corruption and a widening gap between the standard of living of modern, urban centres and rural areas exacerbated the sense of crisis. Neo-conservatives saw the need to run back to the tradition and called for reinstating Confucian traditions, especially its sense of social responsibility and focus on moral virtue, as a foundation on which to rebuild Chinese cultural identity" (To, Yang and Helwig, 405).

There are several routes to illustrate the familiarity of Aristotelian character and virtue frameworks in Islamic contexts. We might start by observing the words of the Prophet Muhammad himself, who said that "I have been sent to fulfil the virtues which go with nobility of character [*masarik al-ahhlak*]."[15] He is spoken of in the Quran as the one who possesses "exalted character,"[16] and he is held up as an example of the moral traits of piety, contentment, patience, thankfulness, clemency, modesty, generosity, courage, self-respect, righteousness, truthfulness and reliability.[17]

Further, the contemporary Iranian philosopher Abdolkarim Soroush makes it clear that there are universal virtues in Islam, which he calls Guiding Values, that should shape our lives as moral human beings.[18] In Islam, there is agreement that the "golden rule" of doing to others as we would have them do to us is foundational for good character.[19] There are also virtue taxonomies, starting with the three main virtues in Islam, which are justice, kindness and charity, and three main vices, which are indecency, wickedness and oppression.[20] Looking deeper into the Islamic tradition[21] we find ethical lists that bear strong resemblance to Aristotelian ones, and include virtues like equity, modesty, compassion, generosity, self-restraint, sincerity, honesty, fairness, humility, patience, courage, endurance, gratitude, dignity, purity, cooperation, hospitality, brotherliness and hard work.[22]

We can also look at some contemporary examples of the affinity between Islam and Aristotle, starting with the importance of community in shaping

---

15. Yaran, *Understanding Islam*, 42.

16. Quran 68:4 (Sura Qalam).

17. Imam Jafar As Sadiq, *Al Kafi*, cited at "Essential Virtues for Developing Nobility of Character: Introduction and Framework," Daily Wisdom for Your Relationships, accessed 12 March 2019, http://www.marziahassan.com/essential-virtues-for-developing-nobility-of-character-introduction-and-framework/.

18. Sarraj notes that Soroush's contention against Western intellectual traditions is reminiscent of Plato's contrasts with the Sophists: "Soroush's meta-ethics depend on Plato's idealistic notion of the virtuous society. Although Soroush does not refer to Plato directly, it is clear that the world ethic he opposes is the same as that called 'Sophistical' in Plato's Dialogues" (Cornell, "Evil, Virtue," 295).

19. "None of you is a believer if he does not like for his brother exactly that which he likes for his own self" (Yaran, *Understanding Islam*, 43).

20. These are found in Surah 16:90: "Allah commands justice and kindness and charity to one's kindred, and forbids indecency, wickedness and oppression."

21. A good summary of foundational virtues and vices is found, for example, in Surah 17 and includes kindness to parents, patience, humility, justice, mercy, moderation, kindness and generosity among the virtues, and lack of trust, indecency, injustice, untruthfulness and pride among the vices.

22. Yaran, *Understanding Islam*, 43.

character. Aristotle's notion of the shaping power of the community is perhaps most clearly seen in some of the more radical proponents of Islam. In the manifesto-treatise *Milestones*, Sayyid Qutb, for example, claims that the only hope for living a just life is found in quarantining oneself off from corrupt communities and living in an ideologically pure Islamic society.[23]

Another fascinating point of contact between Islamic contexts and Aristotelian thinking is the issue of honour. I was initiated to this topic through a conversation over a meal with a common friend (he prefers not to be named but you will quickly identify him). We were together at a training workshop in Malaysia and we got into a discussion on generosity. I asked him, provokingly, if there is any such thing as being "too generous." In my mind, I was trying to reason through the Aristotelian notion of the golden mean, where the excess of generosity can lead to self-effacement. Interestingly, he replied to me that, in his own Arab context, my question made no sense. The only thing that made sense for an Arab was to do the honourable thing and, since generosity is always honourable, it made no sense to enquire about excess.[24] I will not bore you with the rest of the conversation, but I do wish to make a point about how cultures of honour and shame relate to virtue.

As my friend told me, in Islamic contexts virtue is pursued for a number of reasons, most importantly because it contributes to one's honour and preserves one from shame.[25] Being virtuous and being honourable in your community are one and the same thing. If, instead, you follow vice, you have to live with the shame that goes with it, and that is the most painful of all emotions.[26] There are some remarkable points of contact with Aristotle here, for in *Nicomachean Ethics* and *Rhetoric* he writes extensively about shame (*aidos*).[27] Indeed, Aristotle's dealing with the concept of honour and shame is the starting point for most academic discussion on the topic.[28] Although

---

23. Cornell, "Evil, Virtue," 291.

24. Cornell suggests that one of the characteristics of Islamic moral discourse is emotivism, where people are ruled by expressions of preference, attitudes and feelings, rather than more systematic approaches (Cornell, "Evil, Virtue," 287).

25. "While honour might be the most strongly felt motivation, motivation for doing good in Islamic contexts also includes the spiritual growth of individuals, the eternal reward at the Day of Judgement and the peace and security of stable families and virtuous societies" (Yaran, *Understanding Islam*, 43).

26. "Shame is the most painful emotion in the Arab culture producing the feeling that one is unworthy to live. The honourable Arab is the one who refuses to suffer shame and dies with dignity" (Cornell, "Evil, Virtue," 288).

27. Aristotle, *Ethics* 4.9.

28. Nichols, "Shame among the Virtues," 167.

Aristotle makes the point that shame is not a virtue in itself, he clearly indicates that shame is a positive emotion that keeps us away from vice and that activates many of the virtues.[29]

The point is that, in shame and honour societies, Aristotle is no colonial intruder, but a friendly interpreter of widely held dispositions.[30]

A Contemporary Example

I have done some stimulating research in preparation for this letter, and I thank you for the opportunity to put some of this in writing. I conclude with a contemporary example of a particular global trend in character education. This is not directly related to Aristotelianism, but it suggests that issues around character education are universal and that the Majority/Minority World dichotomy is perhaps not as strong as it might seem. I am thinking of the issue of democratization.

If we could single out one educational trend that unites global cultures today, it is, in fact, the subservience of character education to the ends of democracy. Although this is sometimes associated with the American philosopher Dewey, in actual fact it is being developed independently across cultures. In Japan, for example, the traditional practices of Japanese moral education are being revisited to align with the values of democratic character education.[31] In China, the return to Confucianism that I mentioned above is mixed with democratic virtues like open-mindedness and a pioneering spirit.[32] In Korea, the interplay between moral education as a curriculum (MEC) and character education itself (CE) has contributed to making students into good citizens through the development of democratic traits like being self-directed, being creative, and being a cultivated and globally minded person.[33] The same

---

29. Aristotle, *Nicomachean Ethics* 1128b. "In the *Nicomachean Ethics*, Aristotle discusses shame's place in a moral philosophy. Aristotle believed that activation of some virtues, such as a certain species of courage, was dependent on a sense of shame (*EE* 1228b). Aristotle illustrates this observation. According to Homer, 'shame seized Hector' and prompted him to fight, when he faced the danger presented by Achilles (*EE* 1230a) . . . A sense of shame can lead to activation of other virtues. In this case, it is courage" (Nichols, "Shame among the Virtues," 167).

30. "The same can be applied to Confucian societies where cultivation of a sense of shame is fundamental in making decisions about cognition, emotion and behaviour. Confucius himself claimed that 'If they be led by virtue and uniformity sought to be given them by the rules of propriety, they will have a sense of shame, and moreover will become good' (*Analects* 2.11, from Confucius & Slingerland, 2003)" (Nichols, 176).

31. Araki, "Application of Kohlberg's Theory," 310.

32. To, Yang and Helwig, "Democratic Moral Education in China," 406.

33. In, "Moral and Character Education in Korea," 330.

is happening in Europe, where education for democratic citizenship is now considered a top priority for many ministers of education[34] and virtues are being reframed as key competencies, such as those in the OECD's framework.[35] I could find more examples, but I think you get my point. We live in a global village, and good developments in the field of character and virtue education are sprouting up independently and interconnectedly across the planet.

—

I was about to post this letter when I read your wife's Facebook post that says you are in the hospital! I am shocked. Now I understand why I've not heard from you in the last three weeks. It appears that the episode of fainting in the airport and the subsequent fatigue were misdiagnosed and that you were instead dealing with a heart condition. Two days ago, you had a severe stroke while returning home. Your wife has shared a photo that shows you smiling, which is good to see. I will quickly post this letter and then contact you by social media. Let us put a temporary moratorium on our correspondence to allow you to rest.

May life be good to you in proportion to how you have been good to those around you. And should it not be so, may you find peaceful resignation.

---

34. See the 2010 Charter on Education for Democratic Citizenship and Human Rights Education.

35. Edelstein, "Privation Theory of the Vices," 390.

16

A Manifesto for Character and Virtue in Theological Education

My friend Siméon, the summer has passed and, as agreed, we have suspended our conversation to allow you to recover. It is good to see pictures of you hiking with your wife and daughter, and your new pacemaker seems to be ticking away like a charm. I have missed our fellowship but have continued some of my research in the meantime. It seems that you have resumed some moderate activity and that the first meeting with your new board will be taking place shortly. The time has come for you to present a first report of your findings, together with a conceptual proposal that needs approval. You have prepared well for this, combining personal study, research into other theological schools and consultations both with the local university and with churches in your region. Hopefully, my letters have also been useful.

You have asked me to summarize our vision in a manifesto, and I am glad to do so in this letter.[1] Feel free to edit it and improve on it. I've structured the manifesto with a preamble and five key statements, each of which has a set of sub-points.

Preamble

Higher education is undergoing times of great challenge and change, and this includes a renewed discourse around character and virtue education. The university is increasingly a place where students consciously explore their ethical selves and consolidate their identities as individuals and citizens for personal flourishing and societal engagement. Indications suggest that

---

1. "To change the world, we need an 'I have a dream' speech, not 'I have a complaint' speech" (Volf, 55).

character and virtue education in the university is growing in importance and that the late twentieth century and early twenty-first may constitute a revival phase for moral education.

Theological education is also facing times of great change. Despite the historical connection between character, virtue and theology and the contemporary needs of the church and society, the discourse around character and virtue has, so far, been timid. Although character and virtue education appears as a golden thread both in the literature and in the practices of theological education, the thread is thin. Character education occasionally appears in articles or in book chapters, mentioned as a secondary theme, dealt with in limited aspects, or it appears as a side motif in support of other subjects. It is often unhelpfully confused with spiritual formation. Concerning practices, efforts remain mostly marginal, poorly focused and aspirational. The cultivation of virtue in theological education is generally relegated to the extra-curricular domain and moral education is frequently reduced to courses in comparative ethics. Although there is an encouraging revival in practices of spiritual formation, these are often narrowly focused on devotion to God and miss the explicit focus on human virtue and character.

The following convictions underlie this Manifesto for Character and Virtue in Theological Education:

- There are universal virtues that contribute to humans flourishing and that are necessary for a healthy society and a faithful church.
- Virtue can be taught, and character can intentionally be formed through adult education.
- Character and virtue education is firmly grounded in Christian theology and has characterized most of the history of higher education and theological education.
- Contemporary social and educational contexts are calling for a renewal in the tradition of character and virtue, and theological education is strategically poised to lead in this renewal.
- Academic engagement, development of professional skills and practices of spiritual formation have taken precedence in Christian theological education, marginalizing character and virtue education.
- Practical challenges and theoretical objections need to be addressed before character and virtue education can revitalize the future of global theological education.
- For deep change to happen, it is necessary to explicitly focus on theoretical and practical work in character and virtue education.

In summary: we have a tradition; we have a need; we have potential. This Manifesto seeks to bring these together and reclaim the centrality of character and virtue in theological education.

Statement 1: The Aims of Character and Virtue Education Should Be Central in Global Christian Theological Education

1. Character and virtue education should rise from the margins to a place of prominence in theological education but should not be sought to the exclusion of the traditional aims of academic engagement, professional training and spiritual formation.

2. Character and virtue education should be sought within the diversity of Christian traditions. Theological education varies greatly within Catholic, Protestant and evangelical approaches, within pietistic and non-pietistic contexts, within different visions of the nature and purpose of the church and within competing visions of the Christian's relationship to culture. Political visions that are embedded in theological traditions will also take different views on character and virtue, as will theological and philosophical conceptions of morality. Despite all this, the aims and practices of character and virtue education are broad enough to be shared by different theological traditions.

3. Character and virtue education should be both regulatory and non-prescriptive, providing a central hub of principles and standards while at the same time allowing for differences and subjectivity. The centrality of character and virtue education should be seen in all aspects of theological schools, including curriculum design, course content, approaches to teaching, learning and formation, assessment and accreditation, graduate profiles and certification strategies, community strategies, leadership and management approaches, facilities and use of technology, training and recruiting of staff and faculty, and relationship with stakeholders.

4. Character and virtue education should require a radical re-envisioning of theological education from the centre to the periphery. Many changes are necessary, and they will not take place as long as character and virtue education is considered secondary.

Statement 2: The Impact of Theological Education Should Be Seen through Character and Virtue Education

1. The impact of theological education is diminished in the absence of the formation of graduates of character and virtue. While recognizing the value of theological content, academic knowledge alone is insufficient. Similarly, skills and competences alone are incomplete, and theological graduates must demonstrate character qualities alongside skills and competences. Spiritual formation, if defined strictly in terms of a relationship with God, can also reinforce attitudes of other-worldliness and fail to contribute to the formation of moral character.

2. The impact of theological education should correspond to the needs of the society and the church. Contemporary societies are facing crises that can be addressed through an injection of citizens of virtue. Many challenges of the church are also addressed by providing virtuous leaders. No one wants more corruption, more pride, more violence or more envy. Both church and society want more virtue and less vice. When measured against felt needs in society and in the church, character education is the most desired outcome.

3. The impact of theological education needs to be realistic. Character and virtue education cannot be conceived as a mechanism that yields predictable outcomes. Human beings are formed differently, at different paces and different rhythms, and virtue and good character can take on many aspects. Character and virtue education is a concrete enterprise but it is not an exact technique and we must keep our educational expectations within reason.

Statement 3: A New Vision of Character and Virtue in Theological Education Should Be Worked Out and Justified

1. Historical work is needed to reappropriate the tradition of character and virtue education. Research should extend to different cultures and epochs, giving special attention to those traditions that have deeply shaped the history of Christianity, Christian theology and practice and Christian theological education. Educational history can provide a narrative for the rise and decline of character education together with the necessary theoretical foundations, practical

models, case studies and scholarly literature. Historical work will also lead contemporary theological educators to innovate within a tradition, rather than reinvent the wheel.

2. Theological work is needed to ground the concepts and practices of character and virtue education within Christian theology. This should include, for example, a biblical theology of virtue and an exploration of the relationship between biblical genres and character education. Systematic theology should also explore how character education relates to anthropology, pneumatology and ecclesiology. Practical theology is also required to work out the distinctive potential of Christian character education in the context of a theological school.

3. Philosophical work is needed to develop suitable theoretical frameworks for the implementation, evaluation and operationalization of character and virtue education. Particular attention should be given to a neo-Aristotelian framework, as one that is historically rich, potentially universal to global cultures, widely embraced in the Christian tradition, well suited within a framework of Christian theology and popular in contemporary education.

4. Lexical work is needed to reclaim, understand and make popular a vocabulary of virtue that is sufficiently clear but that resists the temptation of excessive definition. This includes both methodological terminologies (such as "habituation" and "wisdom"), taxonomies of virtues and vices, and rich descriptions of the conceptual, emotional, volitional and practical dimensions of the single virtues. Character education also needs to be understood in distinction from spiritual formation.

5. Contextual work is needed to support the claim that character and virtue education should be a universal feature of theological education across the world. Sensitivity needs to be exercised against cultural imperialism and the claims of situationism need to be carefully heard out. This work needs to ground a discussion on universal virtues and vices on the one hand and work out culture-specific visions and versions of character and virtue education on the other.

6. Interdisciplinary work is needed to draw on a vast body of literature, research and practice that relates to character and virtue education.

Examples are found in moral ethics, virtue epistemology, positive psychology, developmental psychology, political philosophy and sociology.

7. Apologetics work is needed in two distinct tasks. The first is an apologetic of character and virtue education which responds defensively to a number of objections. These objections might be (1) theological: entailing, for example, issues of "secular" terminologies and frameworks over against "biblical" language and categories; (2) educational: involving issues such as the appropriateness of moral education in the university or the age-old question of whether virtue can be taught; (3) philosophical: including objections to educational practices that seem moralizing, nostalgic, authoritarian, paternalizing, unduly religious, illiberal and indoctrinating. The second apologetic task is to showcase character and virtue education as an apologetic of the Christian faith, demonstrating its relevance to contemporary society through the outcomes of theological education. The unique way in which theological education can contribute citizens of character and virtue to society could represent an effective apologetic strategy in postmodern contexts.

Statement 4: Theological Schools Should Have Action Plans to Implement Character and Virtue Education

1. *An action plan for community.* Theological schools should intentionally create the kinds of communities where virtue can be "caught" and character can be formed. Attention needs to be given to the qualifications of those leading and serving in these communities in order to generate a context of emulation. The community should feature, for example, the use and display of vocabularies of virtue and vice, role modelling, character development portfolios, practices of habituation, reflective practices, structured dialectic reflection, personal tutoring, peer-mentoring, community service, disciplinary codes, sports activities, musical activities, literary clubs and accountability structures.

2. *An action plan for curriculum.* Character and virtue should be a core, integrated aim of the curriculum and should be explicitly formulated in learning (growing) outcomes. In order for virtue to be taught,

schools should have action plans both for explicit courses and for the integration of character and virtue learning outcomes throughout the curriculum.

3. *An action plan for andragogy.* Andragogical means that are fit for the purposes of character and virtue education should be investigated, experimented with and employed by theological schools. Teachers and mentors should understand and prioritize teaching and learning practices that contribute to character and virtue education with the understanding that these may be radically different from familiar practices.

4. *An action plan for assessment, certification and accreditation.* Character and virtue should be adequately assessed and made a compulsory feature for certification. Learning outcomes related to character and virtue need to be identified as well as means to assess them. Although numerical grading may not be an appropriate means of assessment, ways need to be found to "fail" students in areas of character and virtue where necessary and not allow them to graduate until these area are satisfied. Measures should be in place to include character and virtue in accreditation processes. It should be acknowledged that character and virtue education are intrinsically different and that the familiar "measurement" paradigms of assessment may not be fit for purpose.

5. *An action plan for the formation of theological educators.* Theological educators should be adequately equipped with a new vision and formed with the qualities that are necessary to support character and virtue education. Traditional formation routes for theological educators that do not address issues of character and virtue education should be revisited and training measures should be put in place for both current and prospective theological educators. Theological educators should also be active lifelong learners and researchers in the area of character and virtue education.

6. *An action plan for all modes of delivery.* Character and virtue education needs to be pursued in all forms of delivery. Theoretical work is needed to explore the dynamics of character and virtue education in delivery settings that are different from the traditional, face-to-face residential context, such as evening classes, theological education by extension, intensive delivery patterns and online education.

Statement 5: Students and Stakeholders Should Support Character and Virtue Education

1. *Student support.* Applicants to theological schools should demonstrate a commitment to grow in character and virtue, with an attitude of humble expectation that their character will be formed alongside their academic achievements and professional training. Students should commit to being active participants of a learning community where virtue is pursued, committing both to being formed by the community and to contributing to peer formation within the community. Students should support the notion that they will not be allowed to "graduate" until outcomes in character and virtue are satisfied, and that the formal certification of their studies will include character assessment.

2. *Church support.* Churches (including denominations, charities, parachurch, mission organizations and other employers) need to articulate their need for leaders of virtue and character in light of their vision and purpose. Within the richness of their traditions, faith communities should continually dialogue with the world of theological education to provide input on character and virtue outcomes and make themselves available to support schools insisting on outcomes in terms of character and virtue from their graduates.

3. *Accreditation support.* Accreditation agencies involved in the quality assurance of theological education should define and consistently apply standards for character and virtue education. Theological schools whose aims and practices do not include character and virtue education should normally not be granted accreditation.

4. *Financial support.* Financial supporters of theological education should back initiatives of character and virtue education, contributing practical support for the kind of radical, courageous change that is envisioned.

—

I can imagine your trepidation as you bring all this to the board. You have been breathing, dreaming and thinking about these issues for months. They have not. They have placed in you a huge amount of trust and have volunteered to be on this particular board because they are committed to a new vision of character and virtue education, but now they are at the point where they need to engage in detail. We have both worked under boards and have sat on boards, so we understand that decision-making processes are always . . . how can I say it? . . . interesting.

May you take this as an opportunity to develop civility as you work in respect of others within the appropriate functioning of roles and authority structures. The shortcut of isolation is a losing alternative.

17

Considering Objections

I'm sorry, but I guess this was to be expected. The two-day retreat with your board did not go quite the way you had hoped. While there was excitement and curiosity, there were still many objections and reservations.

Thank you for telling me a little more about who is on the board, as this will help me formulate my response. You have four church leaders representing the main denominational bodies in the region, a professor and former colleague from the school that recently closed, an educationalist from the local university, an accreditation officer from the regional agency specializing in theological education, a local politician, the leader of the largest charity in the region involved in relief work and the principal of the local Christian primary school. All these, with the exception of the educationalist, are Christian women and men, highly esteemed in the region and with a track record of positive response to change and innovation. Six of them are theology graduates themselves. This blend gives a healthy combination of faith and ministry perspectives, appreciation of theological education, educational wisdom and social connection. Each one of them is important for the future of the academy.

By the way, thank you for mentioning me to this good group of people. I do not know most of them, but it was good to hear that they have welcomed me "virtually" into your discussions.

An Overview of Objections

And now, concerning the objections that the board raised, I will not cover the initial set to which you have already responded well. These had to do with character education not being recognizable as higher education, with the threat of never getting accreditation and with the understandable fear that the academy would become intellectually feeble and methodologically shallow.[1] There were also concerns that the broader community might perceive the academy as cultish. The faith-community leaders specifically asked for more theological and scriptural justification (one of them actually said: "Less Aristotle and more Jesus, please"). You were wise to inform them that many of these issues are part of our ongoing investigation and that you and I have not yet worked out the theological and historical grounding of character and virtue yet, nor many of the methodological and practical aspects.

The set of objections that I would like to address in this letter are more philosophical. I've selected the five that seem to have emerged most strongly: (1) overestimation, (2) historical failures, (3) faulty examples, (4) issues of scope and (5) paternalism. I will try to unpack each one and give you some indications on how you might reply. There was a sixth major objection on situationism, and the definition of what virtue is, but, given its significance, I will leave that to a separate letter.

Overestimation

As we enthusiastically launched out on a ground-breaking venture, we should have predicted that the first objection would be that of overestimation. The fundamental question here is whether we really can make a change in individuals and society through character and virtue education. Fortunately, this is not a new question, and even Plato dealt with it as he discussed whether virtue could be taught at all. Granted that virtue can be the object of education, how much can actually be done? What should our expectations be?

There are determinists in the field of psychology who claim that we are the product of our environment, and that we need to live with who we are.[2] These thinkers have low expectations of the ability of education to change individuals. There are also those who point to the adult age of students in higher education and claim that the majority of character formation has already taken place in childhood, leaving little scope for change.[3] On your board, this objection was formulated by the primary school principal who could see a place for character

---

1. Lawrence Kohlberg, considered the founding father of twentieth-century moral psychology, has poured scorn on the traditional conception of moral character as being made up of no more than a "bag of virtues" (Kohlberg, quoted in Walker, *Towards a New Era*, 84).

2. "Mindset: The New Psychology of Success" (by Carol Dweck), https://youtu.be/QGvR_0mNpWM.

3. Students arrive at higher education with "character formation almost completed. They are not blank slates or balls of putty"; our role may be "consolidation of identity ... We certainly do make a difference, but we are not as powerful as we sometimes like to think" (Kiss and Euben, *Debating Moral Education*, 286, 287).

education for children, but not for adults. The church leader from the reformed tradition voiced similar scepticism in theological terms, claiming that there is little hope for change in fallen, unredeemed mankind and that the divine law was given only to show man's incapacity to obey it.[4] I think that this is a short-sighted comment because it misses the fundamental difference between those who are redeemed and those who are not, but that is a topic for another letter.

In any case, you will do well to accept the board's invitation to modesty.[5] Character and virtue education is not a mechanism that will change individuals and the world overnight, nor will it yield predictable outcomes. Human beings are formed differently, at different levels and through different rhythms. For some, change will be dramatic, for others it will be imperceptible. So, while character and virtue education is a concrete enterprise, its outcomes are loosely predictable at best.

More than an objection, this is really a precaution that the board has raised, and you are wise to remember it when you design programme outcomes and prepare publicity for the academy.

Historical Failures

A second objection was raised by your professor friend. As a historian, he was aware of many failures in character education and wondered whether the entire project is flawed. He quoted the example of the "American" variant that was prevalent in the 1980s. This approach was backward-looking and nostalgic, grounded in conservative politics, mainly concerned with fixing individual shortcomings, aimed at behavioural modification and mostly concerned with patriotism.[6] While some good came from this approach, much is probably best consigned to history. He also mentioned the examples of the Cultural Revolution in China and of Italian fascism, in which moral education became a tool for indoctrination. Here, character education demanded passivity, conformity and obedience to authority[7] and was a tool in the hands of political

---

4. Anscombe, "Modern Moral Philosophy," 5.

5. "If efforts at virtue research and development are endangered by underestimation of possible impact, they are no less crippled by overestimation. Well-founded misgivings about virtue education do remain – although those are not the misgivings most commonly highlighted by sceptics. To conclude, we need to take the long view and tread carefully over a bumpy terrain – although that is not the same as treading timidly. At all events, the ambitious transformative aims of current efforts at virtue education, however laudable, need to be mitigated by a substantive dose of intellectual modesty" (Kristjánsson, "Ten Myths," 285).

6. Arthur et al., *Teaching*, 31.

7. To, Yang and Helwig, "Democratic Moral Education in China," 404.

power. Again, these are terrible examples of how character education can go wrong, and we do well to learn from history in order not to repeat its errors.

We are not quite ready yet to respond fully to this objection as we still need to do our historical investigation. Your friend was gracious in agreeing to wait.

Bad Examples and Counterfeit Aristotle

A third objection was targeted at Aristotle. This came from the university educationalist, who had done her homework in investigating some bad examples of current educational systems based on Aristotelian frameworks. I fear, however, that the cases she presented were not genuine instances of Aristotelianism. This is understandable, for there are many counterfeits and several popular approaches to moral education that claim the paternity of Aristotle but have little philosophical affinity to him at all.[8]

Having said that, we have already acknowledged that there are genuine concerns with the Aristotelian framework. I will not treat them here in detail, but they include empirical inadequacies, irreconcilable vocabularies, the assumption of moral inequality, the elusiveness of a grand-end moral theory, the charge of over-systematization, the lack of empathy, the hopelessness of bad education, the lack of a systematic methodology and the lack of measuring instruments.[9] These need to be taken seriously, and your proposal to include ongoing critical research into the field of Aristotelian education in the academy found warm approval.

The Scope of Higher Education

The concern that was probably most widely shared by the members of the board was that character and virtue education might not be recognized as "proper higher education." This may be a genuine problem.

In my trip to China three years ago, I met a secondary school principal who had set up a citizenship and character training programme in his school. As word spread about what he was doing, he was criticized for being strange and he was even called a madman by some, mostly because he was not focusing exclusively on preparing his students for national standardized examinations. The efforts of this principal were classified by the public as messy and as not

---

8. Kristjánsson, "There Is Something about Aristotle," 49.
9. Kristjánsson, 60–65.

helping students with their future career prospects.[10] This is a clear case of character education that does not fit into prevalent conceptualizations of education.

In 2003, an interesting exchange regarding the scope of higher education took place at Duke University. The two scholars involved were Stanley Fish and Stanley Hauerwas and the debate was set off by Fish's article in *The Chronicle of Higher Education* entitled "Aim Low."[11] In this article (later to become a series), Fish argued that universities should not embrace the goals of moral and civic education because the only purpose of the university is academic. Moral purposes, according to Fish, do not belong in higher education and he argues that, while faculty are legitimized in influencing the development of intellectual virtues in their students, they should keep their aims "low" when it comes to their moral character.[12] For Fish, discipleship and indoctrination are wrong, and educators should resist the temptation to dabble in an enterprise that is none of their business.[13] In summary,[14] Fish's main claims are that (1) character education is an unrealistic expectation because there are too many variables;[15] (2) character education is a bad idea because it aims to convince rather than to simply analyse and compare; (3) character education is not the business of the university; and (4) character education violates core norms and requirements of academic work, which is meant to critically understand the world but not change it.[16] I won't spoil the debate (that is publicly available[17]) but I should mention that Hauerwas's main counter-claim was that the role of the university is to foster an educated public and that this must include moral formation, particularly through Christian communities.[18]

I think that the board needs to come to an informed consensus on what "proper education" is. Your academy is breaking with the status quo and will

---

10. To, Yang and Helwig, "Democratic Moral Education in China," 406.

11. Fish, "Aim Low."

12. Kiss and Euben, "Aim High," 58.

13. "You have no chance at all (short of a discipleship that is itself suspect and dangerous) of determining what their behaviour and values will be in those aspects of their lives that are not, in the strict sense of the word, academic. You might just make them into good researchers. You can't make them into good people, and you shouldn't try" (Fish, "Aim Low," 2).

14. Fish, "I Know It," 79–90.

15. "My main objection to moral and civic education in our colleges and universities is not that it is a bad idea (which it surely is), but that it's an unworkable idea. There are just too many intervening variables" (Fish, "Aim Low," 4).

16. Fish warns against the "incursion of virtue" (Kiss and Euben, "Aim High," 69).

17. Kiss and Euben, *Debating Moral Education*.

18. Hauerwas, "Pathos of the University," 106.

be judged accordingly. They need to decide if such a break is needed, and to be prepared to vouch for it.

Indoctrination, Paternalism and Autonomy

A final set of objections was voiced around the issues of indoctrination, paternalism and autonomy. The fear was that character and virtue education would be seen as disrespectful of the autonomy of the individual, that it might become intolerant and abusive and that it could even represent a threat to the climate of political and social pluralism that your region is trying to build. More broadly speaking, character education can be perceived as a return to premodern and modernistic education that saw abuses of authority, excessive self-confidence in formulas, unkept promises of utopias, intolerance of differences, the prominence of power structures, the supremacy of metanarratives, a lack of intellectual modesty and, in general, an approach that is ill-fitting for a multicultural, post-Christian, globalized world.[19] These concerns over "setting back the clock of educational time" were well summarized in the paper that your politician friend circulated.

There are some very good points here and we need to deal carefully with the fear that theological education might be seen as the resurgence of moral *indoctrination* by the religious status quo. This concern is increasingly found in government legislature.[20] Although we unpacked this objection to some degree when we discussed Rawls and political liberalism, let me look at it again from a slightly different perspective.

First of all, we need to defuse the association of morality with religion.[21] Although religion and moral education have often walked hand in hand, the association is neither automatic nor necessary. Aristotle, for example, did not argue from "religious" or divine command grounds, nor was he committed to any form of divine positive law.[22] Morality can be secular, and there are many

---

19. Arthur et al., *Teaching*, 31.

20. "The National Curriculum in the United Kingdom suggests that schools should no longer teach objective values (right and wrong, etc.) in order to assuage pluralistic sentiments" (Spears and Loomis, *Education for Human Flourishing*, 181).

21. "Various misconceptions or 'myths' concerning the notions of character, virtue and character education still remain at large in academic circles and among media pundits. According to those 'myths,' the notions in question are, among other things, old-fashioned, religious, paternalistic, conservative and situation-dependent" (Walker, *Towards a New Era*, 81).

22. Anscombe, "Modern Moral Philosophy," 5; and Arthur et al., *Teaching*, 41.

today who argue for ethics deriving from non-religious sources.[23] Hence it should be clear that the academy is not an exclusively religious project, but one that shares a lay vision of moral formation in society. Second, we need to neutralize the association of moral education with the pejorative category of ideological indoctrination. History provides many bad examples of religious and non-religious indoctrination, but moral education can also be pursued in a liberal, non-partisan way.[24] What we are suggesting is an educational project that trains free moral agents, which is a far cry from indoctrination.[25] Whereas the latter demands unquestioning belief, the former encourages belief on the grounds of understanding and acceptance.[26]

Paternalism becomes a problem when individuals are deprived of rational choice and placed under the authority of someone else.[27] The reaction against paternalism is illustrated by the 1960s' revolts in many residential colleges against all forms of *in loco parentis*. Students wanted to be free, not "parented," and they fought to remove adult regulatory figures from their learning communities. Generally speaking, paternalism is seen as a bad[28] thing in many liberal cultures today and, where education exercises sheer authority over students' moral lives as a form of social control, I think we agree that it is

---

23. "The religious roots of ethical principles can serve well as a lodestar and, for many, an inspiration, necessary as a historical explanation, but not sufficient in themselves as an explanation and a foundation for a system of values and ethics that can bind and direct" (Stückelberger, Fust and Ike, *Global Ethics*, 403). "The decline of a belief in religion as the basis of moral life did not necessarily imply a lowering of moral standards. The Ethical Union (1886) established the Moral Instruction League (1897) comprising many of the leading educational thinkers of the time to provide a secular basis for morality. The intention was to make character the chief aim of school life and to ensure that the outcome was not knowledge of the virtues but their practice in moral behaviour" (Arthur et al., *Character Education*, 6).

24. Kiss and Euben, "Aim High," 63.

25. "There may even be something to be learned from Spartan education, for although it represents an extreme model and has been compared to the twentieth century Fascist and Nazi dictatorships (Gutek 1972: 22), Spartans educated their youth with clarity, duty and discipline which allowed them to recognize integrity in their leaders . . . Facilitating the creation of free moral agents through transitory inculcation of moral habit need not be necessarily illiberal, for as Partington points out: 'the progression from innocence to virtue or from ignorance to knowledge requires initiation into moral or intellectual order'" (Oxenham, *Liquid Modernity*, 210).

26. "Indoctrination is different than education. The process of education seeks as its end true belief with understanding, whereas indoctrination seeks, as its end, mere belief of a sort. Education implies learning without coercion . . . indoctrination implies the opposite" (Spears and Loomis, *Education for Human Flourishing*, 206).

27. "Paternalism is one of philosophy's trickiest concepts. I shall assume here an everyday understanding according to which an intervention X is paternalistic if it involves Person A's forcing X upon Person B against, or at least without regard for, Person B's own will, under the pretext that X is in Person B's best interests" (Kristjánsson, "Ten Myths," 275).

28. Kristjánsson, "There Is Something about Aristotle," 65.

indeed a bad thing.²⁹ Moderate paternalism can sometimes be appropriate,³⁰ and students can thrive under appropriate authority structures, but that is not my point. My point is that extreme forms of paternalism should not be linked to Aristotle, because his framework is based on the reasoned exercise of *phronesis* which is utterly unlike brainwashing.³¹ The heart of Aristotelian education is, paradoxically, non-prescriptive, and liberal societies should welcome an educational approach that maximizes choice between that which is "well" and that which is "un-well."³²

And now for a final word on the concept of *autonomy*. The education of character and the teaching of virtue sound particularly menacing to existential cultures that have placed freedom and human autonomy at the pinnacle of their value hierarchy. Who is anyone to tell anyone else what to do, let alone who to be? As we have seen in the example of Stanley Fish, many educators hesitate to come anywhere near moral deliberation, evaluation and prescription, and prefer the unattached ground of moral description.³³

---

29. The programs of character education in English private schools in the early to mid-1800s were, for example, just for men and just for the elite, and risked being little more than learning to display the right manners. In the Scottish Enlightenment character education aimed at producing character necessary for the world of work and was really not much more than a social control approach (see Arthur, *Teaching Character and Virtue*, 22–24).

30. Carr argues that given the high premium that is placed on character in graduates from the world of employment, students might benefit from being shaped in their character. More precisely he argues that, "insofar as the (new) university recognizes a general responsibility to educate or train students for a wide range of professions and other public services; (ii) such training requires the cultivation of capacities for wise context-sensitive reflection and deliberation (basically *phronesis*) of fundamentally the same order as the practical wisdom that Aristotle takes to be essential for the formation of virtuous character; (iii) [ergo] we should promote or teach virtues of good character conducive to such deliberation in universities and tertiary colleges" (Carr, *Educating the Virtues*, 115).

31. "In an Aristotelian theory . . . truly virtuous persons do not only perform the right actions in a non-reflective way, but they perform them for the right reasons and from the right motives: knowing them, taking intrinsic pleasure in them and deciding that they are worthwhile" (Kristjánsson, "Ten Myths," in Walker et al., *Towards a New Era*, 86).

32. "It is a remarkable feature of liberal thought that it pays almost no attention to the prevalence of evil" (Kekes, *Facing Evil*, in Smilie, "Humanitarian and Humanistic Ideals," 69). "If what citizens really crave . . . is for government to maximize their well-being rather than simply their range of options . . . then 'forcing them to be free to choose' is paternalistic, whereas intervening (apparently paternalistically) in their lives in order to enhance their well-being is the essence of anti-paternalism in action" (Kristjánsson, "Ten Myths," 277). See also Bloom, *Closing of the American Mind*.

33. "Those in higher education often balk at what they may view as tampering with students' morality" (Berkowitz, "Educating for Character," 17). Talking about morality in a society of autonomous individuals feels, as Anscombe puts it, "like someone whose jaws have suddenly come out of alignment; the teeth don't come together in a proper bite" (Anscombe, "Modern Moral Philosophy," 4).

One could argue that there is a place for authority in education and that complete autonomy is not in the best interests of students.[34] We could also develop a theology of authority based on the accounts of the creation and the fall, but that would take us beyond our current purpose.[35] Perhaps the simple answer is, once again, found in the Aristotelian framework, which leaves room for individual autonomy through the practices of *phronesis*. Although the academy will have authority structures and will orient students to the virtues, it will first and foremost train students to become rational agents of their own moral character.[36]

—

I imagine this board meeting must have been difficult but, still, it is wonderful to have such a group working with you. They have raised some very good objections and many good scholars are debating similar issues.[37] Surely, compared with other forms of liberal education, character and virtue education has a price to pay.[38] But the costs are well worth the benefits to society.

May you be unwavering without being stubborn.

---

34. "We often err when designing to exert a moral influence, by substituting . . . persuasion for power; but we soon find that the gentle wining influence of moral suasion, however beautiful in theory, will often fall back powerless upon the hearer, and we then must have authority to fall back upon or all is lost . . . there must be authority" (Hunter, *Death of Character*, 53).

35. See Ott, *Understanding*, 226, for an explanation of endogenic and exogenic views of character education.

36. "How can it be simultaneously true that it is the aim of moral education to develop persons capable of autonomous engagement in rational moral conduct and that this goal might be secured by inculcating from an early age certain ready-made habits of action and feeling? . . . Aristotle does suggest that in order to take the step from habituated virtue to full virtue, we must learn to choose the right actions and emotions from 'a firm and unchanging state' of character [1105a30–1105a34]: that is, after having submitted them to the arbitration of our own *phronesis*" (Kristjánsson, *Aristotelian Character Education*, 277).

37. Kristjánsson, "Ten Myths."

38. "We want character but without the unyielding conviction; we want strong morality but without the emotional burden of guilt or shame; we want virtue but without particular moral justifications that invariably offend; we want good without having to name evil; we want decency without the authority to insist upon it; we want moral community without any limitations to personal freedom" (Hunter, *Death of Character*, xv).

18

Whose Character? Which Virtue?

I come to the last question that was raised by your board, on the nature of virtue. As you can appreciate, the proposal to implement character and virtue education stirs up a number of conversations that are unlikely to be sorted out in the near future. In this instance, we are dipping our toes into the vast debates of moral ethics as we try to define what makes something a virtue. As is fitting to our epistolary correspondence, I will not burden you with an exhaustive overview of the debates, much less come up with a solution. I will simply try to summarize the objections of moral situationism and then explain why moral universalism represents a solid alternative. Hopefully, these explanations will be fitting for a non-specialist audience so you can easily share them with the entire board.

The Nature of Virtue?

Identifying the nature of virtue strikes at the very heart of the objectives of the academy. It is easy to say that we wish to develop character and virtue, but *whose* character and *which* virtue are we aiming at?[1] What vocabulary of virtue will the academy use and what method will guide you in deciding what a virtue is? Should courage be included as a virtue and, if so, why? What about orderliness? Or what about particular civic and intellectual virtues? The big question that looms in the background, as we try to define virtue and vice, is the question of what is right and what is wrong. As Christian theologians there are several ways to respond, and much will depend on our theological method. We can look exclusively to Scripture and compile a specific list of virtues and vices from the Bible, or we can look to a broader reasoned tradition. Since we

---

1. I am intentionally using the same words that MacIntyre uses in his 1988 sequel to *After Virtue* entitled *Whose Justice? Which Rationality?* in which he presents a number of different accounts of justice and of rationality.

will have plenty of space to deal with answers from Scripture in the coming months, allow me to engage here with the latter.

I will immediately put my cards on the table. There are several possible positions on how virtue can be identified,[2] but I will be defending the straightforward claim that there are general moral virtues that are universal. This claim argues that there is a broad-spectrum set of absolute virtues that are not relative to individual preference or subject to local traditions and that are necessary as we pursue moral education.[3] This reflects Aristotle's own position and the so-called "neo-naturalist mainstream" of virtue theory.[4] The main objection to this position is found in situationism, which we will now explore.

The Case for Situationism

Situationism is a variant of moral relativism[5] that claims that all human moral behaviour depends on situations. Arguing, for example, on the results of psychological[6] experiments, situationists deny that morality is universal and claim that there are no generalizable virtues.[7] Situationists are sensitive to the issue of who is deciding what about morality and are quick to point to abuses of power when someone in authority tries to lay down a moral law.[8] Ethical lists and virtue catalogues are seen as instruments of ideology that

---

2. Alasdair MacIntyre holds to a social constructivist version of virtue ethics. He claims that "there is no way to possess the virtues except as part of a tradition" (MacIntyre, *After Virtue*, 127).

3. "In order to pursue moral education, one must believe that absolutes are possible to exist in the world as we know it. We simply cannot teach children right from wrong if there is no such thing as right and no such thing as wrong" (Gretchen and Firmin, "Character Education," 186).

4. "The modern neo-naturalist mainstream of virtue theory follows Aristotle in holding that moral virtues are not relative to local moral traditions and are of general or universal human value . . . Cultivating virtues, in this light, is primarily a matter of teaching positive moral attitudes or dispositions rather than particular points of view" (Carr, *Educating the Virtues*, 112).

5. Arthur et al., *Teaching*, 46.

6. "The most commonly cited are the Milgram experiments" (Kiss and Euben, *Debating Moral Education*, 281).

7. For situationists, "there is no such thing as stable and consistent states of virtues and vices making up character; rather, all human behaviour has now been shown in psychological experiments . . . to be completely situation dependent" (Arthur et al., *Teaching*, 47).

8. "Locke's vision of fundamental human equality and natural rights is seen by critics [as] providing ideological rationalization for dispossession of the native peoples of America, since their failure to make productive use of the land licensed Europeans to claim the land for agriculture and kill or enslave those who unjustly resisted . . ." (Kiss and Euben, *Debating Moral Education*, 272).

need to be done away with in favour of sensitivity to situations and context.[9] The role of the individual conscience is frequently appealed to along the lines introduced by Richard Butler. For Butler, individual conscience is governed by our emotions and should be considered as the sovereign arbitrator. He famously defined virtue as "keeping our heart."[10] Although it would be unfair to consider Butler a fully-fledged moral relativist, his work is illustrative of the shift from universal virtues to individualistic values.

What does situationism look like in educational terms? Allow me to refer to an example from within your own family. I recall that your daughter studied in America in the 1970s and participated in a "values clarification" programme. Schooling in those years was moving away from being a "factory of character" to being a "factory of democracy," and values clarification programmes, rooted in Dewey's vision of morality originating in society and benefiting democracy,[11] were seen as a tool to remove absolute notions of virtue. Values clarification programmes fed off the counter-culture movement of the 1960s that had celebrated autonomy and individual rights rather than responsibility,[12] and what happened in schools was that the classical virtues and ethical lists were gradually replaced by a methodology to clarify values. The approach sought to remove all distinctions between moral and non-moral behaviour and to empower individuals to sort out their own values.[13] I recall you telling me about long conversations with your teenage daughter about the objectivity of virtue and the subjectivity of values (and, given the splendid results in your daughter today, I would say that you were successful). Although the values

---

9. William Blake argued that morality of the "law" is an "ideology serving the hegemonic power of a class" (Kiss and Euben, 211).

10. In Moses, "Keeping the Heart," 614.

11. See Arthur et al., *Teaching*, 22–23; and Jones et al., *Toward Human Flourishing*, 18–19.

12. The social attitude of personalism (1960–70), coming with the counterculture movement, "celebrated the worth, dignity and autonomy of the individual person, including the subjective self or inner life of the person. It emphasized rights more than responsibility, freedom more than commitment . . . It gave birth to 'values clarification'" (Lickona, *Educating for Character*, 9–10).

13. Values clarification programmes were meant to help students clarify their own values, beliefs, feelings and choices on the basis of a shared technique that had three general steps: (1) choosing values freely from differing alternatives; (2) prizing, sharing and affirming one's chosen values; and (3) acting consistently and consciously upon one's chosen values. The seminal text was Raths, Harmin and Simon, 1966, *Values and Teaching*. The movement was distinctively "non directive and value free" (Jones, *Toward Human Flourishing*, 19).

clarification movement did not last long,[14] it did contribute to replacing virtue language with value language.[15]

I will not go further with the critiques that can be made of situationism,[16] nor will I describe the positive correctives that the situationist argument can contribute.[17] I have simply tried to unpack the objection of the board within its broader context.

The Case for Moral Universalism

As an alternative to situationism, here is my case in favour of universal virtues. My argument is mostly based on the common-sense observation that human beings share sets of general universal morals.[18] Wherever one goes, similar character strengths are praised and held up as virtuous.[19] As Socrates claimed, "All humans are good in the same way for they become good by gaining the same things."[20] Moral universalism claims that, notwithstanding cultural situations and individual conscience, there are sets of fixed moral points for all humanity.[21] Justice, for example, is considered good anywhere in the world. So is temperance. So is love. There is also commonality in condemning

---

14. "Values clarification has largely disappeared from the scene, in part due to generally ineffective scientific evidence" (Berkowitz, "Science of Character Education," 56).

15. A study conducted by DEMOS in Britain involving workshops and in-depth interviews with teachers, head teachers, non-formal education providers, education experts, developmental psychologists, policy-makers, social action organizations and a range of experts and policy-makers revealed that there is "resistance among participants to the idea of explicitly referencing or seeking to develop moral virtues among students." Participants were generally "much more comfortable discussing the component parts of moral virtue, such as empathy and respect, than moral virtue as a whole" (Birdwell, Scott and Reynolds, *Character Nation*, 20).

16. "Virtue ethicists have arguably sufficient weaponry in their arsenal to rebut the situationist challenge." Kristjánsson suggests a rebuttal on at least two themes: anti-behaviourism and the concept of a situation (Kristjánsson, "Ten Myths," 281).

17. Cross-cultural research supports the claim that appropriate leadership is "not the same for every culture" (Kohls, "Church Leadership in Africa," 119), and this would be a case where situationism can be positively applied to missiology and character education.

18. Aristotle's empirical universalism about human nature is captured in his much-quoted observation that "in our travels we can see how every human being is akin . . . to a human being" (Aristotle, *Nicomachean Ethics* 1155a20–1155a22, quoted in Kristjánsson, *Aristotelian Character Education*, 281).

19. "It is surely impossible to envisage human societies where character strengths such as conscientiousness or courage are not needed, recognized or held to be of value" (Kristjánsson, 281).

20. Plato, *Meno* 73B.

21. "Taking the [human] race as a whole . . . the human idea of decent behaviour was obvious to everyone" (Lewis, *Mere Christianity*, 9).

certain vices like cowardice, greed and selfishness. Although there are different interpretations, understandings and applications of virtues and vices, there is general agreement over the existence of universal, cosmopolitan and non-religious virtues.[22] Lewis put it well: "In some societies people drive on the right side of the road, in some on the left; yet clearly it would be a myth to claim that there is no such thing as the general skill of a good driver."[23] And again: "Human beings, all over the earth, have this curious idea that they ought to behave in a certain way, and cannot really get rid of it."[24]

Theologically, this is known as the "natural law" theory, which states that "all human beings are naturally inclined toward the realisation of the natural ends for which they are created."[25] This includes a general mindfulness of what is good. Although this inclination is damaged by the fall, most theological traditions still consider it very influential. The role of the conscience is included in this discussion and there is general agreement that the conscience represents an "abiding characteristic which gives a general sense of value and forces one to discover the right thing through reflection."[26] Seen in this way, an educated conscience can be a powerful ally in character education as it speaks through reason and sentiment to inform the will and determine ongoing action.

The universality of virtue is a popular topic of research. A recent study of 458 university students from four different cultures universally acclaimed honesty, welfare and justice as shared virtues.[27] Empirical evidence from moral psychology also supports the universalist position[28] in identifying common

---

22. "Men have differed as regards what people you ought to be unselfish to – whether it was only your own family, or your fellow countrymen, or everyone. But they have always agreed that you ought not to put yourself first. Selfishness has never been admired" (Lewis, 9).

23. In Kristjánsson, *Aristotelian Character Education*, 281.

24. Lewis, *Mere Christianity*, 10.

25. Arthur, *Education with Character*, 50.

26. Arthur, 50.

27. "Our study showed that there are cultural differences and similarities in lay conceptions of moral character. Consistent with our expectations, we found that there were widely shared attributes which are related to issues of justice and welfare. This is in line with the moral universalism perspective (Kohlberg, 1984; Turiel, 1983) and corroborates the widespread 'human obsession' with fairness, reciprocity and justice (Graham et al., 2009) as well as the importance of social cooperation as emphasized by evolutionary theorists (Richerson and Boyd, 2005)" (Vauclair, Wilson and Fischer, "Cultural Conceptions of Morality," 69).

28. "Moral psychology has a long history of advocating a universalism position . . . Kohlberg suggests as the pinnacle of moral maturity to define what is moral or not: justice, rights and welfare" (Vauclair, Wilson and Fischer, 55).

priorities in global morals.[29] The recent work of positive psychology similarly confirms that, across history, there has been essential agreement on what the virtues are.[30] The Children's Morality Code is an interesting example of a universal code that was put together as a result of the popular vote of committees, expert social scientist opinion, academic literature and a compilation of laws of good living that "the best Americans have always obeyed."[31] Although not explicitly linked to virtues, you might also want to take a look at other examples of shared frameworks, such as the Earth Charter[32] or the Common Word[33] project. What is remarkable is that, despite different sources and different research approaches, the results have huge areas of overlap in detecting universal virtues.

If you want to refresh your theological reading on moral universalism, you can do no better than turn to C. S. Lewis's *The Abolition of Man*. In this Christian classic, Lewis shares his search for the independent rise of common moral laws in ancient Egyptian, Babylonian, Hebrew, Chinese, Indian, Greek, Anglo-Saxon and American cultures. He discovered that there are many common virtues, such as kindness, honesty, justice, mercy, courage, loyalty to parents, spouses and family members, an obligation to help the poor, the sick and the less fortunate, and the right to private property. Lewis called these "the universal path to becoming a good person."[34] Should you need to draw on a more heavy-weight theologian for your argument, you will find plenty of material in Hans Küng's explorations of religious traditions that led him to draft the set of universal values that he called the "Global Ethic."[35]

---

29. "The Schwartz values research identifies 10 types of morals in more than 60 countries: power, achievement, hedonism, stimulation, self-direction, universalism, benevolence, conformity, tradition and security. Helkama instead proposes the most important moral values: universalism (resolves values conflicts and justice issues), benevolence and prosocial actions (kindness toward others) and conformity/tradition to control antisocial action" (Vauclair, Wilson and Fischer, 55).

30. "People are more or less the same wherever they go, and . . . the spheres of human life wherein our virtues and vices play out have remained essentially constant throughout history" (Kristjánsson, *Aristotelian Character Education*, 281).

31. This code won the USA National Morality Code competition in 1916 and listed virtues such as loyalty, truth, self-control and duty (Hunter, *Death of Character*, 56).

32. http://earthcharter.org.

33. https://www.acommonword.com. This project reflects dialogue between Christian and Muslim scholars in search of common ground.

34. Lewis, *Abolition of Man*, 83. See also Gretchen and Firmin, "Character Education," 189.

35. See Küng, *Global Ethic*.

The Better Choice

As I mentioned earlier, there are also intermediate positions between situationism and universalism. MacIntyre, for example, offers a social constructivist vision that allows virtues to change between times and cultures, but to still remain binding as universal within that culture.[36] This position forfeits an appeal to the "wisdom of the ages" in favour of the "wisdom of the age."[37] Soviet *vospitanie* is an example of social constructivism where the comprehensive moral culture in Russian society moved from the narratives of Marx and Lenin to new sources of moral culture.[38] Personally, I fear that the shifting sands of culture alone can be misleading. While it is important to have structured goals for life that are context-sensitive, the chosen goal, I would argue, must be the correct goal.[39]

In conclusion, I think that we are better off philosophically, empirically, educationally and theologically in upholding the general universality of virtues. This does not mean that we need to produce a rigid list of all the virtues. The Aristotelian tradition does not call for that. Rather, we should be happy with a stable framework that can be appropriately contextualized and individually engaged by *phronesis*.[40] That is why I've spoken about a general universality of virtues. Nor does it mean that every virtue will be identically understood

---

36. MacIntyre does not combat relativism but takes it on board within a social constructivist interpretation where "virtues (and vices) differ over times and societies or, more specifically, among the prevailing social practices of different cultures" (Arthur, *Teaching Character and Virtue in Schools*, 46).

37. Hauerwas shares this view: "There is no virtue theory in general. Rather the characterizations of the virtues, their content, how they interrelate, will differ from one community and tradition to another" (Hauerwas, "Difference of Virtue," 260). "The courage of a Christian is different from that of a Buddhist" (Hauerwas, "Christian Virtues Exemplified," 338).

38. "Soviet educators wanted to develop in students certain qualities (patriotism, discipline, a strong work ethic, etc.) that would help them reach 'the new socialist future' . . . (see also The Moral Code of the Builders of Communism that Soviet teachers were expected to present each year) . . . With the collapse of communism, Russians are now looking for new sources of moral culture upon which to build their approach to *vospitanie*" (Glanzer, "Moral Education Establishment," 297).

39. Porter, *Recovery of Virtue*, 83.

40. "Aristotle's 'thick but vague' theory of the human good (Nussbaum, 1990) leaves sufficient space for cultural relativity to satisfy all but the most radical relativists . . . The language of virtue thus provides an effective cross-cultural currency of moral evaluation" (Kristjánsson, *Aristotelian Character Education*, 54).

everywhere, for, as Hauerwas reminds us, there are times when a Christian understanding of virtue will be significantly different from society's.[41]

As far as the academy goes, can we settle for a minimalist definition of the virtues?[42] Can we be clear at the core and soft on the edges, being committed both to universal virtues and to socially embedded traditions that generate diversity and richness?[43] Should we do so, it would cohere well with a contextualized gospel in which the core features of Christian holiness will look differently for Moses, Daniel, Peter, Augustine, Charlemagne, Whitefield, Bonhoeffer, Mother Teresa and ourselves.[44]

As I said at the outset, this is a complex conversation, and I look to our philosopher friends to enrich the debates. Although some shadows remain, we have plenty of light to walk confidently. You have been tasked by the board to produce a written response to their objections. Please feel free to take anything I have shared in these last two letters.

This is the last letter of this first set in which we've been working on the vision of our project for the academy. God willing, in the next set we will define the historical and theological tradition of character and virtue and its relationship to theological education.

May we keep our thoughts orderly in what we can know without crushing the mystery of what is beyond us.

---

41. Hauerwas claims that a Christian understanding of virtues, such as courage, does not always align with the understanding of society: "Those who wish to return the church to public prominence by making us serve the public well by being communities of virtue are making a decisive mistake . . . The church must make clear that virtue constituted by the civic order is at best only a pale reflection of what we are called to be. I suspect few polities wish to be so challenged" (Hauerwas, "Difference of Virtue," 249, 262).

42. "Sisela Bok, in *Basic Values*, calls for 'minimalist' ethical standards, perhaps such as found in Boyer (*The Basic School*)" (Pavela, "Renewed Focus," 735).

43. "No two character education programs should look exactly alike. Each reflects the uniqueness of the community it serves" (Gretchen and Firmin, "Character Education," 190).

44. "Christian holiness finally has to take on the characteristics of its host culture in some way" (Neuhaus, *Theological Education*, 183, 186, 189).

Part II

The Tradition

19

A Theology of Character and Virtue – with Method

Dear Siméon, how good to hear that your daughter is now engaged! This is always a tricky passage for us fathers, but I know that you will navigate it well. As you know, I have recently become a grandfather, and this is a thrilling experience. As we think of our theology students, surely let us not forget our own offspring. I have downloaded onto my Kindle a precious little book from Stanley Hauerwas entitled *The Character of Virtue: Letters to a Godson*, and my wife and I are reading a short chapter every evening. It is a lovely collection of letters on different virtues written with Hauerwas's inimitable wit to a growing child. Add this book to your wish list!

It seems like it was only yesterday that we started corresponding, but it has already been a year. You have made good progress despite your health concerns, and your board have been happy with your response to their objections. Well done! You now have a green light from them to proceed along the general lines of our Manifesto.

But we still have some substantial research ahead of us. Before we move into the practical conversation around implementation, there are two bodies of theoretical issues we need to engage with. The first concerns the theological and scriptural grounding of character and virtue education. The board have confirmed that this research needs to be in place before you can proceed. Second, we need to do further historical investigation. Again, the board have shared their concern over the novelty of your proposal and want to know more about the tradition that is behind character and virtue education and what can be learned from it.

I suggest that we divide this work amongst us. How about I work on the historical tradition and you work on the biblical grounding? We can then correspond over each other's work. The combination of our efforts will produce, I hope, a good start on a theology of character and virtue education.

Thinking about Methodology

Before we start, it is useful to think briefly about our method. The question is, what methodology should we use to work out a theology of character and virtue education? Here we have a set of bigger questions about theological method in general, about the tools that we use to theologize on culture, about the place of tradition in theology and about our attitude towards other sources, such as scientific or philosophical work. The question of Scripture is also central, and we need to clarify what exactly we mean when we claim that we want the theories and practices of our theological education to be "biblical."

It is beyond the scope of this letter to scan this topic in depth, but let me suggest some thoughts on the sources we will be using and on how this is part of a broader cultural mandate.

The Sources of a Theology of Character and Virtue Education

Let us start by thinking about our sources in putting together a theology of character and virtue education. There is general agreement that there are four sources of Christian theology, the first being Scripture, the second reason, the third experience and the fourth tradition. This has sometimes been called the "Wesleyan quadrilateral."[1] Although there are differing opinions on how to use them, on how they relate to each other and on which has greater weight or priority,[2] most theological traditions in Christianity would recognize these sources.[3] Let us look briefly at each.

Scripture is the central source in Christian theology, and it is tempting to look exclusively to the Bible to find theories and practices of education. After all, one might reason, if the Bible is the Word of God that helps us in all things, should it not provide answers to the basic questions of educational philosophy and practice? While this sentiment is praiseworthy, it is doomed to fail for its simplicity. It is, in fact, misleading to expect Scripture to provide

---

1. D. Thorsten, *The Wesleyan Quadrilateral: A Model for Evangelical Theology* (Lexington, KY: Emeth Press, 2005).

2. J. Stackhouse, "Theology of Culture" lectures, 2004, available at Regent Bookstore, https://www.regentaudio.com/products/theology-of-culture-1.

3. See P. Allen, *Theological Method: A Guide for the Perplexed* (London: T&T Clark, 2012), 1–22; and A. McGrath, *Christian Theology* (Oxford: Blackwell, 2007), 121.

a full-blown theoretical framework for education or a pedagogical project to nurture virtue. This is because it was never the intent of biblical authors to do so. Moses did not run a school; he led a nation. David did not write educational philosophy; he wrote psalms. Paul did not design curricula; he wrote to edify local churches. To impose questions on Scripture that it is not meant to answer violates Scripture itself. So, if we truly honour Scripture as a source, let us beware of extorting what is not there.

What then? Is Scripture useless for our purposes? Surely not. I think there are at least three legitimate expectations that we need to nurture as we apply biblical sources to educational issues. The first is that we will find explicit or implicit biblical support for educational theories. The second is that we will be equipped with critical filters that will help us spot theological incoherence in educational theories and practices. The third is that we will find original content that will inject new elements of theory or practice that are not present in other sources. As you do your exegetical work in the Old and New Testament, I'm sure you will be meeting all three of these expectations.

A second source that enriches our educational theology is *reason*. In our case, we have engaged mainly with the educational philosophy of Aristotle, but we need to be prepared more generally to discern common grace in all philosophical and educational scholarship that provides categories and content that are not revealed (or even mentioned) in the Bible. Paul's use of a pagan ethical list in the letter to the Philippians[4] is an example of how Scripture itself adopts this methodology.

We then have tradition and experience as the final two sources of our theology of character and virtue education. When it comes to *tradition*, we have the exciting task of unearthing good practice and accumulated wisdom from the history of education. This is what I will be working on in the coming months and, although I have only just begun my historical enquiry, I have already been encouraged beyond all measure. When, instead, it comes to *experience*, I am thinking of the tools of reflective practice and of the data that emerges from empirical research. A balanced theology of character and virtue education will include not only our own experiences as educators but also references to professional journals, empirical research and consolidated

---

4. "The apostle is commending to his Philippian readers what was good in pagan life and morality. H. J. Michael, recognizing that Christians were being persecuted by their pagan neighbours, wondered whether the former were blinded to 'what was good in the heathen life by which they were surrounded' and asserted that the apostle penned this elaborate injunction so that they would keep in mind the virtues of pagan ethics" (O'Brien, *Epistle to the Philippians*, 501).

models of good practice. The latter will be especially useful as we investigate the practicalities of character and virtue education.

All of these sources, Scripture, reason, tradition and experience, contribute to shape the way we think theologically about education. As individuals who respond to our cultures, our histories and our experiences, we have inevitably been influenced by all these sources in our theological thinking. So let us acknowledge them and make good critical use of them.

Using Scripture for a Theology of Character and Virtue Education

Let me probe a little deeper now on the use of Scripture, for it is our most fundamental source. As I mentioned above, being "biblical" in our educational thinking is far from simple. How do we actually go about constructing a biblical theology of character and virtue education? How do we read the Bible to engage with the issue of character and virtue education? I have identified ten possible approaches, which I find easiest to list as a set of bullet points:

- *Key biblical texts.* This approach identifies and applies key biblical texts to issues of character and virtue. There are texts that can be used to engage directly with current educational issues. Examples of this are 2 Peter 1, where we find a clear call to add virtue to our faith, or the book of James, where the relationship between faith and works has much to do with growing in virtue. Care must be taken to respect context and avoid proof-texting and eisegesis of these texts.
- *Key biblical terms.* Here we study key scriptural terms that might relate to character, virtue and vice. These might include words like holiness, sanctification, righteousness, blessing, sin, disobedience and wisdom. There are several important terms in the New Testament, for example, that bear the rich heritage of character and virtue.
- *Biblical heroes and stories.* Another approach is to identify individuals and stories in Scripture that model character and virtue. These need careful contextualization, but we can easily spot stories of virtuous character both in Old Testament heroes and in many Gospel narratives. In the New Testament, we are explicitly called to imitate Jesus and Paul as examples of virtue.[5]

---

5. "Jesus exemplified moral virtue in all that he did. We follow his example, not in doing the precise acts that he did, but in cultivating the same virtues he had and in acting from those virtues in whatever we do" (Austin and Geivett, "Being Good," 3).

- *Biblical patterns of good practice.* A fourth approach identifies patterns of good practice. What we are looking for here are stories and strategies in which character is being intentionally formed. We might, for example, look at the apprenticeship model of Jesus and his disciples and study how their character was transformed during their three years of community life. Or we might look at the pattern of what it might mean to "be imitators" of Paul's character through the life of someone like Timothy.
- *Old Testament patterns.* Here we look at educational patterns that can be seen as a nation is built under God. What were the educational elements in the history of Israel? What was the place of character and virtue? What assumptions are made about human nature and human flourishing? What do we find in terms of both content and method that relate to character and virtue? How do categories like holiness and disobedience relate to virtue and vice? Examples of this might be found in looking at ways in which Deuteronomy is concerned with forming character or in considering the morally rich wisdom narrative of Proverbs. In this approach, it is useful to refer to Jewish culture and contemporary Jewish educationalists like Martin Buber.
- *New Testament patterns in the epistles.* Our method here consists in reading through the letters of the New Testament and identifying issues and dynamics that have to do with character and virtue. This is a very promising approach as we explore, for example, the typical "theory–practice" structure of several letters, the presence of ethical lists or the practical outworking of the gospel in terms of changed lives and relationships. First Corinthians, for example, can be read as a study of a church that is living with many vices and is being called back to virtue.
- *Biblical theology.* In this approach, we look at the broad sweep of God's revelation and try to identify key patterns and relationships, many of which relate to issues of character and virtue. We might, for example, trace the patterns of obedience and disobedience of the people of God to the (moral) law and find direct connections to virtue and vice. We could also look at how character was intended at creation, at what happened with the fall, at how character is transformed as the outcome of redemption and what flourishing human beings might look like in the final restoration of things.
- *Systematic categories.* Here we rely on the categories of systematic theology and use them as frameworks to help us articulate a theology

of character and virtue education. One might, for example, look at creation and the *imago Dei* as an original model of character and virtue, and then revisit the image of the "new man" after the incarnation and the atonement. Anthropology is an important category for education, and we need to formulate a theology of the nature of man, both in his created potential and in his fallen state.

- *Theological systems.* Coherent theological traditions and systems can also be useful as we work out character and virtue issues. One might, for example, look to liberation theology and the works of Freire that deal with fundamental vices related to power. Or we could look to reformed theology as it interacts with culture, articulates a vision of common grace and reflects on human capacity and divine agency.
- *Key theologians.* This approach investigates what specific theologians have written on character and virtue in their historical contexts. Many theologians were also educators, and it is not surprising to find that much of their works deal with these issues. We can find examples of engagement with character in virtue in the early church fathers, in medieval theologians like Aquinas[6] and in contemporary theologians like Stanley Hauerwas.[7]

So, as you can see, there are several tools on our bench. I look forward to reading your letters as you use these tools to contribute to a "biblical" theology of character and virtue education.

The Cultural Mandate and Character and Virtue Education

Let me consider one more general question concerning our work: how do we justify it theologically? In other words, on what grounds are we trying to establish a theology of character and virtue education? Surely we do not want to fall into the error that happened at the time of Abelard, of simply teaching the classical tradition of the virtues with no reference or connection to Christian doctrine.[8] If we are working out a theology of character and virtue education, we must be able to justify the project within the broader scope of Christian theology. Let me suggest that, in articulating a theology of character and virtue

---

6. Aquinas and Aristotle offer an "unsurpassed analysis of how the virtues are acquired to form the self" (Hauerwas, in Porter, *Recovery of Virtue*, 14).

7. Hauerwas writes prolifically on the virtues: *Vision and Virtue* (1974), *Community of Character* (1981), *Dispatches from the Front* (1994), *Christians among the Virtues* (1997), *The Character of Virtue: Letters to a Godson* (2018).

8. Marenbon, *Philosophy of Peter Abelard*, 283.

education, we are responding to the *missio Dei* of creating culture on the basis of the mandate of Genesis 1.

When we speak of "creating culture," different traditions respond differently.[9] Some believe that secular culture is hopelessly corrupted and that we should withdraw from educational dialogue and just "stick to the Bible." Others believe that Christ is alive in every manifestation of culture and that we should uncritically embrace all educational trends as an act of devotion to Christ. I find myself most comfortable with the position that sees Christ transforming what has been distorted in human culture and working through us for its overall growth and improvement. This "Christ transforming culture" stance is not without its paradoxes, but I am encouraged to believe in a "Christ of education."

The main theological support for this position, I believe, is in the creation account, where we have the foundations of a theology of culture. Let me unpack this briefly, for I find it particularly powerful. In Genesis 1, the story begins with a world that was "void" and "shapeless." What the Creator does is fundamentally two things: the first is to *fill the void* with good things, and the second is to *put order* into that which was chaotic. The void was thus filled with light, vegetation, the animal kingdom and mankind. The shapeless chaos, instead, was given order, and the sea and land were separated, the sun and moon were given their cycles, the seasons were put into place and everything began to reproduce according to its kind. The result of God's creation is a world that is full of good things in a well-shaped arrangement. This was "good."

At the end of Genesis, God extends this creative mandate to man, as he tells him to "replenish" the earth and "subdue" it. Man is here called to continue the creational work of God by continuing to fill the void with good things and order what is shapeless. This is how I like to understand the cultural mandate. It has to do with filling the earth with good things that were not there before, such as art, music, architecture and wine. It also has to do with giving order to that which is potentially chaotic through, for example, politics, philosophy and law.

This cultural mandate can be seen in education as well, for what we are doing in education is filling the lives of men and women with good things and helping to create order where otherwise there would be chaos. Character and

---

9. The best-known survey of these positions is found in Niebuhr's famous book *Christ and Culture* (New York: Harper & Row, 1951) in which he outlines five basic stances that different theological traditions have taken towards culture. See also D. Carson, *Christ and Culture Revisited* (Cambridge: Eerdmans, 2008); and A. Crouch, *Culture in the Making* (Downers Grove: InterVarsity Press, 2008).

virtue education falls into the same creational mandate, for it endeavours to fill the earth with the goodness and happiness of virtue and to order the chaos of unrestrained vice to generate well-structured individuals and communities. In doing so, we are participating in the ongoing creation of what God deems to be "good."

—

May you and I find encouragement in seeing that, in a small way, we are continuing the work of God's incomplete creation. May we wear this calling with boldness and do away with false modesty.

20

Virtue in Ancient Cultures

We have divided our tasks in this phase of our correspondence. You will be doing the biblical work and I will try to compile some historical summaries. Here is my first letter in which I begin to tell something of the story of character education.

A Story to Tell

Truly, I feel like I've stumbled into an unexplored galaxy. As I've struggled over the selection of materials, I have decided to keep my letters brief and then send you a complete set of notes and references separately. I must remind myself that I am not writing a history of theological education,[1] nor am I setting out to provide full summaries of some of the great educational thinkers. My objective is to highlight the "dots" of character and virtue education on the map of educational history. I can imagine, however, that, as our study progresses, we will discover that these are not isolated dots but more like a pervasive matrix.

I will proceed roughly in chronological order, beginning with character and virtue in ancient cultures and then proceeding to the classical period, with a particular focus on Greece and Rome. I will then look at the early church fathers and key authors (like Aquinas) and movements (like the monastic movement and the university) in the Middle Ages, and touch on the work of some of the humanist, Romantic, existential and Enlightenment thinkers. Then, I will look into the era of modernity and present a case study of what happened in the nineteenth and twentieth centuries in America. I will conclude my gallop across history with some reflections on character and virtue education after postmodernity.

---

1. González, *History of Theological Education*.

I acknowledge that the story that I will tell is mostly a Western story, and that the main protagonists will be European and American philosophers, educators and theologians. Although their thinking has spread to the world and is relevant to many contexts, it is not the only story to be told, and I trust that my friends in global education will take up the challenge to tell the story of character education in their contexts.

In this letter, I will look at character and virtue education in some of the world's ancient cultures, touching on two significant examples to show that, ever since the dawn of time, human cultures have considered morality and virtue as a route to human flourishing. The choice of great ancient cultures of the world is vast and I might have investigated the Egyptian, Indus, Inca or Mayan civilizations. I have chosen, somewhat arbitrarily, Confucianism and the Mesopotamian culture.

Character and Virtue in Confucianism

I have already written briefly about the links between Aristotelianism and Confucianism but there is more to be said about the commitment of Confucius to character and virtue. Central to Confucius's teaching is the idea of *ren* as the "perfect virtue," also translated as "benevolence," or "goodness," or "humanness."[2] When asked what *ren* is, Confucius replied: "Cherish people."[3] This foundational virtue of love is reflected in the famous passage called *shu*: "What you do not want others to do to you, do not do to others."[4] Other virtues that are constituent of *ren* include ritual order, restraint, respectfulness, loyalty, tolerance, humility and discretion. Confucius summarized the "five ways" of the virtuous leader as follows: "He who can enact five things in the world is *ren*." When asked for details, he went on, "Reverence, tolerance, trustworthiness, quickness, and generosity. He is reverent, hence he receives no insults; he is tolerant, hence he gains the multitudes; he is trustworthy, hence others entrust him with responsibilities; he is quick, hence he has accomplishments; he is generous, hence he is capable of being placed in charge of others."[5]

We note that, for Confucius, *ren* is a quality that is available to all human beings and that can be cultivated and practised. It is not a special endowment for aristocrats or rulers but is the potential of goodness in each human being.

---

2. Luo, "Confucius's Virtue Politics," 15.
3. Confucius, *Analects* 12.22.
4. Confucius, 15.24.
5. Confucius, 17.6.

The outcome of virtue in Confucianism is very similar to what we have been referring to as "human flourishing." For Confucius, in fact, human beings become "more human and more humanised in proportion to their growth in *ren*."[6]

When it comes to education, the cultivation of *ren* is the primary objective. Education for Confucius was considered as moral self-cultivation[7] in communities of like-minded colleagues.[8] Given Confucius's immense influence in Chinese history, this is significant.[9]

For Confucius, virtue is particularly important for those who are in leadership positions.[10] It is, in fact, embodiment of the high moral standards that makes a person fit to lead and to become a *junzi*: a gentleman or a morally ideal leader. Virtuous love of neighbour, for example, is seen by Confucius as the prime mark of a leader.[11] Virtuous leaders, according to Confucius, will be able to transform society as they model virtue. When leaders are virtuous, society will be well ordered.

This is a first remarkable example of an ancient civilization that was deeply committed to a vision of humanity and social well-being that was linked to virtue and developed by educational practice. Indeed, we might label Confucius's teachings and educational practice as "leadership virtue ethics" or "virtue politics."[12]

---

6. Cheng in Luo, "Confucius's Virtue Politics," 15.

7. Confucius used several terms to articulate the idea of moral self-cultivation: *ke ji*, overcoming the self; *xiu ji*, cultivating the self; *zheng ji*, rectifying the self; and *zheng shen*, correcting the self (Luo, "Confucius's Virtue Politics," 22).

8. "The craftsman who wishes to do his work well must first sharpen his tools. When you dwell in a state, serve those of its grandees who are worthy men, befriend those of its gentlemen who are *ren*" (Confucius, *Analects* 15.10).

9. "Education for Confucius is primarily moral education, as he teaches his students to become virtuous persons" (Huang, "Can Virtue Be Taught?," 141).

10. "Abundant textual evidence in the Analects indicates that Confucius's teachings are not mainly about how to become a virtuous person or moral agent, but how to become a virtuous leader" (Luo, "Confucius's Virtue Politics," 17).

11. Love, for Confucius, is the "hallmark of virtuous leadership" (Luo, 19).

12. "The overarching purpose of his [Confucius's] school is not to train moral persons, but virtuous leaders" (Luo, 20).

Character and Virtue in Mesopotamian Culture

A second example is found in ancient Mesopotamian civilization.[13] Here, the field is very broad, and I have chosen to focus on a selection of the literature. To be honest, virtue and character are not a prevalent feature of ancient Mesopotamian literature, for much of what has survived is comprised of religious texts, prayers, rituals and omens that do not deal with educational issues. And yet virtue and moral character are recurring motifs. Let me give you some examples.

In Sumerian praise literature, the virtues are either explicitly praised or taught through the tale of a hero. Lament literature was also often designed to express the loss of virtue or the longing for it. Codes were written to enforce virtues like justice, and the gods were often associated with these virtues. The famous Code of Hammurabi, for example, is one of the most ancient and perfect collections of laws meant to ensure justice, and its divine guardian was Marduk, the Lord of Wisdom.[14]

The myth genre is also focused on the virtues and vices, mostly of the gods. Here we find mostly tales of betrayal, friendship, loyalty, pride, jealousy, wrath, courage, lust, guile and lying. Even the creation myths were often linked to struggles with the vices of laziness, ingenuity, intemperance and pride.[15] Epics also have an important place in Mesopotamian literature, the most famous of which is the Akkadian *Epic of Gilgamesh*. This story tells of the deeds of Gilgamesh and portrays the good life in terms of acceptance of mortality and a disposition to a moderate enjoyment of what is good.[16] Gilgamesh is the hero whose character is to be emulated, and yet Gilgamesh is more than just a natural-born hero.[17] He is a hero who must suffer the consequences of his courageous deeds and, through pain, become wiser, thus learning what it is to be a man, what it means to lead and what it means to die. As he wanders, there is moral growth; and as he learns, he changes.[18] As Gilgamesh accepts the impossibility of becoming immortal, he learns humility and embraces communal responsibility rather than individual heroism.

---

13. T. Jacobsen, "The Literary Legacy: Myth and Epic," under "Mesopotamian Religion," *Encyclopaedia Britannica* online, https://www.britannica.com/topic/Mesopotamian-religion#ref68262.

14. Beaulieu, "The Social and Intellectual Setting," 4.

15. Kikawada, "Double Creation," 43.

16. Abusch, "Epic of Gilgamesh," 614.

17. "Hero in battle, hero in battle, let me sing his song!" (Abusch, 615).

18. Abusch, 615.

Closely linked to these epics, we find collections of wisdom literature that include proverbs, moral precepts, instructions and fables. Here the main themes revolve around human mortality, submission to fate and the need to mediate between gods and humans. Although there is no explicit educational project related to the virtues, the general purpose is to teach the art of leading a successful life, in harmony with society and the divine will.[19] The concept of "wisdom" that is at the core of this body of literature bears a resemblance to Greek *arête* and *phronesis*. Theodicy and human suffering also emerge in the wisdom literature, reinforcing the description of the pious person as one who is prudent, obedient, learned, intelligent and religiously devout.[20]

—

I've not researched other ancient cultures, and surely there is much more to unveil. I am, by the way, interested in supervising doctoral students from the Majority World who would like to do further research on their own cultures as they relate to character and virtue education, so if you hear of anyone who might be interested, please put them in contact with me. I look forward to hearing how your biblical research is going. I have just received the link to your YouTube channel and will look into it now.

May we feel happiness as we drink from the spring that has welcomed so many other travellers.

---

19. Beaulieu, "The Social and Intellectual Setting," 3.
20. Beaulieu, 8.

21

Character and Virtue in the Old Testament

Dear Siméon, what a brilliant idea to set up a YouTube channel to share the results of your biblical work on character and virtue education! Your ten-minute videos are dynamic and profound, and will have a great impact. Although you are aiming at a regional audience, the medium you have chosen will make your work accessible and will stimulate theological educators in many parts of the world. Regarding the fact that you have recorded the videos in English, have no fears! Although this is your second language, you speak impeccably and with a lovely accent.

The Old Testament As a Corrective Source

Before sharing about your videos, I need to say that looking at character and virtue in the Old Testament is particularly significant for a number of reasons: first, because Hebraism has a rightful place among the significant ancient cultures of the world; second, because there are deep links between Hebraism and Christian theology; and third, because Christians believe that the books of the Old Testament are part of the inspired canon and have special prescriptive and normative value. Looking at character and virtue education in the Old Testament therefore goes beyond historical description in shaping a theology of education. While the words of Confucius that I have studied may be inspiring, the words of Moses that you are dealing with are inspired.

But there is more. In my next letter I will be engaging with character and virtue education in the classical tradition. This is, indeed, likely the most important historical source in my study. As I've watched your videos on the

Old Testament, I have revised my evaluation of the Greek culture.[1] This is a case where Scripture has helped me correct pagan sources of theology and, in particular, reconsider the Hellenic heroic figures. In the Homeric tradition, Achilles is the main hero who embodies the prototypical virtues of courage, assertiveness, prowess and lack of self-doubt. In the Old Testament, however, the heroic figures are different, and Moses claims to be the meekest man on the face of the earth, which would be unheard of for Homer. Another good example of this kind of difference pertains to the virtue of courage. Whereas in the classical tradition the virtue of courage was sought as a means of gaining honour and prowess, in Joshua's induction to leadership this was not so. His fear was mitigated not by a virtue that arose from within and that brought glory to himself, but from the assurance that God would go with him and be at his side.[2] So, while we are still technically speaking of courage, the difference is substantive.

Scripture not only corrects us but also enriches our reading of other sources, and this is graphically illustrated in the prototype of Adam. Here we find a "heroic figure" that offers profounder opportunities for emulation than the classic heroes. You mentioned Rabbi Soloveitchik at the end of one of your videos, and I've taken the liberty to look up his fascinating presentation of "Adam-the-first" and "Adam-the-second."[3] In Genesis 1, Adam-the-first is made in the image of God with a mandate to fill and subdue the earth. He represents the creative dimension of humanity that uses reason to improve the cosmos and that finds dignity in mastery.[4] As a heroic figure, he magnificently represents the virtues of assertiveness and boldness.[5]

But according to Soloveitchik, there is more, for we also find Adam-the-second in Genesis 2, who appears as a body that is fashioned from earth, who is charged with the duty to cultivate the garden and who is relationally alone until, through sacrifice, Eve is given to him as a helpmate and complement. Adam-the-second represents humanity in its relational posture as it experiences the breath of God and human companionship. Whereas Adam-the-first is fulfilled through dignity, Adam-the-second finds himself in redemption. Whereas Adam-the-first is driven to produce more, Adam-the-second desires to improve

---

1. "The Character Code with David Brooks," YouTube, accessed 12 August 2018, https://www.youtube.com/watch?v=ELKmuXGzJ3s.
2. Deut 31:6–8.
3. Soloveitchik, *Lonely Man of Faith*.
4. Soloveitchik, 12.
5. "His motto is success, triumph over the cosmic forces. He engages in creative work, trying to imitate his Maker" (Soloveitchik, 13).

himself. Emulation of Adam-the-second refocuses our attention away from success-driven attitudes and calls us to work on controlling ourselves and our relationships with others through a disciplined life of humility.[6]

In these examples we see that Scripture complements, enriches and corrects the secular traditions that we draw on. If we were left alone with the Greek classics, we would miss the meekness of Moses and the depth of Adam-the-second that are sorely needed in an age that privileges the competences of Adam-the-first and the assertiveness of Achilles.

And now for your videos. I might be a bit "old school," but I feel that I need to see what I think, and I have therefore made extensive written notes from your videos. I am sending these notes to you, to ensure that I have captured your research but also to provide a written transcript that might be useful. Here, then, are my notes on your first three videos.

Stories of Virtue in the Old Testament

There are many ways to think about character and virtue education in the Old Testament. Three lines of inquiry are explored here, starting with the Old Testament as a collection of heroic stories, then looking at Proverbs as the most explicit of the Old Testament books on wisdom and goodness, and finally experimenting with a thematic reading of a book of the Old Testament, in this case the book of Deuteronomy.

Let us start with stories. Although the texts of the Old Testament are primarily oriented towards God and living in obedience to him, we can also think of the Old Testament in terms of stories around virtue. As we have seen in Mesopotamian literature, heroic stories were a common device in ancient times. Stories of heroes and villains shaped cultures through emulation and detachment, and Hebrew culture was no exception. It was influenced by the stories of the works of God and by the good and bad examples of the deeds of men and women. These stories, together with the explicit teaching of the law and the historical events in national life, contributed to shape the character of the Hebrew nation.

We can imagine Old Testament stories being told on desert nights by Jewish fathers and mothers to their wide-eyed children. As these stories were passed on to the next generation, children grew up wanting to be prudent like Joseph, wise like Solomon, courageous like David and a good friend like Jonathan. The virtues are everywhere in Old Testament stories. As we read

---

6. Soloveitchik, 18.

them, we find the theological virtues of faith in Abraham, of hope in Moses and of love in David. But we also find the capital vices as we look at the pride of Haman, the greed of Achan, the lust of Amnon, the envy of Saul, the gluttony of Jacob, the wrath of Cain and the sloth of old Eli. And so on. Although these stories contain much more, they also represented a powerful device to enliven the imagination, inform reason, train the emotions and motivate the actions of the Jewish people.

These stories represent a national history that shaped the character of a community around the idea of holiness, both as the distinctive attribute of God and as the benchmark of human virtue.[7] Perhaps, as theological educators, we might consider debating less over the historical truthfulness of these stories and concentrating more on the life of holiness that they inspire.

Wisdom Literature and Virtue

Wisdom literature is another way to think about character and virtue in the Old Testament. Reading the Psalms through the lens of character and virtue, for example, is most enlightening. The well-known tree metaphor in Psalm 1 is a remarkable opening to this great book of Hebrew wisdom as it shows us the way of the wicked and the way of the righteous, the one leading to destruction and the other to flourishing. This is a recurring theme. Consider Psalm 15 as another description of virtuous character:[8]

> LORD, who may dwell in your sacred tent?
> >   Who may live on your holy mountain?
> The one whose way of life is *blameless*,
> >   who does what is *righteous*,
> >   who *speaks the truth* from their heart;
> whose tongue utters *no slander*,
> >   who *does no wrong* to a neighbour,
> >   and casts *no slur* on others;
> who *despises a vile* person
> >   but *honours* those who fear the LORD;
> who *keeps an oath* even when it hurts,

---

7. "In biblical cultures, character was defined in relation to God's distinctive property: His holiness. The expectation was as clear as it was demanding: as God said to Moses, 'You must be holy, for I am holy'" (Hunter, *Death of Character*, 21).

8. C. Stückelberger, "Integrity: The Virtue of Virtuous," Lecture delivered 11 Dec 2015 at the Faculty of Theology of the Protestant University in Congo UPC, quoted in B. Ott, "The Mission of Character Education," unpublished paper, 2016.

and *does not change their mind*;
who *lends money* to the poor without interest;
who *does not accept a bribe* against the innocent.
Whoever does these things
will never be shaken.[9]

We could continue our reading of the Psalms to explore how character is blended with worship, how obedience is linked to a relationship with God and how virtue is defined in practice. But it is probably the book of Proverbs that is the most explicit educational text of the Old Testament. Here, in fact, the main concern is neither theological understanding nor practical ability, but wisdom and goodness.

Starting from the first chapter, we read that Proverbs is intended to give "wisdom and instruction," inform "prudent behaviour" and help the reader in "doing what is right and just." The opening invocation is to heed wisdom and shun wickedness, and this serves as a refrain throughout the entire book. The motivation is also constantly repeated: wisdom will lead to flourishing as "a garland to grace your head," whereas a life of vice and wickedness will lead to disaster that "sweeps over you like a whirlwind."[10]

Wisdom in Proverbs is closely associated with moral goodness and virtue, and this becomes clear as the book progresses. In chapter 2, we find that "turning your ear to wisdom" has to do with being upright, with walking blamelessly and with being right, just and fair.[11] The opposite of wisdom is described as walking in dark ways, doing wrong and being perverted in evil.[12] Likewise, in chapter 8 we are told that wisdom "[walks] in the way of righteousness" and that "to fear the Lord is to hate evil."[13] Although the beginning of wisdom is the fear of the Lord, the fulfilment of wisdom is found in goodness and virtue. Proverbs is, in many ways, a book of moral ethics, pointing to the good life and written to educate in character. Surely a theological programme inspired by the book of Proverbs would be very different from one inspired by the Enlightenment.

It is important to note, however, that Proverbs does not simply furnish a grocery list of good things we need to do and of bad things we need to avoid. Wisdom is not mere prescription of outward behaviour. Rather, Proverbs continually points to the kind of people we should be and to the

---

9. Ps 15.
10. Prov 1:2, 3, 9, 27.
11. Prov 2:7–11.
12. Prov 2:12–15.
13. Prov 8:13, 20.

virtues that should shape our character. Proverbs is not about deontological or consequentialist ethics, but about virtue ethics. We find idealized portraits of what wise women should be,[14] and we find that those who fear the Lord need to be loving, trustworthy, humble, self-controlled, prudent, just, honest, kind, generous, truthful, gentle, patient, faithful, diligent, lovers of knowledge, zealous and moderate.[15] We also find that, in order to avoid futility and punishment, one must not be envious, lazy, false, proud, unjust, corrupt, lustful, violent, wrathful, close-minded or greedy.[16]

It is practically impossible to read a single chapter of Proverbs without being impressed by the massive determination to form character.[17] Several general principles can be seen in this educational project.[18] First of all, God is the source of wisdom, and this wisdom is meant to shape generation after generation. Those who are wise instruct others in wisdom as coming from God. Second, in Proverbs, formation is a communal activity in which those who are wiser have greater responsibilities towards the less mature and where we are instructed to "Walk with the wise and become wise."[19] Third, wisdom concerns the whole of human experience, including work, rest, eating and speaking, each of which is a revelation of our character.[20] Finally, character formation is an urgent matter. Choosing good or evil is a matter of life or death, and there is an incessant sense of educational urgency in the entire book.[21]

The devices that the book of Proverbs employs to educate character are also worthy of notice, especially as we look to our practice. Character is educated through warning. Through straightforward exhortation. Through short stories. Through inspiring poetry. Through comparisons of some things

---

14. "While looking at the models of virtue in Proverbs, it is hugely important to read Proverbs canonically. Surely the wise woman (in counterpoint to the adulteress who tears things apart) has driven more actual women to despair than it has literally inspired. She is surely an idealized figure for the operation of a wise life. And here lies the problem. Read canonically, Proverbs offers a fairly idealized portrait of what should be done; Job seems to say 'I did all of that and look what happened!'; as for Ecclesiastes . . . But this is the real legacy of the OT wisdom literature. It points forward whilst relating an incomplete story until we encounter Wisdom Incarnate and yield to His Spirit" (Robert Willoughby, private correspondence).

15. Prov 10:12; 11:13; 11:2; 10:19; 12:8; 8:15; 11:1; 11:17; 11:25; 12:19; 15:1; 16:32; 20:6; 21:5; 23:12; 23:15; 25:16.

16. Prov 23:17; 6:9; 6:17; 8:13; 13:5; 17:23; 6:25; 13:2; 18:2; 23:2; 23:4.

17. Meye, "Theological Education," 109.

18. Meye, 109–112.

19. Prov 13:20.

20. "Every human activity is a revelation of character" (Meye, "Theological Education," 110).

21. "Proverbs is an abiding testimony to the seriousness with which one community understood the formational task" (Meye, 111).

that are better than others. Through examples of animals. Through promises of reward. Through descriptions of fools, whom no one would want to imitate, and descriptions of wise women and men, whose virtues we all want.

On a more philosophical level, the book of Proverbs also helps us converse with moral ontology and with the objections of situationism and paternalism. Proverbs presents wisdom and goodness as eternal, universal realities. Virtue in Proverbs is not constructed culturally or determined individually, but it is "brought forth" by "the Lord" and "formed . . . at the very beginning."[22] To educate in character and virtue, according to Proverbs, is to realign individuals with archetypal realities.

Reading Deuteronomy for Character and Virtue

A third line of inquiry tries to read an Old Testament book through the lens of character and virtue. Although caution needs to be exercised here against *eisegesis*, this kind of thematic reading is not without its benefits, for it can help us see how single books of the Old Testament contribute to our theme. Let us try an experiment with the book of Deuteronomy.

Deuteronomy is the re-reading of the law to the children of Israel who survived the forty years in the desert and were preparing to enter the promised land. As they prepare to become a nation, the law is read to them so they can "Observe [it] carefully, for this will show your wisdom and understanding to the nations, who will hear about all these decrees and say, 'Surely this great nation is a wise and understanding people.'"[23]

The point of re-reading the law had several purposes, among which was to consolidate a covenant agreement based on constancy and faithfulness, in which the categories of moral virtue and vice played a significant part.[24] Whereas Leviticus was a "God-directed" book that focused on ceremonial duties, Deuteronomy was a book of moral education. We notice, for example, that the narrative parts of the book include stories of virtue and vice, with a clear indictment of the lack of courage and faith (which led to the desert experience), and the tragic story of worshiping the golden calf as an expression of rebellion, disbelief, disobedience and stubbornness. From the selected stories of Moses and Joshua we also learn about mercy, goodness, humility, strength and courage.

---

22. Prov 8:22, 23, 31.
23. Deut 4:6.
24. Deut 29.

The instructional parts of the book are also virtue-rich, even though this is not their main theme. At the heart of Deuteronomy we find, of course, the Ten Commandments. These might initially appear as a set of rules to obey and do, but a careful reading shows that they point to the importance of being. If we are who we should be, then we will do what we need to do. Thus, the person who has no other gods is the person who is *faithful*. The person who does not use the name of God in vain in making vows is the person who is *honest*. The person who rests on the Sabbath is the person who is *temperate, prudent* and *self-controlled*. The person who honours her or his parents is the person who is *obedient* and *humble*. The person who does not murder, commit adultery or steal is the person who is *temperate, chaste* and *just*. The person who does not give false testimony is the person who is *truthful*. The person who does not covet is the person who is *not greedy*. Without these virtues, submission to the Ten Commandments was bound to be shallow, opportunistic and short-lived. The Ten Commandments were calling for a change in being, which then became possible through the new covenant and the work of the Spirit.

What, then, does a wise and virtuous community look like in Deuteronomy? What was the vision that Moses left to the children of Israel that would shape their identity as they moved into the promised land to become a nation? Although Deuteronomy does not have ethical lists beyond the Ten Commandments, there are clear references to virtuous character throughout. So, for example, we find a community that is to be *disciplined* in their worship, their diet and their tithes; *pugnacious* against those who would entice them to worship other gods; and *constant* in observing their festivals.[25] They are to be *generous* in solidarity, *fair* in their judgments, *just* in their social dealings, *compassionate* to the poor and needy, and *merciful* and *fair* in administering punishment.[26] They are to be *respectful, moderate, temperate* and *modest*.[27] They are to be *courageous* in battle but should prefer *peace*.[28] They are to be *good*, to exercise sexual *self-control* and to be *faithful* to their promises.[29] In short, their character is to be holy.[30]

---

25. Deut 12:8, 13, 14, 16.
26. Deut 15; 16:18; 19:15; 24:14; 17:19.
27. Deut 17:10; 24:20; 17:14.
28. Deut 20; 20:10–11.
29. Deut 20; 24:21; 23:21.
30. "In biblical cultures, character was defined in relation to God's distinctive property: His holiness. The expectation was as clear as it was demanding: as God said to Moses, 'You must be holy, for I am holy'" (Hunter, *Death of Character*, 21).

Whereas many of these virtues are found in other traditions, the Old Testament has a distinctive focus. In other traditions, the main motivation to be virtuous is either because of human flourishing or as a means to prosperity. In the Old Testament the emphasis is that we are to be virtuous because of the presence and actions of God. We are to be holy because God is holy. We are to be generous to strangers because God has been merciful to us. We are to be courageous because God is with us.

Deuteronomy also provides a lovely array of educational practices. These include watching oneself closely, reinforcing memory with repetition, educating children through stories, and using symbols and liturgical calendars and festivities to build character.[31] Underlying all this is the notion that obedience to the ways of God is "not too difficult" nor out of reach.[32] Obedience and education of character go hand in hand, and Deuteronomy places great importance on educating the next generation to be holy. This is an appropriate response to the unique wonders of the Lord,[33] but it also carefully accounts for the consequences. The continual refrain that accompanies the invitation to be obedient is "that it might go well with you" and that you "might avoid curses and incur blessings." The final blessings and curses from Deuteronomy 27 onwards clearly set out the consequences that were seen in the history of the children of Israel in the Old Testament. When the people acted faithfully, they were blessed. When they gave in to vice and disobeyed the law, they were cursed and led into captivity.

Hebrew Humanism

Let me conclude this letter by mentioning Martin Buber, the Jewish educationalist.[34] Buber was formed both in the Jewish Hasidic tradition and in modern humanism and brings a unique blend of the notions of human flourishing and the Hebraic tradition. Indeed, Buber suggests that we should think of a "Hebrew humanism" that works out a vision of humanity from the ancient texts of the Bible, rather than from the Latin and Greek classical texts as is often the case in Western cultures.[35] Buber believes that true humanity

---

31. Deut 4:9; 6:7; 6:20; 31:10.
32. Deut 30:11.
33. Deut 4:34.
34. Ott, "Martin Buber on Character Formation."
35. Buber, "Biblical Humanism," 47.

is found in the return to the God of the Hebrew Bible,[36] and he claims that we need to look to the transformative Mosaic man who will lead us beyond the cognition of the Socratic man.[37] He invites us to move beyond the Greek dualism that has caused Christians to give up much of what is material and human, to the Hasidic notion that affirms and praises all that is true and God-oriented in earthly life.[38] Character education, according to Buber, is about recovering full humanity and nourishing all that is good in being *this-worldly*. It is about finding the power from God to enter into an I–Thou encounter with the God who can transform us.[39] For this, Buber would suggest, we must look to the Old Testament.

May we be open-minded in our biblical scholarship and not be threatened by what we might not yet have seen.

---

36. "The educator who helps to bring man back to his own unity will help to put him again face to face with God" (Buber, *Hebrew Humanism*, 160).

37. Stern, "Becoming a Mensch."

38. This critique is expanded by Buber in the article "Socratic and Mosaic Man," in *Israel and the World* (New York: Syracuse University Press, 1997).

39. Ott, private conversation.

22

Virtue in the Classical Era

I'm attending a conference organized by the Aretai Center on Virtues[1] in Rome next week, and I am excited to come back to one of my favourite cities in the world. It also conveniently coincides with my research around the virtues in the classical era, so parts of this letter will actually be penned from a balcony overlooking the Tiber River!

I've been looking forward to writing about the Graeco-Roman classical tradition, as one of the best-developed examples of character and virtue education in the world. We have seen other instances in ancient cultures, but it is rare to find the systematic approach that was developed in Athens[2] and later in Rome. In Athens, Plato, Socrates and Aristotle developed fully-fledged educational philosophies that centred on the formation of character and virtue.[3] Their philosophies were then picked up by some of the great Roman thinkers and spread far and wide to set the course of Western education. Also, as the Roman Empire was Christianized, these philosophies deeply influenced theological education. So let me start with Athens and then move to Rome.

Why Athens?

We will organize our exploration of Athenian education around the practices of *paideia*.[4] Although there were many educational trends in fourth-century Athens, what has come to be known as *paideia* is the one that has stood the test of time. The term *paideia* in its most simple definition means "culture,"

---

1. http://filosofia.dafist.unige.it/?page_id=1540.
2. "We have to be wary of speaking too easily of 'the Greek view of the virtues' . . . because we often say 'Greek' when we should say 'Athenian'" (MacIntyre, *After Virtue*, 135).
3. There were at least four views on virtue in Athens: "those of the sophists, of Plato, of Aristotle and of the tragedians" (MacIntyre, 135).
4. Jaeger, *Paideia*, vols. 1, 2, 3.

and it encapsulates the wealth of the educational thinking of Plato, Socrates and Aristotle. Before we launch into a more detailed description, let me stop, once again, to consider why, as Christian theological educators, we should consider this as part of our enquiry. I have already addressed this question in my letters about Aristotle, so forgive the slight overlap.

I think there are several reasons to study *paideia*. First of all, we can explore it as an instance of common grace. Although there is much in Greek philosophy and pagan cultic practice that we should do away with, there is also much good, especially in educational terms. Furthermore, the underlying ontology, epistemology and moral vision of *paideia* coheres well with Christian theology.

Second, *paideia* reflects a great deal of the cultural context in which the early church came into existence. As I'm sure you will point out, the New Testament writers were deeply embedded in the classical culture of their times, and many New Testament texts on character and virtue are connected to *paideia*, both in language and in content.

Third, *paideia* is respected all over the world as a global legacy.[5] Fourth, *paideia* offers an articulated vision of character and virtue, in terms of both theory and practice. In addition to a comprehensive theoretical framework, *paideia* offers motivational emphasis, pedagogical implementation, rich definitions, consideration of objections and a rich corpus of epic and philosophical literature. Fifth, in the current postmodern climate, many educators are looking back to premodern times and, as we've seen, the neo-Aristotelian tradition has sparked the greatest interest.

Finally, there is much in theology and in theological education that makes explicit reference to *paideia*. Beginning with the church fathers and passing through Aquinas and more recent authors like Farley and Kelsey, many have engaged with the language and categories of *paideia* to cast a vision of theological education.

Educational Responses to Athenian Crises

As we look at some of the key features of *paideia*, it is worth considering the context of fourth-century Athens, for it offers fascinating parallels with our society today. Athens was experiencing a crisis of democracy, which had led into extreme forms of individualism, subjectivism and hedonism. But there

---

5. Marx claims that "the reason why Greek epic poetry has the power over us which it still retains, derives from the fact that the Greeks stand to civilized modernity as the child to the adult" (MacIntyre, *After Virtue*, 130).

were also ontological and philosophical crises in Athens that had cast doubts on the notion of fixed, eternal order and were making room for relativistic and subjective views of reality being governed by social conventions. In terms of moral thinking, the so-called heroic age had generated a set of disordered inconsistencies around virtue and had given rise to Greek tragedy.[6] Most significantly, there was a crisis of education in Athens arising from the teaching of the Sophists, a group of teachers who were intellectually nomadic, unregulated in their character, and individualistic and utilitarian in their educational outlook.[7] The parallels with our times are remarkable, and we can follow the steps of Socrates, Plato and Aristotle as they developed *paideia* to tackle these crises through an approach to education that placed character and virtue at the centre.

What follows are some of the key features of *paideia*. I've mentioned some of this already in dealing with the Aristotelian framework, but here you will hopefully gain a fuller view.

Paideia, Plato and Aristotle

In *paideia*, there is one thing that really counts: the soul. Plato continually repeats that the soul is in danger, that the soul is the highest interest of man, and that there must be a "conversion" in which the soul turns to the light and is shaped according to its essential form. For Socrates, the end of education was the "perfection of the soul," and not utility as the Sophists were suggesting. *Paideia* was, in brief, an educational endeavour to cultivate the human soul. But, you may ask, by what standards is the soul perfected? Here is where the virtues come in. *Paideia* claims that, just as there are excellences of the body (such as health, strength and beauty), so there are excellences of the soul that

---

6. Authors like Sophocles highlighted conflicts in virtue and denied solutions. Even though occasionally the gods intervene in Greek tragedy, they never provide solutions to the incoherencies, but just put an end to the action. "The divine verdict always ends rather than resolves the conflict" (MacIntyre, 143).

7. "They [the Sophists] were finely cultured and knowledgeable teachers, but they were sceptical, and their teaching insinuated that social conventions were arbitrary and that goodness (intended as virtuous living together in the polis) was open to re-definition. They were not ontological realists and they had no specific worldview to propound. They accepted the dictum that morality (like religion) was a personal thing and were quite ready to challenge traditional moral values and to advocate individualistic, subjective and hedonistic behavioural patterns. Educationally, they had no systematic approach and their methodology adapted to the changes in the social, political and economic environment and to sense experience" (Gutek, *Western Educational Experience*, 33).

are called *arêtai* – "virtues."⁸ Education is fundamentally about moulding the soul into its ideal form in harmony with the nature of the universe.⁹

How might we think theologically of what Plato is suggesting? Although it is not presented in biblical or theological language, *paideia* coheres well with a Christian vision. We agree, for example, that the soul counts. While we may not fully share Plato's soul–body dichotomy, we do agree that what counts in a human being is not just physical well-being but the flourishing of the soul. We also agree that the spirit must be nourished and that the "inner man" must be moulded. Furthermore, the doctrine of the fall supports the notion of restoring humanity to a condition of flourishing that corresponds to a lost ideal. While we may not fully embrace Platonic idealism, we are surely closer to Plato in many respects than we are to Sophocles, Rousseau or many other contemporary educators.

So far, I have spoken mostly about Plato. There are a few additional points to be made about Aristotle and *paideia*. In the first place, for Aristotle, *arête* is less idealized than for Plato and has more to do with concrete situations. For him, virtue is the best balance available to human beings given the circumstances and options that are available to them. We also note that Aristotle distinctively starts with the intellectual virtues and with the capacity to use one's reason as an expression of the gift that distinguishes us from animals and makes us uniquely human. For him, the contemplation of truth is the most important virtue, followed closely by the moral virtues that extend into all other areas of human life. It is also worth recalling that, for Aristotle, the virtuous life is the key to politics, which is why education is so central to the community and why virtue should be developed within the community.¹⁰

Rome and Cicero

I hope you enjoyed that brief taster of the Greeks. Let me now transport you from the *agora* of Athens to the *forum* of Rome. For the Romans also play a very significant part in the story of character and virtue education. Although their approach was rooted in Greek thinking, they developed their thinking and practice in new ways and, given the political dimension of the Roman Empire, were able to diffuse their ideas far and wide (the influence of Roman

---

8. MacIntyre, *After Virtue*, 122.

9. For Plato, the soul is "no less plastic than the body, and therefore capable of receiving form and order" (Jaeger, *Paideia*, vol. 2, 44).

10. "A city can be virtuous only when the citizens who have a share in the government are virtuous" (Aristotle, *Politics* vii, 13).

culture can still be seen, for example, in the vocabulary of many languages, where the Latin root *vir* is used for the word "virtue"[11]). Two of the main figures who stand out in this tradition are Cicero and Seneca, and I will now focus briefly on each.

Few thinkers have been more influential than Cicero (106–43 BC) in building on the Greek tradition of *paideia* to establish a truly Roman philosophy of character and virtue. Cicero believed that virtue was that which contributed most significantly to the public *salus*, and this conviction echoed throughout Roman imperial history – printed in documents, engraved on coins and featured in art.[12] Rome was notoriously concerned with both power and virtue, and Cicero established the connection between the two. To be virtuous was to be powerful and, in republican Rome, the main claim to superiority of the noble class was the possession of *virtus*, understood as the supreme quality that a man could enjoy and that was personified in the gods themselves. The *princeps*, for Cicero, was the one who derived his authority not so much from brute power or military prowess, but from his virtue and moral capacities.

Cicero's main work on virtue is likely the *Tusculanae Disputationes*.[13] This collection of five books presents virtue as that which leads to coherent thought, to stability and to the equilibrium of the soul. In Book 2 of the *Disputationes*, Cicero argues that we must not fear pain and that we must have control of ourselves as we cultivate the four cardinal virtues of *prudence*, *justice*, *temperance* and *courage*. Shortly thereafter, he makes the claim that virtue is desirable in itself and can be obtained by rational effort. In Book 3, he comments on the fact that man, by nature, is not far from virtue and that vice is neither natural nor necessary. Education is important, he adds, and a wrong education can lead away from happiness. In Book 4, he lashes out against the passions that distract us from wisdom and provides a taxonomy of the vices in connection with human passions. These vices include jealousy, laziness, fear, malevolence, wrath, hate and instability. The virtue that enables us to obey our reason and resist vice and passion is *temperance*, which stands as the foundation for happiness. In Book 5, Cicero, in full Stoic tradition, makes his most explicit claim that "virtue is of itself sufficient for a happy life"[14] and

---

11. *Vir*, in fact, roughly translates the Greek term for "hero." In Latin, a virtue is quite literally equated to "manliness" (Racelis, "Developing a Virtue Ethics Scale," 17).

12. The golden shield of the great Emperor Octavian, for example, features the four virtues *virtus, clementia, iustitia, pietas*.

13. Available at Project Gutenberg, https://www.gutenberg.org/files/14988/14988-h/14988-h.htm.

14. Cicero, *Disputationes* 6.1.

that poverty, banishment and loss cannot deprive a man of virtue. Complete comfort, for Cicero, can be found only in philosophy that leads to virtue.[15]

One cannot speak of Cicero and his contribution to the classical culture of character and virtue without mentioning *De Officiis*. This stands as an irreplaceable tract when it comes to understanding the moral issues of honesty and utility. This is actually Cicero's last piece of writing, drafted for his son Marcus. In it, he summarizes the best model of aristocratic education and reminds the new generation of Roman leaders of the four cardinal virtues that represent the moral foundation of the empire.[16] *De Officiis* not only deeply influenced Roman culture, but it also shaped the vision of clerical education in the early church, through authors like Ambrose, who wrote his own version of *De Officiis* for the training of clergy. Many future generations of educationalists would be shaped by Cicero's works on character and virtue.[17]

Rome and Seneca

I conclude this letter with Seneca. Here is a writer I have learned to love for his immediacy in talking about virtue. There are several factors that make Seneca particularly relevant to our study: his Stoic heritage, his personal tragedy, his contemporaneity to New Testament writings, his influence on later Christian theologians and the enduring power of his writings. Let me touch on these briefly.

First, Seneca was a Stoic, and for him the road to virtue begins with the search for happiness. In *De Vita Beata*, he claims that human happiness is the fruit of a life lived in respect for one's own nature. This happiness can be

---

15. "O Philosophy, thou guide of life! thou discoverer of virtue and expeller of vices! What had not only I myself, but the whole life of man, been without you? To you it is that we owe the origin of cities; you it was who called together the dispersed race of men into social life; you united them together, first, by placing them near one another, then by marriages, and lastly, by the communication of speech and languages. You have been the inventress of laws; you have been our instructress in morals and discipline; to you we fly for refuge; from you we implore assistance . . . For one day spent well, and agreeably to your precepts, is preferable to an eternity of error" (Cicero, *Disputationes* 5.2).

16. "But all that is morally right rises from some one of four sources: it is concerned either (1) with full perception and intelligent development of the true; or (2) with the conservation of organised society, with rendering to every man his due, and with the faithful discharge of obligations assumed; or (3) with the greatness and strength of a noble and invincible spirit; or (4) with the orderliness and moderation of everything that is said and done, wherein consist temperance and self-control" (Cicero, *De Officiis* 5).

17. "In the 12th century when the university was being founded, textbooks like the *Moralium Dogma Philosophorum* owing much to Cicero's *De Officiis* were written (perhaps by William of Conches)" (MacIntyre, *After Virtue*, 167).

found in virtue and requires that reason dominate passion.[18] In typical Stoic fashion, Seneca claims that virtue thrives when the mind seeks knowledge[19] and is exercised through self-control. This is why we find him continually inviting his readers to be moderate in their passions and to focus on a life of harmony that fulfils the duties of wise living. Seneca illustrates the connections between Stoicism and the education of character and virtue as found in a constant attitude of reflection on our weaknesses and the rediscovery of the fundamentals of virtue and interior freedom.

Seneca is also relevant because his personal tragedy with his pupil Nero vividly reminds us that theory and practice often do not meet. Despite his sterling formation, in fact, Nero became a villain full of vice who commanded that Seneca, his mentor, commit suicide (which he promptly did, slitting his veins open and drowning in his bathtub). This was at the time when some of the New Testament writings were being drafted, and this sad story of human failure was sure to have made a profound impression regarding the limitations of the Stoic educational project.

Despite his tragic end, however, Seneca's legacy was vast and enduring. As with Cicero, his writings had a deep influence on medieval thought and can be found in ethical and political culture even today. Some of his writings were interpreted in a Christian frame and taken up by theologians like Augustine.[20] But perhaps the best argument for the strength of his legacy is found in reading his work. *Letters to Lucilius* stands out as a classic epistolary treatise on virtue and is among my all-time favourites. These delightful short letters could be easily transposed to our work with theology students today. Consider these titles: "On the Blush of Modesty" (11); "On Brawn Or Brains" (15); "On Practising What You Preach" (20); "On Allegiance to Virtue" (37); "On Values" (42); "On Quiet and Study" (56); "On Various Aspects of Virtue" (66); "On Virtue As a Refuge from Worldly Distractions" (74); "On the Fellowship of Wise Men" (109); "On Self-Control" (116); and "More about Virtue"(120).[21]

I conclude with a wonderful little quotation from Seneca on the greatness virtue:

> The power and the greatness of virtue cannot rise to greater heights, because increase is denied to that which is superlatively

---

18. Trombino, *La Filosofia Greca Arcaica e Classica*, 72.

19. "Virtue, for the Stoic, is a corollary of knowledge" (Charles, "Language and Logic," 64).

20. For the connections between Seneca and Paul, see Dodson and Briones: *Paul and Seneca in Dialogue*.

21. Seneca, *Moral Letters to Lucilius*.

great. You will find nothing straighter than the straight, nothing truer than the truth, and nothing more temperate than that which is temperate. Every virtue is limitless; for limits depend upon definite measurements. Constancy cannot advance further, any more than fidelity, or truthfulness, or loyalty. What can be added to that which is perfect? Nothing otherwise that was not perfect to which something has been added. Nor can anything be added to virtue, either, for if anything can be added thereto, it must have contained a defect. Honour, also, permits of no addition; for it is honourable because of the very qualities which I have mentioned. What then? Do you think that propriety, justice, lawfulness, do not also belong to the same type, and that they are kept within fixed limits? The ability to increase is proof that a thing is still imperfect . . . Therefore, virtues are mutually equal; and so are the works of virtue, and all men who are so fortunate as to possess these virtues.[22]

—

As you can see, my friend Siméon, even the format of our correspondence has solid antecedents, both in Cicero's letters to Marcus and in Seneca's letters to Lucilius. I conclude as Seneca does in all his letters: "Fare well."

May these great minds inspire us in our desire for excellence.

---

22. Seneca, 56.

23

Virtue in the New Testament

You've taken an entire week to read through the New Testament looking for traces of character and virtue. I'm impressed! I watched your videos while in Rome, and you have shared some very powerful thoughts! You have, indeed, begun to dig in a gold mine, and many of us will be extracting from it in the future.[1] Here are my notes, summarizing your first three videos. The fourth, enlightening video on Romans deserves a separate letter.

Heroes in the New Testament

We all agree that the New Testament is a document with religious and spiritual weight, but perhaps we have not considered it sufficiently as an important literary source on the topic of character and virtue. In particular, the narrative components of the New Testament represent one of the richest collections of stories of virtue of all times. Throughout the ages, in looking for examples of virtue to imitate, many have considered the New Testament as a source of great inspiration.

As we look at the story-telling power of the New Testament, however, we must reiterate the point that was made about stories of virtue in the Old Testament. For although the New Testament authors were aware of, and influenced by, the classical context of their times,[2] the biblical vision is not

---

1. "I hope to have reminded readers of the New Testament that the great tradition which discusses behaviour in terms of virtue has more to offer than they may have thought, and also to have reminded people who have theorized about virtue that the New Testament has more to offer them than they seem to have supposed . . . The New Testament invites its readers to learn how to be human in this particular way, which will both inform our moral judgments and form our characters . . . the name for this way of being human, this kind of transformation, is virtue" (Wright, *After You Believe*, x, 18).

2. MacDonald, for example, argues that Luke's literary models include not only the Septuagint, the Gospel of Mark and Q, but also Homer's *Iliad* and the *Odyssey*, Euripides's *Bacchae* and Virgil's *Aeneid* (MacDonald, "Luke's Antetextuality," 155 onwards).

the same as the classical vision. Jesus, in fact, is not an Achilles,[3] and there are aspects of his life and ministry that are unique and inimitable. Nor is Paul comparable to Hercules, for the competitive virtues that prevailed in the Heroic age are dissimilar to the cooperative and servile virtues that we find in the New Testament.[4] We find ourselves, therefore, dealing with two different, but overlapping, sets of character codes, one emerging from the classical literature and one coming from the New Testament. Both codes have shaped the Western tradition of character and virtue, and we should read the New Testament both as confirming *paideia* but also as challenging it with a new vision.

Who are the heroes of virtue in the New Testament? Clearly, Jesus stands as the main point of reference in showing the way of goodness. In him, we not only have a magnificent portrait of virtue, but also an example of how it is possible to grow in wisdom and stature.[5] We must be careful in using Jesus as an example of virtue,[6] for there is much about his life and ministry that is unique, but this is not to say that we should not want to be like him, and, in many aspects, his life and character stand as the timeless example for all humanity.

We should imitate his humility as he comes to be baptized and as he washes the disciples' feet. We should learn about self-control as he resists temptation, about compassion as he unceasingly heals the sick, or about justice as he pays taxes to the Roman Empire. We should want to emulate his courage, zeal and diligence as he cleanses the temple, his truthfulness in all his relationships and his love in his giving of himself as a sacrifice for the salvation of the world. The *mimesis* of the perfect pattern of Christ is a powerful means to transform

---

3. "Jesus is not a heroic figure in the same way as Achilles, Hector, Odysseus, etc. If anything, he may be described as an anti-hero. Not only does this need to be very carefully defined vis-à-vis other heroes, but we also need to consider ways in which he is clearly not available for emulation, e.g. a sacrificial death, a virgin birth, a sinless life, etc." (Robert Willoughby, private correspondence).

4. "The Character Code with David Brooks," YouTube, accessed 12 August 2018, https://www.youtube.com/watch?v=ELKmuXGzJ3s.

5. "Can we speak . . . of the formation of Jesus' 'character' and of his exercising 'virtues'? Luke certainly thinks so, for according to him the young Jesus was subject to his parents and 'Grew in wisdom and stature, and in favour with God and men' (Luke 2:52). He would certainly appear to exercise what we would call virtues, even if not always in Aristotelian form: courage, truthfulness and love, if not impassibility, were Jesus' settled disposition, as the narrative depicts them" (Gunton, "Church as a School of Virtue?," 218).

6. Wright, *After You Believe*, 125–133.

character,[7] and the love of Christ should function as the ultimate motivation to change our lives and be loyal to his example.[8]

Another major figure in the New Testament who is set forth for imitation is Paul. Although commentators agree that his character was far from faultless,[9] we are still invited to imitate many good things about him.[10] In the letters to the Corinthians, for example, we see in Paul the virtues of magnanimity, temperance and constancy, compassion, decency, prudence, patience, benevolence, love, truthfulness, loyalty, humility, and endurance in difficulties.[11] A quick search in the other epistles reveals many other virtues in Paul, such as his intellectual humility, fairness, temperance, contentment and sincerity, love and generosity.[12]

Other minor heroes can also be seen throughout the historical books of the New Testament, including Joseph as an example of discretion, John the Baptist as an example of courage and justice,[13] Nicodemus as an example of intellectual virtue, the Samaritan woman as an example of curiosity and zeal, Peter as an example of one who moves from cowardice to courage, the apostles and deacons as examples of diligence, Barnabas as an example of benevolence, Cornelius as an example of generosity, the Bereans as an example of open-mindedness and those who were healed as examples of faith.

There are also plenty of stories of vice that the New Testament sets forth for avoidance. We have Herod as an example of envy, wrath and pride; Judas who is greedy; Peter and Pilate who are cowards; Ananias and Sapphira who are false and cunning; Mark who is inconstant; the false prophets who are greedy, lazy, arrogant and intemperate; preachers who are envious; and leaders who are proud. The Pharisees are frequently reprimanded for neglecting justice, mercy and faithfulness,[14] or for being jealous, proud, deceitful, self-indulgent and hypocritical. Of all the communities that are struggling with

---

7. Erasmus believed that this was the primary function of Scripture and the way to truly reform the church of his day (Herdt, "Virtue's Semblance," 141).

8. "When Christians read and study the New Testament as a guide to their lives, they discover therein both the admonition and the stories to support loyalty to a concrete person, rather than to a set of abstract dispositions, such as the virtues may appear to be" (Hauerwas, *Christian Virtues Exemplified*, 335).

9. Some state, for example, that Paul was a rather intolerant and irritable person (Robert Willoughby, private correspondence).

10. 1 Cor 4.

11. 1 Cor 2 and 9; 2 Cor 2 and 11; 1 Cor 8; 2 Tim 4; 2 Cor 1, 4, 6, 7, 10.

12. Gal 1 and 2; Phil 4; 1 Thess 2.

13. Luke 3.

14. The "important matters of the law" in Matt 23:23 are three virtues.

vice, surely the Corinthians stand out, and we read in 1 Corinthians of their incivility, strife, pride, jealousy, lovelessness, indecency, injustice, revenge, lust, intemperance, lack of compassion and empathy, negligence and non-prudence and disorderly lifestyles.

There is much to be learned, therefore, from the heroes of virtue and the villains of vice in the New Testament. Truly, it is difficult to find such a concentration of good and bad examples in other ancient literature.

Ethical Lists in the New Testament

But the New Testament is more than a collection of stories of virtue. One of the most common devices in character education is so-called "ethical lists." These were very popular in ancient literature, and the New Testament makes ample use of them. An ethical list is simply a catalogue of specific virtues that are listed, recommended or exemplified.[15] Clearly, the New Testament's starting point in providing ethical lists is different from that of the classical context, for whereas Aristotle or Seneca presupposed that good lists would be sufficient to inspire good character, the New Testament presupposes that there must be a transformative work of the Holy Spirit in the life of an individual to empower good practice. The ethical lists in the New Testament are there to tell us what kind of people we need to be as we cooperate with the work of God's grace in our lives. The educational aim is similar to what we see in the classical world, but the pathway to transformation presupposes conversion and divine intervention.

Let us look at these lists. In the New Testament there are at least fourteen lists of virtue and eight lists of vices. The Beatitudes surely represent the most famous virtue list as they provide an unparalleled depiction of goodness leading to happiness,[16] effectiveness[17] and perfection.[18] Most of the lists, however, are

---

15. In his *Letters to Lucilius*, for example, Seneca provides the following list: "We have separated this perfect virtue into its several parts. The desires had to be reined in, fear to be suppressed, proper actions to be arranged, debts to be paid; we therefore included self-restraint, bravery, prudence, and justice – assigning to each quality its special function . . . Virtue has been manifested to us by this man's order, propriety, steadfastness, absolute harmony of action, and a greatness of soul that rises superior to everything" (Seneca, 120).

16. Matt 5–7.

17. "Jesus says little about the qualities particular to ethical leadership, and more about the need for the individual to manifest faith and ask the Holy Spirit into his or her heart in order to do the work of inner transformation" (Mabey et al., "Having Burned," 762).

18. "The beatitudes could be mistaken for a set of rules. They aren't, however. They are much more like virtues" (Wright, *After You Believe*, 107).

found in the epistles. In Romans, for example, the four chapters following the exhortation to offer ourselves as a "holy sacrifice"[19] feature a list of virtues that includes humility, civility, service, teaching, encouragement, generosity, diligence, mercy, love, zeal, hope, patience, faith, solidarity, magnanimity, compassion, civility, equity, justice and patience. In 1 Corinthians the final exhortation lists prudence, constancy, courage, strength and love.[20] In Galatians the list of the fruit of the Spirit is love, joy, peace, forbearance, kindness, goodness, faithfulness, gentleness and self-control.[21] In Colossians the "things above" are compassion, kindness, humility, gentleness, patience, forgiveness, love, civility and equity.[22]

In Philippians we are told to walk in a manner worthy of the gospel and to work out our salvation through civility (like-mindedness), love, humility and altruism, decency and gentleness. In Philippians 4 we find an ethical list that comes under the heading of *arête* ("excellence") and that includes truthfulness, nobility, rightness, purity and loveliness (some scholars have suggested that this list is directly sourced from pagan ethics[23]). We then have the appeal of 1 Thessalonians for sexual decency, temperance, justice, love, diligence, civility, compassion, patience and benevolence, and the virtues in Titus, which call elders to be temperate, loving and constant; older women and young men to be temperate; younger women to be loving, temperate, decent, kind and civil; and slaves to be civil and honest.

The letters to Timothy and Titus further focus on the virtues of leaders, who must be faithful, temperate, self-controlled, respectable, hospitable, knowledgeable, moderate, gentle, not quarrelsome, not greedy, diligent, truthful, just and honest, as well as civil, meek, generous and benevolent.[24] Of all the letters, it is James that probably stands out the most as one that is practically an

---

19. Rom 12:1.

20. 1 Cor 16:13–14.

21. Gal 5:22–23. "The 'fruits of the Spirit' in the Apostle's list include forms of human being and action that are recognizably virtues . . . these do overlap with the virtues of the Aristotelian philosopher, as forms of being human which enable a belonging with the other, but take significantly different shape because they serve to make human being truly an image of the being of the triune God" (Gunton, "Church as a School of Virtue?," 228).

22. Col 3:12, 18–25.

23. "Many scholars have claimed that in cataloguing these virtues Paul has taken over a current list from a textbook of ethical instruction and made it his own, using the material in much the same way as pagan moral philosophers of his day when instructing their adherents" (O'Brien, *Epistle to the Philippians*, 501).

24. 1 Tim 3; Titus 1.

expanded list of virtues, dealing with prudence, humility, patience, temperance, compassion, equity, mercy, peace-making and truthfulness.

The un-ethical lists of vices in the New Testament are equally impressive. In the Gospels, we find that the "evils [that] come from inside" include sexual immorality, theft, murder, adultery, greed, malice, deceit, lewdness, envy, slander, arrogance and folly.[25] We are told that there is judgment coming on every kind of wickedness, which includes evil, greed, depravity, envy, murder, strife, deceit, malice, gossip, slander, God-hating, insolence, arrogance, boastfulness, disobedience, lack of understanding, infidelity, unlovingness and lack of mercy.[26] Then there are the vices of the flesh: intemperance, lust, strife and jealousy,[27] as well as sexual immorality, impurity, debauchery, idolatry, witchcraft, hatred, discord, jealousy, fits of rage, selfish ambition, dissensions, factions, envy, drunkenness and orgies.[28] The "wrongdoers [who] will not inherit the kingdom" are sexually immoral, idolaters, adulterers, thieves, greedy, drunkards, slanderers and swindlers.[29]

There are the vices that need to be dealt with in the church, such as discord, jealousy, fits of rage, selfish ambition, slander, gossip, arrogance and disorder, impurity, sexual sin and debauchery.[30] And there is also the "earthly nature" that needs to be put to death, with its vices of sexual immorality, impurity, lust, evil desires and greed, anger, rage, malice, slander, filthy language and lying.[31] There are the vices of false leaders who are lovers of themselves, lovers of money, boastful, proud, abusive, disobedient to their parents, ungrateful, unholy, without love, unforgiving, slanderous, without self-control, brutal, not lovers of the good, treacherous, rash, conceited and lovers of pleasure.[32] And so on.

In addition to these ethical lists, there are innumerable references to single virtues and vices. All this contributes to making the New Testament a true treasury of moral education.[33]

---

25. Mark 7.
26. Rom 1:29–30.
27. Rom 13:13.
28. Gal 5:19–20.
29. 1 Cor 6.
30. 2 Cor 12.
31. Col 3:5–9.
32. 2 Tim 3.
33. Among single virtues mentioned in chapters of the Bible, we find justice, honesty, generosity (Matt 20; Luke 21; 1 Tim 6), humility (Matt 23), diligence (Matt 25), mercy (Matt 25), constancy (Luke 14), courage (Luke 12), justice (Luke 18), loyalty (John 6, 10), fairness (John 7), truthfulness and honesty (John 9), constancy (John 21; Acts 1), civility and generosity

Shared Language

In addition to stories and ethical lists, the New Testament features a set of keywords and concepts that overlap with those that we have found in the Aristotelian framework. Happiness, for example, stands in dialogue with *eudaemonia*. Although there are significant differences between the teaching of Jesus and that of Aristotle (such as the emphasis on the "here and now" in Aristotle compared to the emphasis on future reward in the Beatitudes), there remains a clear shared link between happiness and goodness.[34] The term *arête* is also used in the New Testament,[35] and some commentators have suggested that, when Paul uses it, he is borrowing it directly from Stoic moral philosophy to build a Christian theology.[36] It is also remarkable to see striking parallels between Athenian thinking on virtue and vice and the New Testament use of the words righteousness (*dikaiosune*) and sin (*hamartia*).

Notably, the New Testament presents a concept of wisdom that is very similar to Aristotelian *phronesis*. We recall that, for Aristotle, wisdom is necessary to help us discern the virtues that need to be deployed in specific situations. In the New Testament, there are several key passages that illustrate this kind of wisdom. Jesus, for example, tells us that we must be shrewd as snakes and innocent as doves,[37] but we clearly cannot deploy them both at the same time, and we need the wisdom to know in which circumstances we need to be shrewd and when we need to be innocent. Jesus also talks about alternating between justice, mercy and righteous anger,[38] and about choosing between equity and generosity.[39] Jesus also demonstrated this kind of wisdom, as he moved between compassion for the sick and justice towards the self-righteous;

(Acts 2), courage (Acts 4), equity (Acts 4), wisdom (*sophia*, Acts 6), intellectual virtues (Acts 15), generosity (2 Cor 9), civility (1 Tim 2), contentment (1 Tim 6), magnanimity (Phlm) and love (1 John). Among the single vices, we find anger, lust, injustice, violence, pride, worry, envy (Matt 20; John 12; Phil 1:15), pride (Matt 20; Luke 18), sloth (Matt 25), greed (Luke 12), love of money (Luke 16; 1 Tim 6), cowardice (John 7), injustice (John 18), deceit (Acts 7), wrath leading to murder (Acts 8), pride (Acts 8), deceit (Acts 13), obstinacy (Acts 19), sloth (2 Thess).

34. Another difference is that Aristotle considers happiness mainly in relation to the fulfilment of the human *telos*, whereas, in the New Testament, the prime source of beatitude is divine approval. The two, however, are not incompatible.

35. Phil 4:8 is the only place where Paul uses this term. The other two instances in the New Testament are in 1 and 2 Peter.

36. Although Paul "borrows" these terms from the pagan traditions, he then "builds" them in a way which is distinctively Christian (O'Brien, *Epistle to the Philippians*, 502).

37. Matt 10:16.
38. Matt 18.
39. Matt 20.

between zeal for service and the need for rest;[40] or between the prudence of hiding himself and the courage of exposing himself to public danger. It might not be without significance that Paul chooses the term *phronesis* to exhort the Philippians to have the same "mindset" as Christ.[41]

We can also find examples of *phronesis* in the epistles, where Israel is shown as a bad example of zeal without knowledge,[42] or where Paul is pointed to as a good example of choosing wisely between the rod of discipline and a gentle spirit.[43] James explicitly calls us to exercise judgment together with mercy,[44] and, although the interpretation is not unanimous, some have also seen *phronesis* in the spiritual charisma of *sophias*.[45]

So far, we have seen the imitation principle in the New Testament, the enumeration of ethical lists and the existence of some shared terminology. Although these are valid elements to construct a New Testament vision of character and virtue education, a much richer approach is found in considering whether the main themes of the epistles have any connection with the notions of character and virtue. This method yields some surprising results. Although we acknowledge that the epistles have a variety of purposes and themes that are completely extraneous to our topic, we also observe a relentless orientation to character and virtue in the life of the church and in Christian discipleship.[46] Let us then take a thematic cavalcade through the New Testament.

Virtue in Galatians

We have already mentioned the well-known ethical list in Galatians 5 that is connected to the fruit of the Spirit. But there is much more to be seen here. We notice, for example, that both human agency and divine intervention are involved in this kind of fruit-bearing. On the one hand, it is the responsibility of the follower of Christ to "not indulge," to "watch out," to "walk by the Spirit," and to govern the "conflict" between competing desires. On the other hand, it is the work of the Spirit to "lead us," "shape our desires," and give us the ability to

---

40. Mark 6.
41. Phil 2:5.
42. Rom 10.
43. 1 Cor 4.
44. Jas 2.
45. 1 Cor 12.
46. Stückelberger has produced a comparative table of the theme of virtue in the letters of Colossians, Ephesians and Galatians (Stückelberger, "Integrity," 313–315).

bear virtuous fruit.[47] As this interplay occurs, the desires of the Spirit influence our own desires in such a way that the desires of the flesh, which once came naturally to us, are replaced by a Spirit-driven desire for virtue.

Through these new, Spirit-infused desires, the fruit of the Spirit comes "naturally." We find an interesting parallel here with Aristotle's definition of character in the *Nicomachean Ethics* in the natural enjoyment of good things. For Aristotle, virtue was not a constant victory over temptation through the exercise of the will, but a state of doing the right things "naturally."[48] What Paul is saying is similar. To bear the fruit of virtue, our desires must change to *want* virtue. But the difference with Aristotle is also prominent. Whereas Aristotle believed that the power to shape our desires is found in education and habituation, Paul teaches that the Spirit comes alongside our efforts and *supernaturally* shapes our desires, enabling us to enjoy virtue and helping us become "naturally" virtuous.

So what can we do? In Galatians 6 we find what might be considered to be the educational contribution of this letter on how to "live by the Spirit." This chapter is extremely practical and reveals an eight-fold process in shaping character. It requires (1) gentle restoration, (2) carrying each other's burdens, (3) having teachers of integrity, (4) testing actions through self-assessment, (5) finding legitimate pride in the achievement of good character, (6) staying away from comparative assessment with others, (7) receiving instruction by word, and (8) having a specific focus on communities of believers.[49] As we design a theology of educational practice, there are some great ideas here.

Virtue in Ephesians

Let's move on to Ephesians, where the key theme of the opening chapter is the "praise of his glorious grace" and the "incomparably great power for us that believe."[50] What follows tells us how to do this, and we do not have to look far to recognize a rubric of virtue and vice. Paul, in fact, claims that we were dead in transgressions (vice) and we have been made alive in order to become holy and blameless and to do good works (virtue). For this reason we should live a life worthy of our calling, which is unpacked as a life of humility,

---

47. Gal 5:17, 18, 22–25.
48. Racelis, "Developing a Virtue Ethics Scale," 22.
49. Gal 6:1, 2, 4, 5, 6, 10.
50. Eph 1:6, 19.

gentleness, patience, civility, truthfulness and love (virtues).[51] If we do not live this kind of life, God is grieved.[52] If, instead, we do, he is glorified. Is Paul saying that the route to showing the incomparable riches of God's grace is found in walking virtuously?

As in Galatians, several chapters of Ephesians tell us how to learn this way of life.[53] This is, once again, educational content that we can inject into our educational philosophy and practice. The "learning" that we find in Ephesians entails being taught, putting off the old self and putting on a new mindset.[54] It also involves removing habits of vice[55] and following new examples of virtue.[56] Virtue appears as the natural outworking of being transformed. Ephesians also includes the community in the learning process, and we are told to not partner with the disobedient[57] but to walk together in unity.[58]

Intriguingly, even the concluding discourse in this letter about spiritual warfare is connected to virtue, for our "spiritual armour" includes the virtues of truthfulness, righteousness, diligence and faith.[59]

Virtue in Philippians and Colossians

Philippians and Colossians are also virtue-rich. Philippians tells us to work out our salvation and to walk in a manner worthy of the gospel[60] through the virtues of civility (like-mindedness), love, humility, altruism, decency and gentleness. These virtues are the expression of the fact that God is working in us to will and to act to fulfil this good purpose.[61] Virtue, however, is not just the work of God. We are also responsible over the way we choose to walk, and we need to strive with constancy towards the prize. Again, we find practical educational tips on how to do this, including the practice of continually

---

51. Eph 4.
52. Eph 4:30.
53. Eph 4:20.
54. Eph 4:21–23.
55. Eph 4:25–31.
56. Eph 5:1.
57. Eph 5:6–7.
58. Eph 4:3.
59. Eph 6:14–16.
60. Phil 1:27.
61. Phil 2:13.

focusing the mind[62] on that which is related to virtue[63] and the call to imitate the practices of those who have both taught and demonstrated a virtuous life.[64]

Colossians contains a strong message about virtue,[65] as we read of the importance of living a life worthy of the Lord and of pleasing him in every way.[66] These are inspiring words, but what do they actually mean? How do we do it? Paul's reply is that we should bear fruit in every good work.[67] In other words, we please the Lord by being good. There is a great three-fold curriculum in Colossians 1: it starts with growing in the knowledge of God, then moves to learning wisdom and exercising spiritual discernment, and finally involves practising good works. This happens as we are strengthened with supernatural power from God to have constancy and patience that will allow us to give joyful thanks for our redemption.[68] In chapter 3, we are called to have our mind set on "things above," which corresponds to an ethical virtue list[69] and is in contrast with a list of earthly vices.[70]

Virtue in Other New Testament Books

Skimming through the rest of the New Testament we find that 1 Thessalonians tells us to please God more and more through a sanctified and holy life of virtue.[71] First Timothy reveals that being "contrary to the sound doctrine" has to do with behaviour full of vice which requires correction from leaders of virtue.[72] Second Timothy tells the tragic story of leaders who have fallen into falsity and vice,[73] and Titus reminds us that we used to be enslaved by passions,

---

62. The "continual dwelling of the mind" on virtue (Phil 4:8) does not carry the sense of a critical engagement with moral philosophy so much as "a careful taking into account and reflection on these positive characteristics so that . . . conduct will be shaped by them" (O'Brien, *Epistle to the Philippians*, 507).

63. The Greek term "if anything is excellent" in Phil 4:8 uses *arête*, described as that which is true, noble, right, pure and lovely.

64. Phil 4:9.

65. Colossians is "Paul's main exposition of Christian virtue" (Wright, *After You Believe*, 139).

66. Col 1:10.

67. Col 1:10.

68. Col 1:11–12.

69. Col 3:18–25.

70. Col 3:5–9.

71. 1 Thess 4:1.

72. 1 Tim 1:3–11.

73. 2 Tim 3:2–4.

but that we have been renewed in the Holy Spirit in order to carefully devote ourselves to doing good.[74] James provides a wonderful set of metaphors about virtue as he teaches us how works make our faith alive[75] and how important perseverance and wisdom are.[76] Hebrews also reminds us that perfecting our faith requires the virtues of perseverance, peacefulness, decency, temperance, love, magnanimity, hospitality and decency, for which God equips us as we do his will.[77] First Peter, instead, makes a forceful call to be holy,[78] to get rid of the past way of debauchery, envy, malice and lust, and to embrace a life of virtuous civility before the pagans.[79] Revelation closes the canon by praising churches that have embodied virtues of constancy, faithfulness, love, faith, diligence and patience, and denouncing churches that demonstrated acedia, tolerance of vice and pride, and lack of courage.[80]

Virtue in 2 Peter

We end with 2 Peter, for here we find one of the clearest statements in the entire New Testament about character and virtue. Against the backdrop of immoral teachers in the church and the "endless sin"[81] at the highest levels of the Roman Empire (such that not even the great teacher Seneca had been able to stop it[82]), the author of 2 Peter blends Stoic thinking[83] and Christian doctrine to instruct us on how to grow in virtue.

The letter rotates around the straightforward directive to make every effort to add virtue to our faith.[84] Notably, the author chooses the term *arête* to speak about virtue and then exposes a creative, deep, sincere and sustained

---

74. Titus 3:3–8.
75. Jas 2:14–20.
76. Jas 1:4–5.
77. Heb 13:21.
78. 1 Pet 1:15.
79. 1 Pet 2:12.
80. Rev 2, 3.
81. 2 Pet 2:2, 3, 8, 10, 13, 14.
82. We recall that Nero was likely the emperor at the time of writing 2 Peter and that Seneca had been his tutor. We also note scholars' debates over whether 2 Peter was actually written in Rome.
83. In this letter, the author touches on several of Seneca's key themes, such as escaping from passion and evil desires (1:4), being unreasoning like animals that are ruled by instinct (2:12), the promise of freedom (2:19 – interior *libertas*) and the scoffing at future judgment. Overall, some have suggested that 2 Peter "mirrors interaction between Stoic and Christian moral thought-worlds" (Charles, "Language and Logic," 55).
84. 2 Pet 1:5.

commitment to the "educational" process of shaping character. The exhortation to add virtue to our faith comes with an ethical list of private and public virtues,[85] which involve being knowledgeable, self-controlled, persevering and godly, but also being mutually affectionate and loving. Throughout the letter we find descriptions of the vices that we are to shun and the associated dangers if we do not. Adding virtue to our faith is the most important thing we can do as Christians. It confirms our calling and election and keeps us from becoming ineffective, unproductive and carried away from our secure position.[86]

What is most significant in 2 Peter, however, is that we find a distinctive perspective on how the power of the gospel relates to character and virtue. In Galatians, we saw how the power of the Spirit shapes our desires, and in Ephesians we considered how the new, God-given life empowers our efforts to be virtuous. In 2 Peter, we see even more explicitly that it is the power of the gospel that shapes our character. Peter tells us that we have received divine power *in order* to live a godly life of virtue.[87] He is saying that, in the gospel, we have everything we need to be good, not just to be saved. This is the less-familiar side of the gospel. The good news is not just that we can receive a rich welcome into the kingdom,[88] but also that we get to add virtue to our faith. The gospel is not just that we get to go to heaven, but also that we get to be good people as we partake in the divine nature.[89]

Simply put, 2 Peter shows us that the Christian gospel provides the power to fulfil the quest of the classical philosophers. Aristotle, Plato, Cicero and Seneca wanted to know how to obtain *arête* and be virtuous. They looked to philosophy to fulfil their vision. They devised habituation practices to educate the soul. And they sought to create a healthy *polis* to instil change by emulation. But although all these things were good, their power was limited, and the failure of Seneca with Nero was a contemporary case in point. What 2 Peter tells us is that the power to add virtue to our faith comes from Jesus. This is the difference between the message of Jesus and that of the classical world.

---

85. 2 Pet 1:5–6.
86. 2 Pet 1:8–10.
87. 2 Pet 1:4.
88. 2 Pet 1:11.
89. "With the aid of the Holy Spirit, through our knowledge of God, on the basis of the Word of God, we may become 'partakers of the divine nature' . . . A chief effort required for growth in Christlike character is intentional attention to the virtues and cultivation of them in an atmosphere of grace in partnership with God" (Austin and Geivett, "Being Good," 297).

Socrates wrote that "*arête* comes to the virtuous by the gift of God"[90] and, although he did not know the gospel of Jesus, he anticipated its wonder. Indeed, there is something new that goes beyond good examples of heroes of virtue, ethical lists and educational tools. There is power in the gospel to become good. This sets the New Testament apart from all other literature on character and virtue education and lays the foundations for our educational theology.

A Few Disclaimers

These, then, are my summaries of your work. It has been a good exercise for me to write all this down. I feel like I have a treasury at my fingertips, and in your last video it felt like you "had a sermon coming on." Well done! I might preach from 2 Peter 1 myself in the near future. You have fed an ongoing conversation[91] and, hopefully, our New Testament scholar-friends will pursue it further. We are used to reading the New Testament as a "religious" text, but you have reminded us that it is also deeply connected to education and to the moral philosophies of the time. I have often wondered whether classical studies should be propaedeutical to theological studies, and your study endorses my instinct.[92]

Might I suggest that at some point you insert a couple of disclaimers? You might want to make it clear, for example, that you are not presenting a fully-fledged theology of virtue in the New Testament, and that your summaries of the New Testament books are not meant to be exhaustive. You are chasing a particular theme and submitting evidence around the tradition of character and virtue education in Christian Scripture. Although the theme of virtue is recurrent, variously expressed and spoken of with great force, it is not the main theme of the New Testament, nor should we read the canon as if it were an intentional treatise on virtue.

You might also want to reassure your audience that you are aware of grace, and that God's providential work is operating in the background of all this. The last section of your work on 2 Peter made that clear. Too much talk about working on our character might sound like salvation by works and we do not want to encourage Christians to use virtue as a device to establish hierarchies of merit or to foster legalistic attitudes. Make sure that hatch is closed tightly.

---

90. Plato, *Meno* 98b.

91. O'Brien, *Epistle to the Philippians*, on Phil 4:8–9.

92. Henry Oxenham made this case in 1860, arguing that adequate clerical education could only happen through grounding in the classics of ancient and modern literature (O'Sullivan, "Henry Nutcombe Oxenham").

Be prepared to receive critical reviews as you go public with this. Hopefully, once the bones have been picked, many will see the fish on your platter. May you and I be accountable for our words, firm in our convictions and happy to correct our errors.

24

The Roman Road to Virtue

I come now to your short video on the epistle to the Romans, which I was fortunate to watch in Rome. I am writing this letter on a park bench just outside the Basilica of San Crisogono. This particular church was built on the ruins of an ancient *domus* that historians claim hosted one of the earliest Christian churches in Rome. So who knows: maybe the letter to the Romans was read for the first time only a few metres away from where I now sit!

I have already referred to this video as "revelatory" and I've watched it several times. You are reading this widely commented-on letter through the lens of virtue and I find the results startling. You rightfully say that, as an educator, you are tiptoeing into the sanctuary of Christian theology and biblical scholarship, and I share your sense of fear and trembling.[1] As before, I will attempt to summarize in writing what you have shared.

Words of Virtue in Romans

Although the words "virtue" and "vice" never appear verbatim in the letter to the Romans, they are an important theme.[2] There are good reasons, for example, to use "virtue" as a synonym for the Pauline word "righteousness."[3] Paul, in fact, is not making an original use of the term *dikaiosune*, nor should

---

1. Wright, *After You Believe*, 61–66.
2. "Virtue talk is settled comfortably in the middle of some of the most profound and forceful reflections ever written about justification by faith" (Hauerwas, *Christian Virtue Exemplified*, 335).
3. "Using 'virtue' as a synonym for 'righteousness' is tricky since in Romans 'righteousness' stands for God's declaration upon us, although, of course, in other places it is a description of the acceptable human behaviour . . . there are similarities but ones which risk skewing the matrix of Paul's thesis" (Robert Willoughby, private correspondence).

it be considered an exclusively theological notion.[4] In Romans, *dikaiosune* is associated with being a person of justice, integrity, moral uprightness and virtue,[5] and this is similar to the way the term was used by the philosophy of the time. Although there are many variations in the literature, the term *dike* was generally used to refer to the moral order of the universe,[6] and the Greeks used it to describe the ethical and virtuous life that demonstrated conformity to the claims of a higher authority.[7] This is not far from the Pauline thought that righteousness has to do with becoming the sort of person that God wants us to be[8] and that it is the ultimate delight, hope and happiness of Christian believers.[9]

When it comes to the term "vice" the linguistic mathematics are quickly done. If virtue can be seen as righteousness, there are good reasons to find parallels between *hamartia* and vice.[10] In Romans, in fact, sin does not refer simply to isolated wrongful acts but to habituated character traits such as lust, a depraved mind, greediness, envy, malice, arrogance, infidelity, unlovingness and mercilessness.[11] Again, the term *hamartia* is not exclusively theological, and Aristotle uses it in *Poetics* to describe a person who misses the marks of good character. Just as virtue has its rewards, so character that is full of vice is the recipe for misery,[12] wrath, trouble and distress.[13]

If we are happy to consider these synonyms, they can have some surprising effects on familiar texts. Consider the following:

---

4. There are broad parallels between the Greek and the Christian protoevangelical use of *dikaiosune* (Black, *Theology of Dallas Willard*, 125).

5. W. Mounce, "Righteousness," *Concise Greek-English Dictionary of the New Testament*, https://billmounce.com/greek-dictionary.

6. "*Dike* means basically the order of the universe . . . and the *dikaios* is the man who respects and does not violate that order. At once the difficulty in translating *dikaios* by 'just' is clear; for someone in our own culture may use the word 'just' without a reference to or belief in a moral order of the universe" (MacIntyre, *After Virtue*, 134).

7. Aristotle reinterpreted *dikaiosune* as *arête*, using the two terms as broadly synonymous. For Plato instead, *dikaiosune* was the "allocation of each part of the soul to its particular function, and no other" (MacIntyre, 141).

8. "Righteousness . . . consists not in right relation with God but in becoming (throughout the whole of one's character) the sort of person God wills us to be and commits himself to making of us" (Hauerwas, *Christian Virtues Exemplified*, 337).

9. Rom 7:22; 5:3; 2:10.

10. Abelard's *Ethics* deals with the relationship between sin and vice.

11. Rom 1:29–30.

12. Rom 7.

13. Rom 2:9.

> Therefore no one will be declared *virtuous* in God's sight by the works of the law; rather, through the law we become conscious of our *vice*. (Rom 3:20)
>
> For all have *been habituated in vice* and fall short of the glory of God. (3:23)
>
> While we were still full of *vice*, Christ died for us. (5:8)
>
> Offer every part of yourself to him as an instrument of *virtue*. For *vice* shall no longer be your master . . . You have been set free from *vice* and have become slaves to *virtue*. (6:13, 14, 18)

A Structured Treatise Leading to Virtue

One way to understand the book of Romans is to start from the end. The latter part of Romans is, in fact, a comparatively straightforward invitation to character and virtue. The invitation is based on the exhortation in chapter 12 to be transformed and renewed in our minds, and, as we read on, we find that our "holy sacrifice" requires the virtues of humility, civility, generosity, diligence, mercy, love, zeal, hope, patience, faith, solidarity, magnanimity, compassion, civility, equity, justice, patience, tolerance, peacefulness, benevolence and constancy.[14] Through these virtues, Paul paints a vision of the church in which the extraordinary effects of salvation are expressed in a life of character. The time has come, claims Paul, to put aside the deeds of vice and darkness and to put on the armour of light and good character.

Let us now return to the beginning of the letter. What is the hinge on which the "therefore" in chapter 12:1 revolves? What is the connection between the ethical list in the last part of the letter and the doctrines in the first part, in particular with the doctrine of the atonement? The hypothesis is that, whereas the second part of Romans deals with the aims and outcomes of virtue and character, the first part presents the gospel road to achieve them. Concerning the aims and outcomes, there is substantial agreement between Paul, Plato and Aristotle, but when it comes to how to achieve these outcomes, Paul takes a radically new route. In doing so, he grounds moral education in theological understanding. There are several points to be made here.

First of all, Paul clarifies the source of sin/vice. It the outcome of judgment on mankind.[15] It is not simply the lack of education or the result of poor

---
14. Rom chs. 12–16.
15. Rom 1:24, 26, 28.

philosophy. It is not just an issue of the untamed will or lack of self-control. There is something deeply wrong in the nature of man who has not only lost his *telos* and is no longer what he should be,[16] but who has also lost the will and the ability to be righteous/virtuous. This is in stark contrast with much of the contemporary literature on virtue education that ignores innate vice and builds on the conviction that human beings are intrinsically able to be good.[17] This is not a secondary matter, and the doctrine of the fall and of original sin must seriously weigh into our educational philosophy.

Second, Paul makes a point concerning human ability. Whereas Plato and Aristotle suggest that the path to virtue is found through a combination of human knowledge, education, community and individual willpower, Paul states that knowledge of what is good alone cannot make us virtuous in God's sight.[18] We are, in fact, in a condition of slavery to vice, and are not controlled by righteousness.[19] There are sinful passions that are working in us, and our mind is bound and governed by the flesh.[20] So, whereas the classical and humanistic traditions tend to focus on human ability to flourish, Christianity looks to the grace of God.

Incidentally, this issue of human agency was sharply debated in the early modern period, most notably by Luther. Could the pagans truly acquire virtue through education? Did schooling in goodness not simply give rise to the vices of pride and vanity? Was true goodness possible outside of "a dramatic displacement of human agency"?[21] Luther believed not and denied that external practice could lead to interior transformation. For him, Aristotle and Paul were in direct antithesis[22] and "the honest sinner is closer to righteousness than the

---

16. "To be fallen is to act in a way that one essentially – that is to say, eschatologically – is not" (Gunton, "Church as a School of Virtue," 219).

17. Interestingly, research of some virtue ethicists confirms the theological stance in Romans about innate evil. "One notable exception to the general tendency of virtue ethicists to marginalize the moral significance of vice, evil and the immoral is the work of the American moral and political philosopher John Kekes . . . [who] provides one of the most profound investigations of the subject available" (Gilead, "Countering the Vices," 272). See Kekes, *Facing Evil*.

18. Rom 3:20.

19. Rom 6:20. In *Facing Evil*, virtue ethicist Kekes "emphasizes that in most cases people do not consciously choose to regularly cause evil. They are led to do so because they cannot control their selfishness, cowardice, cruelty, envy, malice, jealously and other negative, but natural, human inclinations" (Gilead, "Countering the Vices," 274).

20. Rom 7:5; 8:6.

21. Herdt, "Virtue's Semblance," 138.

22. For Luther, "the image of God in us has been utterly destroyed by Adam's fall . . . it is not sufficient to recognise the partial and provisional character of human virtue . . . nor is it the case that the active practice of neighbour-love can foster virtue of the heart . . . instead the

aspirant to virtue."[23] Whereas Luther might have been right in questioning the capability of fallen humanity to be virtuous,[24] his view might be too pessimistic. Erasmus offered a more balanced view, claiming that the pagans were capable of imitating true virtue and that, even though their progress would never *constitute* piety, it could *foster* piety.[25] Although human effort might not lead to perfect virtue, it could contribute to self-improvement and represent genuine "fruits of repentance."

The third point of distinction concerns divine intervention. None of the great classical writers looked to the gods to become virtuous. It was an entirely human affair. Christianity, instead, looks to the work of Jesus on the cross to find the grace to be righteous. The message of Romans is that the will is simply not enough.[26] There is something that stands between our will to do good and our ability to be good.[27] That is why we need a gospel. The good news of Romans is that, in Christ, we receive the ability to be the virtuous people we would like to be.[28]

This, of course, is foundational for Pauline thinking and for Christian theology. The gift of righteousness/virtue is imputed through Jesus and received by faith.[29] This gift allows us to reign in a flourishing life, to be freed from the slavery to sin/vice and to reap the benefits that lead to holiness.[30] Since the power to be virtuous is not in us, the Spirit has put to death the misdeeds of the body, has aligned our minds with right desires and has given us a new life of righteousness.[31]

Seen in this way, the gospel is the solution to the weaknesses of moral philosophy, and it is what is needed for human flourishing. In his wonderful little booklet *After You Believe*, N. T. Wright claims that Christian behaviour

---

starting point must be a moment of utter passivity, in which we utterly relinquish any reliance on human agency . . . As long as we do not acknowledge this point fully, we make no progress at all; we simply mire ourselves deep in sin" (Herdt, 148).

23. Herdt, 148.

24. Studies in social psychology confirm that it is generally difficult for people to be honest, merciful, truthful and good (Mabey, "Having Burned," 761).

25. Herdt, "Virtue's Semblance," 142, 152.

26. Rom 2:4.

27. Rom 7:18–19.

28. "Apart from redemption, our virtues will be but shadows of what they should be" (Gunton, "Church as a School of Virtue," 221).

29. Rom 3:22.

30. Rom 5:17; Rom 6:1–13.

31. Rom 8:5, 13, 10.

and human flourishing are the same thing.[32] Christianity takes the best of ancient wisdom and brings it to a new level, putting it into a framework that becomes possible through grace.[33] In Christ Jesus, human beings are not only called to become what they were always meant to be,[34] but they are also empowered to do so.

Theologically speaking, this is known as the *recapitulation* view of the atonement.[35] The re-reading of Romans through the lens of character and virtue that we've considered suggests that the effects of the atonement are not just to save the lost from eternal damnation, but also to reset humanity on its intended path. If the fall has made us lose *arête*, redemption makes it possible to restore the image of God and for us to become flourishing humans. While this model does not exclude the forensic model of the atonement and its future effects, it spotlights the transformation of our current condition.

Romans 6 weighs in here as a central text that speaks of slavery to sin/vice. It makes it clear that we are born into a natural condition of impotence in which righteousness/virtue has no control over us.[36] This misery is powerfully expressed in Romans 7, where Paul hates himself for not being able to do the good that he wanted to do and for doing the evil that he did not wish to do.[37] Before the Damascus road, Paul was like Aristotle and all the rest, desperately wanting to be virtuous, but unable to be so and condemning himself for it. But, thanks to the gospel of the atonement, Paul claims that we are free[38] from sin/vice. Sin is no longer our master and we have become slaves of righteousness/virtue. The benefit of this new freedom is holiness[39] and a new-found possibility to reach the otherwise impossible standards of character and virtue described in Romans 12–15. Because of the work of the atonement, our "living sacrifice"[40]

---

32. Wright, *After You Believe*, xi.

33. Wright, 25.

34. Wright, 89.

35. When we speak of recapitulation, the key term is *anakephalaiosis* (or *recapitulateo*), meaning the restoration of the image of God. Athanasius spoke of recapitulation, as did Hans Küng in *On Being a Christian*.

36. Rom 6:6–7, 14, 17, 20.

37. Rom 7 is often read as the everyday experience of the Christian life, but there are good reasons to believe that Paul is here describing his frustrating pre-conversion experience as a zealous Jew who wished to keep the law and as a student of Stoic philosophy who desired virtue.

38. Rom 6:7, 14, 18.

39. Rom 6:22.

40. "[In Rom 12:1–2] . . . the telos is not moral perfection, which is too narrow a concept, but virtues, human perfections, in the service of holiness, which is the offering of the whole person to God. Human virtue provides one of the central ways by which God the Spirit may enable anticipations of the end to be realized in the course of the human journey, because it

becomes possible. We can say "no" to sin;[41] we can live a new life of virtue[42] and righteousness; we can choose not to obey the desires of sin;[43] and we can offer ourselves as instruments of righteousness.[44] Although sin[45] is still a possible choice and we are admonished not to offer any part of ourselves to sin as an instrument of wickedness,[46] there is now the possibility of winning that struggle. When temptation comes knocking, we can say "no."

This is a gospel of transformation and not just of forgiveness; of freedom from present condemnation and not just of salvation from future damnation. It is a gospel of getting the kingdom back into humanity and not just of getting humanity back into the kingdom. It is a gospel of anthropological hope and not just of eschatological hope. It is a gospel of hard work, but also a gospel of supernatural help.[47] It is a gospel where we look to Jesus not only as a good example to imitate, but as the one who accomplishes our redemption. It is a gospel where goodness is actually fulfilled, not only imputed. It is, in brief, a gospel of being restored to the image of God.

On these theological foundations we can proceed to design character and virtue education projects for Christian students of theology. While we endorse the secular efforts in character education, we believe that there is special potential in those who have experienced the atoning work of Christ.

—

Dear Siméon, you have brilliantly planted fresh seeds of thought on this issue. I can get excited about preaching this gospel. The hope of recapitulated goodness is indeed wonderful. We can walk with our heads held high and like what we see in the mirror. What a gospel that is!

May we walk in the humility of atoning grace and in the dignity of recapitulated humanity.

---

refers to the way settled dispositions to 'good works' are shaped" (Gunton, "Church as a School of Virtue?," 227–228).

41. Rom 6:1–2.

42. Rom 6:4.

43. Rom 6:6.

44. Rom 6:13, 19.

45. "If Aristotle's virtue entails the impossibility of sin, Kierkegaard's faith depends on the cultivated capacity to sin, along with the willingness, at every moment, not to do so" (Mahn, "Kierkegaard after Hauerwas," 178).

46. Rom 6:13.

47. "Christians are indeed called to imitate Christ, but this act of imitation is not a wilful groping after divine perfection. Instead to imitate Christ is fundamentally to imitate Christ's humility and thus to be dependent, receptive, open to transformation from without" (Herdt, "Virtue's Semblance," 143).

25

Virtue from Cassian to the *Carmina Burana*

In this third letter on the tradition of character and virtue education, I plan to cover the time frame in which classical philosophy met with Christian theology. In my previous letters, I've introduced the educational thinking of the Greeks and Romans and you've done a fantastic job in charting the data from the New Testament. It is now time to look at how these two forces joined hands in the "Christianization" of Europe. As you know, the relationship between pagan philosophy and Christian theology has long been discussed, and positions have ranged from Tertullian's separatism to Aquinas's inclusivism[1] and Petrarch's indecisivism. While acknowledging this complexity, I've selected the inclusivistic part of the story in which Christian thinkers welcomed the classic tradition of character and virtue education. I am therefore guilty of "cherry-picking," but I still think that it is a significant story, and perhaps even the prevailing one.

Before I jump into my overview, I must share with you the thrill I experienced through some of the artwork that I saw in Italy last month. After the conference in Rome, I had an extra week to do some travelling around this country that has produced so much sacred art. I would love one day to teach an entire theology programme that does little more than visit art sites across the Italian peninsula. For now, I will be content to share with you a little bit of what I have admired on the specific topic of virtue. Let me try to describe four works that will help you "feel" the climate of the distinctive time in history that we are about to consider (as you read, please look up each work on the Internet).

---

1. "Great theologians such as Augustine, Aquinas, Calvin and Wesley learned from the work of Plato and Aristotle" (Spears and Loomis, *Education for Human Flourishing*, 63).

Virtue in Art

I began by visiting the Cappella degli Scrovegni in Padua that hosts a set of frescoes by Giotto depicting seven allegorical figures for virtue and seven corresponding figures for vice. The frescoes are placed on two walls, in opposition to each other, as if to illustrate how each virtue can degenerate into vice and how each vice can be overcome by virtue. They are also ingeniously placed to represent two distinct pathways towards the final scene of the Universal Judgment that is featured on the back wall. The fourteen allegorical figures are painted as monochrome statues, and the overwhelming sensation is that of being in the presence of the austere guardians of the afterlife. If one follows the pathway of the virtues one will end up in paradise and obtain a life of blessing, justice and human happiness. If one follows the pathway through the vices, one will end up among the damned in hell.

I then returned to Rome and admired Raphael's three altar-step tables in the Vatican Pinacoteca depicting Faith, Hope and Charity. The figures are amazingly rich in symbolism. *Charity* is depicted as a fertile woman laden with children who loves and serves all life, with a cherub on her left bearing fire to remind us that love is moved by a warming passion, and a cherub on her right that is pouring out abundant grapes, symbol of the generous giving of oneself. The virtue of *Faith* is represented through the living presence of Christ in the Eucharist and the incarnation, and the virtue of *Hope* is shown in prayer as she wins temptation, overcomes short-sightedness and rests in providence. As you know, these three theological virtues were added by Christianity as something that Aristotle had not contemplated, and hold a place of great importance in Christian theology and educational practice.

Finally, I travelled to Naples and spent a quiet afternoon admiring Caravaggio's *The Seven Works of Mercy*. The chapel features seven other paintings representing the different works of mercy, but Caravaggio's work above the central altar dominates the visitor's attention. In it, we see different figures intent on burying the dead, visiting the imprisoned, feeding the hungry, sheltering the homeless, clothing the naked, visiting the sick and refreshing the thirsty. Notably, this painting is found in the headquarters of the Pio Monte della Misericordia, an organization of seven Neapolitan noblemen who practised these works of mercy in seventeenth-century Naples.

While in Naples I also visited the Cappella Sansevero. This was probably my most intense artistic experience. There is usually a waiting line along the small, noisy ally that leads to the modest entrance. Once inside the door, everything becomes quiet and enchanted. At the centre of the seventeenth-century chapel is Giuseppe Sanmartino's masterpiece *Veiled Christ*. This life-size sculpture interprets the body of Christ lying with his face upwards, entirely covered with a thin veil of marble. The veil is so real, so soft and seemingly warm that one wants to reach out and touch it to make sure it is nothing more than cold marble. But one's attention gravitates to the face of the deposed Christ. He is, in fact, caught in the act of breathing in. His eyes are still shut, but the thin veil is imperceptibly being drawn into the mouth as air rushes back into the lungs of the defunct God-man. This sculpture thus captures "the instant of the resurrection," as life comes back and as the Christ becomes the Risen One.

Looking on *Veiled Christ*, the designer of the chapel disposed ten statues representing ten virtues. We see *Divine Love* as an androgynous youth holding up a flaming heart to God. We see *Self-Control* as a soldier who holds a lion in chains at his feet. We see *Sincerity* as a woman dressed in gold, accompanied by a dove and in the act of giving her heart away with one hand and holding the caduceus of eloquence in the other. We see *Disillusion* as a mature man who is trapped in a thick net of sin, passion and deceit and who is being freed by a flaming youth representing the intellect. We see *Modesty* as a beautiful woman, veiled and protected from the eyes of malice. We see the *Sweetness of Marital Love* as a woman holding a plumed yoke combined with two joined flaming hearts. We see *Religious Zeal* as an elderly man, with a priestly oil lamp in one hand to represent the importance of teaching and a whip in the other as a reminder of the importance of discipline. We see *Liberality* as a woman with an eagle at her side, holding both a compass and coins and a cornucopia of goods to be shared. We see *Decorum* as a youth with a perfectly proportioned body representing constancy and moderation. And, finally, we see *Education*, shown as a woman intent on directing a youngster to engage with literature and morals. The woman sits on a pedestal where the phrase "*Educatio et disciplina mores faciunt*" is engraved, to remind us that education and discipline must combine to form good behaviour. The child who is being instructed holds a copy of Cicero's *De Officiis*, in direct reference to the moral impact of classical culture.

I cannot conceal the strong emotions that this art instilled, and it is with this sentiment that I now review with you the pages of history which generated it.

The Desert Fathers and Mothers

In AD 190 Clement of Alexandria wrote about the "Paideia of God"[2] and this is probably the earliest reference outside of the New Testament to the meeting of the classical virtue tradition and Christianity. Around the same time, Origen's works and teaching[3] also featured many references to virtue,[4] but the earliest well-documented examples of a Christian movement that openly pursued character and virtue are the third-century Christian hermits living in the Egyptian desert. These so-called "desert fathers and mothers" lived drawing close to God and teaching others the secrets of the virtuous life. Although their vision was primarily mystical, the control of passions of vice was considered the first step along the path to holiness and union with God. For them, vices were associated with appetites that needed to be dominated through the habits of hard living and by the strength of a relationship with God in Christ. The desert fathers and mothers are the first substantial example of the Christian adoption of the classical practices of struggling against vice and of shaping virtue through habituation.

Although the desert fathers and mothers are frequently associated with mysticism and spirituality, many of their sayings are concerned with morality, with struggling against vice and with pursuing love.[5] Spirituality and morality were, in fact, intimately connected in their understanding. In the *Life of Anthony of Egypt*, for example, Athanasius points to Anthony the Great as a spiritual exemplar who walked the perfect path of virtue.[6] In Athanasius's sayings we can easily spot the language of virtue and vice as he instructs about acedia, courage, humility, wisdom and discernment, fornication, moderation, self-control and pride.[7] Many other sayings of the desert fathers and mothers

---

2. Clement of Alexandria and Origen claimed that "Christianity is Paideia, even by God in Jesus Christ, turning on a radical conversion possible only by the Holy Spirit's help, and taught only indirectly by study of divinely inspired Scriptures in the social context" (Kelsey, *Between Athens and Berlin*, 11).

3. "The teachers of Alexandria were not interested mostly in conveying knowledge or transmitting intellectual skills. They were interested in moral and spiritual formation" (Neuhaus, *Theological Education*, 42).

4. References to virtue in Origen's works include holding fast to perfection in virtues, persevering in acquiring virtues, praying for virtue from God, persevering in preserving virtue, reverencing virtues, searching the Scriptures to ascertain what are the virtues, seeking virtuous works, striving for virtue, training in virtue and working out the opportunities for virtue (see Brattston, *Traditional Christian Ethics*, 511).

5. Ward, *Sayings of the Desert Fathers*, xxvi.

6. Carrigan, *Wisdom*, 1.

7. Athanasius, *Sayings* 1, 7, 8, 11, 13, 18, 37 (in Ward, *Sayings of the Desert Fathers*, 2–8).

make explicit reference to virtue. It is considered an objective,[8] a prize,[9] an outworking of the commandments[10] of God and as something to be taught and spoken about in the community of disciples.[11] Important virtues are frequently listed[12] and ranked,[13] and the effort to turn from vice to virtue is shown as the way that leads to heaven.[14] The desert father Amoun even openly prays to God as the "God of all virtue."[15]

Cassian

John Cassian is another important figure of the fourth century. He interpreted the tradition of the desert fathers and mothers and put it into the systematized form that was instrumental in early theological education.[16] Cassian's works *De Institutis Coenobiorum* and the *Collationes* became classics in the West and

---

8. *Eucharistus* 1 (Ward, 60 onwards) and *Theodore of Scetis* 1 (Ward, 79). Athanasius likewise reminds readers to "not fear the word 'virtue' as if it were unattainable" (Carrigan, *Wisdom*, 20).

9. *Isodore of Pelusia* 2 (Ward, *Sayings of the Desert Fathers*, 98).

10. "Unless he keeps the commandments of God, a man cannot make progress, not even in a single virtue" (*Agathon* 2, in Ward, 20).

11. See *Isodore of Pelusia* 3 (Ward, 98) and *John the Dwarf* 26 (Ward, 91).

12. "I think it best that a man should have a little bit of all the virtues. Therefore, get up early every day and acquire the beginning of every virtue and every commandment of God. Use great patience, with fear and long-suffering, in the love of God, with all the fervour of your soul and body. Exercise great humility, bear with interior distress; be vigilant and pray often with reverence and groaning, with purity of speech and control of your eyes. When you are despised do not get angry; be at peace, and do not render evil for evil. Do not pay attention to the faults of others, and do not try to compare yourself with others, knowing you are less than every created thing. Renounce everything material and that which is of the flesh. Live by the cross, in warfare, in poverty of spirit, in voluntary spiritual asceticism, in fasting, penitence and tears, in discernment, in purity of soul, taking hold of that which is good. Do your work in peace. Persevere in keeping vigil, in hunger and thirst, in cold and nakedness, and in sufferings" (*John the Dwarf*, in Ward, 92).

13. See *Elias* 8 (Ward, 72 onwards), *Theodore of Pherme* 13 (Ward, 75), *John the Dwarf* 22 (Ward, 90) and *Romans* 2 (Ward, 211).

14. See *Isodore of Pelusia* 4 (Ward, 98), *Poemen* 119 (Ward, 184) and *Ammonas*, saying 29 (Ward, 25). "We ought rather to seek after that which will lead us to heaven, namely wisdom, chastity, justice, virtue, an ever-watchful mind, care of the poor, firm faith in Christ, a mind that can control anger, and hospitality. Striving after these things, we shall prepare for ourselves a dwelling in the land of the peaceful, as it says in the Gospel" (*Athanasius* in Carrigan, *Wisdom*, 18).

15. *Amoun* 3 (Ward, *Sayings of the Desert Fathers*, 32).

16. Ward, xix.

were deeply influential in virtue training for many monastic movements,[17] including the Benedictines.[18]

In continuity with the tradition of the desert fathers, a large section of the *Institutis* is taken up with how monks should struggle against eight vices.[19] This work is frequently referred to as one of the sources of the "trees of virtue and vice" (*arbor virtutum* and *arbor variorum*) that were popular in the Middle Ages.

Early Church Training for Ordination

As Christianity became increasingly structured in the Roman Empire, the issue of training ministers became of great significance and particular attention was given to the moral formation of priests. In this period, theological education began to adopt formalized curricula and, although the training of the ordinands was still rather superficial, it is significant that much more importance was given to issues of moral character than to the development of theological knowledge or practical ability. The vice of vainglory, for example, was seen as particularly dangerous and deserving of great attention in theological education.[20]

The literature of the time shows us that good character was paramount for leaders of the early Christian church, and Ambrose of Milan famously claimed that it was useless to look for a spring in the mud, implying that the church

---

17. "The Saint Whose Guide on Virtue Was Read Every Day by Monks in the Middle Ages," *The Catholic Herald*, 23 July 2012, accessed 29 May 2018, http://www.catholicherald.co.uk/news/2012/07/23/the-saint-whose-guide-on-virtue-was-read-every-day-by-monks-in-the-middle-ages/.

18. Cassian's *Collationes* are frequently referred to in the Rule of St Benedict and were read every night in Benedictine monasteries (Ward, *Sayings of the Desert Fathers*, xx).

19. "We now propose, being strengthened by God through your prayers, to approach the struggle against the eight principal faults, i.e. first, Gluttony or the pleasures of the palate; secondly, Fornication; thirdly, Covetousness, which means Avarice, or, as it may more properly be called, the love of money; fourthly, Anger; fifthly, Dejection; sixthly, 'Accidie,' which is heaviness or weariness of heart; seventhly, κενοδοξία which means foolish or vain glory; eighthly, pride" (Cassian, *Institutis*, 350).

20. "Vainglory . . . is 'the greatest obstacle to virtue,' a rock 'more dangerous than that of the Sirens' . . . In vainglory you find the wild beasts: 'they are wrath, despondency, envy, strife, slanders, accusations, falsehood, hypocrisy, intrigues, anger against those who have done no harm, pleasure for the indecorous acts of fellow ministers, sorrow at their prosperity, love of praise, desire of honour . . . doctrines devised to please, servile flatteries, ignoble fawning, contempt of the poor, paying court to the rich . . .'" (Chrysostom, *On the Priesthood*, in Neuhaus, *Theological Education*, 49, 50).

must have priests who were pure in their character.[21] Ambrose was one of three prominent Christian leaders in the fourth century who prioritized moral and spiritual formation. He explicitly referenced classical culture, and his *De Officiis Ministrorum* purposely mimicked Cicero's *De Officiis* as he took the pagan approach to virtue and placed it in a Christian context.[22] He unashamedly looked at the conventions of Greek philosophy, the works of Cicero and the ideas of Platonism, Stoicism and Aristotelian moral philosophy, and put them alongside Scripture as a means to educate in character and virtue.[23]

Two other important figures who focused on moral training in this period were Gregory of Nazianzus and Chrysostom.[24] In his *Second Oration*, Gregory claims that, since the Christian life is spiritual and moral warfare, the aim of teaching and preaching must be to educate others in virtue.[25] Chrysostom, in *On the Priesthood*, tries to understand why the wrong people become priests, and concludes that it is because insufficient attention has been given to their character.[26] He thus recommends the cultivation of the virtuous life as central in priestly training.[27]

Augustine

We cannot consider this period in church history without mentioning Augustine, and it is no surprise to discover that character and virtue were also very important to him. He understood the soul in terms of *ordo amoris*

---

21. "Purity of character enables the priest [to be] the fountain providing the church with the springs of good counsel and the waters of salvation" (Ambrose, *De Officiis*, in Neuhaus, 51).

22. In *De Officiis* Ambrose purposely mimicked the title of Cicero's work and borrowed the same structure: Book 1 concerns duties derived from what is virtuous: Book 2 concerns duties derived from what is useful; Book 3 concerns the relationship between virtue and utility. In this text, Ambrose recaptures Stoic assumptions on virtue and builds on them with biblical patterns of humility, charity and self-denial.

23. Neuhaus, *Theological Education*, 51, 54.

24. The main works are the *Second Oration* by Gregory of Nazianzus and *On the Priesthood* by Chrysostom. In all these works, as in the *De Officiis Ministrorum* of Ambrose, the ideal "revolves not around training or function but around the moral and spiritual character of the ordained person" (Neuhaus, 23).

25. Gregory presents the life of the gospel as involving both the moral life (*tropon*) and the spiritual life (*logon*) (Neuhaus 43, 53).

26. Those responsible for the appointment of priests, according to Chrysostom, "do not all look to the one thing which ought to be the only object kept in view, the excellence of character" (Neuhaus, 51, 52).

27. For Chrysostom, priests are the healers of sick souls through moral reformation and teaching. But how will they be able to do this "unless they far surpass ordinary human virtue"? (Neuhaus, 43). Perfect teaching comes when teachers combine "what they do and what they say" (Neuhaus, 53).

and spoke of virtue and vice in terms of ordered or disordered love as they related to God, neighbour and the world.[28] Centuries later, Dante, in the *Divine Comedy*, would echo this vision, depicting the seven capital sins in terms of "love gone wrong": pride, jealousy and wrath were love that had failed its purpose; greed, gluttony and lust were a distorted love for things; and acedia was nothing more than the lack of love for anything whatsoever. Augustine believed that the virtues were the "best and most useful possessions" in life[29] and that they deserved the highest place in the war against vice.[30]

Although Augustine had great respect for the tradition of character and virtue education, he makes an important theological distinction. In the *City of Man*, he notes that happiness is equated with virtue[31] (this is a clear reference to Aristotle). But this is a mistaken expectation, he says, because complete happiness cannot be found in this life through virtue, but only through salvation.[32] For him, Aristotle was wrong in making too much of virtue and suggesting that *eudaemonia* can be achieved through virtue alone. We live in a fallen world,[33] Augustine reminds us, and if the virtues are not directed towards God[34] and empowered by God, they remain out of reach. True virtue, for Augustine, was found only within a relationship with God[35] and true happiness was found only in the hope of salvation.

---

28. Bennett, *Book of Virtues*, 21.

29. "[T]he . . . virtues of this life . . . are certainly its best and most useful possessions" (Augustine, *City of God* 19).

30. "Virtue . . . holds the highest place among human good things, what is its occupation save to wage perpetual war with vices . . . a war which is waged especially by that virtue . . . [of] temperance" (Augustine, Book 19).

31. "The life of man, then, is called happy when it enjoys virtue and these other spiritual and bodily good things without which virtue is impossible" (Augustine, Book 19).

32. "As for those who have supposed that the sovereign good and evil are to be found in this life, and have placed it . . . in virtue . . . all these have, with a marvellous shallowness, sought to find their blessedness in this life and in themselves . . . Salvation, such as it shall be in the world to come, shall itself be our final happiness. And this happiness these philosophers refuse to believe in, because they do not see it, and attempt to fabricate for themselves a happiness in this life, based upon a virtue which is as deceitful as it is proud" (Augustine, Book 19).

33. Augustine also believed that the virtues are proof of the reality of a fallen world. "Prudence . . . is itself a proof that we are in the midst of evils, or that evils are in us" (Augustine, Book 19). "Evil . . . is removed from this life neither by prudence nor by temperance. And justice . . . does not this virtue demonstrate that it is as yet rather labouring towards its end than resting in its finished work? . . . Then that virtue which goes by the name of fortitude is the plainest proof of the ills of life, for it is these ills which it is compelled to bear patiently . . . [T]he very virtues of this life . . . are all the more telling proofs of its miseries" (Augustine, Book 19).

34. Herdt, "Virtue's Semblance," 138.

35. "That which gives blessed life to man is not derived from man, but is something above him; and what I say of man is true of every . . . virtue whatsoever" (Augustine, *City of God* 19).

In Augustine, we have a robust example of how Christian thinkers began grappling theologically with the Aristotelian vision of character and virtue education.

The Monastic Movement

As we move forward along our timeline, we find one of the most enduring Christian expressions of character and virtue: the monastic movement. First of all, we notice that, in a very dark time in European history, the monastic communities were places of relational friendship in which the monks considered themselves each other's *custos animi* (guardian of the soul).[36] This notion of moral accountability had precedents in the early church, where baptism was preceded by moral instruction and catechetical accountability,[37] and in the monasteries morality was both taught (through a combination of materials from the Gospels and the classical tradition) and enforced within a community of accountability. This was a recurring feature in all monastic communities and replicated the heritage of the desert fathers.

Consider two examples. The first is the Benedictine abbess Hildegard of Bingen. In the formation of her nuns, she privileged virtue over academics and put forward a plan to lead their souls on the path of virtue.[38] The *Ordo Virtutum*, which she wrote as one of the earliest medieval morality plays, is a drama of words and music that illustrates moral medieval monasticism. As the plot develops, we find the soul that falls into sin is rescued by the virtues, who then proceed to defeat the devil.[39]

A second example comes from the opening call of Francis's *Earlier Rule*. This fundamental Franciscan document lays out the fundamental virtues of obedience, poverty, chastity. Throughout the *Rule* reference is made to the virtues of diligence, kindness, love, accountability, humility, joy, liberality, compassion, purity and prudence which should characterize the community

---

36. Ferzoco and Muessig, *Medieval Monastic Education*, 3.

37. González, *History of Theological Education*, 10–11.

38. "Hildegard made it clear that she did not learn anything 'academically' from Jutta, but . . . [she] showed her disciple how to reveal her virtue, and Hildegard would do the same for her community of nuns" (Ferzoco and Muessig, *Medieval Monastic Education*, 91).

39. "The soul falls into sin, experiences a battle between the Devil and rescuing virtues, and returns restored to her community. The principal characters are the Soul, the Devil and personifications of the virtues, such as Humility, Knowledge of God, Charity, Obedience, Faith and Hope. The Soul engages in dialogue with the virtues . . . [A]s the drama closes, the Virtues, led by Humility and Chastity, bind up the Devil" (Ferzoco and Muessig, 78).

of brothers.[40] The importance of a life of virtue is a constant refrain across Franciscan literature and is shown as the key to walking in Jesus's footprints towards eternal life.[41] Francis writes about theological virtues, about the Beatitudes and about the remedial virtues. He also designs his own taxonomy of virtue, classifying the divine virtues, the virtues of Christ and the virtues of the Spirit.[42] Franciscan monasteries offered spiritual programmes for virtuous living, and monastic life and training was arranged around virtues of charity, obedience, goodness, truth, faith, humility, joy, poverty, penance and peace.[43]

The monasteries were also very attentive to vice, and the literature of this period is rich with admonitions. An example of this can be seen in the influential monastic schools in Ireland in the seventh and eleventh centuries which produced the "penitential books" that were used in the private confessional to define sin and the necessary penance.[44] Although this kind of moral listing and penitential practice defies genuine character formation, it remains as an example of how seriously sin and vice were taken at the time.

Medieval and Early Modern Theology

It is probably fair to say that the Middle Ages consolidated the link between the virtues and Christian theology.[45] In the twelfth century, the rediscovery of important classical texts (that had got lost) had a huge influence on the work of the scholastics[46] and shaped Christian thinking in this period. Once again,

---

40. *The Earlier Rule*, Franciscan Intellectual Tradition, https://www.franciscantradition.org/francis-of-assisi-early-documents/writings-of-francis/the-earlier-rule/78-fa-ed-1-page-63.

41. Virtues are key elements in the medieval Franciscan writings. They are the most important building blocks of a life according to "the teaching and footprints of our Lord Jesus Christ" representing steps on the way to the "treasure in heaven" and "eternal life" (Pansters, *Franciscan Virtue*, 2).

42. "[Francis] adds his own scheme of divine virtues (goodness, mercy, gentleness, delight, sweetness, holiness, justice, truth, uprightness, kindness, innocence, cleanness, and strength, greatness, highness, charity, wisdom, humility, patience, beauty, meekness, security, rest, gladness, hope, justice, moderation, richness, refreshment, faith, sweetness); virtues of Christ (humility, poverty); virtues of the Spirit (humility, patience, purity, simplicity, truth, peace, fear, wisdom, love); devotional virtues (love, gratitude, humility)" (Pansters, 171).

43. Pansters, 45, 170.

44. González, *History of Theological Education*, 31.

45. "The Medieval stage... was in a strong sense Aristotelian, and not only in its Christian versions... It is this linking of biblical historical perspectives with the Aristotelian one in the treatment of the virtues which is the unique achievement of the middle ages in Jewish and Islamic terms as well as in Christian" (MacIntyre, *After Virtue*, 180).

46. See, for example, textbooks like the *Moralium Dogma Philosophorum*, owing much to Cicero's *De Officiis* (written perhaps by William of Conches) (MacIntyre, 167).

scholars grappled with relating pagan philosophers and Christian theology. We see this in Abelard, for example, who chose to rely on Cicero in formulating his classification of the cardinal virtues.[47] More generally, the Middle Ages witnessed the production of a substantial corpus of theological work that dealt with the relationship between the cardinal and theological virtues, the integration of new virtues that Aristotle had not considered (such as charity and forgiveness), the connection between sin and vice and the place of the human will in resisting vice and embracing virtue.[48]

As we move into the early modern period, Aquinas is the giant,[49] and he also wrote extensively about virtue and Christian theology. Fundamentally, Aquinas agrees with Aristotle on many issues. He believes, for example, that virtues are necessary to achieve happiness,[50] but, like Augustine, he makes it clear that we need God[51] to supernaturally transform our nature.[52]

We do well to study Aquinas carefully, for there were few theologians like him who systematically revisited Aristotelian virtue theory from a Christian point of view.[53] In the *Prima* and *Secunda Secundae* of his *Summa Theologiae*,

---

47. Although with some important distinctions, Abelard relies on Cicero's *De Inventionae* to classify and define prudence, courage, justice and temperance (Marenbon, *Philosophy of Peter Abelard*, 285).

48. Abelard, in *Dialogue Between a Philosopher, a Jew and a Christian*, takes Cicero's definition of the virtues and critiques it, mostly in terms of the omissions and incompleteness of the account both in terms of the conception of supreme good and the relationship of the human will to good and evil (MacIntyre, *After Virtue*, 168). The main point for Abelard is not good character but the "breaches of divine law and sin." Character may prompt towards either vice or virtue, but it is always the will that assents or dissents. The point is that the "true arena of morality is that of the will and of the will alone" (MacIntyre, 168). This stress on the will looks to certain NT texts and to Stoicism which claimed that ultimately only a will that bends itself to *arête* is unconditionally good. "Virtue is thus conformity to cosmic law both in internal disposition and in external act" (MacIntyre, 169).

49. Aquinas, significant as he may seem to us today, represented a marginal voice in his time as he merged Aristotelian philosophy and Christian theology. "There were many who were at odds with Aristotle, and Aquinas is the 'deviant, marginal medieval figure'" (MacIntyre, 178).

50. Aquinas's desire to address full moral development and human flourishing led him to address the virtues that order our lives to our highest or ultimate end, "the divine good" (Tjeltveit, "Foundations of Moral Selfhood," 73).

51. "Understanding the virtues requires understanding what is good, including the goodness of God. Further, our fullest development as human beings requires grace and a relationship with God" (Tjeltveit, 74).

52. "Aquinas argued that 'the ultimate human good or end is twofold (duplex), one achievable by the human beings' natural capacities, the other beyond the reach of these natural capacities, requiring the influx of divine grace' . . . this is in accordance with Aquinas's famous phrase 'Grace does not destroy but perfects nature'" (Tjeltveit, 73).

53. "[Aquinas] uses Aristotle's account of the virtues in a manner that essentially transforms the structure as well as the content of those virtues . . . for example . . . Aquinas' claim that charity is the form of all the virtues" (Hauerwas, "Difference of Virtue," 256).

he provides an important contribution to a theology of character and virtue (indeed, it might be said that virtue is one of the great topics of this famous work of theology). In addition to a general theology of goodness,[54] Aquinas reflects theologically on many topics that deal with virtue, including the pre-eminence of the cardinal virtues, the priority of the theological virtues,[55] the place of habituation, the classification of the virtues, the relationship of the virtues to spiritual gifts and a theology of the vices.[56]

To be fair, our fascination with Aquinas might lead to the conclusion that all the theologians of the time agreed on these issues. This is not so, and virtue was widely debated and considered from many different traditions and many different theological presuppositions.[57] As in other epochs, there were also those who dismissed the pagan heritage altogether.[58]

The Birth of the University

The last point in this chapter is wholly educational and relates to the birth of the university in the twelfth century. In this period, the world of scholarship began moving away from magisterial virtue in favour of textual knowledge,[59] and this marks the beginning of a dichotomy[60] between academic theology and spiritual formation.

---

54. Aquinas embeds his theory of human good in a general theory of goodness that is linked, in turn, to a theory of nature and of virtue (see Porter, *Recovery of Virtue*, 32).

55. Although necessary for human flourishing and maintaining their integrity, the natural virtues are elevated, perfected, by the greatest of theological virtues, charity (or love), which changes our will and "directs the other virtues, and prudence in particular, to the divine good" (Tjeltveit, "Foundations of Moral Selfhood," 74).

56. See Lagrange, "Reality." Aquinas also wrote an entire book *On Evil* (*Questiones de Malo*) with a complete treatment of capital vices.

57. Medieval thinking on the virtues was "varied and untidy" (MacIntyre, *After Virtue*, 166, 180).

58. MacIntyre, 167.

59. "Generally, education in the twelfth century schools moved the emphasis away from magisterial virtue to textual expertise" (Jaeger, *Paideia*, 130–131). This was the "new learning" (Ferzoco and Muessig, *Medieval Monastic Education*, 89). "The advent of the university in the 13th century is a critical turning point as training is detached from apprenticeship models and monasteries . . . Theology, for the first time, was practiced apart from ministry and divorced from affect and from that compelling correlate of affect, spirituality" (Neuhaus, *Theological Education*, 81).

60. "The invention of academic degrees created credentials that marked you as a professional by what you have achieved (not who you are) in a way that is measured and publicly recognized." "The development of the university marked the beginning of a dichotomy between theological formation and spiritual formation" (Neuhaus, 91).

In the early years of the university, however, the tradition of character and virtue was an important feature. Morality was the only criterion of admission[61] to early universities and the most frequent reason for failure.[62] The links to the church and its moral standards remained strong and all university students were clerics. The church was also the main employer of university graduates, and the *magistri* in the theology faculties belonged to either mendicant or Cistercian religious orders. They were called to be men of intellectual and moral authority,[63] above reproach, avoiding vices and practising all the Christian virtues, especially those that were fitting to their condition. Moral statutes were also generally in place and all universities aimed at decent behaviour among students (*honeste se gerrere*). Sadly, some of the literature that comes to us concerning the moral quality of medieval university students is not encouraging[64] and describes peaks of excesses of vice such as those of the goliards[65] described in Schmeller's *Carmina Burana*.[66] Despite all this, character education remained a central feature of the early universities for many years.

The Decline of Virtue

Around the sixteenth century, virtue began to be unfashionable in Western culture.[67] As I've mentioned, scholasticism likely contributed to this decline, and the attention of scholars gradually diverted from *sapientia* to *scientia*.[68] As the pursuit shifted from the knowledge of God and the formation of God's people to the cultivation of theology as a reasoned philosophical system, the place of virtue in theological studies became increasingly unclear. The Reformation can also be seen as having diminished the emphasis on virtues in Protestant

---

61. See Rüegg, *History of the University in Europe*, 171.

62. The *licentia docendi* was given only if "there was proof of the candidate's blameless mode of life and his progression through a proper course of studies" (Rüegg, 235).

63. "It is by his acts rather than his condition that a doctor earns his 'aureola'" (Henry of Ghent, 1277, in Rüegg, 163).

64. Cardinal Jacque de Vitry (1240) defined the University of Paris as an "international parliament of sin, a rendezvous for vice-ridden souls the world over" (Rüegg, 223).

65. Goliards were roaming satirical university students whose main companions were women, wine and gambling.

66. "I travel the broad path as is the way of youth, I give myself to vice, unmindful of virtue, I am eager for the pleasures of the flesh more than for salvation. My soul is dead, so I shall look after the flesh" (*Carmina Burana*, by Schmeller, 1847).

67. "The whole idea of virtue has been radically out of fashion in much Western Christianity ever since the sixteenth century Reformation. The very mention of virtue, in fact, will make many Christians stiffen in alarm" (Wright, *After You Believe*, 57).

68. Treier, *Virtue and the Voice of God*, 3.

circles, as the emphasis on faith and redemption easily misunderstood virtue education as salvation by works.[69] As Modernity was ushered in, Catholic moral theology also changed its focus, and the attention given to virtues was replaced by an interest in law, sin, conscience and penance.[70] The Enlightenment further excluded virtue as an orienting goal of theology as it praised objectivity and the critical principles of a scientific approach to knowledge. Although virtue remained a desirable outcome, it was methodologically unfit for the emerging paradigms of higher education.[71]

The decline of virtue was further impacted by changes in the broader culture. In particular, three great opinion-forming movements contributed to the weakening of the educational traditions that had been in place for centuries.[72] The first of these was the Romantic movement, which emphasized the importance of inner feeling; the second was the Existential movement, which pointed to individual freedom as the way to human fulfilment;[73] and the third was the Emotivist movement, which claimed that morality has to do with likes and dislikes. In different ways, these three movements diminished the strength of moral education, whether by removing reference to external virtue, by prioritizing new virtues such as liberty and autonomy, or by doubting the value of objective moral experiences.

The formidable combination of many factors thus marginalized character and virtue in Western culture and it is no surprise that it is no longer central in higher education and theological education today.

—

Let me end this letter where I began: with the *Veiled Christ* in Naples. There, in that quiet chapel, Christ lies at the centre, with the virtues standing around him. Just as Christ is caught in the moment of rising from the dead, I was reminded of the fact that the virtues come alive as Christ comes alive. But I also

---

69. "Reformers had replaced virtue-based orientation by an action based solely on faith as redemption" (Stückelberger, "Integrity," 315).

70. "Prominence of virtue receded, even if it did not completely disappear, in the late Middle Ages and modernity. In this period in Catholic moral theology, the Tridentine manuals of moral theology continued to pay some attention to the virtues, but their main focus was on law, sin, and conscience, all with an eye toward the sacrament of penance. With some few exceptions, by the Second Vatican Council there was little focus on virtue in Catholic moral theology, and in Western moral thought in general" (Cloutier and Mattison, "Resurgence of Virtue," 228).

71. Treier, *Virtue and the Voice of God*, 3.

72. Wright, *After You Believe*, 49–50.

73. "Freedom used to mean the power to do what I ought, now it means the right to do what I want" (Tenelshof, "Encouraging the Character Formation," 79).

considered that Christ lives as the virtues live in his church. The virtues live by Christ, and Christ lives through the virtues. All of the goodness of the world, all of the classical tradition of virtue, all of the educational visions of character and all of the efforts of human beings to be good and create just societies: all this comes to life, in a special way, when Christ lives in them.

Our vocation, as those representing the living Christ, is to bring the oxygen of *being* into the solid marble of *knowing* and the muscles of *doing*. Without virtuous works, our faith does not breathe. This is what the academy is about. It is a dream of a resurrection in and through theological education.

May we be the faithful, hopeful and loving channels of such life.

26

The American Case Study

What great news you've shared! It's encouraging to hear that a major donor has stepped forward to provide financial support for the academy. This comes on top of what each faith community has already pledged. This is indeed a relief at a time when so many projects in theological education struggle for funding (indeed, we must pray for the boards of foundations and trusts as they discern where their support should go). Although it is risky to rely on one major donor, you are not in a position to do otherwise, and it is good to share your joy.

Most of the historical research that I've shared so far is premodern, and you are right in asking for something a little more contemporary. I've decided that the best way to give you a sense of what happened with character and virtue education in modernity is to present a case study. I've chosen America, partly because it is well documented in the literature that I have been consulting and also because it illustrates a number of global developments. I will be interested to hear how this resonates in your own region.

For this letter, I unabashedly rely on one main source, which is *The Death of Character* by David Hunter. As he speaks generally about education and not specifically about theological education, I have complemented my study with other sources.[1]

Religious Piety

The American story of character and virtue education can be summarized in various phases.[2] A first phase was marked by strong links with religious piety. In this phase, which began in the early colonial period and ran into the middle

---

1. Neuhaus, *Theological Education*; and McClellan, *Moral Education in America*.
2. See parallels in UK education in Arthur, *Teaching Character and Virtue in Schools*, 22–23.

of the nineteenth century, piety and character appeared together in the general culture, in instructional literature to parents, in educational initiatives like the Sunday school movement (initiated to redeem street children from a life of vice), in the founding of common schools and in the written constitutions of several states. In this phase, America considered itself a Christian nation and its character was mostly derived from Puritan virtues.[3] Moral instruction tended to be prescriptive and directive and relied heavily on the tools of discipline, on the insistence on good habits, on self-restraint, on the force of shame and on the unquestioned authority of the educators.

Religion Meets Secularism

A second phase developed as the result of several changes. First, since the national culture had become saturated with evangelical piety, most Protestant families were happy to allow the state to educate their children, rather than families or the church. Second, psychological motifs began to influence the broader culture, and attitudes towards children began to soften. Themes such as innocence and permissiveness began to appear, together with the notion that education might rest on psychological foundations rather than on religious ones.[4] Third, as American society grew and became religiously pluralistic, the drive to separate church and state bore on the agenda of character education in public schools. Horace Mann, one of the most influential American educators in this period, contributed to this shift. While maintaining that moral education was a "primal necessity"[5] that was legitimately grounded in religious conception, Mann sought to eliminate sectarian representation from public schools, so that no particular religious persuasion was being favoured. As this trend developed, the bonds between character and religion were gradually loosened until, eventually, character was entirely related to general citizenship and detached from Christian discipleship. The motivation for character education also changed and, as the ideals of liberal individualism, classical republicanism and scientific progressivism replaced Christianity, the motivation for virtue shifted from the rewards in the afterlife to material gains in the present world.

---

3. As Benjamin Rush instituted the plan for education in Pennsylvania in 1776 he stated that "religion is the foundation of virtue; virtue is the foundation of liberty; liberty is the object of all republican governments; therefore, a republican education should promote religion as well as virtue and liberty" (Hunter, *Death of Character*, 41).

4. Hunter, 47.

5. Hunter, 49.

An interesting instance of these changes can be seen in the *McGuffrey Readers*, a series of textbooks that were a staple of the nineteenth-century school curricula. The first editions (1836) were clearly religious, sectarian and Calvinistic in both outlook and content. By the third edition (1879), the theistic outlook had completely disappeared, together with almost all references to the Bible and realization in the afterlife. The values and virtues in the Readers also changed in tone and content, moving away from the Protestant emphasis on piety and favouring the civic values of industry.[6]

Despite these shifts, character education remained strong in American culture. This can be seen both in the literature and in the rise of extra-scholastic organizations. Ralph Waldo Emerson's essay "Character" is a prominent example of a popular piece of literature that depicted character as "nature in the highest form."[7] Examples of character-building institutions can be found in the YMCA and in the Scouting movement, which were initially born out of preoccupation with moral degradation in youth and were rooted in Christian commitment. Even as the faith basis became less prominent, these organizations remained anchored in their commitment to character education, and used terminology like "character factory" in their literature.[8]

The Rejection of Religion

A third phase in the American story of character and virtue education came as a result of accommodating religious diversity and responding to the growing pressures of secularization. In this phase, character education became antagonistic towards religious grounding and claimed allegiance to reason and science alone. This was a remarkable shift. In a relatively short time, the foundations of character education in America moved from Puritan Calvinism, to a blend of Christian religiosity and civic morals, to the rejection of religion altogether.

This secularization phase is generally associated with Dewey and with the "progressive" schooling movement. Dewey famously argued that supernaturalism could not constitute the foundation for social progress or

---

6. In 1897 the statute of Washington state claimed: "It shall be the duty of all teachers to endeavour to impress on the minds of their pupils the principles of morality, truth, justice, temperance, humanity and patriotism; to teach them to avoid idleness, profanity and falsehood; to instruct them in the principles of free government; and to train them up to the true comprehension of the rights, duties and dignity of American citizenship" (Hunter, 48, 51).

7. Ralph Waldo Emerson, "Character," accessed 1 June 2018, https://www.emersoncentral.com/texts/essays-second-series/character/#.

8. Hunter, *Death of Character*, 58.

civilization. Concerning morality in particular, Dewey claimed that it could not be imposed or invoked from external "higher" (religious) sources, but that it had to be determined by each individual. Whereas Puritan Calvinism had emphasized the presence of a fallen, sinful nature that needed to be redeemed, tamed and indoctrinated through teaching and shame, Dewey claimed that children were innately capable of moral faculties. Moral authority was internal and needed to be determined individually, independently and subjectively, with the aid of reason and scientific advances. The process of establishing moral objectives was to be rationally thought out by the individual in light of his or her life experiences and social interaction. If there was anything that still counted in terms of character, it was its contribution to democracy.[9]

Personality and Psychology

This emphasis on individuality eventually led to a compulsive interest in personality, which ended up replacing character. Children needed to be developed in their potential as unique individual persons, and education was redesigned to meet their needs, stimulate their interests and cater to their capabilities. Students were regarded as innocent, vulnerable and malleable and were placed at the centre of the educational process. From this point on, the emphasis in moral instruction was to protect children and help them become responsible, rational human beings who could fully express their own personal freedom.[10] In the late 1900s, this shift was marked by the change in language from "virtues" to "values," and this was applied through "value clarification" programmes.

The rising influence of psychology in the mid-1950s took this phase further, and studies in the psychology of moral development emerged, like those of Piaget and Kohlberg. Notably, in this period, the source of authority for educational theory and practice shifted from philosophy to the field of psychology and, today, many important educational reformers are American psychologists.[11]

This influence from psychology contributed to associating bad behaviour with issues of insecurity, trauma and inferiority complexes, rather than to unbridled passions. Many began to consider vice not as a choice, but as a

---

9. What counted for Dewey was measured in terms of democracy, and schooling was not to be seen as a "factory of character" but as a "factory of democracy."

10. Hunter, *Death of Character*, 66.

11. For example, Bruner and Constructivist theories of learning, Kohlberg and moral development theories or Erickson and childhood stages of development.

justifiable reaction. The classical and religious virtues that were associated with moral character gradually gave way to a new vocabulary of psychological well-being, which included words like self-confidence, integration and social adjustment. Virtue was seen as an imposition tied to religious, ideological and cultural sectarianism, and educational methods shifted from the rigour of discipline and prescription to the kindness of guidance, protection and indulgence. Children were left to develop naturally to become good citizens and were supported therapeutically to take care of their emotional disorders. Generally speaking, words like "training" were replaced by a concern for individual happiness, wholeness and realization.

Overall, Hunter's study concludes that character education in America is "dead" due to the disappearance of the social and cultural milieu that had the power to sustain it.[12] In particular, Hunter laments the loss of the Greek, Hebrew and Christian traditions.[13] Although he may be overstating his claims,[14] his study presents a useful example of how some of the broad cultural shifts in modernity have impacted character education.[15]

Character and Theological Education in America

What about theological education? Although it is difficult to map the development of theological education within Hunter's three phases, we can see that liberal arts education[16] and theological education were not immune to these broader changes.

In the nineteenth and twentieth centuries, one of the main aims in Protestant seminaries was to produce Christian gentlemen. In this period, moral formation was integral to the aims of theological education. Moral requirements regulated access, informed discipline, gave rise to student societies, determined pledges to morality and led to the publication of popular

---

12. Glanzer, "Moral Education Establishment," 292.

13. "These communities framed the horizons of people's identity and aspiration and located them within a collective narrative" (Hunter, *Death of Character*, 22).

14. Glanzer, "Moral Education Establishment," 293–295.

15. Likewise, in the UK there was hardly any mention of character in government educational policy between 1950 and 2001. Arthur attributes this to a combination of the rise of cognitive psychology and Kohlberg's theories, Piaget and Erickson's theories of development and progress, pluralistic schools and sensitivity to diversity, the values clarification phenomenon and procedural neutrality in the classroom and prevailing moral relativism (Arthur, *Teaching Character and Virtue in Schools*, 24–25).

16. Koons, "Three Humanisms," 4.

guides on clerical manners.[17] Lectures in pastoral theology began in this period, focusing on the theories and practices of moral formation and featuring standard lists of character traits, virtues and vices.[18] Theological education included practical experiences that were designed to enhance students' capacity for moral judgment[19] and enculturation processes that were meant to teach basic manners to the lower classes.[20]

In the twentieth century, however, this began to change, and theological education generally embraced Schleiermacher's vision of professionalization that gave priority to academic achievement and ministry skills. As academic theology became a respectable university discipline, graduates were trained to provide specialized services and their careers were defined in terms of degrees and status. As this happened, seminaries began to shun prescriptive morality and the insistence on a devotional life. Narrow visions of "the good" were replaced by the abilities of critical religious insight[21] and pastoral theology emphasized ministry skills and practices rather than the cultivation of moral life. If you want to read more about these developments, May and Brown's *The Education of American Ministers* is probably one of the best sources.

After the two World Wars, the emphasis moved from the inculcation of gentleman-like qualities to the breeding of a sort of "muscular Christianity" that prized the virtues of vitality, courage and an entrepreneurial spirit. These were seen as particularly fitting for a new industrial economy and were quickly picked up as the qualities befitting Christian leaders.[22]

The American case study gives us a fairly generalizable example of how attitudes towards character and virtue education have changed in modernity. It also allows us to identify possible factors that are conditioning theological

---

17. Neuhaus, *Theological Education*, 58.

18. Cannon, Lectures on Pastoral Theology.

19. Neuhaus, *Theological Education*, 77.

20. "To serve the middle class churches, theology graduates had to be enculturated and taught etiquette, for example, not to spit, pare their fingernails, pick their teeth or comb their hair in public . . . Moral education and virtues were conflated with . . . a new set of manners so that graduates would never say or do anything which would be offensive to the best bred families in the congregation" (Neuhaus, 61).

21. Neuhaus, 76.

22. "Ministerial manliness, vitality, robustness and virtues such as freedom from fear, simplicity of character, courage of conviction, overcoming of timidity, capacity for self-denial . . . This echoed American culture that was discarding the 'feeble sentimentalities' of the early 19th century and embracing a post-war industrial economy that looked to power and industry barons, [and] growing admiration of sports heroes" (Neuhaus, 71). This was also happening in England where, in the 1820s, character education was seen as the way to elevate the middle class to have "noble character," to be "men of character," and more specifically, a Christian manly spirit (Arthur, *Teaching Character and Virtue in Schools*, 23).

education in our regions. Since many theological schools have been started by American missionaries, the American history may be of greater global relevance than we think. It would be interesting to discover what particular attitudes have been imported into which parts of the world from the historical phases we have seen. I know that some of the schools I have visited have preserved Puritan attitudes and are still very prescriptive in linking morality to religious education. In my region, as you know, there has been very little direct influence from American missionaries, but theological schools that have embraced a secular attitude towards character issues are very similar to their American counterparts. What about your region?

—

In my narrative I have tried to stay away from evaluation. Each phase has had some good things and some bad things, and we need to work from where we are. In re-reading this letter, I realize I may have come down harshly on the therapeutic and human counselling movement. I apologise for that. I was trying to understand how the focus on psychological issues might have contributed to eroding a certain kind of character education; I was not wanting to decry the movement itself. Psychology has done untold good to many people and corrected many errors. Healthy self-esteem and the ability for introspection are virtues in their own right, and we should applaud them wherever they are cultivated.

May we discern the works of mercy that will heal the ailments of our generation.

27

Historical Fragments

It is summertime again, and I am glad to hear that you are taking an extended leave in the coolness of your beautiful mountains. I am also preparing for a break, but I would first like to complete my last two historical letters. I have written about ancient cultures, the classical era, early Christianity, the Middle Ages and American modernity, but I still have a vast collection of scattered notes that span different epochs, countries and sources. I also have notes about movements like humanism, some observations related to the birth of the modern university and some remarkable facts concerning a few key authors from the history of thought. I think that some of these fragments may be useful to you, so I will simply share my notes without trying to string them together into a narrative. I trust that this cacophony of sounds will contribute to you sensing the pervasiveness of our topic.

The Humanists

The humanist movements deserve special mention when we speak of character and virtue education. These movements have come in waves at different times in history, but they have all reaffirmed the models of moral education found in Augustine, Cicero, Aristotle and Jerome and have pointed to the importance of moral education for social responsibility.[1] Petrarch was one of the earliest humanists who wrote significantly on character and virtue. He walked in the path of Socrates and Cicero and indicated that education should aim at creating the *vir bonus* (the good man) as the most useful thing for society.[2] Likewise,

---

1. "The acquisition of a moral education by the *studia humanitatis* enabled one to act responsibly as a member of one's family and one's society" (Rüegg, *History of the University in Europe*, 446 and 449).

2. "The humanities as a whole aim at creating a good man (*vir bonus*), than which nothing more useful (*utilius*) can be imagined" (Proctor, *Defining the Humanities*, 3).

Erasmus, seeing the moral corruptness of the papacy, the hypocrisy of vices that masqueraded as virtues and the powerless piety of religious ceremonies, endeavoured to revive Christian virtue as the means to transform both mind and character.[3]

In the sixteenth century, one of the figures who stands out is Comenius. He has been considered the father of modern education and proclaimed the "teacher of nations." Comenius believed that man was not just a *res cogitans* but a moral entity that has succumbed to evil and vice. On these grounds, he set forth a triple goal for education: true knowledge, true moral integrity and true piety.[4] Perfection, according to Comenius, could be achieved through education and would lead to a world full of light and order characterized by human brotherhood, religious tolerance and peace. In chapter 23 of his *Didactics*, he places moral education at the pinnacle of his pedagogical work and makes it clear that everything that he has written previously is leading to this point.[5] In agreement with the classical tradition, Comenius claims that if education is not held together by morality, it is "miserable," dangerous and incomplete.[6]

It may seem odd to include Rousseau in this list of positive examples, for he ferociously opposed both the practices of habituation and the Christian vision of fallen nature. While dissenting from Rousseau's methods, anthropology[7] and epistemology,[8] however, we share his overall conviction that education is linked to morality. Rousseau wanted his Emile to be preserved from vice,

---

3. Sheldrake, *Brief History*, 109; and Herdt, "Virtue's Semblance," 141.

4. Sheldrake, *Brief History*, 92. For Comenius, moral education and religious piety were intimately connected.

5. Habl, "Character Formation," 142–144.

6. "A person who is well informed but not morally formed is merely a "useless encumbrance on the earth," according to Comenius, even a 'misery' – to oneself as well as to others. For the greater the knowledge, the worse it is when it is used for evil. Therefore, Comenius contended that an educated but immoral humanity goes backward rather than forward, degenerating" (Habl, 147).

7. "Rousseau denies that children are born wayward (originally sinful), insisting that children are, by nature, noble, virtuous beings who are corrupted by intrusive socialization. The untutored child is spontaneously good and graceful "(Sommers and Sommers, *Vice and Virtue*, 499).

8. In Rousseau we see the catastrophic removal of virtue from the realm of facts and into the realm of values. The extent of Rousseau's influence should evoke, according to Lemaitre, "sacred horror" (Koons, "Three Humanisms," 201).

and his final vision of the perfectly educated child is one of goodness, nobility and virtue.[9]

A second and third wave of humanists was seen in the nineteenth and twentieth centuries and produced scholars like Newman, Arnold, Hutchins, Adler and Bloom. Although each of them wrote in different places and in different historical circumstances, they were equally concerned that education should include holistic shepherding of human beings and not just transmission of knowledge. Bloom, for example, called for a return to eternal values,[10] and Arnold indicated that the pursuit of true judgment is one of the primary purposes of the university.[11] Cardinal Newman's landmark *Idea of the University* claimed that the formation of students was more important than the cultivation of studies,[12] and we are indebted to him for a renewed vision of intellectual virtue in the university under the label of "enlargement."[13] Newman also prioritized the formation of noble gentlemen who would steer society away from the miserable deformities of bad morals.[14]

Irving Babbitt was an interesting twentieth-century humanist. His debates with Charles Eliot at Harvard University place conversations on character education within the broader debates of the humanities and the technical/scientific disciplines. Babbitt argued for a return to "humanistic" education against what he saw as the disastrous threat of "humanitarian" education. He believed that humanitarian education had overreacted to Puritan dogmas and was guilty of throwing off all restraints, telling students that they were free, indicating individual interest as supreme[15] and implying that what really mattered was only encyclopaedic knowledge.[16] By contrast, Babbitt argued for

---

9. Rousseau wrote that "the first education should be purely negative ... it consists not in teaching virtue or truth, but in preserving the heart from vice and the mind from error" (Sommers and Sommers, *Vice and Virtue*, 499).

10. Bloom, *Closing of the American Mind*.

11. Arnold, *Culture and Anarchy*.

12. Carr, *Educating the Virtues*, 120.

13. Newman proposed that the university should habituate students in the virtues of breadth of mind, perception of context, clarity of thought, fair-mindedness, intellectual equity, rigour and, most importantly, judgment (Kelsey, *Between Athens and Berlin*, 34).

14. Newman, *Idea of a University*, 105.

15. In *Literature and the American College*, Babbitt ironically comments, "The wisdom of all the ages is to be naught compared with the inclination of a sophomore. Any check that is put on this inclination is an unjustifiable constraint, not to say an intolerable tyranny" (Smilie, "Humanitarianism and Humanistic Ideals," 69).

16. "We see the appearance of a *libido sciendi*, an unbridled lust for encyclopaedic knowledge, in place of the classical quest for *sophia* – wisdom – conceived of as a finite, balanced, integrated and harmonious whole, attainable by individual human beings in each generation" (Babbitt, in Koons, "Three Humanisms," 201).

a return to Greek and Roman classics that would provide restraint, balance and an appropriate shape to students' character. In short, Babbitt believed that the classics had the power to model behaviour and provide norms that would develop students' character and help them flourish.[17] More recent work in humanistic education remains faithful to this holistic vision and looks to the formation of character for moral education, values education and conflict resolution.[18]

There is both fresh and foul air[19] in humanism, and we must think critically and theologically about it. One of the things that we appreciate is the recovery of a holistic vision that gives the virtues a central place in what it means to be deeply human. What we should be critical of is the notion that human beings are innately good and able to fulfil their destiny entirely through philosophy and education. We must take care as we listen to the siren calls of humanism and tie ourselves firmly to the mast of theology.[20] Our Christian anthropology includes the fall, which means that the humanistic vision cannot be fulfilled without the grace of God. Karl Barth warned against those who were optimistically wanting to establish a new Enlightenment humanism after the terrible wars in Europe. He claimed that what was needed was not a new humanism, but a Christocentric humanism of God.[21] Stanley Hauerwas, similarly, refers to a Christocentrically determined humanism that is possible only in Christ.[22]

---

17. For Babbitt, students who meditated upon and contemplated the classics in their education would be much better equipped to develop character, as they would be much better trained in controlling their expansive tendencies (Smilie, "Humanitarianism and Humanistic Ideals," 75).

18. According to the Association for Humanistic Education and Development, humanistic education and character education show several commonalities (Robinson et al., "Humanistic Education," 5).

19. This metaphor is borrowed from Barth: "The outside winds brought not merely fresh air, but notoriously foul air. This meant that errors blew in, were admitted, and made themselves at home." Barth, *Humanity of God*, 19.

20. Reference to Odysseus in Homer, *Odyssey*, Book 12.

21. Barth, "New Humanism," 157–166.

22. "Christ has made us more than we otherwise could imagine by calling us to be a follower. That turns out to be the most determinative formation we could have to be human. And part of what that entails is as Christians we're not called to be more than human. We're called to be human. And that's a modest and realizable way of life" (S. Hauerwas, in Derek Witten, "Interview with Stanley Hauerwas Sets Stage for Laing Lectures," 15 March 2018, Church for Vancouver, accessed 13 February 2019, https://churchforvancouver.ca/interview-with-stanley-hauerwas-sets-stage-for-laing-lectures/).

The University of Berlin

Leaving the trail of humanistic thinkers, let me talk briefly about what happened in the nineteenth century in the University of Berlin. This, in many ways, became the blueprint of modern higher education in many parts of the world, and understanding the University of Berlin helps us understand where we are now in terms of character and virtue education in the university. Despite other areas of discontinuity between the medieval universities and the modern university, character education remained central in von Humboldt's conception. For him, the university was the institution that stood between the state and the individual and whose existence was justified in preparing men and women of character who could empower a state of reason.[23] The central notion in the design of the University of Berlin was that culture featured a two-armed prong: *Wissenschaft*, the unity of all knowledge through scientific-philosophical study, and *Bildung*, the cultivation of character. The first was developed in the university through research and the latter was developed through teaching.

It must be noted, however, that in *Bildung*, teaching for character focused mostly on the process of knowledge acquisition. As was the case with Newman, character building in *Bildung* had to do with the cultivation of intellectual virtues through which man could resist the brutish fragmentation of knowledge.[24] It did not really have to do with the development of moral and public virtues as was the case in the classical tradition. The new university thus built intellectual character and left the formation of moral character to others. Immanuel Kant can be quoted here as one who retained the centrality of moral education[25] but marginalized it to the realm of extra-curricular activities. In *The Conflict of the Faculties* he discards personal formation as one of the core tasks of the university and outsources it to supporting structures. In Kant's notion of education that would serve society (the higher faculties of theology, law and medicine) and pursue knowledge (the lower faculty of philosophy), the place of character formation was somehow lost. I think that we can see this in many theological schools today, where the intellectual virtues are evident in the programme learning outcomes and the moral and public virtues are relegated to the extra-curricular domain.

---

23. Readings, *University in Ruins*, 64, 67.

24. Readings, 66.

25. Character education, broadly conceived, was central to Kant's goals in moral education because he saw that happiness is found in the dignity of performing duty. "Morality is a matter of character" which consists in "the firm purpose to accomplish something and then also in the actual accomplishing of it" (Wolterstorff, *Educating for Shalom*, loc. 2094).

A Final Collection of Thinkers

I conclude this letter with a bullet list of "authors to follow up." They are in no particular order.

- Thomas à Kempis and the Brethren of the Common Life were known for linking education and devotion. Thomas wrote extensively on virtue in the *Imitation of Christ*, claiming that knowledge should be not only intellectual but also affective, and that our character should be shaped after the character of God.[26]
- Philip Melanchthon was one of the main educational figures in the Protestant Reformation, and he claimed that the purpose of education was to help students know Christ better. "He believed that all levels of education should not only study the subject matter at hand but also create virtue and lead students to live out their faith more fully."[27]
- The Jesuit Society of Jesus produced the *Ratio studiorum* in 1599 and set out a comprehensive plan for education that deeply influenced centuries of Catholic education worldwide. The *Ratio* claims that the purpose of education is not just to inform, but also to produce coherent character and deep spirituality.[28]
- Jacob Spener was instrumental at the beginning of the Pietistic movement. In the *Pia Desideria* he considers Scripture to be a guide to our lives and not just a source of answers. He claims that knowledge must be worked out in our experience of Christian charity. He explicitly proposes that universities and schools should be reformed to not only *inform* but also *form*. Ministry candidates, in particular, need to be exemplary, and mentored by professors who "show them, and don't just tell them."[29]

---

26. "What avails it to a man to reason about the high, secret mysteries of the Trinity if he lack humility and so displeases the Holy Spirit?"; "My son, says our Lord, do not let fair and subtle words move you, for the kingdom of heaven does not stand in words, but in good, virtuous works" (Sheldrake, *Brief History*, 65, 66).

27. Sheldrake, 72.

28. "The purpose of education was not only to impart information but also to lead the students to *eloquentia perfecta* – an eloquence requiring . . . a character that is consonant with what has been said and taught and grounded in a profound spirituality. It is for this reason that all Catholic theological education . . . sets 'formation' as a goal parallel to instruction" (Sheldrake, 84).

29. Sheldrake, 96.

- David Hume was a key figure in the eighteenth-century Enlightenment experiments around character education.[30] He openly embraced the ancient ethics of Aristotle, dividing virtues into artificial and natural virtues, and giving reason and passion an equal voice in identifying virtue.[31]
- John Locke can be associated with character education in British Empiricism.[32] He claimed that the most important goal of education was to create a virtuous man.[33] In his highly influential *Some Thoughts Concerning Education*[34] he claimed that there are three educational methods: educating the body, academic teaching and education in virtue and reason.[35] The last constitutes the most substantial part of his work, and he defines the Principle of Virtue as combining self-denial and rationality.[36]
- The Victorian age placed a high premium on character education, at least in terms of the language of character and virtue and of the focus on developing the right kind of character for given social

---

30. "The Scotsmen James Barclay and David Fordyce respectively drew attention to the importance of example, and the role of the imagination in character education. Frances Hutcheson urged an objective study of human nature while John Locke underscored the importance of character formation over intellectual achievement, a distinction neither Aristotle nor Aquinas would have understood. David Hume and Jeremy Bentham were among many during this period who sought to sever the relationship between 'value-laden' religion and 'knowledge-based' education, including character education" (Arthur et al., *Character Education*, 5).

31. "Hume seems to accord them a role that is reminiscent of the Aristotelian view that virtue is a state in which reason and passion speak with the same voice" (Marcia, "Moral Character").

32. Wren, "Philosophical Moorings," 18–20.

33. "Given that Locke is one of the great minds of the last few centuries, we might expect him to put a high value on intellectual development. Actually, though, the strongest message of *Some Thoughts* is exactly the opposite: a child's bodily health and the soundness of his character are far more important, in Locke's view, than the state of his intellect. The primary goal of Locke's education plan is to create a virtuous, well-bred, and wise young man, and not to create a scholar." (Summary: *Some Thoughts Concerning Education* by John Locke, Spark Notes, http://www.sparknotes.com/philosophy/lockethoughts/summary/).

34. *Some Thoughts Concerning Education* (1693) is likely the most important work on education in England of the eighteenth century, having been translated into most European languages, published in fifty-three editions and acknowledged by almost every other writer on education after Locke. This is perhaps Locke's most influential book, and his ideas can be found in Pestalozzi and Montessori. We can safely claim that Locke's work "occupies a canonical place . . . in the history of educational theory" (Tarcov, *Locke's Education*, 1).

35. Locke insists that habits of children be nurtured along the virtues of piety, loyalty, industry and temperance (Hunter, *Death of Character*, 32).

36. "And the great Principle and Foundation of all Virtue and Worth is placed in this, that man is able to deny himself his own desires, cross his own inclinations, and purely follow what reason directs as best, tho' the appetite lean the other way" (Locke, *Some Thoughts*, 33).

roles. This epoch has both light and shadows,[37] and the literature of Jane Austin, although slightly antecedent to this era, stands out as a sparkling example of the struggle of the will to govern good character, emulate virtue and avoid vice.

- Karl Marx considered character education to be a means to resist the capitalist vices of cowardice, intemperance and lack of generosity. For him, a new set of virtues was necessary to transform society through work arrangements. This new social economic community, according to Marx, was naturally congenial to human beings, allowing them to prosper through the virtues of truthfulness and generosity,[38] and leading to happiness and self-esteem. His approach to ethics was distinctly Aristotelian.
- J. S. Mill, known for his contribution to liberal theory and utilitarian ethics, drew on Aristotle to claim a special type of political community for human flourishing. This community was one that cultivated equality and allowed individuals to express deliberative power in order to live virtuous lives.
- For John Dewey and Emile Durkheim, the purpose of education was to transmit cultural continuity and resist the forces of social fragmentation.[39] For them, moral education was urgently needed to keep culture cohesive and maintain a healthy society. Although we may disagree with them on several other fronts,[40] we applaud the vision of the teacher as the interpreter of the great moral ideas of our times.[41]

---

37. In the Victorian age, "the production of persons suited to the needs of work was the dominant purpose of elementary education. Teachers inculcated social roles by requiring obedience without question and punishing deviant behaviour . . . In contrast, amongst the growing middle class there was a marked interest in character formation for the roles their children would inherit. Strong characters were required to support the principled stand they would need to take in favour of the established virtues of society, such as bravery, loyalty, diligence, application and manners" (Arthur et al., *Character Education*, 6).

38. Marcia, "Moral Character."

39. As Dewey and Durkheim observed the negative impact of cultural pluralism, radical individualism and occupational specialization on both American and French societies, they claimed that socialization needed to include a common moral agenda as the best hope for social cohesion (Dill, "Challenge of Contemporary Moral Education," 222–223).

40. Both Durkheim and Dewey were bent on stripping moral education from its relationship with religion and on embedding it rationally either in society or in individual and democratic experiences. In *Moral Education*, Durkheim claims, "In a word, we must discover the rational substitutes for those religious notions that for a long time have served as the vehicle for the most essential moral ideas" (Dill, 225).

41. Dill, 230.

Let me conclude this list with special mention of Stanley Hauerwas who, together with Alasdair MacIntyre, has made the deepest impact in recent scholarship on the subject of virtue.[42] Stanley Hauerwas is no doubt one of the most prolific theologians writing about moral ethics and he has influenced Protestants and Catholics alike.[43] I had considered writing an entire letter just dealing with the evolution of Hauerwas's thinking on the subject, but that might have been too much detail.[44]

Hauerwas's thinking is rich and original, and he stands at a critical distance from virtue ethics, proposing a distinctively Christian approach to virtue.[45] We are indebted to him for many reasons: for his endeavour to connect discourse on the virtues within a broader context of theological reflection; for his making virtue a contemporary discourse while maintaining a critical distance from modern moral paradigms; for his articulation of a robust Christian theological ethic; for his ability to focus the debate on Christian formation; for his originality in linking virtues to liturgical theology; for his renewed emphasis on the role of Christian community; and for his efforts to assimilate virtue language with the languages of justification and sanctification.[46] In addition to all this, Hauerwas's inimitable style and wit have generated renewed attention to topics that might otherwise have remained dry and unengaging.

I will stop here. Surely all these names are more than sufficient to give you a headache and will induce you to leave early for your vacation! The big picture is remarkable. Character and virtue education is everywhere. It has been around for centuries, shaping individuals, societies and cultures. It has occupied some of the greatest minds. It has determined prosperity and decline. It has caused wars and stopped them. It has been the backbone of religion and of secularism alike. In higher education it has been moved around from the centre to the periphery and now perhaps back again.

---

42. Other Protestant ethicists contributing to the resurgence of the theme of character include H. Richard Niebuhr, James Gustafson, James Laney and James Wells (Arthur, *Education with Character*, 47). Catholic moral theologians dealing with virtue include Timothy O'Connel, John Finnis (Cloutier and Mattison, "Resurgence of Virtue," 229) and Jacques Maritain (Arthur, 51).

43. "Perhaps it is ironic that a Protestant . . . would play such an important role in reviving this quintessentially Catholic way of thinking" (Cloutier and Mattison, "Resurgence of Virtue," 232).

44. For a summary, see Herdt, "Hauerwas among the Virtues."

45. "[Hauerwas's] theological objection to virtue ethics responds to a . . . danger, namely that reflection on the virtues . . . could assume a kind of primacy over concrete Christian faith and praxis, such that a formal particularism would displace substantive theological categories" (Herdt, 213).

46. Herdt, 223.

All this is to say that the academy is not reinventing the wheel. We are the bearers of an honoured tradition.

—

I finish this letter with a confession. My presence in Rome last spring was motivated by more than attending a conference. I was interviewed for a job and shortlisted. Last week I received a letter offering me a position in an international consortium operating under the auspices of UNESCO. They want me to direct a global programme in character and virtue education. It is a very well-paid position with remarkable opportunities. But it comes with an extensive travel schedule and the requirement to leave all my current positions and commitments. This would include my university professorship, my consultancy commitments and our correspondence. If I were to accept, the position begins this autumn, and this would be one of my final letters. I am uncertain what to do.

I confess my strain in discerning the greater good at this crossroads. May you stand with me as a friend in our commitment to what is good.

28

Virtue after Postmodernity

I cannot thank you enough for your solidarity in my conundrum. You have demonstrated altruistic character in not thinking about yourself and you've helped me reflect on what is best for me. Although you may be disappointed and even worried about losing my support, you have not let that weigh with you. I have not yet decided about the new job and your prayers are still needed.

This is my last letter on the historical analysis of the tradition of character and virtue education. I thought it would be fitting to focus on the current state of higher education in postmodernity. As you know, I've published in this area,[1] and in this letter I will again turn to one of my favourite authors, the late sociologist Zygmunt Bauman. I would like to employ three of his metaphors[2] to briefly rehearse where higher education is in postmodernity as it relates to character and virtue education. I will then conclude with a fourth metaphor of my own for where we might be headed *after* postmodernity.

Premodernity and the Gamekeeper

Bauman's metaphor of the *gamekeeper* is an image of premodernity. In chronological order, this first metaphor describes the classical era and the Middle Ages. Here is what Bauman says:

> The main task of a gamekeeper is to defend the land assigned to his wardenship from human interference, in order to defend and preserve, so to speak, its "natural balance"; the gamekeeper's task is to promptly discover and disable the snares set by poachers and to keep alien, illegitimate hunters away from trespassing. His services rest on the belief that things are at their best when not tinkered

---

1. Oxenham, *Liquid Modernity*.
2. Bauman, "Living in Utopia."

with; that the world is a divine chain of being in which every creature has its rightful and useful place, even if human mental abilities are too limited to comprehend the wisdom, harmony and orderliness of God's design.[3]

The gamekeeper is one who believes in a world of pre-established wholeness. The land and the forest existed before he inhabited them and will continue to exist in much the same way after he leaves them. The gamekeeper believes in the stability of the world and does his best to understand it. He lives in his habitat with respect and educates the next generation in harmony with the existing realities. Education takes place as a fundamentally conservative task that seeks to understand what is good, preserve it and revive what has been hidden or marred. Gamekeepers educate within a "big story" that provides direction and boundaries.

Character education for the gamekeeper means alignment with a framework of universal virtues. Human flourishing means understanding and living in accordance with truth and virtue, in harmony with how things are and how they will always be. To be happy is to seek virtue as that which fits one's true nature and purpose.

We have seen many gamekeepers in our historical cavalcade, beginning with ancient cultures and carrying through the classical era, Christian theology and medieval culture.

Modernity and the Gardener

As the Enlightenment replaced God and ideals with human reason and autonomy, the gamekeeper metaphor becomes inadequate. Bauman describes the metaphor of modernity as the *gardener*:

> [The gardener] assumes that there would be no order in the world at all, were it not for his constant attention and effort. The gardener knows better what kind of plants should, and what sort of plants should not grow on the plot under his care. He first works out the desirable arrangement first in his head, and then sees to it that this image is engraved on the plot. He forces his preconceived design upon the plot by encouraging the growth of the right types of plants and uprooting and destroying all other

---

3. Bauman, 4.

plants (now re-named "weeds"), whose uninvited and unwanted presence disagrees with the overall harmony of the design.[4]

What we see in the gardener metaphor is a utopia that is determined by human reason. The gardener expresses the human effort to plot out the perfect garden, create the perfect society, engineer the perfect industry, reason to find the perfect political arrangement and educate to nourish the perfect character. Modernity was the time of great discoveries, great conquests and great ideologies. It was the time when mankind set out to dominate the planet, fix broken economic systems, mend the psyche, unearth and control the secrets of nature and set up perfect political systems that would guarantee peace and prosperity to all.

Education for gardeners is about the enhancement of reason and the progress of science in service of society. In modernity, the university becomes the new temple of worship that achieves the utopia. Good character is seen as part of this utopia. The intellectual virtues are considered to be necessary expressions of reason and need careful nourishment. Moral and social virtues are likewise seen as instruments of democracy and, as such, are to be efficiently pursued.

Sadly, modernity and the project of the gardeners did not work out as anticipated. The utopias fell. Two great wars ensued. Terrible genocides were committed. Atomic weapons were invented. Great political systems crumbled. Science polluted the planet and humans fell to their psychological fragilities. Education was also abused. It was used by totalitarian regimes for indoctrination. It became a carrier of cultural exclusivity and colonialism. It undervalued man's existential dimension. It became abstract and irrelevant. It became a tool of power in the hand of the elite[5] and it used the rhetoric of virtue to socialize into conformity, silence differences and homologize human disparity.

The arrogance of modernity made it fragile, and, as rational metanarratives began to crumble, a new form of modesty began to grow. Waves of uncertainty began to flow through culture and a time of general deconstruction followed.

---

4. Bauman, 4.

5. Titanic-like arrogance was "triumphalist, self-congratulating, blind, hypocritical" (Bauman, 12).

Postmodernity and the Hunter

The metaphor for postmodernity (or, as Bauman would prefer, *liquid modernity*) is that of the *hunter*:

> Unlike the two types that happened to prevail before his tenure started, the hunter could not care less about the overall "balance of things" – whether "natural," or designed and contrived. The sole task hunters pursue is another "kill," big enough to fill their game-bags to capacity. Most certainly, they would not consider it to be their duty to make sure that the supply of game roaming in the forest will be replenished after the hunt. If the woods have been emptied of game due to the particularly successful hunt, hunters may move to another relatively unspoiled wilderness, still teeming with would-be hunting trophies. It may occur to them that sometime, in a distant and still undefined future, the planet could run out of un-depleted forests. This is not, however, an immediate worry and certainly not their worry; it won't jeopardize the results of the present hunt, and so surely this is not a prospect which a single hunter or a single hunting association would feel obliged to ponder, let alone do something about.[6]

For the hunter, flourishing is surviving the present. She has no use for the gamekeeper's ideals and no interest in the gardener's utopias. Both have failed. The world has become a small place, where she is at the centre and where her individual needs are all that matters. What counts is having a bag full of hunting trophies, a fire for the night and reduced gear to allow swift movement and adaptation to change.

The world of the hunter is a dystopia in continual change, and nothing is predictable. Survival competences are the only things that are really necessary. In this new world, education is not about discovery, preservation or rational creation, but about dismantling old knowledge and pursuing temporary, tentative and unarranged bits of knowledge and helpful competences. Education is "the un-authoritative activity of learners that, lacking cultural purpose and rational framework, operates outside the bounds of structure in the service of the market."[7]

For the hunter, the relationship with character and virtue education is an uneasy one. On the one hand, she is wary of schemas that might bind her

---

6. Bauman, 5.
7. Oxenham, *Liquid Modernity*, 40.

liberty. On the other hand, she realizes that good character helps one to survive. As the world is continually changing, personal identity is in continual crisis, and virtue and character appear as powerful tools to achieve self-identity and self-realization. The hunter finds inspiration in virtues that may shape her identity, even if only temporarily. She may be inspired by a hero for a while, then perhaps by a movie, a good book, a religion or a new social movement. But it is a temporary identity, and she will readily discard it and move on once it becomes tiresome and binding.

Virtue for the postmodern hunter is chameleonic and she is usually fascinated by one virtue at a time, consuming it for her momentary identity and then discarding it. This makes it very difficult to conceive of the stable dispositions that characterize virtuous character. Constancy does not sit well with the hunter, for hers is a time of many swallows and little spring.

The Infernos of Postmodern Education

I've written an extensive critique of education in postmodernity elsewhere, but I do want to rehearse some of the infernos that you will have to deal with in thinking of character and virtue education in a world of hunters.

The first is the inability to sustain value judgments. Briefly put, in welcoming paradox and absurdity, postmodernity drains the meaning out of life. If everything is equally allowed, then everything has the same meaning, and nothing has any particular meaning. If you can't make mistakes, you also cannot do anything "right," in the strict sense of the word. This goes further than what Weber and Nietzsche did in substituting the language of right and wrong for the language of values, for it abolishes values themselves. When the value of value itself is called into question, then everything is potentially worthless. This situation is devastating for both education and society, and this may be one of the reasons why character education is returning in vogue.

A second inferno in the age of hunters is the lack of motivation. Once learning has become open, self-gratifying and temporary, there is no drive for achievement because there is no finish line to look forward to. Instantaneity, remarks Bauman, breeds inconsequentiality. When we have everything immediately, the level of our interest and motivation fades.[8] If education serves only the momentary satisfaction of desire, these desires will eventually fade through the law of diminishing returns. Character and virtue education can be leveraged as a relief to this inferno, because it provides a slow, constant walk in

---

8. Bauman, *Liquid Modernity*, 118; Oxenham, *Higher Education in Liquid Modernity*, 161.

a worthwhile direction. As character is developed it can defeat acedia, futility and Baudelaire's boredom. Students can find in virtue and character education a project that will provide a lifetime of motivation.

Identity is the final inferno that I'd like to mention.[9] The postmodern commitment to freedom and change makes it difficult to shape social identity. Postmodernity is a night where all cats are grey.[10] It is a night of liberal hunting that is unable to sustain identity. Character and virtue education stands up to say that freedom is not the highest value and that human flourishing requires a richer bouquet of virtues.

After Postmodernity: The Sophisticated Sage

That was a brief rehearsal of the narrative of character and virtue education through the metaphors of the gamekeeper, the gardener and the hunter.[11] But where do we go next? Since the hunter metaphor of postmodernity has so many weaknesses, what might a metaphor for *after* postmodernity look like? I've thought long and hard about this and have come up with several options. I think the metaphor that works best is that of the *sophisticated sage*. Let me explain the two parts of the metaphor.

The *sage* aspect of the metaphor captures the post-postmodern tendency to look back to the past. The sage has felt the bite of rootless autonomy and the uncertainties of future change. The sage is looking for roots and for a tradition. Attachment to that which is ancient seems to ease the unbearable lightness of freedom. That which is old provides a sense of solidity that is desperately needed. The sage thus puts antique flesh on the thin bones of individualism, makes value judgments from consolidated wisdom, finds motivation in unearthing and rediscovering deep traditions and shapes his identity around inspirational heroes of the past. We can see this in the renewed fascination with ancient authors and philosophers, the revival of the classics and reception

---

9. Other infernos relate to the emptying of the cultural agora, the indeterminacy of happiness or the anxieties that are produced by the pressures of postmodern education to stay ahead of the game (Oxenham, 160–184).

10. Jaeger, *Paideia*, xxv.

11. Other metaphors are possible. Walker, for example, speaks of the *sinful pupil* characterized by religious stewardship, the *good pupil* as seen by Rousseau, the *polite pupil* of class-based legitimation, the *morally adjusted pupil* of the early twentieth century, the *cognitively developing pupil* of the late twentieth century, the *emotionally vulnerable pupil* of the early twenty-first century, and finally the *flourishing pupil* which is feeding the rise of virtue ethics, the renaissance of Aristotelianism and the positive-psychology movement (Walker et al., *Towards a New Era*, 82–86).

studies, the rediscovery of ancestral communitarian politics, the search for hereditary roots, the fashionable pilgrimages along ancient routes and – why not? – the revival of Aristotle in education.

The sage metaphor is seen in spiritual and religious trends as well, and many of our Christian friends are looking to the past to shape their faith identity. Many of the younger generation are turning to ancient liturgies, exploring radical orthodoxy, reviving the practices of the desert fathers, rediscovering medieval mysticism and spiritual direction and seeking to integrate their faith with traditional, local spiritualities. The sage metaphor also captures the renewed discourse on the nature of theology itself as *sapientia* rather than *scientia* which sees theology as the cultivation of wisdom rather than as the accumulation of critical knowledge. As postmodernism has eroded confidence in reason, sapiential theology[12] can be seen as "the development of *phronesis* in Christian *paideia*."[13]

The second part of my sophisticated sage metaphor has to do with being *sophisticated*. This is an important qualifier for, without it, all we have is a reloaded version of the gamekeeper. Sophistication means that the sage is selective. He does not feel, in fact, obliged to accept all the ancient menus of wisdom, but acts as a detached customer who is free to come, to go and to complain about the food. There is something of the hunter metaphor that lingers on and, whereas ancient traditions are consumed to ease his sense of rootlessness, they have no real "staying" power over him. Wisdom is taken in sporadic morsels and kept faded, undogmatic and shrouded in mystery. It will feed him but will not bind him. The sophisticated sage is, in many ways, still a child of postmodernism who does not want to be framed into any one particular way of life or tamed by a prescribed set of virtues. He holds tightly to freedom, shuns idealism, despises dogmatism, runs from worldviews and does not renounce individualism. The main difference from the hunter is that his identity survives through ancient wisdom rather than through temporary skills.

So where does that put us with character and virtue education? On the one hand, character and virtue education ticks many of the boxes for the sophisticated sage. It is ancient, it cultivates human flourishing, it is not necessarily religiously committed, it keeps definitions blunt, it allows for differences in the exercise of wisdom, it is found in many local traditions and it allows for the construction of a dignified identity. On the other hand, the

---

12. "The recovery of sapiential theology seems tied to a form of *paideia* in which communities of the virtuous are formed, as they envision responding to God's communicative action" (Treier, *Virtue and the Voice of God*, 28).

13. Treier, 30.

sophisticated sage might miss out on the force of character education, for virtue is not a matter of temporary charm.

—

This letter marks the end of our exploration of the tradition of character and virtue education. As we have considered the history of the world's societies, it seems that the pendulum has swung too far from security towards freedom. This is just like airport controls, where the more you have of one the less you have of the other. Some societies have been very secure but have lacked freedom; others have enjoyed great freedom but have lost their security. Life is unbearable at either end of the pendulum, and history (and education) swings back and forth between these extremes. I think we are in a moment where many societies have swung too far in the direction of freedom and the revival of character and virtue can represent a welcome fluctuation back towards security.

May we be just in dealing with the social sensitivities of our time. Rest well over your break.

Part III

The Practice

29

A Question of Practice

I have returned from my summer holiday and I have good news for you: I have decided to turn down the position with the UNESCO project for now. There was no consolation in my soul and I would not make a decision in desolation. This was a case of exercising *phronesis* as I was tugged between the virtue of constancy on the one side and benevolent ambition on the other. Both were possible, but this time I felt that I should complete what I had begun. I use the verb "*felt*" carefully, because I recognize that God's voice is often perceived in our emotions, and *phronesis* frequently operates together with spiritual discernment. The text of Psalm 15:4 spoke to me about the character of the man who "keeps an oath even when it hurts." So this means that I will stay with the academy and with other projects that I am involved in. The mist has cleared, and I am at peace.

I am now ready and excited to work with you through a final set of letters on the practices of character and virtue education.

The Temptations of Practice

This practical part of our correspondence may seem like the easier task, but it is not, for we must master the difficult art of matching educational theory with practice.[1] After nearly two years in which we've engaged in much theory, we will now "dirty our hands" to see how our theories inform the nuts and bolts of character and virtue in theological education.

As I set out, I have noted a handful of dangers that I want to avoid. First of all, I want to resist the temptation of sketching definitive prescriptions. Should my letters end up reading like a "how-to" manual, let me know and I will change my tone, for character and virtue education cannot be neatly packaged

---

1. Walker et al., *Towards a New Era*, 79–92.

in this way.² Aristotle himself never produced a systematic methodology³ and I purpose to leave many edges frayed. Second, I will try to avoid proposals that are too radical. I recall one of my mentors encouraging me to be courageous in innovation, but to never move so far ahead of everyone that I scare people off.⁴ Third, I will make an effort to not think only about the academy. I recognize that, although I am writing to you with a radical proposal for a new academy that is thoroughly centred around character and virtue, these letters may fall into the hands of theological educators who are not in a place to carry out such radical implementation. Nor may they be called to do so. Hopefully, they will nevertheless find some inspiration for those changes that are possible or desirable in their contexts.

You may recall that, in one of my first letters, I spoke about the parameters of clarity, centrality and intentionality in character and virtue education. In these next letters I will try to show you how we can achieve these in a number of areas, including the vocabularies we use, the structures of our schools, our learning communities, our choices of venue, our curricula, our approaches to teaching and learning, our pedagogical strategies and our assessment and certification.

Can Virtue Be Taught?

Before we come to the practices, however, there is a final theoretical question that we need to address about practice itself. It is the question whether virtue can be taught. Is character too much of a personal thing to be an object of education? Are we born with good character? Is character simply acquired by the environment or by unpredictable forces? Do social and personal circumstances leave no hope for educational intervention?⁵ When we deal with adults, is it too late to influence their character?⁶ Does God sovereignly

---

2. "Character education cannot be isolated, codified, and packaged into tidy little instructional units in a how-to manual" (Gretchen and Firmin, "Character Education," 193).

3. Kristjánsson, *Aristotelian Character Education*, 64.

4. A special thanks to Steve Hardy for these words of wisdom.

5. "Marx, Mill, and Rawls suggest how character can be moulded by antecedent circumstances – Marx by economic structures; Mill by paid work, political life, and family relationships; Rawls by the institutions regulated by the two principles of justice. Yet these insights about the effect of institutions on character seem to raise other, more troubling questions: if our character is the result of social and political institutions beyond our control, then perhaps we are not in control of our characters at all and becoming decent is not a real possibility" (Marcia, "Moral Character").

6. Curtler, "Can Virtue Be Taught?," 47.

change our character regardless of our educational efforts? These are all good questions that we need to face, for, if virtue cannot be taught, our endeavour is pointless.

Thankfully, we are in good company in believing that virtue can be taught. Confucius, for example, believed that virtue can be taught through the power of personal example.[7] In the Bible, we've seen that the book of Deuteronomy prescribes educational strategies that can mould character in accordance with God's laws.[8] Plato also explicitly addresses the question about the possibility of teaching virtue in *Meno*, through the lips of Socrates.[9] Although his answer is tentative, he does end up agreeing that virtue can be taught on the condition of finding adequate teachers. Aristotle is more emphatic and claims that it is possible to learn moral virtues by repetition and that intellectual virtues can be instilled by school teaching. Some go even further, saying that virtue *cannot not* be taught. This view suggests that, especially in an educational context, influence on character is unavoidable; hence it might as well be intentional.[10]

We will move forward on the assumption that character can be taught, displayed, demanded, practised and reflected on.[11] On the basis of your work in the New Testament, I also believe that there is special hope in shaping character and virtue in Christian theology students.

Comenius as a Model of Practice

In this first letter, let's look at some examples of practice. These models show us how others have proceeded and can provide many good ideas.

Comenius is one of the best models I've come across. Not only is he considered the father of modern education but he was also a Christian practitioner who believed that morality and piety are teachable and learnable.[12] He claimed that, under the influence of grace, proper pedagogy can lead to

---

7. Huang, "Can Virtue Be Taught?," 142.

8. The "educational" strategies in Deuteronomy include watching oneself closely (4:9), reinforcing memory with repetition, multi-contextual education (6:7), use of symbols, question-answering (6:20) and liturgical actions (31:10).

9. "Can you tell me, Socrates, is human excellence [*arête*] something teachable? Or, if not teachable, is it something to be acquired by training? Or, if it cannot be acquired either by training or by teaching, does it accrue to me at birth or in some other way?" (Plato, *Meno* 70).

10. "[To] abstain is merely to abdicate control to chance or other influences" (Berkowitz and Fekula, "Educating for Character," 17).

11. Berkowitz and Fekula, 19.

12. Habl, "Character Formation," 148.

the acquisition of personal virtue. In *Great Didactic* he set out a grand plan to enable this. Let me apply some of his practical principles[13] to the academy.

First, Comenius says that virtue is cultivated by *actions*, not by talk. He claims that the virtues are learned through doing what is right. So, just as one learns how to walk by walking, one learns constancy by being constant.[14] Virtuous action is thus both the method and the outcome of virtue. A character education programme will therefore give students occasions to act in virtue-related contexts rather than just listen to lectures about virtue. Lessons will entail structured occasions for virtuous action, and assessment will look at how character grows as a result of these actions. A school of this kind will spend less on building classrooms and more on a fleet of mini-vans to shuttle students to soup kitchens, refugee camps, hospital wards and political gatherings where real-life situations require virtuous action.

Second, Comenius taught that virtue is acquired through interaction with virtuous people in *community*. Comenius believed that humans instinctively imitate others before they can even learn how to learn. Therefore, at the most basic level, virtue is learned by example. This is what the Greeks called *mimesis*. An educational programme must therefore look very carefully at the virtuous character of everyone in the learning community, including the faculty, the leadership, the management team, the administration, the staff and the students themselves. On this view, everyone is a teacher within the community, regardless of their role.

Comenius also believed that virtue is learned by *instruction*, so although it is important to surround those who are growing in virtue with good examples, it is not sufficient. Students must also receive instruction that clarifies what moral behaviour is, explains when certain virtues are appropriate, describes what excess and defect in virtue can look like and provides the motivation to be virtuous. An educational programme of character and virtue will take teaching very seriously and feature classrooms, lectures, books to be read, papers to be written and assessments to pass. In the process of being educated in character and virtue, the mind will be deeply engaged, attentive, critical, open and creative as intellectual virtues develop together with moral and social virtues.

---

13. Comenius outlined ten principles, here condensed into a shorter list (Habl, 143–144).

14. "The virtues are learned by constantly doing what is right . . . it is by learning that we find out what we ought to learn, and by acting that we learn to act as we should. So then, as boys easily learn to walk by walking, to talk by talking, and to write by writing, in the same way we will learn obedience by obeying, abstinence by abstaining, truth by speaking the truth, and constancy by being constant" (Comenius, *Grande didactique*, 367).

Fourth, in addition to action, example and teaching, Comenius taught that virtuous conduct is cultivated by *active perseverance*. Here, the virtue of constancy appears again. Comenius believed that fallen human nature makes us fickle and undependable and that virtue is cultivated by focused discipline. This should not become legalistic obsession but should be a joyfully sustained focus on growth. Educational structures can be put in place to encourage this kind of perseverance, such as accountability groups, personal journaling, artwork, symbols as visual reminders, recurring exhortation from those leading the community and even smartphone apps.[15]

One final insight from Comenius is that virtue must revolve around *service* to others. He claimed that, whereas fallen human nature is expressed in self-love, the heart of the gospel calls us to live for God and for our neighbour. Educationally, this means that everything should pass the test of service to others. This has implications, for example, in thinking of numerically graded examinations that might lead students to compare and rank their achievements. Are we endorsing competition and individual assertion over a spirit of collaboration and shared work? Might more group projects replace individual examinations and foster the virtues of generosity, patience, justice, diligence and reciprocal service?

There is much to learn about moral education from Comenius. He taught about the importance of learning through practice, the influence of peer pressure, the role of active participation, the principles of systematics, appropriateness and imitation, and the significance of moral examples.[16] Surely you will want his books in the library of the academy.

Other Practical Models

Other practical models are also available. One extensive review of successful programmes that implement character education[17] has suggested that there are four common denominators in these programmes: (1) they promote student autonomy; (2) they require student participation; (3) they provide training in social skills; and (4) they aim at social service. Another study of twelve American

---

15. Virtue is a smartphone app that is "designed to help you monitor yourself so you can identify and improve problem areas in your life. Begin by selecting your primary virtue that you want to start working on. Make an effort to improve that quality in yourself each day. Every night, a notification will remind you to review your virtues, and log them in your journal" (Google Play, https://play.google.com/store/apps/details?id=com.listfist.virtue&hl=en). See other apps as well: Virtues Reflection, The Virtues App, Virtues Cards and Ben's Virtues.

16. Habl, "Character Formation," 145.

17. Berkowitz, "The Science of Character Education," 57.

institutions revealed that there are three principles for advancing character education in higher education, namely: (1) it must concentrate on different dimensions of character education (to include moral judgment, emotional intelligence and the ability to work with others); (2) it must involve all aspects of the institutional experience (including curriculum, extra-curricular activity and institutional culture); (3) it must be involved with the local neighbourhood and include the democratic processes of the university itself.[18]

Internationally, we find examples of good practice in Korea,[19] where moral and character education programmes include (1) role-modelling to demonstrate respectable character both through the teacher and through moral stories; (2) exploration and explanation of the concepts of moral values and norms; (3) discussion and debate of moral dilemmas; (4) peer exchange of moral experiences through narratives; (5) project-based action; (6) creation of moral and caring communities; (7) experiencing and practising moral values first-hand; and (8) school–home community partnerships. One might also explore Soviet *vospitanie* that involved communist youth organizations in a variety of social practices.[20]

Individual authors have worked out summaries of practical steps in character and virtue education. Aristotle would have us think of at least four components: (1) identify which virtue is needed in a specific situation to realize the greatest good; (2) think through the options to discern which virtuous practice can best express the golden mean; (3) act consequentially; and (4) reflect on our actions.[21] In *Some Thoughts Concerning Education* John Locke also suggested a practical model that begins with the formation of a virtuous mind through the exercise of reason and then proceeds to exercise self-denial through the tools of habit and example.[22]

Contemporary authors like Baehr suggest that teaching virtue begins with identifying which virtues you'd like to focus on; you then gain clarity on the behaviours and actions that are characteristic of these virtues; and finally you build opportunities for virtue-specific practice as they arise from

---

18. Colby, in Arthur, Wilson and Godfrey, *Graduates of Character*, 14.
19. In, "Moral and Character Education in Korea," 337–341.
20. Glanzer, "Moral Education Establishment," 297.
21. Arthur et al., *Teaching*, 75–76.
22. "By habit, virtue is practiced through self-denial until it becomes natural and instinctive. Example builds on the natural tendency to imitate virtuous people (exposure to bad example is therefore to be avoided). Tutors should be not so much scholars as virtuous, of good breeding and with knowledge of the world. They should, for example, tell stories of men ruined by vice" (Locke, *Some Thoughts*).

the classroom.[23] Lickona, instead, claims that although there is no single script for character education, there are several useful practical components that should be in place, articulated along the axes of moral knowing, moral feeling and moral action.[24]

Practical Components to Consider

You can see that there are a number of models. Here is an initial list of my own for you to consider as you plan for the academy. In the next letters I will be unpacking several of these (note that they are not in any particular order).

1. You are wise to have a contractual agreement with potential students. This is because character and virtue education cannot be forced on unwilling adults. Since students are signing up for much more than what is normally expected in traditional education, they must be fully consensual.

2. You must provide students with knowledge and understanding of what the virtues are and of how they are exercised. You cannot, in fact, hope to transform students in areas they have no knowledge about.[25] So knowledge acquisition and related assessment have their place.

3. You need to generate desire for virtue through the influence of community, example and emotional education. There are many ways in which this can be done, not least through impassioned lecturing in public assemblies.

4. You need to intentionally design virtue-reinforcing habits, so that being will result from doing.

5. You must surround yourself with like-minded colleagues who understand, embrace and endorse what you are doing. Unless your team is fully involved, your project will flounder, so do not simply hire good lecturers and efficient administrators.

6. You need to carefully craft a curriculum and match it with fitting pedagogy. Learning outcomes, aims, curricula, course maps,

---

23. Baehr, "Cultivating Good Minds," 376–378.
24. Lickona, *Educating for Character*.
25. Paul claims that he would not have known what coveting was if the law had not provided the necessary knowledge (Rom 7:7).

assessment strategies, etc., are a crucial part of the process and need careful design.

7. Never forget to cultivate your students' relationship with Christ, for character education is a work of God.[26]

Implementing practices of character and virtue in current academia is a phenomenal challenge and we can easily succumb to anger and frustration.[27] May you find meekness as self-possession in the face of adversity.[28]

---

26. "Vices need more than a process of retraining. Apart from redemption, in other words, apart from a radical redirection of the created order through Christ, death will have the last word" (Gunton, "Church as a School of Virtue?," 223).

27. "[Is it] really possible to undertake moral formation for ordination in an academic setting today?" (Neuhaus, *Theological Education*, 138).

28. Aquinas, *Summa* 2.2.157, on "Clemency and Meekness."

30

Taxonomies of Virtue

Thank you for suggesting Sofia as a possible doctoral student. She sounds like a promising scholar and her father happens to be a member of your new board. I am not sure that her bachelor's degree in education provides sufficient entry qualifications to the research programme in my university, so a bridge programme may be necessary. Too bad that the academy is not yet set up. In any case, I will wait for her to contact me once she decides whether she wishes to do research or take up a job in women's education advocacy.

We've been talking a lot about the virtues and in my initial set of letters I shared a definition, but we've never really described the virtues in any detail yet. This is an important practical step, for our students must have specific knowledge and understanding of what the virtues are. As St Anthony said, you can't just beat on a piece of iron and hope that it will eventually turn into a ploughshare.[1] We need to know what we are aiming for. In the next couple of letters, therefore, I'm going to focus on virtue literacy.

The Importance of Virtue Literacy

Virtue literacy is the collection of language and concepts that inform moral character engagement in real-life situations.[2] Words are very important and we, as theologians, should appreciate this. If we do not have words, we do not have concepts. If we do not have concepts, we will not have a conscience. If we don't have a conscience, we will not have a practice. And if we do not have a practice, our character will never flourish. The following lovely quote

---

1. "Nobody picks up a piece of iron, like a locksmith, and just starts beating on it and says, 'I think I'll beat on this to see if it turns into a ploughshare or a weapon of some sort.' So it is with the virtues. We must decide in advance what it is we want to create and then move in that direction" (in Neuhaus, *Theological Education*, 165).
2. Arthur et al., *Teaching*, 94.

is attributed to Frank Outlaw,[3] late president of the Bi-Lo Stores: "Watch your thoughts, they become words; watch your words, they become actions; watch your actions, they become habits; watch your habits, they become character; watch your character, for it becomes your destiny."

It is important, then, to begin with words. One of the most practical outcomes of a programme in character and virtue education is that students emerge as virtue literates. Studies have shown that teachers often struggle to find the appropriate moral language to address ethical issues in the classroom and wish for a standardized vocabulary such as that which all other subjects normally offer.[4] Research has also indicated that students cherish and enjoy a rich moral vocabulary.[5] Although alternative vocabularies have been suggested, such as vocabularies of self-respect or personality, teachers and students alike are frustrated by a state of linguistic poverty that does not allow for precise and significant meanings. In general, there seems to be an appetite to bring back a richer virtue vocabulary,[6] and some schools are doing this intentionally.[7]

If this is happening in secular schools, how much more should we be resuscitating virtue vocabulary in theological education! My experience is that Christian moral language has become impoverished when it comes to speaking about the virtues.[8] It seems that we have abandoned specific virtue language and speak generally about "integrity," when we could be more incisive by speaking of truthfulness, honesty and equity. Or we speak about "servant leadership" but miss out on the benefits of speaking specifically in terms of generosity, mercy and humility and on how these virtues interact with justice, courage and prudence. We use the terms "spirituality" and "discipleship" but, as we've seen, the moral connotations of these words are often indeterminate.

---

3. Quote Investigator, https://quoteinvestigator.com/2013/01/10/watch-your-thoughts/.

4. Walker et al., *Towards a New Era*, 91.

5. The Learning for Life Project (the largest empirical study of character education to date in the UK, with over 70,000 respondents) has revealed that young people "are themselves aware of their lack of vocabulary to talk meaningfully about those issues [character] – and that, when they were provided with such a vocabulary, they cherished it and enjoyed the opportunity to use it. Many of us may have experienced the eureka-feeling of coming across phrases, previously unfamiliar to us, that enable us to say exactly what we mean" (Kristjánsson, "Ten Myths," 273).

6. "The need may arise to try to resuscitate some old but invaluable ways of speaking" (Kristjánsson, 273).

7. A study in a Jewish day school, for example, reveals the practice of teaching students the meaning of many Hebrew words to promote character development (Roso, "Culture and Character Education," 35).

8. As Meno's fellow citizens, we "know absolutely nothing about what *arête* happens to be" (Plato, *Meno* 71).

Even when we speak about "sin," our language is often nebulous, and we shy away from preaching about the specifics of greed, lust or gossip.

Virtue Language and Theological Education

The social changes that we have seen in previous letters have contributed to weakening virtue literacy and students come to study theology with very hazy or distorted notions of virtue and vice.[9] But there are other specific challenges as well. I've come across a great article on "Educating Virtue As a Mastery of Language" by Vasalou which I'd like to apply to our context. Let me share some of his arguments.

The first challenge Vasalou suggests has to do with redeeming good words with bad connotations. Some virtue and vice terms have acquired negative baggage, and this makes us shy away from using them.[10] So, for example, when we speak of "chastity," we associate it with extreme manifestations of monastic life; words like "charity" bear the twin burdens of peculiar Christian legacies and philanthropic activities;[11] and meekness is more easily associated with weakness than with self-possession in the face of adversity.[12] Sometimes virtues can even bear the burden of appearing as vices, such as when intellectual integrity is misinterpreted as intolerance or when faith is equated with fanaticism. A practical challenge of theological education is to reclaim the true meaning of these good terms.

Vaslau's second point is most interesting in pointing out our hesitance to use big words in small situations. What he means is that we feel that the "weight" of important virtue words is normally disproportionate to the small situations of everyday life. This is one of the reasons why we do not use virtue vocabulary. So, for example, whereas we would find it appropriate to use the word "courage" in the context of a battle against a vicious enemy, it would seem exaggerated to speak of courage when driving into an unknown neighbourhood at night to visit a sick friend. And yet both cases have to do with not allowing our legitimate fears to stop us from doing what is right, and

---

9. "Today, we no longer seem to know what vice and virtue are, we are weaker in the knowledge of morality, and for the first time in history we have lost objective moral law" (Tenelshof, "Encouraging the Character Formation," 79).

10. "Some virtue terms . . . carry the weight of many years and the cumulative voices of numerous participants on their shoulders and have fallen into desuetude or acquired baggage that is onerous to bear" (Vasalou, "Educating Virtue," 72).

11. Vasalou, 72.

12. Aquinas, *Summa* 2.2.157.

so the word "courage" is correct. This sense of discrepancy between the weight of the word and the insignificance of the issues needs to be overcome, and we need to learn to use big words for small events.[13]

As theological educators, we should take the cue and begin attaching extraordinary weight to ordinary situations, even if this may initially sound odd.[14] So, for example, when we teach the historical narratives of Scripture, we should choose to speak of Joseph's *chastity* and *temperance* with regard to Potiphar's wife, of Mardocheus's *modesty* despite his achievements and of Jesus's *magnanimity* in response to Peter's betrayal. We should also help students become aware of virtue and vice in their own everyday lives, in personal conversation and in the context of their formational activities. So, for example, we might speak of *benevolence* when going to visit a boring aunt,[15] of *temperance* in declining the extra pint of beer in the pub,[16] of *civility* when we give up our place on the bus to an elderly person and of *decency* when we keep our living quarters tidy. This apparently disproportionate use of strong virtue language can serve as a character-shaping verbal shock.

I can testify to the benefits of this in my own life. It has now been more than a year that we have been corresponding, and the sustained use of virtue words has made me more conscious of my actions. I catch myself observing a situation and thinking, "Ah, that is an example of temperance." Or, as I reflect on my life patterns, I find myself using wonderful words like "attentiveness" or "meekness." This growing precision in vocabulary has generated a greater awareness in me as I work on my own character.

A third piece of practical advice that Vasalou gives is to use "old" words rather than neologisms. These old words not only tend to be more precise, but they also situate our moral quest within the broader human endeavour towards goodness.[17] This is, admittedly, a tiring task, for using old virtue words is like

---

13. "What seems to get in the way of the application of the word is a sense of discrepancy or disproportion between the force or gravity it carries, and the relatively short stature or insignificance of the situation at issue . . . this response seems unreasonably strong . . . when our interest lies in cultivating character, big words may be needed for small events" (Vasalou, "Educating Virtue," 72–73).

14. "It is only by attaching such extraordinary weights to more-than-ordinary circumstances that we can develop new habits of moral perception and response; and this means that the learner of virtue may need to use language in ways that seem extraordinary or inappropriate to the ordinary ear" (Vasalou, 73).

15. Vasalou, 73.

16. "We should thank God for beer and Burgundy by not drinking too much of them" (Chesterton, *Orthodoxy*, 89–90).

17. Vasalou, "Educating Virtue," 78.

learning a foreign language or wearing someone else's clothes.[18] The more we do so, however, the more natural it becomes. As these words express the actions, reason, emotions, desires and perceptions within theological learning communities, they will help form conscience and character.

As we will see later on, it is very important that virtue words appear specifically in the aims and outcomes of the academy's programmes, in the course syllabi, in the vision and mission statements and in the publicity materials, on the website and on the application forms. But it is also important that your teachers use them in their lectures, mentoring, placements and essay topics. If you do nothing else but improve the virtue literacy of your students, you will have taken a huge step forward in shaping their character.[19]

There are many ways in which we can improve virtue literacy. In this letter I will share a few taxonomies of virtue, and in the next I will try to describe some of the virtues that I've come across.

Classifying the Virtues

When we think about classifying the virtues, we need to exercise caution. Some, like Aquinas, have produced massive taxonomies, but I think that we are wiser not to aim at such precision.[20] For all their love of systematic order, even the Greeks did not produce exact lists, and a superficial comparison of Homer, Aristotle, the New Testament, Jane Austen and Benjamin Franklin shows a great difference not only in the virtues that are included in the different lists, but also in the ordering of the lists and in the different hierarchies that are used.[21]

In one of my first letters I mentioned several ways in which the virtues can be classified. We saw the *cardinal virtues* of prudence, justice, fortitude and temperance, the *Christian virtues* of faith, hope and love, the *moral virtues* such

---

18. "The word 'kindness' or 'humility' or 'fortitude' may feel as strange in my mouth as any other new vocabulary I learn to use for the first time and in which, until it becomes my own through habit, I feel as awkward as if I was wearing someone else's clothes" (Vasalou, 81).

19. This method was used by Comenius. He "first briefly clarifies the individual virtue and subsequently posits the method of its acquisition; together, these then form the crux of his methodology of character formation" (Habl, "Character Formation," 143).

20. "Large classificatory schemes ought always to arouse our suspicions . . . a good deal of our knowledge of the virtues is . . . empirical: we learn what kind of quality truthfulness or courage is, what its practice amounts to, what obstacles it creates and what it avoids and so on, only in part by observing its practice in others and in ourselves . . . there is necessarily a kind of empirical untidiness in the way that our knowledge of the virtues is ordered" (MacIntyre, *After Virtue*, 178).

21. There are "rival lists of virtues, different and rival attitudes toward the virtues and different and rival definitions of the individual virtues" (MacIntyre, 138, 182).

as kindness, compassion and generosity, the *civic virtues* such as decency, loyalty and diligence, the *intellectual virtues* such as attentiveness, open-mindedness and curiosity, and the *foundational virtues* such as prudence, constancy and love. I also mentioned the classifications of *capital virtues* and *capital vices*. This is probably a fair summary of the most common classifications.

There are also other ways to organize the virtues. We might, for example, organize the virtues according to their *authors*. Although Aristotle never produced a definitive list of virtues, in the *Nicomachean Ethics* he clearly identifies virtues such as gentleness, bravery, modesty, temperance, indignation, justice, liberality, sincerity, friendliness, dignity, endurance, greatness of spirit, magnificence and wisdom.[22] Aquinas's *Summa*, as mentioned, offers one of the most detailed classifications of the virtues in Christian theology. In it, we find the *intellectual virtues* that are represented in the first principles of science, wisdom, prudence and art; the *moral virtues* of prudence, justice, fortitude and temperance, which can be infused and acquired; and the *theological virtues* of faith, hope and charity that elevate our higher faculties with God's inner life. Aquinas also introduces the *seven gifts of the Spirit*, consisting in wisdom, understanding, knowledge, counsel, fortitude, piety and fear of the Lord. Authors of other faith traditions also offer robust taxonomies of virtue, such as those that we've mentioned in Confucianism[23] or in the Five Basic Precepts of Buddhism.[24]

Contemporary authors also offer interesting classifications, such as that of Austin and Geivett who suggest *faith*, *hope* and *love* as the main categories, each with a set of sub-virtues, such as open-mindedness, wisdom and zeal under the rubric of faith; contentment and courage under hope; and compassion, forgiveness and humility under love.[25] *New York Times* columnist David Brooks proposes distinguishing between *competitive* and *cooperative virtues* to define the codes used in the classical world and those used in the Christian tradition.[26] According to Brooks, the Homeric virtues privilege an attitude of courage and assertiveness whereas the Christian virtues showcase humility, forgiveness and

---

22. Racelis, "Developing a Virtue Ethics Scale," 28.

23. The main properties of *ren* are propriety; *xiao* as filial piety; *ti* as brotherly love; *zhong* as loyalty; *shu* as tolerance; *yi* as righteousness; *zhi* as wisdom; and *xin* as integrity (Chen and Yu, "Traditional Chinese Philosophies," 31).

24. The Five Basic Precepts are (1) no harming of living beings; (2) no stealing; (3) no sexual misconduct; (4) no false speech; and (5) no drinking of alcohol (Chen and Yu, 40).

25. Austin and Geivett, "Being Good."

26. "The Character Code with David Brooks," YouTube, 16 July 2012, accessed 28 August 2018, https://www.youtube.com/watch?v=ELKmuXGzJ3s.

service. Although some would argue that these two codes cannot coexist,[27] Brooks claims that the Western tradition has tried to fuse them together (Shakespeare's *Hamlet* is an example of this, in that the hero seeks vengeance and honour but also struggles with the wrongness of anger and murder).

We've already come across James Arthur as a scholar who has done much work on character and virtue education through the Jubilee Centre. He classifies virtues as: (1) *moral virtues* that are needed to respond soundly and ethically to experience (such as courage, self-discipline, compassion, gratitude, justice, humility and honesty); (2) *performance virtues* that enable us to manage our lives effectively (such as resilience, determination, confidence and teamwork); (3) *civic virtues* that engage us as responsible citizens (such as service, citizenship and volunteering); and (4) *intellectual virtues* that are the rational prerequisites for right action and correct thinking (such as autonomy, reasoning and perseverance). Arthur also suggests a list of specific virtues that are necessary for *education* and that include intellectual integrity, vocational integrity, moral courage, altruism, impartiality, human insight, assuming the responsibility of influence, humility, collegiality, partnership and vigilance with regard to professional responsibilities and aspiration.[28]

Seligman's "Classification of Strengths and Virtues" is another possible classification that has gained popularity through the Positive Psychology movement and the Values in Action (VIA) test. This classification identifies twenty-four different virtues and places them in six main clusters of *wisdom* (creativity, curiosity, judgment, love of learning, perspective); *courage* (bravery, honesty, perseverance and zest); *humanity* (kindness, love and social intelligence); *justice* (fairness, leadership and teamwork); *temperance* (forgiveness, humility, prudence and self-regulation); and *transcendence* (appreciation of beauty, gratitude, hope, humour and spirituality). The goal of the VIA test is to provide operationalized definitions, measurements and interventions for each of these character strengths. These six VIA clusters have been compared to Jesus's teachings on wisdom and the test itself represents a useful tool.[29]

---

27. Machiavelli, in *The Prince*, argued that the Christian code must be set aside for those in leadership as it simply is not efficient in the kind of fallen world that we live in.

28. Arthur et al., *Teaching*, 10, 37.

29. White and Murray, *Evidence-Based Approaches*, 36. For the VIA test, see VIA Institute on Character, http://www.viacharacter.org.

The Intellectual Virtues as Special

Let me conclude with a brief focus on the *intellectual virtues*. In previous letters we have engaged with some of the debates around moral and intellectual virtues, so I will not rehearse these. Although rarely labelled as such, the intellectual virtues are the natural focus of higher education and theological education.[30] The virtues of *scientia*, art, prudence, intellect and wisdom are virtues that have given rise to the university and have allowed academic practice to flourish. I recommend the excellent recent work on the intellectual virtues that can be found at the Intellectual Virtues Academy (IVA), which lists nine master intellectual virtues, organized in three categories and corresponding to three stages of learning.[31] At the *getting started* stage, we have curiosity, intellectual humility and intellectual autonomy. At the *executing well* stage, we have attentiveness, intellectual carefulness and intellectual thoroughness. Finally, at the *handling challenges* stage, we find the virtues of open-mindedness, intellectual courage and intellectual tenacity as a willingness to embrace intellectual challenge and struggle.

Your Own Classification

So, which taxonomy should you use for the academy? I hope that the variety of approaches that I have just illustrated demonstrates that there is no one right way to classify the virtues. You can use any one of them or, better yet, devise your own taxonomy which is fit for your purpose. You might, for example, create a classification of virtues that are necessary for ministry.[32] Alternatively, you might involve the faith communities in a further consultation to develop a shared taxonomy of desirable virtues in your region. Or, more interestingly yet, you could involve the entire learning community in the academy to create a table of virtues for the community. Such a table would give visibility to the excellences that are praised in the community and be a reminder of the kinds of actions that are praised and those that are not to be tolerated.[33]

---

30. These virtues often appear in programme outcomes under the rubric of cognitive thinking skills, such as the ability to think critically, analyse and interpret texts, integrate and correlate sources or reflect theologically.

31. "Master Virtues: IVA's Nine Master Virtues," Intellectual Virtues Academy, http://www.ivalongbeach.org/academics/master-virtues.

32. Hauerwas suggests that the virtues necessary for ordination are the same as those needed for marriage (Neuhaus, *Theological Education*, 167).

33. MacIntyre, *After Virtue*, 151.

It is hard to go wrong in rearranging the furniture of the virtues, especially once you have appreciated the breadth of the possibilities.

—

Taxonomies are both healthy and dangerous. Healthy, because they help us see how the virtues complement each other. Dangerous, because they can induce us to treat virtues in isolation, as if they were discrete little blocks that we can pile up in different ways. As you know, I'm a fan of G. K. Chesterton, and what he wrote about the "virtues gone wild" makes a fitting end to this letter.[34] He said that virtues go wild when they are isolated from each other. When this happens, they can do more damage than good. Sadly, the plight of the modern world is, according to Chesterton, that the religious schemes that have traditionally held the virtues together have been shattered and have left the world "full of the old Christian virtues gone mad."[35]

May we rectify this madness by creatively holding the virtues together in all their wonderful difference.

---

34. Chesterton, *Orthodoxy*, 34–38.
35. Chesterton, 35.

31

Virtues Described

Sorry for the delay between my letters and for not replying to your emails. I have been trying to pace myself with one letter each month, but I have been silent now for nearly three months. In the meantime, you have been busy with informal meetings with individuals who might potentially staff the academy project, and I commend your diligence. It is never too early.

You may have read about the crisis in my university, but sadly it is uglier than what is known publicly. We had been relying heavily on the donations of one particular corporate family, and last year the business suddenly went bankrupt. As a result, we have faced a serious deficit and have had to make half of our staff and faculty redundant. We have also sold significant portions of our campus to pay off our debts and have had to shut down some good programmes with low recruitment. Saddest of all, the financial crisis has revealed a deeper crisis of trust between the board, the university leadership and the faculty, and this has generated intense relational tension.

I have been involved in mediation and this has drained me, which is why my correspondence has dwindled. This letter describing the virtues has taken three months to write, and while it has focused my soul on the good, it has also made the shortcomings around me painfully clear.

Describing the Virtues

As I began my own venture into character and virtue education, I recall searching for definitions of the virtues. I was very much geared to an encyclopaedic approach, but now, after an extended time of researching, observing and working on my own character, I've realized that virtues change as they encounter life and that we are better off describing them than defining them.[1] I've also realized that virtue words can take on many different meanings, depending on culture, history and context.[2]

In this practical letter, I share some of the descriptions that I've collected over time. I have followed the tradition and placed the cardinal virtues first, followed by the foundational virtues of humility and constancy. Other than that, there is no real classification and the order is random. My descriptions also vary. Sometimes I use words, other times I provide a story, other times I lump similar virtues together and other times I look for the middle ground between the excesses and defects suggested by Aristotle. Often you will find that I seek out the contrasts between virtues and vices and offer some descriptions of vice as well. This is important, for if we believe that character is formed within the competing forces of good and evil, then we must have just as much clarity about vice as we do about virtue.[3] I trust that you will find this carousel enriching.

Prudence

Let me start with *prudence*. This is best described as practical wisdom that helps us discern which virtues are necessary as we meet life's unpredictable circumstances. Prudence is about having discernment in our choices and it is synonymous with *phronesis*, *wisdom* and *discernment*. It is a form of reasoning that mediates between universal virtues and the particularities of real-life situations and helps us find the middle ground in virtue, avoiding both excess and defect.[4] Prudence helps the soldier decide when it is time for courage and when it is time for patience. It helps the care-worker know when it is time for compassion and when it is time for truthfulness. It helps the leader feel when it is time for humility and when ambition is called for. In the words of Ecclesiastes, prudence helps us discern when it is time to sow and when it is

---

1. Aristotle never produced a list of defined virtues, but kept them open-ended and context-sensitive (Arthur et al., *Teaching*, 37).

2. "The characterizations of the virtues . . . will differ from one community and tradition to another. This diversity is often obscured by the fact that the virtues have the same name and may in fact seem structurally similar" (Hauerwas, "Difference of Virtue," 260).

3. "Questions relating to [vice] must be addressed separately. Focusing on the virtues will simply not suffice because it does not necessarily correlate with overcoming the vices. Character education, it follows, might greatly benefit from providing a clear image not only of the virtues and the good but also of evil, vice and the immoral" (Gilead, "Countering the Vices," 276).

4. "Prudence . . . guides both the will and the sense appetite in finding the right means in attaining an end" (Aquinas, *Summa* 47.2). Also Heywood, "Educating Ministers of Character," 9.

time to reap, when it is time to laugh and when to cry, when it is time to gather and when to scatter.⁵

Prudence is a virtue that is functional to other virtues. If the virtues are like different tools that hang on a handyman's belt, prudence is the virtue that allows us to deploy the right tool at the appropriate time. It is equivalent to *phronesis* in the Aristotelian framework, as it engages our mind in choosing the appropriate moral behaviours and keeps us off the rocks of indoctrination, paternalism and mechanical adherence to rules. We need to instil prudence in our students, otherwise we will be conditioning them and not educating them.⁶

The vices that oppose prudence are *cunning*, which is finding ways to benefit only oneself; *cleverness*, which gives the appearance of wisdom but has no substance; *negligence*, which gives up on seeking the best in every situation; *stupidity*, which always does the same things in every circumstance; and *over-simplicity*, which is happy for quick, superficial solutions based on hearsay or personal opinion.

Justice

Justice is the actioned desire that what is due should be given in order to favour the ideal interaction between individuals in a community.⁷ It has to do with the *respect* of everyone's rights and with establishing harmonious human relations, and with *equity* in treating one's neighbour for the common good without distinction of rank or position. Justice requires the activation of particular sensitivities in order to deal with economic, physical, relational and social differences.

Synonyms for justice might be found in *equity, fairness, honesty* and in *obedience* to the laws of men and of God. *Severity* should also be included as being inflexible in the infliction of punishment when right reason requires it.⁸ Opposing vices can be found in *illegality*, which breaks rightful laws; *unfairness*, which denies to each what is due; *dishonesty*, which breaks covenants of truthfulness; *partiality*, which accords undue favours; and *corruption*, which bends what is right for personal gain.

---

5. Eccl 3:1–8.

6. "The cultivation of moral virtues without the cultivation of the intellectual virtues of phronesis is not really character education . . . but rather an inferior form of character conditioning" (Arthur et al., *Teaching*, 51).

7. "Justice inclines the will to give everyone his due" (Aquinas, *Summa* 47.2). Also, Augustine, *City of God*, Book 19.

8. Aquinas, *Summa, Second Secundae*, Question 157.

The excess of justice is oppressive *tyranny* and its deficiency is found in *submissiveness*, which passively consents to oppression. Justice is a foundational virtue and is seen by some as the mother of all virtues, especially given its power to produce healthy communities.[9]

Courage

Courage (or *fortitude*) has to do with taming the will to do what is good and right in the face of legitimate fears.[10] It is not absence of fear, but action in the presence of fear. Captain Ahab feared the whale in *Moby Dick*, but that did not deter him from hunting down the beast that had bitten off his leg.[11] Joshua was rightly terrified of the walled cities in the promised land, but he was strong and courageous and moved into the land.[12] Although Timothy faced persecution and danger, he was instructed not to be ashamed of the gospel but to suffer with the spirit of power, love and self-discipline.[13] The virtue of courage is found in our character when we face fearful situations that are larger than we are, and we nevertheless bend our will to do our duty.[14]

Courage stands as the golden mean between the vices of *cowardice*, on one hand, and those of *imprudence, rashness, foolhardiness* and *recklessness*, on the other. The coward does not have enough courage. The imprudent person has too much courage and does not fear the things that she or he should fear.[15] What counts is that fear does not control us.[16]

---

9. "Justice is the optimal interaction between the individual and the group or community" (White and Murray, *Evidence-Based Approaches*, 36).

10. "To despise things that are terrible, and to stand our ground against them, we become brave, and it is when we have become so, that we shall be most able to stand our ground against them" (Aristotle, in Bennett, *Book of Virtues*, 441).

11. Bennett, 441.

12. Deut 31:6–8.

13. 2 Tim 1:8.

14. "Fortitude strengthens the irascible appetite against unreasonable fear" (Aquinas, *Summa* 47.2).

15. "It is appropriate to feel the emotion of fear in the face of what is fearful. Courage tames fear with the will and acts rightly. It is 'acting bravely when we don't really feel brave'" (Bennett, *Book of Virtues*, 442).

16. "Bravery is a scorner of things which inspire fear; it looks down upon, challenges, and crushes the powers of terror and all that would drive our freedom under the yoke" (Seneca, *Moral Letters to Lucilius*, 88).

Temperance

We come to *temperance*, understood as governing ourselves through reason.[17] One could say that temperance is about being content with one's state and with taming our impulses and appetites.[18] Temperance mainly concerns the body, but it is also a foundational virtue for other virtues, working with prudence to keep the golden mean and to restrain the other virtues from excesses and deficiencies. So we will be "temperately courageous" to avoid rashness and cowardice, "temperately generous" to avoid meanness and undue prodigality, and so on.[19]

We find a rich cluster of synonyms for temperance. *Moderation* regulates our attraction to pleasure and balances the use of creation's goods. *Self-control* is being the owner of oneself such that reason tames the will to produce right action. *Abstinence* is knowing how to govern our passions and desires and being able to say "no" at the appropriate times. *Meekness* is being self-possessed in mitigating our anger,[20] and is the middle ground between *irascibility* and bitter sentiments of *wrath*, and *indifference* and the *absence of indignation* over evil.

The defective vices of temperance are *licentiousness* and *self-indulgence*, seen, for example, in the capital sins of *gluttony*, where there is no control in our relationship to food, or in *lust*, where there are no limits placed on sexual impulses. The excesses of temperance lead to *self-denial* and to *unwarranted asceticism* in which all pleasure is avoided.

Humility

We can think of *humility* in many ways, and indeed rivers of ink have flown on this particular virtue.[21] One common description is that humility is a correct assessment of oneself.[22] This can be true both for the good and for the bad

---

17. Timpe and Boyd, *Virtues and Their Vices*, 17.
18. "Temperance rules the concupiscible appetite" (Aquinas, *Summa* 47.2).
19. "Temperance controls our desires; some it hates and routs, others it regulates and restores to a healthy measure, nor does it ever approach our desires for their own sake. Temperance knows that the best measure of the appetites is not what you want to take, but what you ought to take" (Seneca, *Moral Letters to Lucilius*, 88).
20. Aquinas, *Summa, Second Secundae*, Question 157.
21. Church and Samuelson, *Intellectual Humility*.
22. Whitcomb et al., "Intellectual Humility," 3. Not all, however, agree with the self-evaluation view of humility. In *Mere Christianity*, for example, C. S. Lewis argues that humble people are generally not overly concerned with recognizing their limits but with doing good to others (Stephen Pardue, "The Other Benedict Option: Humility," *Christianity Today*, 3 August

aspects of our character. Humility allows us to walk in full disclosure of our faults but also empowers us to wear our abilities and achievements in a spirit of *modesty*.[23] Humility thus avoids both the excesses of *shyness* and *false modesty* and the deficiencies of *pride* and *shamelessness*.

Humility can take many forms. It can be the Socratic admission of ignorance which is the starting point of all *learning*. It can be the recognition of right authority as the basis for *civility*. It can be the *respect* of our traditions as we embrace our identities. It can be the attribution of credit and rights to those around us in a spirit of *altruism*. It has also been defined in very active terms, such as the commitment to being agents of change in society.[24] Appropriate humility is meant to restrain our arrogance, doubt our efforts, curtail our infinite appetites and make us small in order to enlarge our world, but at the same time it is the source of *self-confidence* and *pugnacious* living.[25]

When it comes to character education, humility is recognized as a foundational virtue, for it puts us in a place of growth concerning all the other virtues. Unless we are humble, in fact, we never see our faults and will not be motivated to work on our character. The proud person will never learn; hence humility must be cultivated at the outset. But humility is also crucial *after* we become virtuous. For, as Cassian has reminded us, pride is the vice that most easily ensnares those who make progress.[26]

Constancy

Constancy is one of those beautiful old words that has fallen into disuse. And, with its loss, we lose the trait of firmness and determination in searching for what is good, in resisting temptation, in overcoming sloth, in demonstrating strength of resolve, in bending our will to reasoned choices and in overcoming the obstacles of moral life. Constancy comes together with *loyalty*, both in

---

2018, https://www.christianitytoday.com/ct/2018/august-web-only/benedict-option-humility-public-engagement.html).

23. Modesty is beautifully illustrated by one of the statues of the virtues in the Cappella Sansevero in Naples, depicted as an unostentatious veiled beauty.

24. Pardue argues that true humility should lead to public engagement (see Pardue, "Other Benedict Option").

25. Chesterton, *Orthodoxy*, 36–37.

26. "Pride . . . endeavours to cast down by a most fatal fall, and destroy those who were already at the top of the tree of the virtue . . . it generally attacks those only who have conquered the former faults and have already almost arrived at the top of the tree in respect of the virtues" (Cassian, *Institutis*, 12.3, 24). Humility was also the most prominent of virtues in the Benedictine Rule.

relationships and in causes, and with *perseverance*, if necessary to the point of death, in facing trials, difficulties and persecutions. Constancy is the long walk in the same direction. It is the marathon of life rather than a set of short sprints.

Constancy is another foundational virtue, for it is what makes spring out of passing sparrows. It turns one good act of virtue into a habit of virtue and thereby shapes character. It creates the kind of stability that unifies our life's projects.[27] Seneca suggests that the greatest proof of an evil mind is that it continually wavers between the pretence of virtue and the love of vice.[28] Constancy, instead, keeps us walking on the same path,[29] curing our wavering and steadying our character.[30]

Many contemporary societies have replaced constancy with freedom, and they have seen a proliferation of the vices of *fickleness*, where commitments are made and easily unmade, of *whimsicalness*, where the wind of emotion and circumstance governs choices, of *superficiality* and its thin veneer of virtue,[31] and of *irresponsibility*, where we refuse to be tied down to situations in which others will rely on us. There are also excesses in constancy, and we must put our students on guard against *stubbornness*, *obstinacy* and *close-mindedness* that never changes or backs down.

Love

Love is the first of the theological virtues and occupies a place of prominence among the virtues. Many would claim that all the other virtues can be summed up in love, and Aquinas claimed that any other virtue is false unless it is motivated by love.[32]

Love is committing ourselves to the good of people, projects, things and principles with the same intensity that we commit to our own welfare. It is the embodiment of the golden rule which is shared by many cultures.[33]

---

27. Hauerwas, *Dispatches*, 33.

28. Seneca, *Moral Letters to Lucilius* 120.

29. "I do not say that the philosopher can always keep the same pace. But he can always travel the same path" (Seneca, 20).

30. Hauerwas, in *Dispatches*, speaks about constancy and forgiveness through the novels of Austen and Trollope.

31. "Charm is the quality used by those who simulate the virtues to get by" (Hauerwas, 33).

32. "Aquinas . . . maintains that no true virtue is possible without charity. He notes that if we speak of virtue as that which is ordered to some particular end, then there may be a virtue where there is no charity, but such virtue remains a 'false likeness' to genuine virtue" (Hauerwas, "Difference of Virtue," 256).

33. Bennett, *Book of Virtues*, 741.

Love includes *solidarity* towards neighbours and enemies in need. It includes *friendship* and most other virtues, like loyalty, faithfulness, courage, justice and compassion. Love, like all theological virtues, has no excesses. The definitive biblical text on love describes it as including the virtues of *patience, benevolence, loyalty, truthfulness, justice, faithfulness, hope* and *constancy*, and as excluding the vices of *envy, pride, egoism, wrath* and *vengeance*.[34] Truly, the virtue of love is the most excellent way.

I write the least about this primal virtue, for it is the one of which Christian theologians know most.

Truthfulness

A number of virtues can be brought together when we think about *truthfulness*. It is the disposition of *saying the truth* (in love), of being *genuine* and of living *loyally* in friendship and relationships. It also relates to the virtues of being *responsible, accountable* and *answerable* for what we have, or have not, said and done, whatever the consequences. It is where Adam and Eve failed, hiding their actions, shifting responsibilities and seeking shelter in the crowd.[35] The virtue of *honesty* finds its place here, where our words and intentions match our actions out of self-respect, *respect* for others, *integrity* and *sincerity*.

The opposite vices are easily identified as *falsehood, lying, deceit* and *dishonesty*. Truthfulness is also essential for collective *cohesion*, as nothing will segregate social bonds as much as dishonesty.[36]

Compassion

Compassion is the ability to stand with others in their distress and to take the reality of our neighbour seriously. It is an active disposition towards sharing and supporting those who are facing adverse circumstances.[37] It is synonymous with *mercy*, as expressed in the "Seven works of mercy" of feeding the hungry, giving drink to the thirsty, sheltering the homeless, visiting the sick, visiting the

---

34. 1 Cor 13.

35. "A crowd in its very concept is the untruth, by reason of the fact that it renders the individual completely impenitent and irresponsible, or at least weakens his sense of responsibility by reducing it to a fraction . . . In the *Confessions*, Augustine makes a point about taking responsibility rather than hiding behind peer pressure in justifying the vandalism of his youth" (Kierkegaard, in Bennett, *Book of Virtues*, 186).

36. "Honesty is better than all policy" (Kant, in Bennett, 600).

37. Bennett, 107.

prisoners, burying the dead and giving alms to the poor. The Catholic tradition also suggests seven "spiritual works" of mercy, which include admonishing the sinner, instructing the ignorant, counselling the doubtful, bearing wrongs patiently, forgiving offences willingly, comforting the afflicted, and prayer.[38] Compassion is also related to *empathy*, as the disposition to understand and share the feelings of others.

It is easy to see the deficiencies of compassion in *disregard, selfishness, indifference* and *cynicism*. Perhaps the excesses of compassion are less obvious, but they need to be carefully understood as they can lead to the vice of *self-annulment*. Compassion is foundational to other virtues, for it makes us morally aware of our neighbour, towards whom many of the other virtues are directed.

Faith

Faith is a virtue characterized by the double disposition of *reliance* and *reliability*. Reliance has to do with faith in; reliability means faith towards. The two are connected, as faith in someone or something often serves as the grounds of *faithfulness* (e.g. to God, spouse, a friend or a cause).

Faith includes *loyalty* to another person and is an irreplaceable mark of *friendship*.[39] It also includes the disposition to believe in reliable sources and the choice to act on the basis of those beliefs. Faith finds its synonyms in *trust, trustworthiness* and *obedience* and it is surely one of the main themes in the life of Israel in the Old Testament.

Faith is a virtue that can be difficult to navigate, as we are often called to be faithful to those we may not like. It can also place us in conundrums of conflicting loyalties, and it regularly requires the exercise of prudence as we seek the mean between the excesses of *ingenuity, over-reliance, fanaticism* and *partisanship* and the deficiencies of *betrayal, distrust, cynicism* and *anarchy*.

Hope

Hope is a virtue that projects us towards a positive future. It is the conditioning of our life that comes from an optimistic view of the future even when the

---

38. "The 7 Spiritual and 7 Corporal Works of Mercy," Catechism of the Catholic Church, paragraph 2447, https://fwdioc.org/works-of-mercy.pdf.

39. "Loyalty is the holiest good in the human heart; it is forced into betrayal by no constraint, and it is bribed by no rewards" (Seneca, *Moral Letters to Lucilius* 88).

outlook is grim.[40] For Christians, the sovereignty of God provides a fundamental perspective for hope, because the future is placed in the hands of a loving and powerful God.

Hope is also closely linked to the virtue of *joy*, as the ability to not dwell on present adverse circumstances, and of *friendship*, as seeing through imperfections and offering new opportunities after failure. As with the other virtues, hope also needs wise discernment in order to avoid the excess of *ingenuity* and *gullibility* and the deficiency of *cynicism*.

Patience might be included as a virtue related to hope as it calls for appropriate resignation, for a given time, regarding the evils of a fallen world and its inhabitants. The virtue of patience might be described as the disposition to bear conflicts and to resolve them in peace over time, rather than through rapid conflict. Patience is the opposite of *wrath* that explodes during conflict. Patience is the precious ability to remain controlled and to know how to wait, demonstrating wise discernment between the excesses of *irascibility*, *intemperance*, *impulsiveness* and *haste* and the deficiency of *resignation* and *defeatism*.[41]

Benevolence

As you are beginning to see, many of the virtues overlap and blend into each other as colours on a palette. *Benevolence* is one of those virtues that blends with many other virtues, but it is also distinct enough to be seen on its own. It is best described as a deep satisfaction in what one has, leading to being happy for what others have and to desiring that their conditions improve even further. It is the sincere admiration of others' traits and abilities without any desire to compete or compare.

This is an important virtue in the context of a community where students are being trained in virtue. Comparisons and hierarchies are typical of educational structures where students can easily compete for results. Benevolence turns this around and instils the disposition to rejoice over the achievements of others

---

40. "[Hope] is something we 'lean upon' . . . it speaks less to our difficulty in actively doing something than in bearing or suffering or enduring something" (Hauerwas and Pinches, "Christian Virtues Exemplified," 342).

41. In *The Patient Ferment*, Kreider argues that the patience was the virtue that allowed the early church to grow. "Patience . . . was centrally important to early Christians . . . Christian writers called patience the 'highest virtue,' 'the greatest of all virtues,' the virtue that was 'peculiarly Christian' . . . The sources rarely indicate that the early Christians grew in number because they won arguments; instead they grew because of their habitual behavior (rooted in patience)" (Kreider, 2).

just as much as over one's own. Benevolence also leads to concrete action, as found in *kindness*,[42] *gentleness*, *goodness* and *altruism*, and to the commitment to build others up for their own good.[43] The opposite of benevolence is found in the vices of *jealousy*, which makes us protect what we think we may lose to the benefit of another; *envy*, which wants for ourselves what belongs to another; *malevolence*, which wishes that the other will lose what she or he legitimately has; and *roughness*, *harshness* and *abruptness*, which take no consideration of the needs or feelings of others.[44]

Diligence

Diligence is a zealous attention to one's actions and work. It includes a *work ethic*, a *wise use of one's time* and a sense of *duty*. Its synonyms are *zeal*, *attentiveness*, *work* and *orderliness* and its opposing vices are *sloth*, *acedia* and *laziness*. Aristotle indicated that happiness resides in the work of one's life,[45] and the Bible is well stocked with exhortations to work.[46] *Ambition* can be a positive virtue as it finds legitimate pride in *achievement* and motivation in *desiring excellence*.[47] Quality assurance in theological education is grounded in these virtues.

Together with diligence, we can think about *decency* as living in conformity to right standards of *purity*, *cleanliness* and *dignity*. Decency includes the ordering of one's person, things, speech, sexuality and a right relationship with food and other substances. I have often thought that theological students in a residential context might be judged by their diligence in ordering their rooms, as a reflection of an ordered mind and ordered affections. Teachers, instead, might be judged by the amount of coffee they drink.

---

42. "Kindliness forbids you to be over-bearing towards your associates, and it forbids you to be grasping. In words and in deeds and in feelings it shows itself gentle and courteous to all men. It counts no evil as another's solely. And the reason why it loves its own good is chiefly because it will someday be the good of another" (Seneca, *Moral Letters to Lucilius* 88).

43. Rom 15:2.

44. Porter, *Recovery of Virtue*, 107.

45. "Life's greatest joys are not what one does apart from the work of one's life, but with the work of one's life" (Bennett, *Book of Virtues*, 347).

46. "Our people must learn to devote themselves to doing what is good, in order to provide for urgent needs and not live unproductive lives" (Titus 3:14).

47. *Pleonexia* is seen as the vice of wanting more than your share to the detriment of your neighbour, but it can also be seen as the virtue of taking pride and desiring to win in the context of the *agon* – the contest.

The deficiency of diligence can easily be seen in *laziness*, but the excesses of diligence are not that easy to spot. Christians can be particularly vulnerable to *obsessive-compulsive* behaviours and *overly controlling* attitudes. These are vices that drain the vitality out of life. Diligence and work need to be mitigated by the practices of *rest* and *Sabbath*,[48] for diligence is also about resting well and enjoying the goodness of life.

Magnanimity

Magnanimity is the nobility of soul and action whereby one does more good to others than they deserve and refrains from returning evil even to those who may deserve it. It includes the Christian virtue of *forgiveness*,[49] as refraining from vengeance, and *generosity*, as quickness to give of one's own time, resources and money. *Liberality* and *philanthropy* are synonyms of magnanimity, whereas *avarice*, *greed* and *violence* are its opposites.

The excess of magnanimity is found in *vanity*, and Jesus admonished us to do our good deeds in secret. The deficiency is found instead in *pusillanimity*, where we measure out only what we think is fair, and *stinginess*, where we avoid giving if at all possible.

Knowledge

In listing the virtue of *knowledge*, we include most of the intellectual virtues: *scientia*, as the identification of axioms and supreme principles that provide unity and harmony to all things; *art*, as the ability to produce something with our hands; *intellect*, as the intuitive process that allows us to deduce/induce universally valid truths from observation; *wisdom*, as scholarly intelligence that gives lasting insight into the most important causal relationships; and *prudence*, as the acquired characteristic of choosing the correct course of action (prudence is both a cardinal virtue and an intellectual virtue).

We also find *curiosity*, as a disposition to wonder, ponder, and inquire; *intellectual humility*, as a willingness to own up to one's intellectual limitations

---

48. "*Hesuchia* is the term used in the New Testament to exhort us to work (e.g. 2 Thessalonians 3:12). In Greek mythology, she was the goddess who represented the 'peacefulness of spirit to which the victor in a contest is entitled when he is at rest afterwards'. The notion is that we strive to be at rest, not just to struggle from one goal to the next" (MacIntyre, *After Virtue*, 136).

49. Some, like Hauerwas, argue that forgiveness is at the very heart of Christian virtues (Arthur, *Education with Character*, 46).

and mistakes; and *intellectual autonomy*, as a capacity for active, self-directed thinking. *Attentiveness* is included, as a readiness to be personally present in the learning process; *intellectual carefulness*, as a disposition to notice and avoid intellectual pitfalls and mistakes; and *intellectual thoroughness*, as a disposition to seek and provide explanations.

Also worthy of inclusion are *open-mindedness*, as the ability to think outside the box; *creativity*, as the commitment to filling the void and ordering the chaos in new ways; *intellectual courage*, as a readiness to persist in thinking or communicating in the face of fear of embarrassment and failure; and *intellectual tenacity*, as a willingness to embrace intellectual challenge and struggle.[50]

Civility

The last virtue on my list is *civility*, which can be described as knowing how to live in harmony, peace, tolerance and respect for others within the right roles and authority structures. It is a cousin to justice and has to do with giving to everyone what is owed them, whether respect, honour or part of our resources.[51]

Civility is applied in *respect* towards parents, elders and authorities, but also in *peace-making* activities, in *civil obedience* and in initiatives of *social cohesion*. Civility can also include very basic actions of *courtesy* and *social etiquette*.

Civility is a virtue that deals with the right relationships to power. This is a highly sensitive issue in many parts of the world and a recurring theme in postmodern writings in philosophy, politics and education. Civility operates at both ends of the power spectrum, regulating the dispositions of the powerless and redressing the abusive dispositions of the powerful.[52]

The opposite of civility is found in *isolation, social slothfulness, strife, rebellion, tyranny* and *war*. The excesses of civility are instead found in *timidity* and *cowardice* in the face of abusive authorities and arrangements.

—

This has been a long letter. Forgive me. Consider it an opportunity to exercise constancy, diligence and patience! Hopefully I have stimulated your

---

50. "Master Virtues: IVA's Nine Master Virtues," Intellectual Virtues Academy, http://www.ivalongbeach.org/academics/master-virtues.

51. Rom 13.

52. "*Sophrosune* was an aristocratic virtue that had to do with the man who does not abuse his power" (MacIntyre, *After Virtue*, 136).

imagination and prodded you to engage with some of the great literature that focuses on the virtues.[53] You can see what a rich canopy we have before us. Lecture on this, encourage further research, find biblical examples, tell stories of heroes, invent tests, identify familiar virtues and vices and bring to the light what virtue and vice look like in your region.

In my current virtue-deficient context, may I find the hope of a better future.

---

53. See Stückelberger, Fust and Ike, *Global Ethics*, for a description of dozens of specific virtues within a theological and sociological framework of reference (https://www.globethics.net/documents/4289936/13403236/GE_Global_13_web.pdf/).

32

Character as Sought

Life is ironic. As I describe a wonderful vision of virtue, I totter close to the abyss of burn-out. This is a dark night of the soul and I apologize again for my silence in the last couple of months. I have succumbed to the pressures of constant conflict in my university and I have taken an extended sick leave. I recognized the chasm I was heading towards just in time and I've pulled back before plunging into despair.

My mind is now strangely clear, and I can see what I want to write in these final letters. I have recommendations that concern organizational issues, community, the role of venue, curriculum, teaching and learning, and assessment and accreditation. There is an odd sense of urgency in my soul and you can now expect my letters to come in rapid succession. I hope to complete all this by the end of this summer.

I realize that, in discussing virtue literacy in my previous two letters, I've not yet given you any ideas of what to actually do in the academy. I have found three verbs to be very useful in describing what needs to be done, and I will use these as a structure in my next set of letters. I will hence be speaking of character and virtue as something that is *sought*, *caught* and *taught*. In my "character as sought" letter I will be sharing about what can be done to structurally support a culture of character and virtue. In my "character as caught" letters I will write about generating a community of character and about practicalities such as the choice of a venue. And finally, I will write to you about "character as taught," addressing what can be done in terms of teaching and learning, curriculum, delivery and assessment.

Let's start, then, with character and virtue as *sought*. Rather than immediately thinking about how we can teach character and virtue, it is important that we begin with some structural issues. For, just as a plant needs the right climate to grow, so the soul requires the right environment to flourish.[1] Here are some suggestions as to how to intentionally and explicitly structure the academy in a way that will support growth in character and virtue.[2]

A Good Plan

A first important ingredient is strategic planning. As I wrote in one of my first letters, character education can lack clarity, centrality and intentionality, but a solid strategic plan is of great help.

This plan should have several elements.[3] First of all, there must be a *vision statement* that outlines where you want to be in the future. This is the big, bold dream that will provide inspiration to you, to those who will work with you and to your students. Your vision statement should use specific virtue language[4] and be concise enough so it can be easily understood by stakeholders, employees and students. You can write fuller explanations and position papers to support your vision, but the statement itself should communicate quickly and clearly.

Together with the vision statement, you should also have a *mission statement* that spells out clearly what you are planning to do in the present to fulfil your vision. So, whereas your vision statement might speak about changing your region through graduates of character and virtue, your mission statement might say that you will develop a training programme and a learning community meant to form virtuous character. In formulating your mission statement, it might be a good idea to write a SWOT analysis, in which you identify strengths, weaknesses, opportunities and threats to your mission. It will probably take some time to get the mission statement to the point that you and your board are happy with it, but, once it is in place, it will provide a clear direction for the academy.

Third, you should think about your *core values*. These describe the things that are really important in the academy and that need to be in place to achieve

---

1. The "conversion" of character requires, according to Jaeger, "a slow vegetable growth" that needs "a climate and nutrients that can only be provided by a society and its culture" (Kelsey, 9). "In the final book of the *Nicomachean Ethics* (X.9), Aristotle observes that reasoned arguments alone are not enough to make people good . . . there is little chance of becoming good if one does not grow up under good laws" (Curren, "Aristotle's Educational Politics," 546).

2. Birdwell, Scott and Reynolds, *Character Nation*, 27–35.

3. Dan McCarthy, "7 Elements of a Strategic Plan," The Balance Careers, 2 November 2018, https://www.thebalancecareers.com/strategic-plan-elements-2276139.

4. "While several Christian schools may currently have terms like discipleship, leadership, or Christ-likeness in their mission statements, these terms are not as precisely related to character development" (Roso, "Culture and Character Education," 47).

your mission and vision. These might be expressed in short sentences about what you believe in, such as: "We believe that every human flourishes in being virtuous"; "We believe that character can be intentionally shaped"; "We believe in the special power of grace to become women and men of virtuous character"; or "We believe in the dialogue between Christian theology and educational philosophy." You could also express your core values in a selection of slogans, such as: "Virtue, the purpose of human life"; "Character, the essence of discipleship"; or "Theology, transforming who you are."

Finally, your strategic plan needs *curricular aims*, yearly *objectives* and detailed *action plans*. Think of a Russian babushka doll. You need to first set out the big picture and then gradually move inwards to reveal its specific components. Your action plans will fulfil your objectives and these, in turn, will achieve your curricular aims. All of this is pretty standard strategic planning and you might use a Gantt chart or similar software to plot it all on a timeline.

A Good Organization

Once you have a plan, you have a structural foundation for the academy. It is important at this point to work out the organizational elements of the academy, for it is often at the management level that our ambitions fail. To ensure that your organizational structure is indeed facilitating the education of virtuous character, you should be able to trace every element back to its main vision.

So, for example, when you look at the facilities, the library and even the furniture, you should be able to justify the choices that are being made. The same should be true when you look at the yearly calendar, the weekly schedule and the daily routines: you should always be able to explain what they have to do with virtue. It is easy to simply imitate the models we are familiar with, but these models are often designed to fit other purposes and they can clash with your mission. Let me give you an example. The fixed deadlines and assessment dates of a traditional semester timetable are designed in line with distinct academic assessment aims, but they might stand in the way of the unpredictable dynamics of a dialogical model of communal growth.[5]

The composition of your staff is also an important indicator, and it might be a good idea to hire someone whose main job is to monitor and enhance quality assurance processes that focus specifically on character and virtue.[6] It is

---

5. "The unintended effect of timetables will be to move what is of the essence to the periphery" (Pazdan, "Wisdom Communities," 25).

6. "An office, staff and dedicated resources" are essential in creating an environment that nourishes good character (Arthur, Wilson and Godfrey, *Graduates of Character*, 15).

also very important to organize the budget to clearly reflect your priorities and for the budget itself to be an example of virtue, avoiding gross inequalities in salaries or expensive technological "toys" that are not matched by their utility.

There are many other organizational elements to be considered. Your board meetings, for example, should have standing items around character and virtue education. Your course evaluation forms should be designed to collect feedback from students with explicit reference to character and virtue. In terms of accreditation, you should seek out arrangements that will hold you accountable to your goals. You also need to be careful when it comes to the bureaucratic load of administration that is placed on teachers, for it is easy for them to lose heart under the pressures of regulatory demands.[7] Organizing workloads is also important, and you need to make sure that your team has the necessary space for the activities that support character and virtue education. Should your teachers not have sufficient time to conduct research in character education or to engage in personal mentoring, this would be a structural impediment that would need to be redressed.[8]

There are so many things that can happen in the life of a school, and the urgencies can easily distract us from what is important. That is why we need managerial foresight.[9]

Good Extra-Curricular Activities

The final area I will write about here concerns the extra-curricular activities of the academy. I have argued that the objectives of character and virtue education need to be curricular, but that does not mean that extra-curricular activities are not also of great importance. I will write about the curriculum in a separate letter, but here I would like to focus on the extra-curricular activities of the academy. This is a very important area to develop well in structuring a culture of character and virtue.

There are many examples of extra-curricular activities that contribute to character and virtue education. These might include assemblies and chapels that regularly refresh the vision for what is happening; structured worship;

---

7. "Wisdom is subverted by bureaucratic measures that focus on compliance with instrumental ends . . . [This] risks taking the fight out of some good teachers and takes other good teachers out of the fight" (Arthur et al., *Teaching*, 7).

8. "It is rare to find incentives for faculty members in higher education to engage in mentoring relationships" (Pazdan, "Wisdom Communities," 32).

9. Arthur, Wilson and Godfrey, *Graduates of Character*, 15.

the use of liturgy and the sacraments;[10] award schemes to encourage the development of character skills and virtues; "elder brother/sister" arrangements for individual mentoring and accountability schemes; music programmes;[11] and involvement in voluntary character-shaping activities in the local community.[12] Let me, however, focus on two that have particularly captured my attention: art and sports.

The use of *art* as an extra-curricular structure to support a culture of character and virtue offers great opportunities. I saw a fantastic example of this when I visited the Pio Monte della Misericordia in Naples. A sixteenth-century artisan had created a heptagonal table and had carved the seven works of mercy onto each of the sides. The noble governors of the Pio Monte used the table for their meetings, rotating around it each year to mark their taking turns in administering the seven works of mercy. As they each sat facing the engraving of the particular work of mercy they were committed to, the piece of art became a visual symbol of their duty.

The use of art and symbols is not childish, for it builds on how humans respond to visual environments. One need only think of the opposite effects of an environment saturated with perverse, lewd and violent images to understand the power in decorating our spaces. Our environment is not neutral, and we should carefully structure physical and digital artefacts to press home the message of virtue. Sadly, the spaces in many universities and theological schools are drab and functional.

A second example is found in *sports*. This may be surprising, but the educational force of sport is recognized in many cultures. In Athens, for example, gymnastics was one of the main components of the curriculum, and through the practice of sports youths grew in the virtues of self-control, discipline, love of harmony and respect for rules. In the British Empire, sport was seen for many years as having an even greater importance than academics, and was considered a crucial influence in forming English gentlemen.[13] When

---

10. Hauerwas suggests that worship and sacrament have a formative character in the community and that virtue education might be approached through the lens of liturgy. "Ethics knows that people are bad, worship tries to make them good" (Hauerwas, "Christian Ethics as Informed Prayer," 4).

11. "Rhythm and melody supply imitations of anger and gentleness, and also of courage and temperance, and of all the qualities contrary to these, and of the other qualities of character . . . in listening to such strains our souls undergo a change . . . music is able to modify the character of the soul; and if it has this power we must certainly use it in educating the young" (Aristotle, *Politics* 8.5).

12. Birdwell, Scott and Reynolds, *Character Nation*, 12.

13. "As in Athens, sport and exercise helped mould the character of English gentlemen" (Arthur, *Teaching Character and Virtue in Schools*, 23).

travelling across England, one is still impressed by the huge playing fields outside most English schools.[14] Other examples can be found in Sumerian and Roman cultures, and I'm sure you would have no difficulty finding regional examples as well. All over the world, people admire sports celebrities, and this reminds us of the importance of heroic models in emulating virtues but, sadly, also in imitating their vices.

Sport is a powerful vehicle to teach virtue, and I recall admiring the influence of my son's basketball coach in the lives of disruptive children.[15] Sport helps to shape human communities through the civic virtues of self-control, justice, human cooperation, obedience, courage and endurance,[16] and helps us to embody a careful balance between cooperation, competition and individual achievement.

You and I have personally experienced the impact of sport on our own characters as we completed our marathons (by the way, I am still far from your fantastic 3h. 23 min.). As we've trained in the heat and in the cold, in the early morning and late at night, when feeling good and when struggling with fatigue, we've developed virtues of self-discipline and endurance. We both know what it means to "hit the wall" at 30 km during a race and how to find the constancy that is necessary to continue in the face of pain. We've been diligent in researching training plans, and temperate in our diets. Surely our occasional injuries have made us humbler, as have the races which we've never won and the ones which we did not complete. Perhaps courage might even be listed, as we both faced the fear of failure in our first race and discovered the positive power of dignity that drove us to complete competitions that we were dying to quit. All our training has been a wonderful illustration of habituation. Neither of us was a born marathon-runner. We became runners through the habit of running, and now it has become a part of who we are.

I've said this before, and I'll say it again: if it were up to me, I would have every theology student run a marathon with her or his teachers.

---

14. Gillespie, "Players and Spectators," 302.

15. Albert Camus once remarked that the only place he had ever learned ethics was in sport (Gillespie, 298).

16. "[Sports] teach us the value of skill and cunning but also hardness, stamina, courage, loyalty, and rule-abidingness, virtues that sustain us through our lives" (Gillespie, 298).

An Example of a School of Character

Let me conclude with a lovely example of character and virtue in a real school.[17] This is not a theological school, but a Jewish day school that undergirds the teaching of character with the Jewish tradition and the Torah. The school handbook stresses virtues and character traits as they relate to Judaic philosophy and community, and the Torah and Judaic values are the keys to the curriculum, to academic classes and to all extra-curricular activities. Jewish values are also modelled for students through the example of teachers, who not only ask their students to live according to good virtues but also model these virtues themselves.

In this school, good character is conceived of in terms of knowing, being and doing. Students are taught how to think morally (through discussion of the Talmud and Jewish traditions), how to feel (through practising empathy with others) and how to act (through projects like collecting money for coats for the poor or reading to the elderly). Values of respect are continually taught, practical projects are regularly put in place to help "repair the world" and students are constantly given opportunities to apply moral principles to daily life through conflict resolution, ministry to nursing home residents, and community outreach. The school aims to be a caring community through positive peer relationships, through outreach in the surrounding community and through the observation of Jewish traditions and customs. Character is explicitly taught as a distinct course and virtue literacy is promoted by teaching the meaning of many Hebrew words that promote character development. Character is also integrated throughout the curriculum and most classes and activities are directly or indirectly related to character.

I've found this to be a helpful example of an educational project that grounds ethical values in religious absolutes, uses Scripture, integrates character training throughout the academic curriculum, shapes a caring community, provides multiple opportunities for moral action, models good character by teachers and leaders, and designs in-service activities that will shape moral leaders.

—

Albert the Great summarized the spirit that animated the first universities as *in dulcedine societatis quaerere veritatem*, that is, "the sweet and blessed company

---

17. The school is the Heritage Academy in Longmeadow, Massachusetts (Roso, "Culture and Character Education").

of those who seek truth."[18] There are many things that make company sweet and blessed, and in my next letter I will look at the kind of community that will make the academy prosper. Having good people is clearly more important than having a good organization, but a good organization will make it easier for good people to achieve good things. There is admittedly little joy in sitting down to manage the planning of a tower, but there is great joy in seeing it inhabited.

May you endure the discipline of management in order to reap its good fruits. This is, sadly, not my current experience, but I wish it for you.

---

18. Rüegg, *History of the University in Europe*, 354. The central idea of the Sorbonne college (1257) was summarized as *vivere socialiter et collegiater, et moraliter, et scholariter*: "A study community organized in the form of a brotherhood and living together in regulated and moral fashion" (Rüegg, 214).

33

Character as Caught

My thoughts on how character is caught in community come to you on the back of my previous letter. I have had a few sleepless nights and writing this letter has been therapeutic, as it has reminded me of one of the things that many theological schools, in normal circumstances, do very well. A typical theological school, in fact, offers unique opportunities to experience meaningful community, relational growth, worship and service. For many students, communal life is the factor in their education that has the deepest impact on their development and many consider it the best part of their theological training. This is especially true for younger students who come to study theology in their early twenties and leave their homes and families for the first time. What great hopes there are in this kind of community!

Where Community Fits In

As theologians, we draw important instruction about learning communities from the life of Israel and the church,[1] but we can also learn from educational literature and, in particular, from authors who deal with how character and virtue are caught in community. I have grown up in an individualistic culture in which we tend to think of ourselves as abstract and independent personalities for whom community is often little more than an object of consumption, a means to utility or a therapeutic crutch for individual well-being.[2] It has been refreshing to compare my dismal view of community with Plato and Aristotle's views. For them, friendship in community was a constituent dimension of

---

1. Theologians like Craig Dykstra argue that, fundamentally, character is formed in and by the Christian church community (Dykstra, *Vision and Character*). See also Bondi, "Elements of Character."

2. Jaeger, *Paideia*, xix.

humanity itself[3] and a man without a *polis* was no more than a barbarian.[4] Community was the primary source of human identity and fulfilment and prosperity were found only in being gregarious.[5]

This vision of man as a political animal fed the educational practices in Athens.[6] Plato and Aristotle, in fact, never considered education as a personal possession to be acquired in competition,[7] but as something that was done by the community, for the community, and which generated conformity to the community.[8] This conformity included the formation of character that transpired as individuals emulated the virtues of the surrounding community. Indeed, we could say that Athens did not *have* an educational programme; Athens *was* the educational programme, and the greatest character-shaping power was found in active participation in the *polis*. The main component of *paideia* was simply to live in Athens,[9] which is why it was so important for Plato to safeguard Athens as a virtuous community, even resorting to censorship if necessary.[10]

How does this model relate to the academy? The main lesson that we learn is that we need to nourish communities of virtue. No amount of organization, regulation or curricular innovation will substitute for a virtuous learning

---

3. "The milieu in which the virtues are to be exercised and in terms of which they are to be defined is the polis . . . to be without a community was to lose your humanity" (MacIntyre, *After Virtue*, 135).

4. MacIntyre, 135, 158.

5. "Although Greek culture was the first to strongly lay out the value of human individuality and freedom, they did not claim that each individual was a law to himself (as happened after the Renaissance), but that he was fully himself vis his community" (Jaeger, *Paideia*, xix).

6. "Aristotle's *Politics* begins with his famous claim that human beings are 'political animals' (*politikon zôon*). What this means is not that human beings naturally engage in political activities, but that they are gregarious, need to live together in cities in order to live the best kind of life, and are equipped by language to live as a community consciously organized in pursuit of the best kind of life" (Curren, "Aristotle's Educational Politics," 549).

7. Heywood, "Educating Ministers of Character," 16.

8. "Education is the process by which a community preserves and transmits its physical and intellectual character . . . the essence of education is to make each individual in the image of the community; the Greeks started by shaping human character on that communal model" (Jaeger, *Paideia*, xiii, xxv). "It is to, for and with specific individuals that I must do what I ought" (MacIntyre, *After Virtue*, 126). See also Gutek, *Western Educational Experience*, 28; and Arthur et al., *Teaching*, 26.

9. "As the source of group norms, values and behaviour, the *polis* served as an informal educational agency and exercised a strong formative effect on the shaping of human conduct and character. Since all citizens were expected to participate in the community, the *polis* stimulated each man to develop his potentialities . . . much Athenian education resulted informally from the experience of living in Athens" (Gutek, *Western Educational Experience*, 20, 26).

10. Virtue could only be practised within a society that "permitted and encouraged excellence," which is why Plato was in favour of censorship of certain kinds of plays (Gutek, 20).

community, and you should never forget that. The academy should not only have an educational programme, it should be one. The main shaping force on students in the academy is the community, and you need to work hard on shaping and safeguarding the community according to virtue. Virtue will breed virtue, and if you get that right, your educational task is mostly done.

The community in the academy will be composed of two main groups: your team of staff and faculty, and your students. Here are a few thoughts that can help you.

A Good Team

In my previous letter, I spoke about strategic planning and organization, but they will avail nothing if you do not have good people in the right places. The use of the word "good" is intentional and loaded with meaning. Often, when we think of a "good" team in a theological college, we think of effective leaders, efficient administrators and seasoned academics. I am instead using the term "good" in its moral sense, to intend a person of virtue. This does not exclude the excellences that come with being professionals, but it goes deeper in describing a certain kind of person. How, then, do you go about getting a team that is made up of women and men of virtue? This seems like an easy question, and all theological colleges aspire to this, but how intentional are we in shaping and preserving this kind of community? Here are some ideas.

Think first of all of your hiring processes. Within a year or so you will be creating job descriptions, advertising posts and interviewing candidates for a number of positions in the academy. You need to find ways to ensure that there is explicit understanding and consensus about the priority of character education among all those you hire.[11] Job descriptions should be explicitly matched to your mission and everyone, not only teachers, should be contractually committed to being actively engaged in formational conversations, role-modelling and virtue-related practices.[12] You are building a community of character that shares vision, a mission and a set of core values,

---

[11]. Pavela indicates that "Ethical development programs will fail if not grounded in a broad community consensus" (Pavela, "Renewed Focus," 735). "Ryan and Bohlin (1999) predict that 'Character education can take root in a school only when the administration, teachers, and staff believe in what they are striving to accomplish'" (Gretchen and Firmon, "Character Education," 192).

[12]. "Comenius spoke of a process of character education in community that included working on being a living example for imitation, providing an adequate explanation of what good is and what we are to do and then providing an opportunity for practice where doing meets knowing" (Habl, "Character Formation," 25).

and this should never be forgotten. You should never hire someone who is simply good at the job, and, if you need to choose between character and ability, always prioritize the former.

Together with the hiring process, you will need to plan the ongoing nurture of your team. Virtue is not a status but a process, and being part of the staff team in the academy should entail an ongoing experience of growth, accountability and renewal around character and virtue. For many on your team, this might be a novelty, so an initial induction will be necessary. You will, unfortunately, also have to devise firing policies and contractual articles that will allow you to legally remove people who damage the community.

Let me zoom in now on the teachers, for they represent the single most powerful tool that we have to impact a student's character.[13] As we've seen, Plato doubted the possibility of teaching virtue because he wondered about finding virtuous teachers.[14] Teachers of character and virtue education must, in fact, not only be able practitioners of character education but, first and foremost, they must be women and men of virtue themselves.[15] They will be the models from whom the next generation will learn,[16] and they should never forget that who they are, and how they conduct themselves, will shape those in their care.[17] Although we've seen that virtue and character are desirable for many professions, the stakes are particularly high for teachers in theological education because the practices for which they are training students are inseparably bound to issues of character.[18]

---

13. "Unless professors recognize the importance of moral education, unless they personally participate by treating ethical issues in their classes, counselling students, helping to define and administer rules of behaviour on campus, any effort along these lines will lack credibility and force" (Bok, "Ethics," 1). See also Ott, *Understanding and Developing*, 229; and Arthur et al., *Teaching*, 16.

14. "I have, at any rate, often sought out whether there were any teachers of it but, doing everything, I have not been able to discover any, and indeed I have searched with many – with those I supposed to be the most experienced in the matter" (Plato, *Meno* 89e).

15. "Moral development . . . is not accomplished . . . by classroom teachers who cover units on moral education . . . Character education must be embedded in the teachers' lives so that it is taught as a part of who they are" (Gretchen and Firmin, "Character Education," 192). "In Africa, we have many teachers who possess impressive diplomas, but what we need are models that Christians can imitate" (Ferdinando, "Theological Education and Character," 59).

16. Plato's *Meno* 93. Here Socrates is comparing the evil training in virtue that is done by professional Sophist mercenaries with the imitation of true Athenian gentlemen.

17. "Every class to some degree is a class in ethical conduct. For it is not so much the content but the conduct of the classroom discourse that shapes students' conceptions of how to conduct their lives" (Kiss and Euben, *Debating Moral Education*, 258).

18. "The role of both teacher and minister is not just to execute a particular task or skill efficiently, but precisely to exemplify to or for others what it is to be a virtuous, honourable or admirable human being" (Carr, *Educating the Virtues*, 117).

Having stated the obvious, let me get a little more practical for, as you recruit and train teachers, you will face several challenges. The first is that most theological educators are not trained in education, let alone in character education. Theologians normally prepare for their vocation by completing eight to ten years of academic studies in theology, and they rarely engage with the discipline of education. We've discussed this problem many times, and both of us have spent much time and energy in trying to build the educational capacities of theological educators. But the problem you will face in the academy is even more complicated, for you are looking for theological educators who have specific understanding of the theories and practices of character and virtue education. This profile might be very hard to fit.

Most theological educators have never been trained in character and virtue themselves and the virtues that are found in their characters are likely to be the outcome of other processes and of the work of God in their lives, but not of an intentional educational plan. Even if you are lucky enough to identify local theological educators who have completed a teacher-training programme, it is very unlikely that they will have been trained in how to nourish personal character qualities in themselves or in their students.[19] There are several challenges, as you can see, but do not lose heart, for you are doing something that is relatively new, and this kind of difficulty is to be expected. Also, most theology teachers will *want* to help their students grow in character and virtue, so at least you are not dealing with a recalcitrant audience.

So how might you proceed? You should begin by selecting women and men who lead lives of character and virtue. This is your prime material. You have already identified a pool of potential co-workers and have begun informal conversations with some of them. This is good but, as you proceed with formal interviews, make sure you look for character before you look for academic achievement and professional experience. I have no experience in this kind of interview myself, but I know that normal hiring protocols are insufficient. All the job applications I've come across say very little about character, and interviews are structured to tell us little more than how a person behaves during an interview. As far as references go, unfortunately many are quick, overly positive and focus on things that we are not really interested in. None that I have seen, for example, deal with issues of humility and pride, even though this is probably the greatest area of character weakness for qualified

---

19. Walker et al., *Towards a New Era*, 90–91.

academics.[20] Although we are not looking for perfection or for moral geniuses, our hiring processes need to be longer, more honest, potentially more invasive, and should include more robust probationary periods during which we can observe candidates as they interact with students.[21]

There is probably no getting around the fact that you will need to train your teachers in the specifics of character and virtue education yourself. This might even require extended retreats, during which you and your team experience the educational formulas that you plan to use with your students. This may take months or years and I agree that the logistics are daunting, but it is vital in the founding of the academy.

Good Students

Let's think now for a moment about the second group that will make up the community: your students. Here, again, you need to think carefully about selection processes, for it is very important to have students in the academy who are committed to character and virtue. You will need to be wise in gatekeeping, and think carefully about who you will let in and who will be allowed to stay in. This means that you need to work out both admissions criteria and disciplinary procedures to safeguard the community.

In the application process, you may investigate whether students have given evidence of commitment to grow in their character. A student whose main motivation is academic study might not be best served by the academy nor necessarily be the kind of community member you are looking for. Likewise, you might discourage applicants who are convinced that they "have it all together," for they might be lacking the humility that is a prerequisite to all growth. Although this might sound discriminatory, a learning community committed to virtue needs to be made up of those who are committed to virtue. Although you are not looking for students who are perfect, you should not

---

20. In some African contexts where literacy is low, a theology degree can become an instrument of discrimination and status and a "trap for God's servants" (Kohls, "Church Leadership in Africa," 111). "The higher the qualification, the greater the danger of pride and self-sufficiency" (Ferdinando, "Theological Education and Character," 47).

21. "For educating character you do not need a moral genius, but you do need a man who is wholly alive and able to communicate himself directly to his fellow human beings" (Buber, *Between Man and Man*, 105).

accept everyone on the basis of their entry grades and there are cases when you should refuse applicants on the grounds of their character.[22]

Discipline also plays an important role in the community for, just as we need to have the right people entering the community, we must also have ways to protect the ongoing identity of the community.[23] Although disciplinary codes and statutes[24] have lost force and content over time,[25] they still maintain a place of importance in many theological colleges. A disciplinary code for the academy should not simply look at the infringement of rules. What you are not looking for, in fact, is not a policing system in which students are under surveillance, rules are multiplied and routines are enforced on everyone in the same way.[26] This is not beneficial to character and will do little to elicit virtues.[27] You are not worried about students breaking rules, for just as single good actions do not make virtue, so isolated transgressions do not make vice. The infractions that you should be concerned about are related to an ongoing lack of commitment to the virtues that are holding the community together. You are looking out

---

22. Plato's abortive attempt to educate Dion's son in Syracuse is instructive. "These repeated attempts failed because the young man was already vain, undisciplined and self-absorbed by the time Plato started to work with him. The last attempt nearly cost Plato his life and, later at the Academy, the story probably made a powerful impression on Plato's pupil Aristotle. In addition, Aristotle had a number of other examples of bright and promising young men gone awry – notably Alcibiades, for whom not even the friendship of Socrates could be a palliative" (Curtler, "Can Virtue Be Taught?," 44).

23. In suggesting the "shalom community" as the centre of character development, Wolterstorff includes discipline (together with reasoning, modelling and empathy) as a necessary ingredient to cultivate dispositions (Wolterstorff, *Educating for Shalom*, loc. 2214).

24. "In the early universities in Europe, it was common to have statutes aimed at *honeste se gerrere* (decent behaviour) that generally aimed at four things: avoiding contact with women, prohibition to bear arms (to limit cases of student wars), prohibition of wearing and displaying fashionable clothes and [prohibition of] insults in word and deed against students and professors" (Rüegg, *History of the University in Europe*, 226). "The early university had *denunciantes* who were the proctors, and although students were mostly fined for infractions, sometimes positive punishment was given such as serving at tables, cleaning rooms, going to mass, weekly sermons and confessions, and in extreme cases detention cells and exclusion was also occasionally practiced" (Rüegg, 113).

25. In *Excellence without a Soul*, the former dean of Harvard University claims that whereas Harvard once aimed at making students better "youths of learning and virtue," the relativization of the meaning of "better" has vaporized that purpose. "Much has been lost today," claims Lewis, "through the combined effect of the consumer culture and the drive for perfection. Because we strive to make students happy, we cannot say they are wrong." The main moral issue confronting many universities today seems to be the definition of rape under the influence of alcohol (Lewis, *Excellence without a Soul*, 147).

26. "Transformation is about Christian character – about wisdom – and not about Christian rule-keeping" (Ferdinando, "Theological Education and Character," 53).

27. In 1860, Henry Oxenham wrote against the "principle of police" in Catholic seminaries as "It does little for eliciting the manly virtues; it helps deaden the sense of responsibility; it checks rather than fosters the development of character" (H. Oxenham, "Catholic Education," 248).

for unrepentant and unchanging character and will apply discipline when vice has become a constant replacement for virtue. In accordance with the Augustinian motto *Humanum fuit errare, diabolicum est per animositatem in errore manere*,[28] we need to protect our communities from those who are unrepentantly unwilling to grow.

As you think of disciplinary codes, make sure they are well adapted to your context. The leader of one theological school once told me that in her culture punctuality is a sign of respect for authority, and they have sent students away for regularly showing up late for classes unexcused. As you can see, the issue is not the lateness, but the lack of commitment to the virtue of civility that is customary in that culture.

A Community of Friends

In conclusion, I'd like to talk briefly about friendship. This is a worn term today that can mean anything, from emotional attachment to affirmation through social media. I hope that the academy will be a community that rediscovers the deeper meaning of friendship[29] and a place where long-term relationships are the basis for moral training.[30]

Once again, Aristotle is useful in defining friendship as the bond between those who recognize and pursue goodness.[31] For him, only the good binds, and a true friendship can only develop between good people.[32] Although friendship can involve utility and affection, these are secondary bonds. The main glue of friendship is found in a common alliance around that which is good.[33] I love this. You and I have been friends for over two decades now, and if you think about it, what has bound us together so deeply has been our

---

28. "To fall is human nature, but to persist in one's error because of pride is diabolical" (Augustine, "De Verbis Apolstoli Gal 6:2–5, *Sermo* n. 164, par. 14, http://www.augustinus.it/latino/discorsi/discorso_213_testo.htm, accessed 30 May 2019).

29. "The major seminary should strive to become a community built on deep friendship and charity so that it can be considered a true family living in joy" (John Paul II, *Pastores Dabo Vobis*, 36).

30. "Ethical training is not just teaching; it is the habituation of desires, and it requires not just a few inspirational lectures per week but a closer, long-term relationship" (Gillespie, "Players and Spectators," 297).

31. Friendship for Aristotle is "that which embodies a shared recognition of and pursuit of a good" (MacIntyre, *After Virtue*, 154).

32. Jaeger, *Paideia*, 175.

33. "Friendship of course, in Aristotle's view, involves affection. But that affection arises within a relationship defined in terms of a common alliance to and a common pursuit of good... In the modern perspective affection is often the central issue: our friends are said to be those whom we like" (MacIntyre, *After Virtue*, 156).

shared commitment to that which is good. We have shared spaces of virtue in the way we've been husbands, fathers, leaders, teachers and Christian men in our societies. We've responded with similar virtue under duress. We've demonstrated kindred intellectual virtues in our academic pursuits. We've persevered through the pain of marathons. Although imperfectly, we've habituated humility, constancy and self-control, and we've loved each other for it. We've been like Jonathan who, being a man of courage, loved David when he saw courage in him.[34]

If this is true, what better place is there to cultivate genuine friendships than in an educational community committed to the good of character and virtue?[35] In all the pain of imperfection and growth, the commitment to the project of creating and sustaining a virtuous community will allow students to consider each other and their teachers as friends.[36] Such a climate will facilitate learning.[37] Friendship, in fact, influences feelings, desires and motivations, promotes deep change and naturally replaces self-interest with cooperative pursuit and social virtue.[38] Small groups of friends provide the relational space to be humble, vulnerable and teachable.[39] They offer the ideal contexts for discussion around the virtues and their application in day-to-day events. They create zones of proximal development[40] in which learning can happen thanks to the presence of meaningful members of the community who come alongside to scaffold learning.[41] They can also bring concreteness to the theories that are being studied, furnish accountability structures for personal projects, encourage confession and provide support in cases of failure, and they represent the ideal context for peer assessment.

—

Community is a great thing, but it can also be dangerous. Those leading this kind of community need to make sure that the force of the community does

---

34. Jonathan "loved [David] as himself" after David had demonstrated courage in defeating Goliath (1 Sam 18:3). This was the same kind of courage that Jonathan had demonstrated in fighting the Philistines (1 Sam 14:1–14).

35. Curren, "Aristotle's Educational Politics," 549.

36. See MacIntyre, *After Virtue*, 156. Virtue-based friendships can also generate threatening role reversals for which teachers need to be prepared (Pazdan, "Wisdom Communities," 25).

37. Baehr remarks that shaping fundamental beliefs, attitudes and feelings is deeply personal, and needs a friendly, caring and safe environment, with the teacher and with fellow students. "Susceptibility to personal change occurs more readily in contexts marked by respect, care, and trust" (Baehr, "Cultivating Good Minds," 280).

38. Aristotle, *Rhetoric* 2.4.

39. MacIntyre, *After Virtue*, 156.

40. L. Vygotskij, *Mind in Society* (Cambridge, MA: Harvard University Press, 1978), ch. 6.

41. Heywood, "Educating Ministers of Character," 16.

not wipe out the agency of the individual. Some of my suggestions in this letter may sound cultish, and, indeed, the academy may face this criticism. Cults, in fact, typically use the strength of community to conform, brainwash and dominate the will of their members. They also create boundaries, approve the chosen elite and discriminate against all others. May this horrify you.

We are dealing with individuals who are made in the image of God and we must always respect their will. God himself does not coerce. If people change and conform to a community, they must do so in full awareness and self-ownership. Make sure you keep the practices of *phronesis* up front, involving everyone in rational dialogue. Ask your students to subscribe to learning contracts. Ask for continued critical feedback and listen to it carefully. If you have virtue tables in your community, strive for agreement, but allow for difference. Be firm in your exhortations, but tolerant in demanding detailed obedience. Speak with meaningful vocabulary, but keep the edges blurred. Consider discipline and expel those who disrupt the community if necessary, but never make it personal. Be trusting as a dove, but also careful as a serpent about the legal issues that might include anti-discrimination laws, infringement of liberty or personal vexation. Never forget to be hospitable and accepting of everyone, especially of those who are different and are not a part of your learning community.

Always remember that no amount of structuring, planning or good intentions will stop sin. You may do everything right to build and maintain an intentional community of virtue. But you can be Seneca and produce a Nero. You can be Plato and educate Alcybiades. You can be Paul whose associate was Demas, or Jesus who spent three vain years with Judas. Temptation will be there, and people might fall and fail. Even the most committed will falter. Always frame all that you think, feel and do in a balance of grace and forgiveness on the one hand and justice and truthfulness on the other.

I've purposely kept from sharing a piece of news with you until the end of this particular letter. I have, in fact, lost my community. After twenty-seven years of work in my university, I have been made redundant and, three months from now, I will be leaving. For the first time in my adult life, I will be an orphan. I harbour no hard feelings towards my beloved community, although I hurt from the injustice that has been done. What I feel most is genuine bereavement.

I've written and torn up parts of this letter several times. I am still unhappy with it overall. Hopefully, you will glean some good from it. As you lead the new community in the academy, may you grow in justice and create right interactions in the community so that even the burden of leaving may be bearable.

34

A Venue for Virtue?

How lovely of you to invite me to come and join the academy. No, my friend. Although I will consider it and pray about it, this is your dream, and I must look elsewhere. Thank you also for not diverting our correspondence to my personal situation. You know me well enough to understand that I am best helped by focusing on the tasks at hand. Answering your questions about venue is a welcome task.[1]

You are in a privileged position where all the options are still on the table, so let us think about *where* you will establish yourself physically. This is important, because the whereabouts of the academy will not only contribute to its identity but will also determine your delivery mode. There are a number of models that I would like to explore under the following names: the *cloud* model, the *retreat centre* model, the *embedded city* model, the *local community* model and the *residential campus* model. Notice that I have listed them in rough order from an "outward" to an "inward" focus, with at one end of the spectrum the cloud model, in which students are kept in their local contexts without any physical contact with a learning community, and at the other end the isolated campus model, where students are kept together in a close-knit community with relatively little contact with the outside world. Let us review them briefly and consider their benefits. I will then suggest the one that I think is the most promising for the academy.

The Cloud Model

The *cloud* model refers to online education. Here the venue is "in the cloud" and there is no physical campus. If you choose to go with this model, all you need is an open office space where tutors can operate from behind computers

---

1. C. Taylor, "Location of Theological Schools."

and a nice meeting room for your team. Beyond the advantages related to finances and access, this model may seem unworthy of consideration when it comes to character and virtue education, but I think there are some things going for it. Since it is probably the most counter-intuitive model, I will write a little more to explore it.

In this model, I imagine a careful blend of online taught components, well-crafted discussion forums, habituated reflective exercises linked to local practices and close one-to-one tutoring through social media. The convincing argument for this approach is that students are not pulled out of their normal life situations and are called to develop virtue where they live. I can think of other advantages as well, such as ubiquitous access and instant communication through smartphones, which can favour constancy, good habits, accountability, reciprocal support, a sense of equality, the capacity to allow introverts to participate more fully, the ability to drip-feed input and reflection in bite sizes, the facility to intervene at the moment of need and the opportunity to develop new kinds of remote, bi-directional friendships that can be just as powerful in terms of educational impact as face-to-face relationships.[2]

If you choose this model, make sure you carefully craft the virtual learning environment to intentionally reinforce a culture where virtue can be caught. This will be your virtual home, and it must be curated to exhibit virtue. This can be done in many ways, such as exhibiting *creativity* in your learning design and site art, crafting *order* in the structures of the categories and courses, committing your teaching team to *constancy* in feedback to queries, encouraging *curiosity* in Internet searches, modelling *respect* in forum netiquette, reinforcing *integrity* and *dignity* in anti-plagiarism rules, appealing to *friendship* in issues of discussion forum lurking, offering *care* and *love* in sharing written prayers or in naming *resilience* as a character trait that can help deal with attrition and drop-out issues. Forgive the irresistible play on words: your virtual environment must itself be virtuous.

Your online delivery should also be contextualized to the digital culture and speak into its specific vices. These vices include being fake, distracted, unaccountable, intolerant, entertainment-prone, fragmented, superficial, careless, impulsive, ego-centric, homophile and shallow. As you train digital natives in character and virtue, your ethical lists should include virtues that counter these vices, such as genuineness, attentiveness and intentionality, accountability, commitment, discipline, unified thinking, scrupulousness,

---

2. Ellison, *With a Little Help*.

thoughtfulness, reflectiveness, other-centricity, acceptance of difference and depth.

The whole issue of relationships looms in the background of online delivery, especially when we imagine character and virtue education. Many, in fact, believe that, without physical presence, deep relationships are not really possible. If this were true, it would be a severe blow to online character education. I am not, however, sure of this conviction, and I have not seen it well supported by research in the social sciences or in theological consideration. A growing body of research is actually demonstrating the opposite, suggesting that it is possible to have meaningful online relationships and that there are unique online relational opportunities that are not available in face-to-face contexts. What we have seen about friendship in the pursuit of the common good, for example, might be favoured by the ubiquity of online contexts that provide unique opportunities for attachment, companionship, emotional support and help.[3]

Online character and virtue education is therefore possible, but I admit that it is not the delivery method of my choice. If you do use it, we should talk further about a number of issues, such as the means to reinforce community and to avoid individualistic isolation.

Let us think further now about three other models: the retreat centre model, the embedded city model and the local community model.

The Retreat Centre Model

If you should choose the *retreat centre* model, you need to find a nice, isolated place that can provide lodging, catering and meeting rooms. You probably also want to have permanent accommodation for your team, library space, and offices for your administration staff and faculty. This kind of venue is conducive to a delivery approach where you bring your students together for weekends and intensive sessions in combination with individual study and projects done at home. On the "outward–inward" spectrum, this model is strongly outward, as it assumes that your students are mostly living in their natural contexts where they are engaged in habituation, service-learning and reflective practice.

Bringing students together for regular retreats offers the opportunity to build virtue friendships, to enjoy intensive experiences in an intentional community of virtue and to benefit from intense instruction, structured reflection, interaction, mentoring, encouragement and planning. The retreat

---

3. Matook and Butler, "Social Media"; Wright, "Self-Referent Motivation," 115–130.

centre offers a virtuous cycle where students are motivated and equipped with precise plans, sent back into their contexts for practice, and then called back again into the community to report, reflect and move forward.

The Embedded City Model

The *embedded city* model is similar to the retreat centre, with the difference that it places itself inside a big city. The idea is that we establish a highly accessible learning centre that can offer innumerable opportunities to develop habituation practices for all the virtues. The embedded city model strategically takes advantage of the unique opportunities of a big city to exercise virtue in social services, law enforcement centres, charities, hospitals, parishes and schools. Students in this model engage with the academy on a part-time basis, and then develop character and virtue in their professional activities and in new and challenging contexts. A lawyer, for example, might work intentionally on character virtues that relate to her profession, such as diligence or magnanimity, and then she might be stretched into developing new sets of virtues, like mercy, through prison visitation.

In terms of logistics, this model requires learning and office space but no accommodation, as your students would be attending evening sessions or day-long retreats over the weekend.

The Local Community Model

The *local community* model moves closer on the inward spectrum by creating many small local communities within a larger network. This model is comparable to the new church expressions that we spoke about in a previous letter and fits well with theological education by extension models (TEE) that focus on the local delivery of shared programmes.

The model sets up dedicated venues in several places, which need be no more than a room where the local cohort can meet several times a week. The local group is typically led by a trained facilitator who relies on shared guidelines to engage in both personal and group work. This model commits the academy's teachers to regularly travel to different small communities. Their tasks during these visits are similar to those in the retreat centre model but distributed in smaller bites to a smaller group. Should the number of local community groups grow significantly, you can train local group leaders; but be cautious about expanding too quickly, for inadequate preparation of these leaders would be highly detrimental.

The strong point of this model is the integration within the local community and the church. Ideally, you should find local churches that share your vision and actively participate in the project. Without this, this particular model will not work, because the virtue-practising activities will take place mostly through the ministries of the churches. A nice addition to this model might be an annual conference that gathers the small communities together in a hotel somewhere for a time of encouragement, testimony and further equipping.

The Residential Campus Model

As you can see, each model has advantages and disadvantages. Some are embedded in outward contexts and keep the academy from becoming insulated, ingrown and overly intellectual, while others focus on the internal context and enhance the possibilities of building the kind of community of virtue that we have been talking about in the last couple of letters.

This leads me to the final model of the traditional *residential campus*. This involves having a self-contained venue with all the trimmings of a traditional higher education campus, including accommodation and catering facilities, libraries, learning spaces and sports fields. This model uses a delivery approach in which students live full-time with their peers, teachers and the staff team. An ideal venue for the academy would be in relative isolation, but still situated within an easy commute from a large city and with access to multiple churches in the vicinity. This would allow you to reap some of the benefits from the embedded city and local community models and make sure that you engage with outward contexts as your students seek to practise a wide range of virtues.

There are, of course, historical precedents for this model. The founders of American colleges, for example, chose bucolic locations and built high walls around their campuses because they believed that a virtuous community could be best sought out, created and protected in isolation.[4] Similarly, the Second Vatican Council encouraged the existence of "the religious house" for the formation of priests, as a place where detachment could take place and growth could occur within a community.[5] A sort of commune is what I have in mind here, reminiscent of monastic traditions. In cultures that are particularly distracting, damaging and dark, there is indeed something to be

---

4. Kiss and Euben, *Debating Moral Education*, 126.
5. John Paul II, *Pastores Dabo Vobis*, 36.

said about the Benedictine model of virtuous communities that survive by retreating into the desert.[6]

I think that this might be the slightly better solution for the academy. The advantages are the intensity of focus and teaching, the ongoing context of accountability and emulation, the possibilities for providing structure to the educational process and the ongoing community life in which character and virtue education can be lived out.[7] Given the novelty of the academy, I fear that the other models might dilute the process and lose its focus. Clearly, there are also disadvantages to the residential campus model, but I think that they are outweighed by the benefits.

—

I recall visiting a Benedictine monastery with you in your region; did you say something about it recently being shut down? Before I forget, thank you for letting me know that Sofia will not be pursuing doctoral studies at this point. May God open unexpected doors for this young lady.

May you guard your soul from the love of bricks that is the root of many evils.

---

6. MacIntyre, *After Virtue*, xiii, xiv; Dreher, *Benedict Option*.

7. "Real character education is not preached at you, but rather lived with you" (Gretchen and Firmin, "Character Education," 192).

35

Virtuous Curriculum

I really like the recruitment and training plan that you have shared with me. I highly commend your intention to spend an entire year with your newly formed team before opening the academy to students. I look forward to seeing this happen and I would be honoured to respond to the invitation to join you, as a guest, for a term.

Speaking of good things in community, I have just come back from a two-day retreat with my former university. The entire staff and faculty, leadership and board, together with those of us who have been made redundant, have come together for a time of truth and reconciliation. I admit that I have been surprised by grace, moved in my soul and rejoined in love to this community. I have seen many virtues again. My hope is rejuvenated.

Challenging the Standard Curriculum

Now for the topic of this letter, which is the curriculum. Although I have written about the dangers of too much systemization in character and virtue education, this does not mean that we should abandon curriculum design. Indeed, there are few things that have more impact in the world than well-designed educational curricula, so this is our challenge.[1]

But where to start? Can we look for models elsewhere? I recall how, in a brilliant publication a few years ago, you dealt with the "Roman occupation" of the curriculum in theological education. In the article you argued that, just as the Roman troops marched in standardized formation to conquer the world, so most theological schools across the world have designed their curricula in

---

1. "An important fact was first adumbrated in Plato's *Republic*: to understand any cultural conflict, one must look first to the design of the curriculum . . . Any profound change in the character of a civilization will, therefore, express itself most clearly in a reform of who teaches what to whom and how" (Koons, "Three Humanisms," 199).

standard fashion. With relatively little variation, this usually includes the four categories of systematics, biblical studies, dogmatics and practical theology. Although this occupation is not a bad thing, it is not very useful for the academy. The mission of the academy, in fact, demands that we challenge this standard arrangement, first because the four traditional disciplinary silos of theology have little room for character and virtue education, but also because it is frustrating to achieve holistic educational aspirations within such clear-cut boundaries.

In a thought-provoking video,[2] Martin Seligman (the founder of positive psychology) asks his audience two questions: (1) What do we want most for our children in life? and (2) What do our schools actually teach children? Whereas the responses to the first question included things like joy, fulfilment and happiness, the answers to the second question catalogued things like teaching competences, facts and knowledge. The difficulty in matching the two lists is apparent. How is joy connected to knowledge, or how do competences produce happiness? A similar mismatch can be found in theological education. If asked what our greatest aspirations are for our theological graduates, we would list that they might become flourishing men and women who love God and neighbour and who will impact the church and society. When it comes to the curricula that we design to achieve this, however, we typically fill them with facts of church history, critical debates over the atonement and techniques for creating good sermon outlines. Again, how do the two lists match? If it is not clear how our aspirations are met by what we are teaching, we may need to reconsider our curricula.

Where to Start

How, then, can we go about designing innovative curricula that take character and virtue education seriously? Our common friend Perry Shaw has suggested that we start curriculum design by asking the right questions. In our correspondence so far, we've pretty much answered his basic questions about the church, the contextual challenges, the Christian leader, the learners, the destination of graduates, the time frame, the learning environment, the facilitation of learning and some of his "what" and "how" questions.[3] What we have not done yet is to think strategically about the aims and outcomes of

---

2. "Martin Seligman: Highlights from Grit and Imagination Summit, 2016," Vimeo, https://vimeo.com/192522856.

3. Shaw, *Transforming Theological Education*, 20–42.

the programme, nor have we designed a map of learning activities. That is the purpose of this letter.

We will start with aims and learning outcomes, but before we do so, let me throw another variant at you. I would like to suggest that the term "learning" outcome might be deceptive. For, although "learning" has broad connotations, it is most naturally associated with the cognitive and practical domains. We tend to think of "learning" as gaining knowledge and understanding, as sharpening thinking skills, as absorbing practical skills or as acquiring generic competences. We do not naturally relate the word "learning" to the domain of character and virtue. It sounds slightly odd, in fact, to speak about "learning" courage, constancy and temperance. Or, worse yet, we might misunderstand the intent of the word we are using, and conclude that we are learning *about* courage, *about* constancy and *about* temperance, which would be a dramatic shortfall in respect to the aims of character education. Might I suggest that, for clarity's sake, we speak of "growing outcomes" instead of "learning outcomes"? *Growth* language, in fact, brings us nearer to what we have in mind. Better yet, we could speak about "growing-in-grace" outcomes.[4]

So now that we have got our terminology straight, let's look at aims and growing outcomes.

Aiming Right

A few letters ago we discussed the importance of a strategic plan with curricular aims. I gather that you're still working on the overall plan, but the draft that you sent me looks great. I especially like the three aims that you have set for your programme. I quote your draft:

1. The programme of the Theological Academy for Character and Virtue aims to provide an experience of theological education in which character and virtue education is prioritized and integrated with academic knowledge and understanding, with ministry skills and competences and with appropriate spiritual formation.

2. The programme of the Theological Academy for Character and Virtue aims to foster knowledge and understanding of theological, theoretical and historical frameworks for character and virtue

---

4. "To grow in grace is to develop virtues, provisional perfection, and those settled dispositions [which] are the matrixes for forms of human action which enable us to be that which we were created to be" (Gunton, "Church as a School of Virtue," 231).

education, which include vocabularies of virtue and strategies for character growth.

3. The programme of the Theological Academy for Character and Virtue aims to nourish personal growth in character and virtue that includes intellectual, moral and public virtues. It also aims to equip students for a lifelong journey of character and virtue development in order to flourish as human beings, achieve increasingly deep happiness, contribute to the well-being of their communities and glorify God.

That is really good. I think you have covered the basic areas that we have been discussing. Although you might have opted for a more simplistic division of aims related to knowing, doing and being, I much prefer your nuanced approach in which the "being" component is integrated into each aim.

From Aims to Outcomes

Now let me try to map out some examples of growing outcomes. My list is not exhaustive, and I have not tried to order or categorize it, so take it as a brainstorming exercise. I start my list with the standard phase: "Students completing this programme will . . .":

1. Have a theologically informed vision of character and virtue that is worked out through a narrative of creation, fall, redemption and restoration and is expressed in a *missio Dei*;

2. Be able to articulate how human agency and divine grace interact in the process of growing in character and virtue;

3. Understand how the aims of character and virtue integrate with other aims of theological education, including the overlap with and difference from spiritual formation;

4. Understand the history and philosophy of character and virtue in various cultural contexts;

5. Be able to articulate and implement frameworks for character and virtue education that are contextually relevant, theologically justified and educationally sound;

6. Be articulate in a vocabulary of virtue;

7. Understand what wisdom is as it relates to virtue;

8. Be wise in making choices related to virtue, avoiding both excess and defect;
9. Grow in the realm of intellectual virtues;
10. Grow in the realm of personal moral virtues;
11. Grow in the realm of public virtues;
12. Be motivated in the pursuit of virtue and the avoidance of vice;
13. Be virtuous and integrated members of a community;
14. Be able to self-assess their growth in character, identify areas of weakness in virtue in their personal lives and develop strategies for growth;
15. Understand habituation dynamics and be able to intentionally plan and enact habit-forming strategies for growth in virtue in self and others;
16. Grow emotionally so that their affections are aligned with virtue;
17. Know how to implement strategies to help others grow in character and virtue in various contexts;
18. Be able to reflect contextually on virtue and implement strategies of character growth that are appropriate to various cultures.

As you can see, I have not included many of the typical outcomes that are found in programmes of theological education (e.g. knowledge and understanding of Christian Scripture and theology, and ability to interpret texts and apply theology in relevant ways), but this does not mean that they are not important, nor that you should exclude them. I have restrained myself from going any further, in order to allow you to complete the exercise for yourself.

A Radical Curriculum

Once you have aims and outcomes, you can imagine a curriculum. In dreaming this up, I may have gone too far and fallen into educational fiction. Still, this kind of radical exercise is helpful. I leave it to you to land it all back in reality.

The curriculum I've imagined entails a three-year, full-time programme in a residential context. Each year features six to seven courses, which I have briefly described in light of the growing outcomes above. I have not specified the credit weighting of each course, but that is an easy detail to add once you have made your certification choices.

Year 1

- *Understanding Character and Virtue Education:* this foundational course gives students a basic induction to the programme, its aims and objectives, its practices and how it is assessed; it also sets the aims of character and virtue in the context of their broad historical roots and demonstrates how this is a bona fide programme of theological education.
- *The Theology Degree You Will Not Get:* this course provides an overview of a traditional theological degree; in telling students what they will not get you will indirectly provide it in a condensed form that will prime them for further study.
- *Conceptual Frameworks for Character Education:* this course introduces the Aristotelian framework, compares it with other possible frameworks and critically engages with the framework from a theological and multicultural standpoint.
- *Introducing the Virtues:* this course provides students with a vocabulary of virtue and includes thematic work on the virtues through Old and New Testament biblical theology.
- *Engaging Growth in Community:* this course aims at growth in understanding and practising virtue in community.
- *Sport for Character:* this course organizes sporting activities with a focus on nourishing the virtues of self-control, discipline, cooperation, teamwork and perseverance.
- *Habituation Practicum 1:* this course leads students to self-assess their character through a virtue-related project in the learning community.

Year 2

- *Understanding Habituation:* this course provides a basic induction to the principles and practices of habituation; it also relates growth in virtue to how students function emotionally, to how their reason elaborates, to how their desires work, to how their will determines courses of action, to how their perception picks up situations and to how others perceive them; it also deals with the work of the Holy Spirit in character growth.
- *A Theology of Character and Virtue:* this course provides training in theological method and helps students to develop a theology of

character and virtue; it includes work on the relevance of character and virtue in the *missio Dei* and how soteriology relates to character transformation.
- *The Cardinal Virtues in Theology and Practice:* this course does specific work related to the cardinal virtues; it works out specific theologies and practices of justice, courage, prudence and temperance.
- *Capital Vices and Corrective Virtues in Individual and Communal Life:* this course does specific work related to the capital vices and virtues in the context of a theology of sin and human nature; it also engages with virtue and vice in personal life, community life and society.
- *Art and Music for Character:* this course organizes artistic and musical[5] activities with a focus on nourishing the virtues of harmony, beauty, creativity and reflection; it also allows students to engage with some of the world's great art and helps them produce their own artefacts.
- *Habituation Practicum 2:* this course leads students to work on a project in the local community to grow in specific virtues.

Year 3

- *Understanding Wisdom:* this course provides a basic induction to the principles and practices of wisdom and *phronesis*; it engages with the golden mean, with discernment practices and with biblical wisdom literature, like Proverbs, and classical wisdom literature.
- *Virtue in Church and World:* this course provides students with a vision of the impact of virtue in the church and the world; it also helps students engage with issues of context and culture as they relate to character and virtue.
- *The Intellectual Virtues as Scholarship:* this course does specific work related to the intellectual virtues, in particular as they relate to academic work; it habituates students in these virtues and equips them to produce a significant academic artefact that requires the exercise, cultivation and demonstration of these virtues. The artefact

---

5. Aristotle writes extensively about the capacity of music to shape character and judgment (Curren, "Aristotle's Educational Politics," 551).

- *Literature for Character:* this course exposes students to stories and key texts about character, both biblical and otherwise; it includes stories of inspiring heroes of virtue and villains of vice; this course can be used to deepen students' knowledge of the basic biblical narrative and of the relevant secular literature.
- *Reading Project:* this course allows students to practise the intellectual virtue of attentiveness through extensive reading in academic theology; this course will contribute to achieving knowledge and understanding outcomes related to academic theology.
- *Demonstrating Virtue in Communication:* this course sets students on a variety of communication projects, equipping them with the skills of writing, teaching and rhetoric, and reinforcing the virtues necessary for communication.
- *Habituation Practicum 3:* this course helps students devise, implement and assess a lifelong habituation plan that they will engage with after the completion of the programme.

(or dissertation) entails a critical discussion of character and virtue education.

As usual, my list is indicative and not exhaustive, and I look forward to your revision. There are no electives, of which I am generally cautious.[6] There is also a progression from year 1 to year 3, featuring more content in the first years and more practice in the last part of the programme. Although the courses may seem like a series of lectures, each course should feature no more than 30 percent total lecture time, with ample space for projects, personal work and structured reflection. This will vary from course to course, depending on the outcomes. You will note that there is also a major habituation project every year and a strong emphasis on self-reflection and assessment. I have not listed the courses in chronological order, although some topics are propaedeutic to others and several topics are best scheduled simultaneously.

What we need next is to populate these courses with learning activities and then think about the difficult topic of assessment. I will write about this shortly.

—

As you meet with perplexity, remember that we are not on a war of conquest. Not all curricula need to look like ours, and there is also no harm in finding creative blends with a more traditional curriculum.

---

6. "In place of the spacious vision offered by the Grand Canyon of the classical curriculum, the elective system drops students down a succession of scattered oil wells" (Koons, "Three Humanisms," 203).

As I conclude this letter, I am reminded of the story in Judges 15 where Samson uses the fresh jawbone of a donkey to strike down his enemies. What is remarkable is that, after Samson finished his battle, he threw the tool of his victory away. He did not write a book about it. He did not design a course on using jawbones as the ultimate methodology. He did not offer seminars in which he showcased the jawbone. He threw it away. And here is a lesson for us. We can design good curricula that will help us accomplish our task, but let us never enshrine methods as keys to success.

May our trust in God make us trustworthy.

36

Character as Taught

Greetings from Dubai airport! I am taking a brief trip to pursue employment opportunities and I have a long stopover in which I aim to complete this letter.

We have come at last to the issue of teaching virtue. As I argued previously, character can be taught, displayed, demanded, practised and reflected on. But what are some explicit teaching strategies that can be used to help students grow in their character and virtue? In simple terms, how we are to go about this business?[1] Happily, there are many good practices to be explored and, although the shaping of the human soul escapes the rigidity of technique, there are some very useful things that can be done through education.

In the next letter we will look at practices of teaching and learning. Here I'd like to focus on course design.

Naturally Taught

Before we look at how to design courses that teach character and virtue, it is useful to consider how growth in character and virtue occurs as a natural byproduct of other teaching activities. What I mean is that there are some things that we are already doing in most theology courses that naturally contribute to teaching character and virtue. This is encouraging, since it means that we are not entirely starting from scratch.

The first of these has to do with knowledge. Knowledge, on its own, in fact, changes character. Regardless of what is taught, people change simply because of what they know. And if what they know is good, they will change for the good. Good knowledge influences emotions, tempers dullness,

---

1. "People no longer question if character should be taught . . . the question is how character should be taught in the daily school setting" (Roso, "Culture and Character Education," 31).

corrects parochiality, impacts our habits and shapes our mental nature.[2] This is particularly true when it comes to the knowledge of God and of truth that is imparted in courses of theological education. Whether we realize it or not, the act of teaching theological knowledge impacts the character of our students.

Engaging with culture also has a natural impact on character. This, again, happens spontaneously in many theology courses as students engage with the humanities, read great books, understand great philosophy, are moved by great history and enjoy great art.[3] Culture contributes to making them better people and we should deeply value these things in our teaching. Speaking personally, my "virtue reservoir" is deeply replenished every time I take an art history trip to Italy.

Third, virtue is a natural byproduct of theological education through the cultivation of the intellectual virtues. This has to do with the characteristics that students develop as they engage with truth. Courses in theological education make students read, take notes, conduct critical research, engage in academic writing, memorize for exams and engage in intellectual struggle. These things do much more than prepare students for a life of tests; they shape them intellectually for the tests of life.[4] Intellectual virtues such as perseverance, attentiveness and intellectual thoroughness are an essential part of virtuous character and there is no better place to develop them than in an academic programme.

Although knowledge acquisition, cultural engagement and development of intellectual virtue may not be identified as direct virtue-teaching activities, they are important allies that need to be recognized. This kind of character education is already happening, and we should name it, support it and help students become more conscious of it.[5]

Planning and Teaching Specific Character and Virtue-Related Courses

We come now to what can be done *explicitly* to teach virtue through specific courses. Since this is not happening in many theological schools, some

---

2. "Education implies an action upon our mental nature, and the formation of character" (Maskell and Robinson, *New Idea of the University*, 25).

3. "Character is cultivated and developed as a result of the study of culture" (Readings, *University in Ruins*, 15). The acquisition of a moral education by the *studia humanitatis*, for example, "enabled one to act responsibly as a member of one's family and one's society" (Rüegg, *History of the University in Europe*, 449).

4. "Schooling should prepare students for the tests of life rather than just a life of tests" (Arthur et al., *Teaching*, 27).

5. Baehr, "Educating for Intellectual Virtues," 22–23.

innovative thinking is needed. What I have in mind here are specific, identifiable courses in the curriculum (such as those listed in my previous letter) whose main outcomes are related directly to issues of character and virtue.

The greatest danger in teaching a course related to virtue is that you end up telling students about character and virtue rather than helping them to grow in character and virtue.[6] We have a funny way of fooling ourselves that knowledge about something is adequate in itself.[7] Indeed, when it comes to character and virtue, the opposite may be true, and too much rational engagement with the theories of virtue may desensitize the soul to the realities of virtue. Many ethics courses run this risk, as they deal with theories that leave students satisfied with their abilities to reason well in moral terms but with little grip on the formation of the kind of character necessary for them to deal with real-life moral situations.[8] This is a fatal mistake.[9] While we certainly need to teach things about the good, our main aim should be to nourish persons who are good.

Having dealt with this danger, let me be a little more positive and explore a process of creating courses that will foster growth in character and virtue. I have found some good work done by the Jubilee Centre for Character and Virtue and I would like to apply it to theological education. The Centre has drawn heavily on Aristotelian thinking to identify a three-fold process of mutually interrelated aspects in course design that have been labelled the "caterpillar" process.[10] Let me unpack this process briefly.

First, courses in character and virtue should feature *virtue knowledge*. This cognitive domain includes elements such as basic definitions and vocabularies, metaphors and examples, understanding of frameworks, historical analysis and explanations of what each virtue looks like and why it is important. Socrates at first thought that virtue was not knowledge, but he then changed his mind

---

6. To defuse the danger of a cognitive drift, teachers might consider developing a mission statement referring to virtues. It might read as follows: "We are a community of inquirers tasked with philosophical learning and reflection. As your instructor, my primary aim is not to impart a body of knowledge; rather, it is to nurture your relationship to learning by providing ongoing opportunities for you to practice . . . virtues" (Baehr, 367).

7. "The development of reason can detach a man from the sentiments of his heart so that he becomes dehumanised and desensitised" (Kiss and Euben, *Debating Moral Education*, 284).

8. "The incorporation of formal courses of ethics in programs of professional training – while arguably necessary for satisfactory professional education – may not be sufficient to ensure the development of morally appropriate occupational sensibilities" (Carr, *Educating the Virtues*, 121).

9. Buber, *Between Man and Man*, 105.

10. Harrison, Bawden and Rogerson, *Teaching Character*, 7.

and admitted that thinking skills are a key part of virtue.[11] Virtue knowledge also includes looking at what each virtue does particularly well, and which emotions are alerted to call for their practice. Elements of virtue knowledge in a course should respond to the question: "Do I know virtue?"

Second, courses should include *virtue reasoning*. Here, we are helping students think about what the virtues look like in the real world and in their experience. This might also be called "virtue perception" and it happens as we triangulate the perception of virtue, the observation of the world and the self-understanding of the individual. As we have seen, it is not enough simply to know about virtue, and we must help individuals to learn how to continually "read" themselves in real-life situations. Virtue reasoning answers questions about our basic dispositions and inclinations towards particular virtues, about how to act in specific situations, about how the golden mean operates in specific circumstances, about cultural contextualization, about how circumstances are important and about handling conflicting virtues. Virtue reflection is ingrained in the practices of *phronesis*, prudence and wisdom, and keeps us away from the rocks of indoctrination. A student's growth in the ability to reason around virtue is an important marker of character development.[12] Virtue reasoning in a course responds to the question: "How do I understand virtue in my world?"

Lastly, courses on virtue need to include *virtue practice*. This is perhaps the most important aspect because it is here that our teaching makes sure that knowledge and reflection around the virtues actually engage with the student's life and character.[13] Virtue practice builds into a course opportunities to exercise the virtues, engage in self-examination and to reflect on practice and character development. To do this, we need to imagine situations where students can habituate particular virtues over time. These situations, such as an extended internship in a refugee camp, a year-long neighbourhood cleaning project or even a semester spent cataloguing books in a library, will allow students to respond to specific virtues over an extended period of time. This will generate opportunities for habituation of the right kind of emotions as students repeatedly choose to do the right things. This kind of practice will

---

11. Arthur et al., *Teaching*, 12.

12. Kohlberg's stages of moral development include the ability to reason around morality as an important stage of moral growth. Kohlberg, *Philosophy of Moral Development*.

13. "Practicing virtues remains among the most important and powerful steps we can take to cultivate virtues. While we can sometimes develop virtues in the absence of role models or 'exemplars,' or without an especially supportive community, we rarely if ever do so in the absence of virtuous practice. For this reason, practicing virtues is perhaps the most important means of developing virtues" (Baehr, "Cultivating Good Minds," 376).

have a deep effect on students' identities as they develop constancy in virtue and are affirmed by their community as they do so.

I have come across a five-fold set of descriptors of genuine growth in character that are really helpful as we design virtue practice in a course.[14] The first descriptor is *attention* and it reminds us that courses on character and virtue should teach students to notice and attend to situations that require specific virtues. The second descriptor relates to the *emotions*, meaning that the courses we teach should help students cultivate and recognize the kinds of feelings that are roused by both virtue and vice. The third has to do with *desire*, meaning that virtue practice in a course should contribute to making students want to change things. Then we have *actions*, which are most evident as we seek to design experiences that generate commitment to ethical goals. And, finally, the last descriptor is *expression*, meaning that courses should devise ways to help our students develop the kinds of personalities that are perceived as virtuous by those around them.

The elements in this caterpillar process of course design are not necessarily in chronological order, and you should blend them together as courses develop. If you look back at the radical curriculum that I described in my previous letter, you will be able to recognize this three-fold process in most courses. You may find a brief review of those courses helpful at this point.

Teaching Character and Virtue across the Curriculum

In addition to teaching specific courses, it is also important to think about designing virtue-teaching across the curriculum. You may, in fact, choose to mix virtue-specific courses and traditional theology courses. Here, it is important to think about an integrated teaching strategy in which character and virtue remain as an outcome of all courses. Whatever you do, you want a cohesive, integrated programme and not a set of independent courses. To be effective, the objectives of character education need to be transversal and curriculum-wide.[15]

It may be helpful to sketch a little diagram here.

---

14. Arthur et al., *Teaching*, 28.

15. "To be effective, character education must be comprehensive, intentionally making use of every phase of school life as an opportunity to develop good character" (Lickona, "Religion," 23). "Insofar as character lessons are grafted onto the course load and have no meaningful connection to the core curriculum, they make ethical concerns appear artificial – something reserved for particular occasions, rather than part of the warp and woof of everyday life" (Roso, "Culture and Character Education," 30).

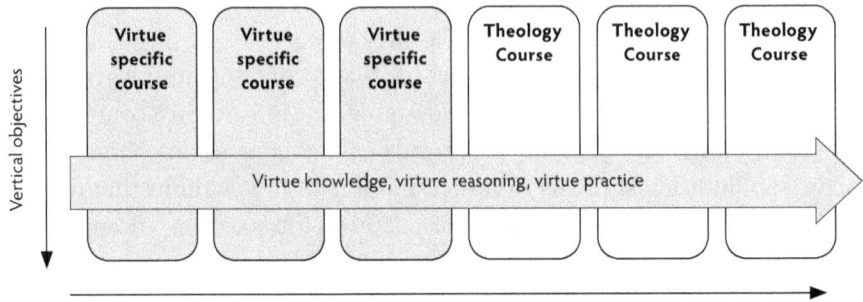

Horizontal (transversal) objectives

As you can see, I've distinguished horizontal objectives that are transversal and curriculum-wide, and vertical objectives. The vertical objectives are related to individual courses. So a virtue-specific course might aim at engaging with the cardinal virtues, whereas a traditional Old Testament Survey course might aim at knowledge of the books of the Old Testament. The horizontal objectives, however, cut across the curriculum and are found in every course. So, even in an Old Testament Survey course that has other kinds of aims, you will blend in some aims that relate to character and virtue. My argument is that, whatever combination you make of virtue-specific and traditional theology courses, you need to maintain transversal objectives that deal with character and virtue.

We've seen how the Greeks did something similar when they linked music, gymnastics and literature with character virtues. They had different subjects they were dealing with, but they all shared transversal objectives related to virtue. There are also some contemporary examples of this kind of integration.[16] I found an example of a secondary school curriculum in which all the subjects were mapped onto a matrix of virtues. This meant that each subject was taught with a specific emphasis on a particular virtue.[17] Mathematics, for example, was seen to help students grow in the virtues of integrity, focus and perseverance; history became the vehicle to develop respect, curiosity and resilience; and science dovetailed with the cultivation of honesty and curiosity. In theological education we could do something similar. Let me give you some examples of how to design traditional theology courses that integrate this approach within the three-fold objectives we have seen above of virtue knowledge, virtue reasoning and virtue practice.

---

16. Berkowitz, "The Science of Character Education," 46.
17. Harrison, Bawden and Rogerson, *Teaching Character*.

Example 1

Let us imagine a course in the Gospels that, in addition to a set of traditional objectives, focuses on the virtue of compassion. Here is what you could do. In terms of virtue knowledge, ask students to do some research on what compassion is, then have them write a 500-word definition of compassion (using Greek terms, classical definitions, etc.). Then have them read the parable of the Good Samaritan, work in groups discussing what compassion looks like, what feelings it generates, and so on, and prepare a small presentation to the rest of the class on "Compassion As a Theme in the Gospels." These learning activities should enhance the students' knowledge of the virtue of compassion.

Concerning virtue reasoning, point students to relevant sources and ask them to do some research in the recent news to find good and bad examples of compassion in society. Then lead your students in a brainstorming session on why compassion is central to a flourishing society. Once you've done that, divide your class in two and have them prepare a debate, dealing with issues of excess and defect in compassion and how they can discern the right actions in particular circumstances. By the end of these activities, students should be better able to recognize compassion in the world around them and reason on what compassion really looks like in real-life situations.

When it comes to virtue practice, build community service activities into the course, engaging the students in a socially deprived context. This could be a soup kitchen, an immigration centre or a service to the homeless. Ask students to keep a personal diary in which they focus on their emotions and on how they feel about the needs of those who have suffered undeserved misfortune. At the end of the course, build a reflective essay into the assessment in which they reflect on their feelings of compassion.

In this example of integrated course design you can see that I've done several things. First of all, I've identified sets of specific outcomes related to character and virtue. Second, I've taken a familiar course and focused on one main virtue. Third, I have used the three-fold caterpillar process to develop learning activities related to virtue knowledge, virtue reasoning and virtue practice. Fourth, I have chosen one of the five-fold descriptors of a virtuous character and made it the focus of the virtue practice element (in this case it was *emotions*). Finally, I've tailored the importance of character and virtue in the course. Depending on the course, this may vary in intensity. In some courses it may be marginal, whereas in other courses virtue-related outcomes might represent a principal feature.[18] In the example I have just given, I would not argue that compassion is one of the main themes in the Gospels, so the bulk of the course would likely focus on other outcomes. Should we be thinking of a course in Proverbs, however, it might be appropriate to make the virtue of prudence prominent.

Sorry if this all sounds a little complex. Here are three more examples, which I promise to keep briefer. In the last two examples I've imagined online courses in order to show how this kind of teaching can also work with different delivery modes.

Example 2

Imagine a course on the letters to the Corinthians that includes a focus on the virtue of friendship. Concerning virtue knowledge, ask students to write a paper on bad friendship using the behaviour of the Corinthians towards Paul as an example. They should include a list of bad qualities with appropriate references to commentaries and journal articles. Then examine together Caravaggio's painting *The Taking of Christ*. These two activities should provide a basic vocabulary to speak about bad friendship.

Then move to activities related to virtue reasoning and ask students to search the Internet on the topic of "Facebook friendships." They should also find and comment on the lyrics of at least one contemporary pop song on a friendship gone bad. They then need to produce a 500-word paper on why friendship is important today and what new forms of betrayal look like. This will help them to reason around friendship in today's world.

When it comes to virtue practice, choose the area of *attention* from the fivefold set of descriptors and help your students grow in noticing and attending to situations that require virtue. To help them in this, structure daily small groups over a period of two months where students can share instances of when they have noticed bad friendships in the learning community, alongside examples of actions that constituted virtuous friendships. Although students are not directly practising the virtue of friendship, they are growing in their character as they become more attentive to their surroundings.

---

18. Gregory's commentary on Job focuses in great part on the issue of morals and virtue (*The Books of the Morals of St Gregory the Pope; or An Exposition on the Book of Blessed Job*, Lectionary Central, http://www.lectionarycentral.com/GregoryMoralia/Book21.html).

Example 3

Here is an example of an online Church History course focusing on the virtues of courage and humility. Begin, as usual, with virtue knowledge and provide an online video lecture on the courage and humility of Luther and Calvin, with links to book chapters or journal articles on the topic. Create a discussion forum where students can share about what the courage and humility of the reformers looked like.

Continue with virtue reasoning and provide another video lecture showing negative instances of where courage and humility did not balance each other out and where the golden mean was missed. In a discussion forum, ask students to share a testimony about a contemporary church situation that evidences the interchange between courage and humility.

Finally, deal with virtue practice by focusing on *expression* and how the students' characters are perceived by others when it comes to courage and humility. To facilitate this, ask them to approach a mentor or spiritual guide in their church and ask to be evaluated in terms of how much humility and courage emanate from their character. Ask students to share the results of this conversation in a forum and to write prayers for each other.

Example 4

For this final example, imagine an online Homiletics course that focuses on the intellectual virtues of attentiveness and tenacity. Concerning knowledge, point students to Internet sources that define and illustrate what focus and tenacity are (articles, videos, blog posts, etc.).

For virtue reasoning, provide articles, links, TED Talks, and so on, about distractions in today's world. Also ask students to contribute to a forum discussion on (1) the features of a distracted generation and (2) what kind of world is shaped by leaders who lack focus and tenacity.

Finally, concerning practice, choose to focus on *action*, the fourth element of the five-fold set that deals with the commitment to doing things that will achieve ethical goals. Ask students to spend two hours working on the exegesis of their sermons with all their devices turned off. They will not check their emails, their phones should be put in another room, and they should not have a coffee break or any social interaction. Then ask them to share in a forum about sermon preparation and distractions. Have students write a decalogue of things they will do/not do when they are doing biblical exegesis. Then pair up the students into accountability groups for the rest of the semester to hold each other to their plans.

Many further course plans can be imagined, but I hope that these have sparked your understanding and imagination.

—

We are nearing the end of our planned correspondence and I think that we are beginning to see the tip of the iceberg after much theoretical work. It is a thrill to imagine these practices and I happily envy you for the possibility of seeing this all come to fruition with real students.

May you find deep joy in loving those students whom you have not yet met.

37

Andragogy of Virtue

You've asked about my employment, and I have good news. I've been offered a two-year writing contract and a substantial writing grant. I have many books and articles in mind, and I feel wonderfully energized by the prospect of being able to share my modest legacy. Andragogy in theological education is one of the areas I will be focusing on, and this letter is the prelude to more writing on the subject.

Having looked at the content of the curriculum and at course design, we now explore the methods and practices that we should employ as we educate adults in character and virtue.[1] It is, in fact, important to combine what we are teaching with *how* we teach it. This is especially true when it comes to methodologies in the area of formation, which are different from the traditional methodologies that we use in academic teaching and practical instruction. As I have warned you before, please do not take the practical tools that I have selected as techniques. As important as it is to plan our teaching practices carefully, there is nothing worse than reducing character and virtue education to the application of techniques. We need to keep our tools blunt and not kill our patients with the cure. Aristotle himself reminds us that building character is an inexact and messy science and that each student is unique.[2] Here, then, are some ideas.

---

1. Arthur et al., *Teaching*, 81.

2. "Any taught course in character can only hope to offer the vaguest of outlines about what is required or recommended to live a life of virtue, or in the building of character. As Aristotle observed, building character is a most inexact and messy science. The emphasis has to be on the students owning the issues raised, colouring, detailing and reshaping them with the unique stories of their own lives" (Arthur et al., 70).

Understanding Habituation

Let me start with habituation, which is likely the less familiar practice but probably the most important. I wrote to you briefly about habituation nearly two years ago, introducing it as a fundamental practice in Aristotle's vision of moral training thanks to which the virtues become second nature through repetition.[3] Habituation practices are not frequently mentioned in theological education today, but they are well established in educational literature. Dewey, for example, defined character as the "interpenetration of habits."[4] Locke spoke about the importance of established habits[5] and Farley defines the habits of medieval theologians in cultivating intellectual virtue as "an enduring orientation and extremity of the soul."[6] Contemporary educators have also redefined habituation in many ways, such as "the pedagogy of habit formation"[7] and a "neo-classical approach to compliance."[8] Theologians have also spoken about habituation, and we discover that Aquinas stated that "human virtues are habits"[9] and Abelard wonderfully described the virtues as "the best habit of the mind."[10] N. T. Wright similarly defines virtue as that which happens "when wise and courageous choices have become second nature."[11] Across the ages and the variety of sources, the widespread agreement is that, since moral development is ongoing and unstoppable, it is essential that we intentionally form good habits. The issue then is not *whether* we learn morality or not, but

---

3. Wright, *After You Believe*, 33.

4. See Dewey, *Human Nature and Conduct*. "Without the continued operation of all habits in every act there can be no unified character, but only the juxtaposition of disconnected reactions to separate situations" (Buber, "Between Man and Man," 112).

5. "But pray remember, Children are not to be taught by Rules, which will be always flipping out of their memories. What you think necessary for them to do, settle in them by an indispensable practice, as often as the occasion returns; and if it be possible, make occasions. This will beget Habits in them, which being once established, operate of themselves easily and naturally without the assistance of the Memory" (Locke, *Some Thoughts*, 66).

6. "It was natural then to see theology as a habitus, a cognitive disposition and orientation of the soul" (E. Farley, *Theologia*, 35).

7. "[Habituation] is the 'repetition' of good acts that develops moral virtue as 'second nature' and character. It can be educated by discipline, motivation by rewards and punishment, good example, reasoned explanations and simple consistent repetition – this is the 'pedagogy of habit formation'" (Nucci et al., *Handbook*, 18).

8. "Although it is not crude behaviourism, [this kind of strategy] does fundamentally look for compliance" (Hunter, *Death of Character*, 108).

9. Aquinas, *Summa* 1–3, 55.1.

10. "Abelard is quoting Boethius as he defines the virtues as *abitus animus optimus*, and by contrast, vices are the worst habits of the mind" (Marenbon, *Philosophy of Peter Abelard*, 284).

11. Wright, *After You Believe*, 21.

what kind of morality we learn and how we can best promote positive rather than negative growth.[12]

What, then, is habituation and how is it related to character and virtue education? Before giving you some practical guidelines, let me rehearse some of the theoretical background from my earlier letter on the Aristotelian framework. First of all, Aristotle claims that those who are not yet virtuous can perform virtuous actions and thereby become virtuous. Many of us have been raised to believe that who we are precedes what we do, but Aristotle turns this around and claims that doing leads to being.[13] This is reminiscent, in some ways, of the motto of Alcoholics Anonymous which encourages its members to "fake it, until you make it." The key to genuine change is seen in purposeful action, even if initially it is nothing more than external conformity.[14]

Second, Aristotle claimed that the virtues can be perfected through repetition. Hence the importance of habit. Just as one swallow does not make a summer, so one virtuous action does not shape character.[15] Good actions that are repeated become habits and then become ingrained in character. This is a slow process with no shortcuts[16] and, as the contemporary motto goes, "it is practice that makes perfect."

Third, habituation has to do with the will. In habituation, we select actions and contexts that force us to exhibit a certain virtue, and this shapes our character. We effectively choose who we want to be by choosing the things we repeatedly do. Habituation means constantly choosing right actions rather than yielding to the instinctive paths of familiarity, pleasure and self-protection. This is especially true for adults.[17] As Abelard would later say, the settled state

---

12. "[As] the teaching and learning of ethics goes on whether we like it or not, the question is not whether we should be taught, but how, when and by whom" (Kiss and Euben, *Debating Moral Education*, 14). "Everyone who teaches is modelling ethics, whether good or bad" (Holmes, *Shaping Character*, vi, viii).

13. "On Aristotle's view, we develop virtues by practicing virtuous actions, and by practicing them at the right time, in the right amount, in the right way, and so on. Eventually, he thought, such actions will become a matter of habit and virtues will be formed" (Baehr, "Cultivating Good Minds," 373).

14. "Aristotle claimed that virtues are developed over time, direction and knowledge of the teacher and that good actions are the key, even if they begin with conformity without inner conviction" (Arthur et al., *Teaching*, 12).

15. "For one swallow does not make a summer, nor does one day; and so too one day, or a short time, does not make a man blessed and happy" (*Nicomachean Ethics* 1.7).

16. Wright, *After You Believe*, 35.

17. "The foundation of character, as Aristotle knew, is laid in the moral training of childhood through the habits that were formed by authority and discipline. Then, in adolescence, the method changes, and Aristotle points out that behavioural habits must be developed by choice" (Tenelshof, "Encouraging the Character Formation," 83).

of virtue must be gained through care and deliberation.[18] The will, therefore, has an important role in choosing to act in concrete ways in order to govern the passions and shape the mind.

Fourth, habits precede reason. This is something that we observe in children, who do not need to understand everything before learning simple habits like saying "thank you." The same applies, to some degree, to adults. Although virtue reasoning and *phronesis* are vital elements in our educational project, we can implement good habits even before there is full understanding. It is appropriate to recall here what Aristotle taught about the nature of the soul as being both rational and non-rational.[19] Both parts need to be trained in virtue, with the rational and intellectual part being trained through a life of study while the appetites and desires are being trained through the repetition of right actions.[20]

Fifth, habituation eventually produces spontaneous action. That is the entire point of character education that I've laboured in my previous letters. Habituation is not necessarily a lifelong battle of the will. Once virtues are habituated, they become second nature and we no longer need to continually call on the will. Once our desires are changed, we become naturally attracted to virtue.[21] Once our emotions are changed, they will resonate instinctively with virtue. I am not saying that we will never again need to draw upon our will. But I am saying that after a steep learning curve that requires education, discipline and willpower, there is a plateau where goodness becomes more spontaneous. After repeatedly willing to do that which is good to become good, we eventually enjoy doing what is good – because we are good.

Sixth, habituation does not guarantee character growth for everyone. Sixteenth- and seventeenth-century thinkers were particularly preoccupied with dissimulation and pretence and with the possibility that social role-playing would lead to acting in virtuous ways for the sake of praise and honour, not

---

18. Abelard, *Collationes* 116: 190–192, quoted in Marenbon, *Philosophy of Peter Abelard*, 285.

19. Aristotle, *Nicomachean Ethics* 1097a–b.

20. This is one of the points of disagreement between Plato and Aristotle. Although both agreed that character could and should be cultivated, "Plato's focus is seen to be on the teacher helping to improve the pupil's thinking skills, while Aristotle's central idea is the teacher helping the pupil practice good actions. The implication is that one emphasizes moral reasoning without moral action, and the other conformity without inner conviction" (Arthur et al., *Teaching*, 12).

21. External conformity is not to be mistaken for character growth. "Self-controlled students . . . often act virtuously, but they do so with a kind of reluctance that virtuous people have overcome, as they now do what is virtuous gladly and with pleasure" (Arthur et al., 61).

because of genuine change.[22] Luther's pessimism, for example, was in contrast with Aristotle's conviction that there is a visible difference between those who are truly virtuous and those who are simply aping the virtuous.[23] But Aristotle had foreseen the possibility that habituation might not work. He claimed that, in relation to moral development, there are four categories of people.[24] There are "the many," who are morally indifferent and with whom little moral progress can be made. There are the "weak-willed," in whom self-control is emerging and who, given an appropriate level of ownership and a healthy reliance on a virtuous community, can benefit from habituation practices. And then there are the final two categories where habituation is seen to work: those who are "self-controlled" and habitually do what is virtuous, and those who are "practically wise and virtuous," who act virtuously with pleasure.

Practising Habituation

So much for the conceptual analysis. In practice, it is actually quite simple. Let me illustrate a six-step process that you can apply in most of the academy's courses.

Start by helping your students understand how the process of habituation can be a part of their growing and learning journey. Adult students learn as they understand how they learn, and learning by habituation is likely to be unfamiliar. It is important to expose students early on in their studies to some of the theories that we have been discussing in order to give them ownership of the process. You do not have to do this on every course, but frequent reminders would be helpful.

Second, it is good practice to help students focus on one virtue at a time. You can either choose this virtue for them in a particular course or provide self-assessment exercises to help them identify areas of growth (more on this below). In identifying the virtue on which they wish to focus, it is important that students do some theoretical and theological work on the chosen virtue, working out a definition, illustrating areas of praiseworthy functioning, finding stories and examples, and naming defects and excesses. They might also follow

---

22. Herdt, "Virtue's Semblance," 139.

23. Erasmus aligned with Aristotle, accepting "a habituation in virtue that proceeds from 'outside-in,' from engaging in formative practices and emulating models to transformed character." Luther, instead, "insisted that we must not begin by 'acting the part' of virtue, but by seeming to be what we are in fact – sinful . . . Only when we focus on God and neighbour rather than on acquiring virtue can we begin to make progress in true goodness" (Herdt, 140).

24. Arthur et al., *Teaching*, 62–67.

the five-fold set of descriptors that we saw in a previous letter.[25] This phase of rational engagement before embarking on habituation practices is essential for *phronesis* and reflective growth. This step might work well in a small research and writing project, perhaps followed by group work and discussion.

A third step is to identify certain kinds of activities that are characteristic of the chosen virtue and a set of specific opportunities to practise those activities.[26] So, for example, if a student is seeking to habituate the virtue of intellectual carefulness, she might identify activities that involve detailed avoidance of errors. Specific opportunities for practice might be proofreading a manuscript, writing computer code or verifying the accuracy of a library catalogue. The act of linking specific virtues with practices is an important skill in itself, and it helps students identify spheres of human life where virtues might (or might not) be operative.

At this point, we can start the fourth step, which is the actual habituation. This is the easiest step, for the student simply plans the repetition of the specific activities that have been identified in step 3. The student working on the virtue of intellectual carefulness will simply choose multiple manuscripts to proofread, and consciously revise her work multiple times to ensure that she finds and corrects even the smallest error, perhaps even keeping a log of errors. It is important to plan this step realistically to ensure feasibility. Constancy, in fact, must be possible, and timetables or other planned school activities need to be considered to make sure that habituation can take place with the necessary time commitment and focus. This is normally a process that takes many months, and it is conceivable that a student will work on habituating a single virtue for even an entire year.

The fifth step in habituation is that of reflection. I will come back to this when we discuss assessment practices in my next letter, but I mention it here to close the loop of growth. Through reflection, the student looks back and consciously realizes how her character has been shaped.

---

25. (1) How our perception picks up situations where a particular virtue is necessary; (2) how the virtue functions emotionally; (3) what the virtue makes us desire; (4) how our will determines courses of action relative to the virtue; and (5) how others perceive us when we exhibit this virtue.

26. Baehr gives some examples of characteristic activities linked to some of the intellectual virtues. Attentiveness, which is understanding and engaging with content, is enhanced in note-taking, questions and mind maps. Curiosity is enhanced by asking thoughtful and insightful questions. Intellectual humility, which is awareness of your limitations and mistakes, can be habituated by small-group discussion, agreeing/disagreeing and debating. Open-mindedness, which gives a fair hearing to opposing views, might be cultivated by arguing for the view opposite to yours (Baehr, "Cultivating Good Minds," 387–388).

The final step is something which students should do during the entire process. It has to do with prayer. As we focus on the educational dynamics and the practices of character and virtue education, we must not forget the spiritual dynamics. We are working with students who have the incredible asset of being indwelt by the Holy Spirit and who benefit from God's transforming grace and guiding voice. Students should therefore pray through each phase of habituation. They should pray that God will grant them understanding of how their character will grow; they should pray to discern which virtues God would have them work on and which activities are most suitable to determine their growth; they should pray for power and ongoing constancy as they practise actions of virtue; they should pray to ask God to shape their character during their practice; and they should pray as they reflect on their progress to ask God to grant them clarity, humility and wisdom. So, although prayer is not the main topic of our correspondence, let us not lay aside the unique weapons of our Christian faith.

Habituation is, indeed, a Christian practice. In the New Testament, we have seen the repeated call to virtuous action; we have seen that perseverance produces character;[27] we have seen that the Spirit changes our desires; we have seen exhortations to govern our will; we have seen that, in addition to thinking about the virtues, we need to keep putting them into practice;[28] and we have seen that the power of God supports our commitment to add virtue to our faith. So it is entirely fitting that we pray as we work on changing our character.

In the second half of this letter, I'd like to discuss four more andragogical practices for character and virtue education. The first one takes place outside the classroom, the second takes place around the classroom, and the final two can take place in the classroom.

Service and Project-Based

Let's start with service and project-based learning as a practice that takes place outside the classroom. Service and project-based practices are a popular device in schools that support character education.[29] Similar practices are also found

---

27. Rom 5:4.

28. Phil 4:8–9. See O'Brien, *Epistle to the Philippians*, 511. Interestingly, Paul is using an imperative as he prescribes continuous actions of truthfulness, nobility, justice, purity, loveliness and admirability.

29. Many schools connect their character agenda with their service opportunities. Although service learning is a common vehicle for character education, any form of service may support character education (Berkowitz, "Science of Character Education," 46).

in many theological schools under the labels of Christian service, placement opportunities, internships or community service. The difference is that, in theological schools, these practices usually focus on developing skills and competences and are seldom linked to developing character and virtue. A theological student will normally be sent on a placement assignment with the aim of gaining ministry experience of some kind, but not with the explicit intent to grow in a particular virtue. Although the learning might *also* entail growth in virtue, this is not the explicit objective.

The academy should design service and project-based opportunities that are linked to the character habituation practices we have just seen. So, for example, a student who intends to grow in courage could be involved in a service project in a difficult neighbourhood where some danger is involved. A student focusing on the virtue of justice could be given the opportunity to take part in advocacy-related projects. The projects need not be complex or original, and even a simple placement opportunity with a youth group or in a local church can provide many opportunities to habituate virtues like patience, diligence and hope.

There is a slight difference between service learning and project-based learning that might give you further ideas. Service learning normally requires students to get involved in a social problem to help find solutions.[30] Students in the academy might therefore support your local farming communities that are struggling against land-grabbing tycoons. This would be a great opportunity to grow in the virtues of justice and equity. Project-based learning is broader terminology that can describe many creative forms of planned experiences,[31] ranging anywhere from hospitality of refugees, to physical labour or to personal projects of spiritual discipline. The procedures for both service and project-based learning are fairly standard and involve phases of theoretical work, planning, implementation and subsequent reflection.

Role-Modelling

Another practice that I'd like you to consider is role-modelling. This takes place around the classroom in the broader life of the community. Role-modelling is

---

30. In America, the term is used in this sense (Nucci et al., *Handbook*, 395).

31. "Project-based learning is defined as planned learning and growth in virtue that moves away from being knowledge-based to being experience" (J. Lee, "Moral and Character Education in Korea," 340).

generally acclaimed as a core practice[32] in most of the literature on character education and that is confirmed by what we've seen in the Christian Scriptures about imitation.[33]

How can this be intentionally built into our andragogies of virtue? We have already touched on the kinds of teachers that are needed in a virtuous community and, indeed, there is no replacement for the person of the teacher as the most effective means for character education.[34] But in addition to just being virtuous, what can teachers do to encourage imitation? One suggestion is that they can explicitly draw attention to their own character growth. Although this may sound like immodesty, it is important that teachers are more than just silent examples.[35] They should speak out from their own lives, commenting on their own actions with a vocabulary of virtue. This might mean pointing out, for example, that when they return assignments on time, it is part of their effort to habituate diligence. Or they might share areas of virtue that they are working on in their lives, or how they have overcome a particular vice. Students need to be shown, and showing might entail a small amount of explicit telling. This is not showing off; it is a precious sharing of our own character growth in the context of respectful, caring and trusting relationships.

I've come across a nice little acronym, MELA, to describe a four-step model for this kind of role-modelling.[36] Teachers start with modelling (M), which means that they think about which virtue they wish to model and why it suits them well. Then they commit to explaining (E), to themselves and others, how they have put this virtue into action. Third, they legitimize (L) and justify why they have chosen this particular virtue, how it fits a particular situation and what they have wanted to achieve. And, finally, they help apply (A) as they equip and motivate others to habituate the same virtue.

---

32. "Character education is unambiguous [in] advocating role modelling as a fundamental method to help students develop character traits" (Arthur et al., *Teaching*, 102).

33. Phil 4:8–9: "These things which have been mentioned generally as being excellent and worthy of praise, the Philippians also learned specifically from Paul by teaching and tradition, spoken word and living example" (O'Brien, *Epistle to the Philippians*, 508).

34. "The single most powerful tool you have to impact a student's character is our own character" (Arthur et al., *Teaching*, 16).

35. "Teachers as role models are not just virtuous, they attract students' attention because they make them notice something about virtue that they had not seen before" (Arthur et al., 103).

36. Developed by Swennen, Lunenberg and Korhagen (Arthur et al., 104).

Dialogue

I conclude with two specific practices that you can use in the classroom. The first is the practice of dialogue. Moral virtue is not a mindless process of memorization and emulation, but the result of active engagement with a community. That is why dialogue is so important. When students come together, teachers need to be careful not to monopolize learning spaces with lectures and instructions.[37] Without necessarily embracing everything that connectivistic theories say about student-centred learning, we recognize that much moral learning occurs as students dialogue with each other. As you can appreciate, this is a huge topic, so let me just offer a few simple comments that relate to practice.

First, privileging dialogical rather than didactic practices enhances the contextualization of moral commitments and avoids indoctrination.[38] It is important, for example, that students work together to identify universal virtues and vices within their contexts and discuss peculiarities of their cultures, age groups and social circumstances.

Second, dialogical activities engage students in *phronesis*. As we've seen, it is important that students develop reasoning skills around virtue, and this happens in discussion with the community.[39] We must allow students to struggle together in small groups, discussing concrete circumstances of everyday life where virtue can be seen and practised. We should set up debates and focus groups around conflicting virtues, present case studies for discussion where virtues are seen to balance each other, or brainstorm together to generate ethical lists that identify defects and excesses of virtue. This does not mean that teachers should never lecture, but that lectures should be seen as an entry point to spark dialogue.[40] Creating learning spaces where meaningful dialogue happens is hard work for teachers. They must learn to lay out significant discussions, carefully choose questions, provide discussion materials and identify critical issues that will help conversations go deep and

---

37. "But who is so stupidly curious as to send his son to school that he may learn what the teacher thinks?" (St Augustine, quoted in Arthur et al., 4).

38. "Deliberative and dialogical pedagogies . . . cannot be pursued through techniques of discipleship and indoctrination" (Kiss and Euben, "Aim High," 62).

39. "Virtue terms cannot be absorbed through a form of rote learning, as the very life and soul of these virtues is likely to be lost" (Arthur et al., *Teaching*, 95).

40. "Lecturing . . . will require grappling with questions like: 'How can my students become active participants in the process of direct instruction? How can I build opportunities for thoughtful engagement and participation into this process?'" (Baehr, "Cultivating Good Minds," 378).

wide. Dialogue should not fall into pointless exchanges of opinion and it is the teacher's responsibility to make sure that the conversations are substantial.[41]

Third, dialogue gives students an opportunity to share about their personal journeys in virtue. Used in this way, group dialogue reinforces emulation, motivation and determination. Groups may discuss, for example, the outcomes of their habituation practices or the difficulties encountered in working out some of the theories. This is also an opportunity to confess failure and to receive support and prayer. Teachers should participate openly in this sort of dialogue in a climate of openness and trust. Used in this way, dialogue becomes habituated practice in its own right in which civic, democratic and relational virtues are practised.

Story-Based Lecturing

The final practice that I would like to lay before you has to do with story-based lecturing. Lecturing is the main tool whereby theology teachers seek to inform and convince their students. And, despite some recent bad press about the lecture,[42] it still remains a very good educational tool. Even in character and virtue education, the lecture is probably one of the best tools to help students conceptualize frameworks, appreciate virtue traditions and understand habituation. Although most lecturing is propositional, rational and linear, lectures can also be delivered in another way.

I'd like to suggest that there are great advantages in story-telling lectures. Lectures that are biographical and narrative, in fact, are probably more useful in describing virtues than sets of propositional statements.[43] How, for example, might a student whose first language is not English understand the meaning of the word "gentleness"? Certainly, one could provide more words and offer a verbal definition of what gentleness is, but it might be more effective to describe things that are gentle or, better yet, to tell a story, parable or historical event that shows what gentleness does.[44]

---

41. "Sometimes, a small group doesn't involve a very efficient or effective use of class time. Nor does it always demand very deep or engaged thinking. Nevertheless, small groups can be an excellent context in which to practise intellectual virtues" (Baehr, 379).

42. See, for example, Eric Mazur in Craig Lambert, "Twilight of the Lecture," *Harvard Magazine*, March–April 2012, accessed 8 February 2019, http://harvardmagazine.com/2012/03/twilight-of-the-lecture.

43. "Hauerwas is right to insist that if we are to have a satisfactory concept of a particular virtue, we must be able to tell stories about persons whose lives exemplify that virtue" (Porter, *Recovery of Virtue*, 108).

44. Porter, 105–106.

Stories are a great way of illuminating morality[45] and the stories of Greek heroes are a great example of this. These stories typically engage the listeners in identifying with characters who face complex situations and live between virtue and vice. So, in the *Iliad*, we are naturally led to keep our distance from the lack of temperance in Helen and Alexander as their lust sets off unending tragedy. We warm instead to Priam, who demonstrates prudence in making difficult decisions and who embodies the kingly wisdom of old age. We condemn the wrath and pride of Achilles but cannot help also being drawn to his commitment to honour and justice. We want to be courageous and loyal like Hector, but none of us wants to imitate the blind fury of Menelaus or the baseness of Agamemnon who kills his own daughter and betrays his promises to the Trojans. As we read stories of this kind, we are not allowed to stay indifferent. We find ourselves continually either attracted or repulsed as we struggle with the dilemmas of life. As we engage with stories, we also find a safe place to project our own virtues and vices onto other characters without feeling directly confronted and without having to reveal personal information.[46]

Educating through story-telling is a well-established practice and there are plenty of examples. We find examples of such stories in school programmes,[47] in the work of theologians,[48] scholars[49] and educators,[50] in classical culture,[51] in pagan literature,[52] in popular writing,[53] in some of the great literature[54] and in edited collections.[55] Stories from the Bible have also frequently been used

---

45. Students need to develop a personal understanding, not be preached at: "The use of stories and literature adopts such an approach and was advocated by Aristotle himself. He believed that stories have a power to illuminate morality and other aspects of human motivation, such as feeling and agency, in a way that natural or social scientific sources of knowledge and insight are not necessarily equipped to do" (Arthur et al., *Teaching*, 95).

46. Arthur et al., 95.

47. Knightly Virtues programme, Jubilee Centre, https://www.jubileecentre.ac.uk/1641/character-education/resources/knightly-virtues.

48. Stanley Hauerwas engages with Trollope and Austen as he claims that "Novels are an irreplaceable resource for training in moral virtue" (Hauerwas, *Dispatches*, 31).

49. Coles, *The Call of Stories*.

50. Baehr, "Cultivating Good Minds," 136.

51. MacIntyre, *After Virtue*, 121.

52. "There is much wisdom in the pagan literature consistent with the Scriptures, which might be collected and used . . . But at the same time there is much 'immorality,' 'godlessness,' and 'blindness'" (Comenius, in Habl, "Character Formation," 145).

53. M. Smith, *Tolkien's Ordinary Virtues* (Downers Grove: InterVarsity Press, 2002).

54. M. Adler, "Great Books Approach," Center for the Study of the Great Ideas, http://www.thegreatideas.org/.

55. Bennett, *Book of Virtues*.

as educational tools and theological educators might have something to learn in this area from Sunday school teachers.

—

You can see that there are many exciting opportunities to structure and plan growth in character and virtue. There are many other methodologies that have also emerged in recent pedagogy. These include practices such as peer-to-peer tutoring, problem-solving, learning by doing, role-playing, brainstorming, flipped classrooms, laboratorial and cooperative teaching, mind-mapping (conceptual maps), heuristic lessons, inquiry-based learning, situated learning, authentic learning and cooperative learning. Although many of these pedagogical practices are designed for constructivist and student-centred learning strategies in children, there are many good ideas that can be applied to the education of character and virtue in adults. I will leave it to you to do further investigation.

Keep in mind, as you plan your teaching and as you train your teachers, that no single strategy works on its own and that virtues are best formed when different factors and methods converge.[56] But also remember that genuine change happens through very simple means. Just yesterday I was preaching in my church and, as I spoke from 2 Peter 1 about adding virtue to our faith, I found myself wondering how the members of my church, many of whom are unschooled, would benefit from my simple half-hour exposition. They know nothing about habituation practices, and we do not have a training programme in the church that could put into practice any of the methods that I have just presented. This question buzzed around in my mind all day, and my thoughts turned to the letters in the New Testament. What, in effect, was happening in these letters from the point of view of andragogy? I re-read the epistles quickly, looking for the verbs that would give me an answer, and here is what I found. The main educational devices in the epistles are direct teaching, exhortation and warning. We also find many other verbs,[57] but most of them are accomplished by direct speech (whether we call it a lecture, sermon, video, podcast or written artefact). This does not mean that we can lay aside all sophistication and educational planning and just preach, but it does remind us of the simple things.

---

56. Baehr, "Cultivating Good Minds," 376.

57. "Andragogical verbs" in the epistles include beseeching, pleading, inviting, appealing, thanking, scolding, urging, commanding, rebuking, critiquing, explaining, fact-telling, referencing, illustrating, example-setting, consoling, questioning, declaring, reminding, praying and encouraging.

So, as you are pugnatious in sophisticated learning design, may you also embrace the power of simplicity.

38

The Assessment Dilemma

You have asked me why I have been handwriting my letters to you instead of sending you a series of emails. The latter would have been more efficient, but there is something nostalgic, personal and slow about writing by hand on paper, putting a letter in an envelope with your address, and walking down to the post office to send it. It all felt more befitting of the climate of slow nurture that we are seeking in virtue. Writing by hand has also allowed me to think more carefully, and the time that has passed between sending and receiving letters has helped me mature. Finally, crafting an artefact is a way of saying that our correspondence is special. Thank you for playing along with my little oddities and replying in similar fashion. I have kept all your letters in a tin box that I have carefully placed in the bottom drawer of my office desk. At the beginning of our correspondence I purchased a substantial block of loose-leaf paper which is now nearly used up. I do not plan to purchase another one, since I feel that most of what I wanted to explore with you is now done. This letter, on the important topic of assessment, will be one of my last.

The assessment of character and virtue education is a very difficult topic, and I am far from having satisfactory answers on many issues. I have, however, given it much thought and I have done some research that I would like to share with you. In structuring my reply, I will use the fundamental distinction between self-assessment and assessment which is carried out by others. Self-assessment is where students are given tools to look at themselves, to evaluate where they are in terms of character and virtue and to make plans for improvement. Assessment done by others is based instead on external input from someone in the community. When we think of assessment, we normally think only of the latter, but the two are equally important, especially when it comes to character growth.

Self-Assessment through Humility and Prudence

You may recall that among the growing outcomes in our curriculum are the ability to self-assess growth in character and virtue and to make plans for improvement. These are important outcomes. We do not want the graduates from the academy, in fact, to provisionally conform to the expectations of the community for the sole purpose of satisfying certification requirements. Our vision is to shape individuals for whom virtue is an ongoing way of life, and that is why we must teach self-assessment as a character habit. Our hope is that students will carry this with them once the external constraints of a programme and a community are removed.

Self-assessment requires the cultivation of two virtues: humility and prudence. Humility allows students to see themselves honestly and admit their flaws and achievements, and it is therefore essential for healthy self-assessment. It removes a spirit of self-justification, self-defence and false modesty and allows students a clear vision of their strengths and weaknesses. Self-assessment, in fact, will never be beneficial in the presence of pride. Self-assessment also embodies prudence (*phronesis*) for it requires rational reflection around the practices and expressions of virtue in everyday life. It applies the famous Delphic maxim "Know thyself" and reflects Socrates's famous words about the unexamined life that is not worth living.

Self-assessment is also found in Scripture. The metaphor of looking at ourselves in a mirror in the book of James skilfully outlines the main features of self-assessment. First, James shows us that self-assessment begins with instruction. "Hearing the word" is the first step that points us to right behaviour. Second, there is an "intense" activity of looking at our "natural" faces[1] where we concentrate to see who we really are. Third, self-assessment should lead to action. In looking at ourselves, we should be "doing the word"[2] and looking "intently into the perfect law."[3] This is potentially the weakest spot in self-assessment, which always runs the risk of remaining mere evaluation without self-improvement. Self-assessment without self-improvement is, in the words of James, self-deceit.[4] Finally, self-assessment, when properly done, leads to happiness. James claims that we can thus be "blessed" in our doing.[5] This four-fold sequence, "learn–look–do–and be happy," tells us that, as we

---

1. Jas 1:23.
2. Jas 1:22.
3. Jas 1:25.
4. Jas 1:22.
5. Jas 1:25.

self-assess and improve our walk in virtue in accordance with God's laws of morality, we will find deep happiness. This fits very well with Aristotle's vision of wisdom, virtue and flourishing.

What might self-assessment look like in the academy's programme? There are many ways in which this can be done, one of which is to follow the template of the "caterpillar" design we discussed a few letters ago and to think of self-assessment in terms of virtue knowledge, virtue reasoning and virtue practice. Self-assessing virtue knowledge means asking students to reflect on what they know about virtue. This is probably the easiest kind of self-assessment and it helps students identify areas of ignorance and make plans for further investigation, observation and study. Students can also self-assess virtue reasoning, which entails evaluating their abilities to reason about virtue. Here we want to teach our students to applaud their growth in themselves, to recognize what virtue looks like in their lives and in the world around them, and to be able to evaluate their abilities in understanding which virtues need to be deployed. Finally, and probably most significantly, we want to teach students to self-assess their growth in virtue practice. Here students should learn to evaluate themselves in terms of their response to the call of virtue in particular situations, in terms of feeling the right kind of emotion in the right situation in the right way, and in terms of seeking out further opportunities to practise and strengthen particular virtues.

The five-fold set of descriptors of virtue that we've seen provides a further template for this kind of self-assessment. Students should learn to respond to questions such as the following:

1. What do I notice in relation to virtue and how do I attend to situations requiring a particular virtue (*attention*)?
2. What feelings are aroused in me that relate to virtue from particular situations (*emotions*)?
3. How am I motivated to change things in myself and in the world to align with virtue (*desire*)?
4. In what ways have I demonstrated commitment to doing things that will achieve ethical goals (*acts*)?
5. What is there about me in terms of style, communication and perception by others that relates to the kind of virtuous character I would like to exhibit (*expression*)?

There are also some practical tools that you might consider for self-assessment – most importantly, questionnaires and reflective essays.

Questionnaires for Self-Assessment

Questionnaires are usually designed by the teacher to help students conduct specific self-assessment exercises. The example given just above of the five-fold set of descriptors might be one such questionnaire. Another example might be an "entry questionnaire," where students assess their own characters in terms of virtue as they enter the academy, and then do the same again on exiting the programme to observe their growth. I once used a two-page questionnaire of this type in which I listed a set of virtues, along with a brief definition of each, followed by a set of possible choices whereby students evaluated each virtue as either "missing," "barely visible and poorly practised," "visible but not constant" or "visible and constant." We then used this questionnaire within a mentoring programme in which my students chose to work on their weaker areas.

Although I would encourage you to develop your own questionnaires, there are existing resources that you might want to look at. The Intellectual Values Academy has developed self-assessment questionnaires to diagnose intellectual virtues.[6] When considering intellectual humility, this questionnaire asks students whether it is easy for them to admit that they are wrong. Or, when considering tenacity, they are asked whether they stick with problems when they are frustrated and cannot find solutions. The Curiosity and Exploration Inventory is an example of a specific self-reporting instrument on the virtue of curiosity, assessing "the recognition, pursuit and integration of novel and challenging experiences and information."[7] Another popular questionnaire of this kind is the "Values in Action (VIA) Survey of Character Strengths"[8] based on Seligman's work in positive psychology. This simple questionnaire helps to identify strengths and weaknesses in each virtue. Some researchers have also found moral dilemma tests useful, and you might consider these as well.[9]

Reflective Essays for Self-Assessment

Reflective essays are another useful tool for self-assessment. There is plenty of

---

6. Baehr, "Cultivating Good Minds," 536–537. For an extended discussion on assessing intellectual character growth, see Baehr, 524–541.

7. http://www.midss.org/content/curiosity-and-exploration-inventory-cei-ii (accessed 30 May 2019).

8. At VIA Institute of Character, http://www.viacharacter.org/www/Character-Strengths-Survey.

9. Kohlberg's moral dilemma tests are not designed to test virtue, but they can be used to establish a useful critical distance in self-assessment (Arthur et al., *Teaching*, 113; Birdwell, Scott and Reynolds, *Character Nation*, 27).

material available in the area of reflective learning[10] and theological reflection,[11] and I will not rehearse these trends here. Here we are interested in reflective writing as a formative tool that contributes to self-assessment abilities and character development.[12] When students write about themselves in relation to their character and to virtue, in fact, they grow.[13] As we've seen above, students can write reflectively at different intersections of the formative process: they can reflect on their understanding of virtue, on their ability to reason around virtue and on their growth in the practice of virtue. Reflective essays might be assigned to meditate on growth in deep happiness, about the feelings associated with virtues, about the experience of *phronesis*, about growth in specific virtues following service learning or about the process and outcomes of habituation.

Reflective writing on virtue can also be used for assessment purposes (for example, as the evaluation piece of a habituation practicum) or to accompany an entire period of study through journaling practices. Although reflective essays are more open-ended than questionnaires, they require some structure and guidance, and you should make sure that you provide this, especially for beginning students. Although apparently simple, reflective writing is one of the most powerful and sophisticated tools in your assessment kit.

External Assessment and the Measurement Captivity

Let us now turn to assessment of character and virtue done by others. This is both important and problematic. It is important because it gives value to the feedback from the community and provides a corrective dimension to self-assessment. Self-assessment alone, in fact, can be partial, biased and even delusional,[14] and we need to be evaluated by "significant others." But this is also where the problems begin.

Being evaluated by others, in fact, can lead to a climate of comparison and competition in which, paradoxically, students compete with each other to be the humblest in the community. Being evaluated by others can also generate a

---

10. Donald Schon, *The Reflective Practitioner*.
11. Ballard and Pritchard, *Practical Theology in Action*; Laurie Green, *Let's Do Theology*.
12. Heywood, "Educating Ministers of Character," 15.
13. Aquinas taught that "learning is self-activity on the part of the student" (Arthur, *Education with Character*, 48).
14. "Self-report measures are typically grounded in anti-realism . . . Moral naturalists complain about possible response biases in such measures caused by self-deceptions and self-fabulations. Even if I consistently think I am a duck, this does not make me a duck" (Kristjánsson, "Ten Myths," 283). Just reporting that you are honest does not mean that "in reality" you are honest (Arthur, *Teaching Character and Virtue in Schools*, 110).

culture of conformity where students surrender to external codes for approval without any real character change. The more significant problem, however, has to do with *how we measure* character and virtue. This problem does not emerge as long as students are assessing themselves through questionnaires or reflective writing, but it becomes a significant issue as soon as multiple third parties are involved in assessment. At that point, the "how" of measurement must be solved and the issue of fairness arises, meaning that we need exact measurement tools to guarantee objectivity and justice for everyone.

This is a general problem, both in higher education and in theological education. The quest for exactness in measuring is historically linked to the combined forces of the Industrial Revolution[15] and the rise of scientific determinism which claimed that everything that exists can be measured, including human existence and education. In the name of concreteness, scientificity and exactness, the measurement paradigm of education claims that intangible goals are worthless and that we can know our students only as we are able to measure their abilities and capabilities.[16]

This is what I call "the captivity of numbers" in which educational experience is dominated by numbers. Course credits are *counted*, study years are *enumerated*, learning hours are *tallied*, words are *calculated* in essays and books are *totalled* in bibliographies. Nowhere is this seen more clearly than when it comes to assessment. *Grades* are given for courses, *calculations* are made to establish grade point *averages* and degree classifications, and educational performances are generally ranked through a *numeric* value. This influences teachers and students as well as employers, who look at academic performance computations to evaluate graduate attractiveness.[17] Even though the measurement paradigm is a relatively recent phenomenon in education, it has pretty much subjugated the landscape with its emphasis on scientific exactness, efficiency and total quality management. Nowhere is this captivity more strongly felt than when it comes to assessing character and virtue education.

How, in fact, can we measure virtue numerically? How can we ascribe a grade to character? How can we place happiness on a histogram or arrive

---

15. West-Burnham, "Understanding Quality," 313–324.

16. In *How to Measure Education*, McCall claims that "Whatever exists at all, exists in some amount. Anything that exists in [an] amount can be measured. Measurement in education is in general the same as measurement in the physical sciences. To the extent that the pupil's initial abilities or capabilities are unmeasurable, a knowledge of him is impossible. To the extent that any goal of education is intangible, it is worthless" (in Spears and Loomis, *Education for Human Flourishing*, 178).

17. Arthur, Wilson and Godfrey, *Graduates of Character*, 10–12.

at moral education from utility functions?[18] What sort of grid or rubric can external assessors get hold of in order to fairly and consistently compare students in their growth? All the questions are simply wrong. The aim of monitoring students as they become wise saints and grow in wisdom, ability to love and deep happiness escapes the exactness of numerical assessment.[19] While there is much good to be said about accountability and external assessment, it is clear that numerical assessment is not fit for the purposes of character and virtue education.[20] Aristotle's framework is foreign to contemporary measurement paradigms[21] and assessing virtue through numbers is like trying to measure heat with a microscope.

Ways Forward in Assessment

This leads us to a crossroads in terms of certification (more on this in my final letter). If, in fact, you want the programme of the academy to be recognized as a higher education programme in your region, you will have to find a satisfactory way to assess the learning (growing) outcomes of your programme. It is very unlikely that you will obtain accreditation or recognition in the current higher education scenario without this. How, then, can you deliver learning that is recognized and, at the same time, escape the captivity of numbers? You are operating between the horns of a dilemma, for, on the one hand, you want to encourage growth in character and virtue that is personalized, messy and organic, but, on the other, you want to provide learning that is recognizable in today's structured educational systems. So what can you do? Let me share with you some thoughts on ways forward. I have two easy responses and a more difficult one.

The easy responses have to do with the assessment of content and the assessment of intellectual virtues. When it comes to acquisition of content,

---

18. "There is an obvious problem for the quantity adjuster and social engineer. How do we measure value? On what scale do we weight a sentiment? What cost variables are assigned to beauty and happiness? Under what quantitative criterion is spiritual growth assessed? How do we get sound ethics or moral education out of utility functions?" (Spears and Loomis, *Education for Human Flourishing*, 176).

19. G. Smith, "Character Matters: Theological Education and Formation for Wisdom," Theological Education.net, June 2017, http://theologicaleducation.net/articles/view.htm?id=28.

20. M. Berkowitz, "There's No Accounting for Character Education," Center for Character & Citizenship, https://characterandcitizenship.org/about-us/blogs/item/there-s-no-accounting-for-character-education.

21. "Aristotle's age was not as obsessed as ours is with measurements" (Kristjánsson, *Aristotelian Character Education*, 65).

we know that this can be assessed numerically, and we do so regularly. In previous letters, we've seen that there are necessary components of knowledge and understanding in a character education programme. Students need to know and understand the history and tradition of virtue, a framework for character education, what the virtues are, how habituation works, and so on. These content-related components can be easily assessed by traditional assessment means, such as academic essays or exams, and be given a numerical value. The same can be said about the assessment of intellectual virtues. These virtues, which include intellectual honesty, attentiveness, open-mindedness, thoroughness, and so on, can be measured and assessed numerically using traditional means. This is probably already being done in most theological colleges, and most marking grids contain these intellectual virtues under the name of graduate skills or transferable competences.[22] In assessing content and intellectual virtues, we can measure some important components in a character and virtue education programme without compromising its nature.

The more difficult response relates to other kinds of virtues. How can we assess moral, public or theological virtues? Although we cannot, and should not, try to impose numerical assessment on these virtues, we must find ways to assess them externally. Self-assessment alone, as we've seen, is insufficient and we should not follow the tempting route of moving character and virtue education into the extra-curricular. External assessment is important for many reasons: it formalizes learning, it gives students a way of knowing how they are doing, it defines the criteria for failing, it provides teachers with a way of evaluating students' work, it reassures employers that learning and growth have occurred and it informs stakeholders on whether the academy is achieving anything at all. We thus need to find a way forward that keeps students accountable and evaluated with regards to character and virtue growing outcomes, but without using numerical assessment.

I am still searching for ways to do this, but here is a bullet list of ideas that I have come up with so far. None of these is sufficient in itself, so read them thinking of possible combinations.

- Compose a list of loose descriptors that indicate what success looks like in character and virtue education. These might include descriptors like: "There has been growth over time"; "There is evidence of constancy"; "There is emotional awareness linked to virtue." These descriptors can be applied by teachers and peers.

---

22. Such descriptors typically include knowledge of pertinent literature, creativity, wide reading, good critical engagement, logical argument, support by evidence, good grasp of concepts, and so on.

- Use assessment words rather than numbers – or, better yet, sentences. Paradoxically, it is much more precise to say, "You have made substantial progress in this virtue" than to indicate, "You have achieved 68 percent in courage."
- Make substantial use of pass/fail assessment components.
- Develop a loose descriptive grid/rubric of what might count for a pass and what might qualify to say that a student has failed in relation to a particular character and virtue outcome.
- Creatively use the formative and summative assessment distinction, using the formative assessment as a necessary requirement for the summative. So, for example, you might have a formative assessment that is related directly to growth in a particular virtue and that needs to be satisfied with a pass. Satisfying the formative component will permit a summative assessment, such as a reflective essay, that can be numerically marked.
- Award credits for courses and learning activities related to character and virtue as a necessary evil.
- Combine several types of assessment in a portfolio. If you ask students to be involved in a project and a journal, also require a reflective essay. A grade can be given overall, but you will avoid being numerically specific in each component.
- Use self-assessment as grounds for external assessment. Ask students to share their self-assessment with you as a teacher or with their peers and make this the grounds of assessment.
- Make self-assessment count in evaluating the achievement of learning outcomes. Ask students themselves whether they think they have achieved the outcomes and passed the course. Answers should normally be accompanied by justification and examples of evidence, and teachers will determine whether the self-assessment is appropriate.
- Use community dynamics. Allow students to evaluate one another within the boundaries of a safe community. I have come across a phone app that is meant to use peer feedback in practising virtue.[23] You might imagine a communitarian covenant around which students meet regularly for open conversation and formative

---

23. The NOVA phone app (Networked Virtue Assessment) is set up to allow User 1 to observe virtue in User 2, who receives a notification and is asked for the intention and the emotion behind the action (Arthur et al., *Teaching*, 117).

feedback on their growth in virtue. This practice can be given summative value and the entire community can assess each other.
- Tailor formal and informal assessment, giving more emphasis to the latter. The more informal assessment is taking place, the more you will establish a culture of accountability that can then express itself in formal assessment.
- Be careful in applying some of the traditional assessment criteria to character and virtue education. Think carefully, for example, about how attendance requirements might fit in.[24]
- Always provide generous feedback on any assessment, making sure you use virtue language. Perhaps even underline the virtue words you use in marking up written submissions.
- Think carefully about your assessment criteria. Are you looking for growth? If so, is it quantitative? Will positive assessment mean that there is "more virtue"? Are you looking for "more frequent" instances of virtue reasoning? Are you checking that virtue vocabulary is "used more consciously" and that habits are "more regular"? Or will you use a qualitative language of development, and give positive assessments wherever you see change and improvement? Are you looking for deeper and more sophisticated reasoning around virtue, a broader virtue vocabulary and virtue practices that are difficult and deeply transformative? Both approaches are correct, but it is helpful to distinguish them.
- Make sure your initiatives and assessments are well matched to the outcomes you have set out. This seems obvious, but it is far from easy.

A Decalogue

In conclusion, here is a further decalogue of generic suggestions that relate both to self-assessment and to assessment done by others. These might be used to explain your assessment philosophy to students both at the outset of the programme and every time a numerical assessment is scheduled.

1. Keep your tools blunt.[25] Resist the temptation of accurate measurement and assessment. Remember that this is an organic

---

24. Berkowitz, "No Accounting for Character Education."
25. Tools need to be "necessarily inexact, but useful nevertheless" (Arthur et al., *Teaching*, 76).

process. Be happy even if you appear to be inefficient, as this might be the best safeguard.

2. Keep your expectations real. What does ideal growth look like exactly? What kind of impact can we expect in the given time of our teaching contact?

3. Use a variety of approaches.[26] Triangulating various instruments and activities usually works best.

4. Discuss assessment with your students. Do this either alone or in a group. Students need to own and accept the evaluation of their character as part of the process, not as a pass or fail exercise to gain credits. Where possible, downplay the value of numerical assessment.

5. Stay away from comparison, competition and conformity. No student should compare her or his growth in character to that of anyone else. We are all on different journeys, and growth for one person might look like failure to another. Arrogance and pride are around the corner and the last thing you want is a pecking order. Students have different starting points, and someone with a difficult past may struggle more than someone who has grown up in a family and community where virtue was regularly habituated and exemplified.

6. Use the full five-fold set of virtue descriptors of emotion, desire, motivation, behaviour and perception. The "enjoyment" of virtue might, for example, be an interesting benchmark.[27]

7. Keep an eye on overall character, not just on virtue. The Aristotelian framework is based on different virtues interacting with each other, and even if one virtue is strong, it might not be an indication of the overall development of character. A student might give a great show of resilience but be a confident egotist.[28]

8. Look for constancy. Is change in character stable and consistent across domains?

---

26. Arthur suggests a complex ideal set that includes (1) measuring moral perception by analysing a novel, poem or film and identifying moral issues; (2) measuring moral emotion and desire by implicit testing; (3) measuring moral self-concept by self-testing; (4) measuring moral understanding and reasoning through a deep interview; (5) measuring moral motivation by dilemma testing; (6) measuring moral behaviour by longitudinal observational study corroborated by peer reports (Arthur et al., 120).

27. "What I particularly enjoy will of course depend upon what sort of person I am, and what sort of person I am is of course a matter of my virtues and vices" (MacIntyre, *After Virtue*, 160).

28. Arthur et al., *Teaching*, 110.

9. Be gradual in your expectations. Early on in the programme you may wish to have more generic goals to simply help students understand what you are doing. Then you can gradually increase expectations across the full set of programme outcomes.

10. Decide beforehand about public communication of assessment outcomes. Will the school issue a transcript, a letter or a reference? Who will write this and sign it off? The student? The community of peers? The teachers? The school leadership? Who will see the documentation that you produce? What is the purpose of sharing the data you have collected?[29] Make sure you ask for the written consent of entering students to make these results known as they graduate. This is important both in respect of students and as a safeguard from legal retorsion.

—

When all is said and done, assessing character in contemporary educational contexts is fraught with uncertainty. We need to recognize the imprecision of our approaches and that, despite a good deal of research,[30] very few assessment approaches have been developed to deal with character and virtue.[31] This may come with the territory, given that current assessment philosophies do not sit well with character and virtue education. But we should not lose heart, for there are some very good things that we can do. I hope this letter has encouraged you.

May you be patient as you move forward, for changing people is an erratic process.[32]

---

29. "We need to be cautious in how we use the data we collect. How much we share with students could shame them into change or decrease their internal motivation" ("Assessment," Educating for Intellectual Virtues, http://intellectualvirtues.org/guiding-principles/assessment/).

30. "Can Virtue Be Measured?," papers of conference, Oriel College, Oxford, 9–11 January 2014, Jubilee Centre, https://www.jubileecentre.ac.uk/485/conferences/can-virtue-be-measured.

31. Some promising research is being done through "The Spiritual, Character and Virtue Formation of Seminarians" project, led by David Wang and sponsored by the Templeton Foundation. This research project aims at adapting "tools from psychology and philosophy and insights from the field of spiritual direction in order to help seminaries gather longitudinal measures of their students' character development" (see https://www.templeton.org/grant/the-spiritual-character-and-virtue-formation-of-seminarians).

32. "Character defies hasty acquisition . . . the very idea of character in this historic sense ridicules the 'ethical fitness seminar' or the 'ten steps to character' now hustled by the merchants of direct-mail morality" (Hunter, *Death of Character*, 19).

39

Assuring Quality

I think this might be my last letter for now. This is the end of our third summer of correspondence. You fell ill during the first summer. I had a vocational crisis during the second summer. Now you are entering the executive phases of the foundation of the academy. We've covered a fair bit of ground in these three years, starting with a new vision for theological education, then moving on to consider the tradition and theological grounding of character and virtue education, and now considering its practice.

We have both served for a long time as quality assurance officers in our respective regions, so it is appropriate that the topic of this final letter is accreditation and certification. A couple of months ago, you asked me to outline standards and guidelines that might pertain to the accreditation of the academy. That is a very good request and I will come to it in a moment. First, however, let me deal briefly with the issue of certification, since it is closely connected to accreditation.

Certification of Character and Virtue

Here is the question: should a theological programme focusing on character and virtue education aim at being certified in order to grant a recognized degree? Should you be thinking of offering, for example, a BA in Theology, Character and Virtue that is accredited by an official agency? Or should you free yourself from the restraints of higher education accreditation and offer a non-formal programme whose main value is found in its benefits to the students and to the communities they serve? There is a broader question here about the place of theological education within contemporary higher education. This is not a painless issue, and we have had these discussions at many international conferences.

On the one hand, there are clear benefits to a certified degree. Formal certification itself is, in a way, a commitment to a set of virtues, such as quality, truthfulness, faithfulness and attestation of constancy. But certification also benefits students with a formal title that is recognized by society, justifies years of effort and expense, enhances their mobility, allows them to continue to higher level studies and permits them to move forward in employment.[1] In addition, higher education recognition gives the discipline of theology respected status in society and confers the sense of offering a "proper" degree.[2]

And yet I've often wondered whether the secular certification of theology programmes might represent a Babylonian captivity. Are there constrictions in the standards and expectations of today's higher educational systems that hinder us from achieving our true mission as theological educators? The question is even more pertinent as we consider a programme focusing on character and virtue. Might it lose its efficacy altogether under the constraints of certification? Perhaps. We can envision, for example, difficulties in designing recognizable learning outcomes within subject benchmarks, awkwardness in credit-counting procedures or some of the assessment conundrums that we considered in my last letter. We might also imagine conflicting views around staff discrimination, expulsion criteria, student-centred policies, graduation documentation and degree classification. It seems that there are many quality standards in tertiary accreditation that might not be the best fit in terms of the purposes of the academy.

As we work through these certification conundrums, it helps us to keep the main stakeholders in mind. Who are we certifying *to*? If our main audience is the world of higher education, then there is no doubt that we need to certify the fitness of our programme for the university, using its language and following its expectations. But if our main stakeholders are faith communities, then certification should speak first and foremost to them. And here the expectations are probably different from those of higher education. As we've seen, many church leaders are keener on developing spirituality and character

---

1. Over 65 percent of potential theology students indicate that accreditation is extremely/very important in the choice of a college. Most indicate that receiving credit is essential (Kinnaman and Hempell, "Perceptions").

2. "The largely Western, and more specifically American, model of accreditation weighed large in the desires and hopes of the majority world. An accredited degree, even a bad one, somehow felt 'real.' A different type of certification, even when a much better education and process, felt second class" (Higgins, "Majority World Theological Development," 106).

than academic skills, and many practising Christians are simply interested in theological education for personal growth.[3]

I don't have an answer to the certification conundrum as it relates to the academy. There are good arguments either way, both for offering a certified degree and for offering a non-certified programme. The question is clearly connected to the issue of accreditation, to which I now turn.

State Accreditation

Concerning the accreditation of character and virtue education, I am assuming that you will pursue some sort of quality assurance, and this means that you have two options. The first is state accreditation and the second is accreditation through an agency that specializes in theological education.

Should you decide to pursue state accreditation, the first step is to contact the state agency and renew your contacts with the university rector. Keep in mind that things are still relatively new when it comes to quality assurance of character and virtue education, and you might encounter obstacles. Character education normally operates below the radar of quality assurance (in the extra-curricular), and quality assurance officers will struggle to fit your programme into their standards.[4] You might also find diffident attitudes, which arise from the (mistaken) impression that character and virtue education is grounded in religion and is not a legitimate expression of higher education.[5]

There are, however, some interesting precedents that are emerging in the accreditation of character issues that you might want to take a look at. In the UK, for example, a proposal is in place to renew the criteria of Ofsted assessment within the "Character Nation" project[6] which could easily be used for accreditation purposes. Another useful template for accreditation is found in the "Schools of Character" programme, which has established

---

3. Accreditation ranked 11th place in a survey asking prospective theology students what was "very important" in deciding which theological college to attend. The higher considerations were "academic rigour," "evangelical position," "spiritual climate" and "mission and purpose" (Kinnaman and Hempell, "Perceptions," 71).

4. "What stands as character education is highly variable and infrequently meets the standards for quality" (Berkowitz, "Science of Character Education," 47).

5. "Accrediting associations have struggled to see moral education grounded in religion as bona fide higher education" (Kiss and Euben, *Debating Moral Education*, 38).

6. Birdwell, Scott and Reynolds, *Character Nation*, 51–66.

eleven principles by which to accredit schools offering character education programmes.[7]

Should you go down this road, be mindful that you might be asked to pay a price in terms of the nature and content of your programme. Although it would be great to offer a bachelor's degree in theology that focuses on character and virtue, you may find that the accreditation parameters will alter your outcome. If this happens, have the courage to make difficult choices. Is it better to have a non-certified programme that is genuinely offering a chance to grow in character and virtue, or to have a certified programme that bears a promising title but ends up being a scholarly study of character and virtue? Not that there is anything wrong with the latter, but it is different from all that we have been discussing so far.

Accreditation through Specialized Agencies

The second strategy is to consider certification through agencies that specialize in the accreditation of theological education. There are several of these across the world, and we have served on their visitation teams. I believe that there is a desire to creatively accredit programmes in character and virtue education in these circles. I know, for example, that the International Council for Evangelical Theological Education has worked on global standards for accreditation of theological programmes that include quality standards and guidelines for character education.[8] In addition to at least one explicit accreditation standard that deals specifically with character education,[9] this remarkable document makes frequent reference to character and virtue in relation to school

---

7. The guide comes complete with principles and key indicators which make it a very practical document. The principles include promotion of ethical and performance values, clear definitions of character, evidence of comprehensive, intentional and proactive approaches, the presence of a caring community, the opportunity for students to be involved in moral action, the existence of a fitting curriculum that develops character, the fostering of self-motivation, appropriate staff as an ethical learning community, appropriately supportive leadership, engagement of families and communities and ongoing internal assessment of its culture, climate, functions and efficacy in developing good character (Lickona et al., "Character Education Partnership").

8. ICETE, "Standards and Guidelines for Global Evangelical Theological Education, 2019," https://icete.info/resources/sggete/.

9. "Institutions include and monitor outcomes and learning activities in their programmes related to character and virtue education, both through specific courses dealing with virtue knowledge, virtue reasoning and virtue practice and through the integration of character and virtue education across the curriculum. Learning communities intentionally provides [sic] a context where character and virtue are modelled and can be emulated" (ICETE, "Standards and Guidelines," Standard B1.3, 20, https://icete.info/resources/sggete/).

leadership, staff and faculty, learning communities, integration in programme design, learning outcomes, admission criteria, graduation requirements and certification. This is a relatively new development, and a promising one. Accreditation can be a powerful agent of change, and we are hopeful that character and virtue education will gain a new place of priority in theological schools. Your school might serve as a pilot for other schools.

The Association of Theological Schools is another specialized agency that deals with the accreditation of theological education in America and I've looked for character and virtue education in their "Standards of Accreditation." The "Standards" are not uninterested in the virtues and we find both implicit assumptions around character[10] and indirect appeals to virtue.[11] They encourage the cultivation of habits of theological reflection, the nurturing of wisdom in practice, the growth in moral sensibility and character, the encouragement of learning in communal settings, the development of formative aims in the curriculum and the inclusion of moral development.[12] The demands for intellectual virtues are also clearly present and include critical thinking, ability to conduct research,[13] scholarly collaboration[14] and freedom of enquiry.[15] The "Standards" also feature recurring appeals to personal formation and spiritual formation.[16] In a few cases, formation is explained as "emotional maturity, personal faith, moral integrity and social concern."[17] The words "growth" and "depth" are also frequently used as descriptors in formative outcomes.[18]

Although these are encouraging signals, the current version of the "Standards" makes no direct or explicit appeal to character or virtue, and there are some lacunas, such as the lack of formational outcomes in the higher-

---

10. Meye, "Theological Education," 118–119.

11. The ATS "Standards" make an indirect appeal to truthfulness in purpose statements (1.1.3), diligence in planning and evaluation (1.2), overall integrity (2), justice and equity in dealing with diversity (2.4–2.6) and in governance (7.2.2), and responsibility in governance (7).

12. ATS "Standards," 3.1 and 3.2.

13. ATS "Standards," 3.1.

14. ATS "Standards," 3.3.1.

15. ATS "Standards," 3.3.2.

16. In the "Admissions" section, care is given to personal and spiritual qualifications (ATS "Standards," 6.2). Residency is linked to possibilities for spiritual and personal formation (ES 2.1.2), and distance education mentions enhancing personal and spiritual formation (ES 4.2.3).

17. ATS "Standards," ES 1.2.1.

18. For example, the "Goals of Programmes" section includes spiritual depth and moral integrity (ATS "Standards," A1.2) and growth in personal and spiritual maturity (B1.2.1).

level degrees and the absence of moral requirements for faculty members or governing boards.[19]

Generally speaking, agencies that specialize in the accreditation of theological education represent a great opportunity.[20] However, there has not yet been a focused effort on developing detailed criteria or examples of evidence to define quality assurance parameters for this kind of programme. You have asked me what criteria I would adopt, so I will make a small list here. Quality in a school that offers a theological education programme that centres on character and virtue should feature:

- A clearly articulated theoretical framework for character education in theological education that includes key definitions, educational procedures and theological grounding;
- Visible statements with explicit and consistent vocabulary related to character education in key strategic documents, the school mission statement, curricula and courses, student handbooks, disciplinary codes, library regulations, chapel topics, publicity, website, public events, newsletters and buildings (art work);
- Documented input from stakeholders (staff, students, church, broader society) related to the identification of core virtues that are relevant to the context of the school;
- Documented input of staff and students related to ongoing planning, reflection and evaluation of character education strategies;
- Senior positions in the school that hold responsibility for the development and monitoring of character education strategies. The senior leadership is a visible and supportive champion of character education;
- Pastoral support measures to enhance a loving and virtue-shaping community;
- Staff hiring criteria, review and disciplinary procedures that include explicit reference to character. New and existing faculty receive training and ongoing professional development in character education;
- Learning outcomes pertaining to thinking, feeling and doing in relation to character and virtue education present in curricular

---

19. Meye, "Theological Education," 116.

20. See also the Alliance for the Certification of Lay Ecclesial Ministers, "National Certification Standards for Lay Ecclesial Ministers," which includes the "demonstration of basic human virtues" as one of its standards (4).

maps and traced to specific course outcomes. Graduate profiles make reference to good character and the associated virtues. In addition to explicit courses, character education strategies are mapped onto all school activities, including curricular, co-curricular and community service;
- Teaching and learning strategies and andragogical practices in place that are carefully thought-through so as to contribute to growth in character and virtue;
- Provision for students of habitual opportunities for moral action and service learning in the learning community and in surrounding faith communities and society;
- Specific multi-method assessment strategies in place for character education, and personal feedback for students relating to their character growth;
- Certification measures in place at graduation that include character assessment of the graduates;
- Research occurring in the area of character and virtue both as a distinct subject and in dialogue with other theological disciplines.

This is no more than an initial sketch. As I've said, certification and accreditation of programmes centred on character and virtue education is a new venture. Often, schools will not experiment with radical change because of accreditation constraints. So there is a great responsibility for accreditation agencies to be agents of change. What we need are visionary schools working together with courageous accreditation agencies who will embrace disruptive innovation. There is a special opportunity for accreditation agencies that specialize in theological education to take the lead and experiment with more holistic accreditation criteria. Although there are some positive signs, we recognize that the resources are limited in meeting these new challenges.[21]

You are well beyond the state where you need me to tell you what to do, and I have been honoured to be your conversation partner in all of this. On the specific issues of this letter, I really do not know whether you should pursue certification or not, nor am I sure whether accreditation by the state or by a specialized agency is the better choice for the academy. You are surrounded by a good board and you have done your research. I would encourage you to sit down with the educationalist from the local university and the accreditation officer from your regional agency and discuss these issues candidly with them.

—

---

21. Meye, "Theological Education," 118.

I think I have completed what may be useful to you. It has been a long journey of two and a half years in which we've enjoyed each other's mind and dreams. Now it is in your hands to act and, by God's grace, to determine what will come. If deeds are doors and the handles are their doing,[22] it is up to you now to turn those handles.

This is no time for nostalgia, but I will miss our conversation. I will stand on the sidelines and prayerfully cheer you on. Several major pieces still need to fall into place. Your board needs to commit to a final detailed strategic plan. You need to host another consultation and share your work with the regional faith communities. You need to finalize your initial team. You are waiting for the confirmation on the purchase of the monastery (by the way, thank you for the pictures). You need to develop a curriculum and decide on certification and accreditation. Then, if all goes well, you will need to build your team and start marketing your programme.

You've indicated next year as the target opening date. May that be so. May you find peace as you discern the next steps, modesty to backtrack should you discover that you have taken the wrong direction, resilience to withstand obstacles and sufficient rest to enjoy your life and your family.

Next year, I hope to fulfil my dream and run the New York marathon. Might we run together to celebrate the inauguration of the academy?

---

22. Attributed to George MacDonald. "It is not enough for us to talk – the test will be in how we translate our concern into deeds" (C. Taylor, "Sources of Renewal," 323).

40

Ten Years Later

Dear sir, my name is Sofia and I am one of the first graduates of the Theological Academy for Character and Virtue. I had the privilege of being formed under the leadership of the late Dr Siméon and his team. Since then, I have pursued a career in education and politics and have had the good fortune to rise to my current position of Senior Secretary of Education for our region. I am now doing doctoral research in the area of character and virtue education for our government and I am investigating the origins of the Theological Academy for Character and Virtue which was the first school in our region to systematically engage with this kind of formation.

As you know, Siméon died five years ago, after repeated strokes. I recall that he began to weaken while I was still enrolled at the academy, shortly after he returned from a marathon in New York and his daughter married. It was as if he had met three significant targets, and his heart began to let go. His funeral was a massive event, and thousands came to honour him from all over the region. I recall you being there, but we did not meet. In accordance with his wishes, the funeral eulogy was a tribute to the virtues that he had tried to embody. What a legacy he has left us.

His wife has kindly allowed me to browse through his personal archives and I have found your letters. They were carefully kept in a tin box in the bottom drawer of his office desk. I have read through them and would like to ask your permission to translate and publish them. They are both scholarly and personable, and I'm convinced that they can be of inspiration and instruction to many others as they obviously were for Siméon.

The Difficult Years

Our region has been deeply impacted by the academy. Initially it was not so, and the first years were very difficult. I belonged to the first cohort who walked into the beautiful monastery that had become the home of the academy, and I recall how my ears were buzzing with reports from local newspapers about a new cult that was being established under the guise of an educational venture. The government at the time would have nothing to do with us, and the academy had not even been granted formal school status, let alone higher education accreditation for a formal degree. The association of university rectors would have nothing to do with us either, and Siméon's personal reputation as an academic and a scholar had taken a serious blow.

The beginning was bumpy in the relationships with the faith communities as well. Despite the initial support and consultation, the test of reality met with less enthusiasm. You may recall that the board split shortly before the property was purchased. I've been granted access to the minutes that reflect the rising tensions that were mostly caused by the radical curriculum that Siméon was proposing. There were also financial issues, but thankfully the main donor remained constant and the academy never suffered a financial crisis.

Within the faith communities there were wide-ranging reactions. Some denominations felt that the project was too radical and decided to send their ordinands abroad for traditional training. Others preferred church-based training and resisted the residential nature of the academy, trying to replicate similar projects on a smaller scale. Some of these have prospered, but others floundered. There were also many young people who simply did not understand what the academy was about, and either pursued discipleship programmes or joined the growing "spiritual direction" movement that rose up in our region at about the same time as the academy.

A Golden Start

Siméon remained undeterred by these difficulties, and a significant group of people stayed with him. This included a good part of the board, many donors and church leaders. The staff team that Siméon trained also never wavered. My impression is that Siméon's wife and daughter were among his main staying forces in the darker moments. And then, of course, there were the first students.

I recall when Siméon and two others on his team came to my community to advertise the academy. The team had already been living together for almost a year in the monastery, carefully planning and shaping themselves as a community of virtue. I had seen the website, watched their YouTube videos, followed their Facebook page and read some of their leaflets. Given that my father had been on the board of the academy as the local politician, I had been curious about it for some time. But it was meeting Siméon and the others that really made a difference for me. I arranged a two-day visit to the monastery and, through encountering the rest of the team, I immediately felt that I wanted to be part of this community of virtue for the next three years of my life. I wanted to grow in character and virtue as a Christian woman. I wanted to know God and the truth of my faith, but I also wanted to see how this knowledge would change who I was as a person. I wanted to bless the world around me by embodying the virtues that the world needed. At the time, I was working with underprivileged young girls, and I was thinking mainly about growing in the virtues of compassion and justice. But that was soon to expand.

On a late September morning, fourteen of us joined the community of the academy and began our journey. Reading your letters, I can now see that many of the things that Siméon did were direct outcomes of your encouragement and advice. He spoke of you often and kept telling us that, one day, you would come to visit the school yourself. I don't believe you ever have done, but your legacy is here with us. Here is a brief list of some of the things that we experienced at the academy.

From day one, there was no doubt that the central purpose of our time at the academy was to shape our character towards virtue. Everything spoke to this end: clearly, centrally and intentionally. When I read your letter on the radical curriculum, I could not believe my eyes, for it was almost identical to what we experienced. We had courses on virtue, on community, on the church and the world and on literature. We had an entire course on the Aristotelian framework and Siméon worked hard to convince us all that this was not a Western/Greek importation. In all our courses, theology was woven throughout and, as I've compared myself with friends who have studied theology elsewhere through a traditional degree, I've never felt that my theological understanding was inadequate. We grew in character through participation in sports and art, but our favourite courses were always the habituation practicums.

Siméon's team also scrupulously worked out what they taught us, and all of our courses blended virtue knowledge, virtue reasoning and virtue practice. They also used creative combinations of lecturing, habituation practices, service learning, role-modelling, dialogue and story-telling. We did a lot of learning through projects and in the community, and our classroom time was seldom taken up with long lectures. The monastery had been fitted with sets of lounges rather than formal classrooms, and I vividly recall our worship in the beautiful little chapel where the sun would come through the stained-glass windows as we focused daily on the virtues of the Trinity. The library was not large, but everything we needed for our research was there. I recall my initial reaction to the assessment approach at the academy that was based mostly on self-assessment and reflective writing. To me it seemed flimsy and subjective, and I initially resented the fact that I could not demonstrate my achievement through grades. But now, looking back, I realize that I have never grown so much in my life and the outcomes that were set out in the programme have been met by all of us who were serious and committed.

Sadly, not all of the initial fourteen students stayed for the entire three years. Five left during the first year: one for financial reasons, one because he was offered a high-paying job in his father's company and three who candidly admitted that they could not share the level of commitment in the community.

Yes, because, above all, there was the community. I think that is what shaped me the most. I saw virtue in action and in construction. I saw what virtue can look like in the messiness of real life. I saw the conundrums of lived-out morality and the exercise of painful wisdom. I saw both failure and the grace of God that was working to transform the characters of those around me. I saw the gospel at work in shaping righteousness. I saw humility, constancy and love. I wanted to emulate what I saw. I became a friend. A friend who was bound to others through a commitment to what was good.

None of us graduated with a degree of any kind. We were awarded the academy's "Letter of Completion." This was Siméon's invention and consisted in a rather long report that described our journey. It was written by the entire team, subjected to the community for comment, and then given to each of us for the final edit. That was it. No transcript of grades. No degree to hang on the wall. No credits to transfer elsewhere. Just a changed character and a community that stood to verify it. I hold that letter as one of my most precious keepsakes and have left a signed agreement with the academy that anyone can request a copy of it at any time.

If I recall correctly, in one of your letters you spoke about the golden thread of character and virtue education. Well, what we experienced was a golden start – small and insignificant to many, but precious and strong for us. Personally, I had struggled with lack of constancy my entire life, and that was slowly changed through many activities, not least by the early morning running routine with my fellow students and the teachers. I managed to complete my first half-marathon in my third year, and I was celebrated by the community for what they called a character milestone in my life. It was true: the benefits of this habituated discipline have extended to other areas of my life where I can see what it means to "run the good race" of faith.

When I entered the academy, I was a person who strongly felt the passion of fear. I was easily intimidated by situations that might cause me pain, and this hindered me from doing my duty. At secondary school, I often would not submit my assignments for fear of being evaluated poorly, and in my university years I avoided close relationships to avoid being hurt. I had undergone some helpful counselling for these issues, but it was in the first year of the academy that I was able to name the vice of cowardice. I dedicated two of my habituation projects to the virtue of fortitude and, during the second project, when I spent four months in a very dangerous context of human trafficking, I began to perceive that the passion of fear was being tamed and that my emotional responses to fearful situations were being re-educated. Today, I consider myself a brave woman.

The academy also changed the way I viewed my Christian walk. I had been brought up to rejoice in the fact that we were going to heaven and that Jesus was there to provide for our needs, and most of the worship songs that I had been taught spoke either of future hope or of present providence. I have now embraced a gospel that I like to define as "more muscular," and I have discovered that Jesus has come to transform me and not just forgive me. God has a design for my life that is to be Christlike in my character and not just pave my way with desirable surroundings. My prayer life has changed, and I rarely pray that the circumstances of my life will change. What I pray is that God will change me as I walk through them, whatever they may be. Grace, for me, is the power to change. Socrates did not know the gospel of Jesus, but he was right in concluding that "*arête* comes to the virtuous by the gift of God."[1] The academy has taught me to receive this gift.

The Mustard Seed

The early years were good for us, but they must have been very difficult for Siméon. And then things began to change. The mustard seed developed roots and began to sprawl. It all began shortly before Siméon died, and he was blessed to see the first signs of what was soon to become a massive movement in our region. Several things began to come together. Our country had a season of violent unrest in the outskirts of all our major cities. Many died, and when the dust settled, social analysts pointed to a widespread moral malaise as one of the main causes of the violence and called for a renewed focus on moral education. Shortly before this, the university rector with whom Siméon had met so many times also had a change of heart and, after a three-day visit to the academy, wrote a glowing article about character and virtue education.

---

1. Plato, *Meno* 98b.

The article appeared in the region's main educational journal and sparked a wave of debate.

As this was happening, the accreditation process also bore fruit. Siméon had applied to the accrediting agency in our region that specializes in theological education. At the time of our application, the agency had no specific standards or criteria that related to what the academy was doing. Nor did they have the resources to develop them. But they caught a vision to do so, applied to a foundation for a grant, obtained the necessary resources and set out to develop a whole new set of accreditation standards and assessment criteria that enabled them to engage in quality assurance of character and virtue education. The academy was the first school in the world to obtain this kind of accreditation, and it happened the year after I left and just months before Siméon's death.

As I write, the process is now underway to obtain government accreditation and degree status. This is because our government has begun to take character and virtue education very seriously. The department of which I am Secretary has several branches that aim to implement programmes for character and virtue education in primary and secondary schools as well as in higher education. Many schools have already begun to put such strategies to work, and a flurry of research is now taking place. Including my own.

Oddly, the faith communities have been a little slower than secular society. But, as graduates are returning to their communities, the reputation of the academy is growing. Engaging in theology together with character and virtue education is gradually being acknowledged as a genuine response to the needs of the church, and the academy has a waiting list of prospective students.

—

I trust you will receive this letter. I have found it very difficult to locate your contact details. Even the Internet has gone silent about you for the last two years. That is why I am writing this hard copy and sending it to the return address I found on your letters. We have never met and perhaps never will, but I would like to thank you on behalf of our society and the faith communities in our region.

Your letters to Siméon have shown virtue and sown virtue. May you find deep happiness in having contributed to ours.

Select Bibliography

Abusch, T. "The Development and Meaning of the Epic of Gilgamesh." *Journal of the American Oriental Society* 121, no. 4 (2001): 614–622.

Adler, M. *The Paideia Proposal*. New York: Touchstone, 1998.

The Alliance for the Certification of Lay Ecclesial Ministers. "National Certification Standards for Lay Ecclesial Ministers." 2011. Accessed 10 August 2018. http://lemcertification.org/docs/aclem_final_standards_20111115.pdf.

Ambrose. *De Officiis Ministrorum* (On the Duties of the Clergy). New Advent. Accessed 23 May 2018. http://www.newadvent.org/fathers/34011.htm.

Anscombe, G. E. M. "Modern Moral Philosophy." *Philosophy* 33, no. 124 (Jan 1958): 1–16.

Aquinas, T. *The Summa Theologica*. Accessed 11 July 2018. http://www.documentacatholicaomnia.eu/03d/1225-1274,_Thomas_Aquinas,_Summa_Theologiae_%5B1%5D,_EN.pdf.

Araki, N. "An Application of Kohlberg's Theory of Moral Dilemma Discussion to the Japanese Classroom and Its Effect on Moral Development in Japanese Students." In *Handbook of Moral and Character Education*, edited by L. Nucci, 308–325. New York: Routledge, 2014.

Aristotle. *The Nicomachean Ethics*. Los Angeles: Enhanced Media Publishers, 2017.

———. *Politics*. In *The Works of Plato and Aristotle: 35 Works*. Edited by B. Jowett. C&C Web Press, 2009. Ebook.

Arnold, M. *Culture and Anarchy*. Cambridge: Cambridge University Press, 1932.

Arthur, J. *Education with Character*. London: Routledge, 2003.

———. "A Framework for Character Education in Schools." The Jubilee Centre for Character and Virtues, 2017. Accessed 5 February 2018. https://www.jubileecentre.ac.uk/media/news/article/5514/New-A-Framework-for-Character-Education-in-Schools-Published.

Arthur, J., K. Wilson, and R. Godfrey. *Graduates of Character*. Birmingham: University of Birmingham, 2009.

Arthur, J., et al. *Character Education: The Formation of Virtues and Dispositions in 16–19 Year Olds with Particular Reference to the Religious and Spiritual*. Report to the House of Lords, Canterbury Christ Church University and University of Bristol, 2006.

———. *Teaching Character and Virtue in Schools*. London: Routledge, 2017.

Association of Theological Schools (ATS). "Standards of Accreditation in the United States and Canada." 2010.

———. "Voyage: Vision: Venture Report of the Task Force on Spiritual Development." *Theological Education* 8, no. 3 (Spring 1972): 153–197.

Augustine. *The City of God*. New Advent. Accessed 1 April 2018. http://www.newadvent.org/fathers/120119.htm.
Austin, M., and D. Geivett. "Being Good: Christian Virtues for Everyday Life." *Journal of Spiritual Formation and Soul Care* 6, no. 2 (2013): 296–336.
Baehr, J. "Cultivating Good Minds." Accessed 10 June 2018. IntellectualVirtues.org.
———. "Educating for Intellectual Virtues." 2015. Accessed 10 August 2018. www.jasonbaehr.wordpress.com.
Barnett, R., and K. Coate. *Engaging the Curriculum in Higher Education*. Maidenhead: Open University Press, 2015.
Barth, K. *The Humanity of God*. Louisville, KY: Westminster Press, 1996.
———. "The New Humanism and the Humanism of God." *Theology Today* 8, no. 2 (1951): 157–166. https://doi.org/10.1177/004057365100800204.
Bass, D., et al. *For Life Abundant*. Cambridge, MA: Eerdmans, 2008.
Bauman, Z. "Living in Utopia." Ralph Miliband Public Lecture, London School of Economics and Political Science, 2005. Accessed 31 May 2019. https://digital.library.lse.ac.uk/objects/lse:vob876pub.
———. *Liquid Fear*. Cambridge: Polity Press, 2006.
———. *Liquid Modernity*. Cambridge: Polity Press, 2000.
———. "Universities: Old, New and Different." In *The Postmodern University*, edited by A. Smith and F. Webster, 17–26. Maidenhead: Open University Press, 1997.
Beagles, K. "Growing Disciples in Community: A Review of Scripture and Social Science." *Andrews University Seminary Studies* 48, no. 1 (2010): 81–108.
Beaulieu, P. "The Social and Intellectual Setting of Babylonian Wisdom Literature." In *Wisdom Literature in Mesopotamia and Israel*, SBL Symposium Series 36, edited by R. Clifford, 3–19. Atlanta: SBL Publications, 2007.
Bebbington, D. *Evangelicalism in Modern Britain*. New York: Routledge, 2005.
Belcher, J. *Deep Church*. Downers Grove, IL: InterVarsity Press, 2009.
Bennett, W. *The Book of Virtues*. New York: Rockefeller Center, 1993.
Berkowitz, M. "The Science of Character Education." Hoover Press: Damon, 2014. Accessed 30 May 2019. http://media.hoover.org/sites/default/files/documents/0817929622_43.pdf.
Berkowitz, M., and M. Bier. "Toward a Science of Character Education." *Journal of Character Education* 13, no. 1 (2017): 33–51.
Berkowitz, M., and M. Fekula. "Educating for Character." *About Campus* (Nov–Dec 1999): 17–22.
Birdwell, J., R. Scott and L. Reynolds. *Character Nation: A Demos Report with the Jubilee Centre for Character and Virtues*. London: Demos, 2015.
Black, G. *The Theology of Dallas Willard: Discovering Protoevangelical Faith*. Eugene, OR: Pickwick.
Bloom, A. *The Closing of the American Mind*. New York: Simon & Schuster, 1987.
Bok, D. "Ethics, the University and Society." Accessed 16 May 2018. http://www.drbachinese.org/vbs/publish/229/vbs229p015e.pdf.

Bondi, R. "The Elements of Character." *Journal of Religious Ethics* 12, no. 2 (1984): 201–218.
Bonhoeffer, D. *Discipleship*. Minneapolis: Fortress, 2003.
Bott, D., et al. "The State of Positive Education." World Government Summit. Accessed 13 February 2019. https://www.worldgovernmentsummit.org/api/publications/document/8f647dc4-e97c-6578-b2f8-ff0000a7ddb6.
Boyd, W., and E. King. *The History of Western Education*. London: A&C Black Publisher, 1980.
Brattston, D. *Traditional Christian Ethics*. Vol. 3. Bloomington: WestBow Press, 2014.
Brown, W. *Character in Crisis*. Grand Rapids: Eerdmans, 1996.
Buber, M. *Between Man and Man*. London: Kegan Paul, 1947.
———. "Biblical Humanism." In *The Martin Buber Reader: Essential Writings*, edited by Asher D. Biemann, 158–159. New York: Palgrave Macmillan, 2002.
Campolo, A. *Seven Deadly Sins*. Wheaton, IL: Victor Books, 1988.
Cannon, J. *Lectures on Pastoral Theology*. New York: Charles Scribener, 1858.
Carnegie, S. C. *The Ideal Seminary*. Louisville: Westminster John Knox, 2002.
Carr, D. *Educating the Virtues*. New York: Routledge, 1991.
Carr, D., et al. "Return to the Crossroads: Maritain Fifty Years On." *British Journal of Educational Studies* 43, no. 2 (Jun 1995): 162–178.
Carrigan, H. *The Wisdom of the Desert Fathers and Mothers*. Brewster, MA: Paraclete, 2010.
Cassian. *Institutis*. Accessed 18 July 2018. http://www.documentacatholicaomnia.eu/03d/0360-0435,_Cassianus,_De_Coenobiorum_Institutis_Libri_Duodecim_[Schaff],_EN.pdf.
Chan, F. *Multiply: Disciples Making Disciples*. Colorado Springs: David C. Cook, 2012.
Charles, D. J. "The Language and Logic of Virtue in 2 Peter 1:5–7." *Bulletin for Biblical Research* 8 (1998): 55–73.
Cheesman, G. "ME7501 Perspectives in Theological Education." Course materials. London School of Theology, 2015.
Chen, G., and J. Yu. "Traditional Chinese Philosophies and Their Perspectives on Moral Education." In *Handbook of Moral and Character Education*, edited by L. Nucci, 43–60. New York: Routledge, 2014.
Chesterton, G. K. *Orthodoxy*. London: Hodder & Stoughton, 1996.
Church, I., and P. Samuelson. *Intellectual Humility*. Reprint, London: Bloomsbury Academic, 2017.
Cicero. *De Officiis*. Accessed 12 May 2018. https://www.loebclassics.com/view/marcus_tullius_cicero-de_officiis/1913/pb_LCL030.1.xml.
———. *Tusculanae Disputationes*. Accessed 8 April 2018. https://www.gutenberg.org/files/14988/14988-h/14988-h.htm.
Cloutier, D., and W. Mattison. "The Resurgence of Virtue in Recent Moral Theology." *Journal of Moral Theology* 3, no. 1 (2014): 228–259.

Colby, A., et al. *Educating Citizens: Preparing America's Undergraduates for Lives of Moral and Civic Responsibility*. San Francisco: Jossey-Bass, 2003.

Coles, R. *The Call of Stories: Teaching and the Moral Imagination*. Boston, MA: Houghton Mifflin, 1990.

Comenius, J. *La Grande didactique*. Translated by M. E. Bosquet-Frigout, D. Saget and B. Jolibert. Paris: Editions Klincksieck, 1992. Accessed 12 August 2018. http://www.ibe.unesco.org/fileadmin/user_upload/archive/Publications/thinkerspdf/comeniuse.PDF.

Committee on Priestly Formation of the United States Conference of Catholic Bishops (USCCB). *Program of Priestly Formation*. 5th ed. Washington: United States Conference of Catholic Bishops, 2006.

Confucius. *The Analects*. Accessed 15 July 2018. http://www.indiana.edu/~p374/Analects_of_Confucius_(Eno-2015).pdf.

Cornell, V. "Evil, Virtue and Islamic Moral Theology." In *Probing the Depths of Evil and Good: Multireligious Views and Case Studies*, edited by J. D. Gort et al., 281–304. Amsterdam/New York: Rodopi, 2007.

Crawford, P. "Educating for Moral Ability: Reflections on Moral Development Based on Vygotsky's Theory of Concept Formation." *Journal of Moral Education* 30, no. 2 (2001): 118.

Cunningham, S. "Who's Mentoring the Mentors? The Discipling Dimension of Faculty Development in Christian Higher Education." *Theological Education* 34, no. 2 (Spring 1998): 31–50.

Curren, R. "Aristotle's Educational Politics and the Aristotelian Renaissance in Philosophy of Education." *Oxford Review of Education* 36, no. 5 (Oct 2010): 543–559.

Curtler, H. "Can Virtue Be Taught?" *Humanitas* 7, no. 1 (1994): 43–50.

Davis, M. "What's Wrong with Character Education?" *American Journal of Education* 110, no. 1 (2003): 32–57.

Dewey, J. *Democracy and Education*. [n.p.]: Simon and Brown, 2011.

———. *Human Nature and Conduct*. Cosimo: Cosimo, 2007.

Dill, J. "Durkheim and Dewey and the Challenge of Contemporary Moral Education." *Journal of Moral Education* 36, no. 2 (Jun 2007): 221–237.

Dodson J. R., and D. E. Briones. *Paul and Seneca in Dialogue*. Leiden: Brill, 2017.

Dreher, R. *The Benedict Option*. New York: Penguin, 2017.

Dykstra, C. *Vision and Character: A Christian Educator's Alternative to Kohlberg*. Eugene, OR: Wipf & Stock, 2008.

Edelstein, W., and T. Krettenauer. "Citizenship and Democracy Education in a Diverse Europe." In *Handbook of Moral and Character Education*, edited by L. Nucci, 386–400. New York: Routledge, 2014.

Ellingsen, S. T. "The Privation Theory of the Vices." Filosofisk Supplement, 2019.

Ellison, N. B., et al. "With a Little Help from My Friends: How Social Network Sites Affect Social Capital Processes." In *A Networked Self: Identity, Community, and*

Culture on Social Network Sites, edited by Z. Papacharissi, 124–145. New York: Routledge, 2010. Accessed 19 May 2018. https://www.academia.edu/1195111/With_a_little_help_from_my_friends_How_social_network_sites_affect_social_capital_processes.

Elshtain, J. "A Call to Civil Society." *Society* 36, no. 5 (1998): 11–19.

Emerson, R. W. "Character." In *The Works of Ralph Waldo Emerson*. Vol. 10, *Lectures and Biographical Sketches*. 1904. Accessed 30 May 2019. https://www.bartleby.com/90/1004.html.

———. *Delphi Complete Works of Ralph Waldo Emerson*. Hastings: Delphi Classics, 2013.

European Union. "Charter of Fundamental Rights of the European Union." Official Journal of the European Communities, 2000. C 364/1.

Farley, B. *In Praise of Virtue: An Explication of the Biblical Virtues in a Christian Context.* Grand Rapids: Eerdmans, 1995.

Farley, E. *Theologia*. Philadelphia: Fortress, 1983.

Ferdinando, K. "Theological Education and Character." *Africa Journal of Evangelical Theology* 27, no. 1 (2008): 45–63.

Ferzoco, G., and C. Muessig, eds. *Medieval Monastic Education*. London: Leicester University Press, 2000.

Fish, S. "Aim Low." *The Chronicle of Higher Education* (16 May 2003). Accessed 17 February 2019. https://www.chronicle.com/article/Aim-Low/45210.

———. "I Know It When I See It: A Reply to Kiss and Euben." In *Debating Moral Education*, edited by E. Kiss and P. Euben, 76–91. Durham, MD/London: Duke University Press, 2010.

Gallati, R. *Rediscovering Discipleship*. Grand Rapids: Zondervan, 2015.

Gilead, T. "Countering the Vices: On the Neglected Side of Character Education." *Studies in the Philosophy of Education* 30 (2011): 271–284.

Gillespie, M. "Players and Spectators: Sports and Ethical Training in the American University." In *Debating Moral Education*, edited by E. Kiss and P. Euben, 296–316. Durham, MD/London: Duke University Press, 2010.

Glanzer, P. "Did the Moral Education Establishment Kill Character?" *Journal of Moral Education* 32, no. 3 (Sept 2003): 291–306.

Goodrich, R. "Neo-Thomism and Education." *British Journal of Educational Studies* 7, no.1 (Nov 1958): 27–35.

González, J. *The History of Theological Education*. Nashville: Abingdon Press, 2015.

Graham, G. *The Institution of Intellectual Values*. Exeter: UK Imprint Academic, 2005.

Gretchen, W., and M. Firmin. "Character Education: Christian Education Perspectives." *Journal of Research on Christian Education* 17 (2008): 182–198.

Gunton, C. "The Church as a School of Virtue? Human Formation in Trinitarian Framework." In *Faithfulness and Fortitude*, edited by M. Nation and S. Wells, 211–231. Edinburgh: T&T Clark, 2000.

Gustafson, M. "Reflections on the Literature on Theological Education Published between 1855 and 1985." *Theological Education*, Supplement 2 (1988): 9–88.

Gustavsson, B. "What Do We Mean by Lifelong Learning and Knowledge?" *International Journal of Lifelong Education* 21, no. 1 (2002): 13–23. Accessed 26 December 2009. http://dx.doi.org/10.1080/02601370110099489.

Gutek, G. *A History of Western Educational Experience*. Long Grove, IL: Waveland, 1972.

Habl, J. "Character Formation: A Forgotten Theme of Comenius's Didactics." *Journal of Education and Christian Belief* 15, no. 2 (2011): 141–153.

Hall, D. "Theological Education as Character Formation?" *Theological Education*, Supplement 1 (1988): 53–79.

Harrington, D. *Jesus and Virtue Ethics: Building Bridges between New Testament Studies and Moral Theology*. Lanham, MD: Sheed & Ward, 2005.

———. *Paul and Virtue Ethics: Building Bridges between New Testament Studies and Moral Theology*. Lanham, MD: Rowman & Littlefield, 2010.

Harrison, T., M. Bawden and L. Rogerson. *Teaching Character through Subjects*. Jubilee Centre. Accessed 12 September 2018. https://issuu.com/creativecause/docs/teaching_character_through_subjects.

Hauerwas, S. *The Character of Virtue: Letters to a Godson*. Cambridge, MA: Eerdmans, 2018.

———. *A Community of Character*. Notre Dame, IN: University of Notre Dame Press, 1982.

———. "The Difference of Virtue and the Difference It Makes: Courage Exemplified." *Modern Theology* 9, no. 3 (July 1993): 249–264.

———. *Dispatches from the Front*. Durham, NC: Duke University Press, 1994.

———. "Happiness, the life of Virtue and Friendship: Theological Reflections on Aristotelian Themes." *The Asbury Theological Journal* 45, no. 1 (Spring 1990): 5–48.

———. "The Pathos of the University: The Case of Stanley Fish." In *Debating Moral Education*, edited by E. Kiss and P. Euben, 92–110. Durham, MD/London: Duke University Press, 2010.

———. *Vision and Virtue*. Notre Dame, IN: University of Notre Dame Press, 1974.

Hauerwas, S., and C. Pinches. *Christians among the Virtues*. Notre Dame, IN: University of Notre Dame Press, 1997.

———. "Christian Virtues Exemplified." *Pro Ecclesia* 5, no. 3 (1996): 334–348.

———. "Virtue Christianly Considered." In *Christian Theism and Moral Philosophy*, edited by M. Beaty, C. Fisher and M. Nelson, 287–304. Macon, GA: Mercer University Press, 1993.

Herdt, J. "Christian Ethics as Informed Prayer." *The Blackwell Companion to Christian Ethics*, edited by S. Hauerwas and S. Wells, 3–12. Malden, MA: Blackwell Publishing.

———. "Hauerwas among the Virtues." *Journal of Religious Ethics* 40, no. 2 (2012): 202–227.

———. "Virtue's Semblance: Erasmus and Luther on Pagan Virtue and the Christian Life." *Journal of the Society of Christian Ethics* 25, no. 2 (2005): 137–162. http://www.jstor.org/stable/23561604.

Heywood, D. "Educating Ministers of Character." *Journal of Adult Theological Education* 10, no. 1 (May 2013): 4–24.

Higgins, K. "Majority World Theological Development." *International Journal of Frontier Missiology* 34, nos. 1–4 (2017): 103–111.

Holmes, A. *Shaping Character*. Grand Rapids: Eerdmans, 1991.

Huang, Y. "Can Virtue Be Taught and How? Confucius on the Paradox of Moral Education." *Journal of Moral Education* 40, no. 2 (June 2011): 141–159.

Hull, B. *The Complete Book of Discipleship: On Being and Making Followers of Christ*. Colorado Springs, CO: Navigators eBook Collection, 2006. EBSCOhost. Accessed 7 May 2018.

Hunter, J. D. *The Death of Character*. New York: Basic, 2000.

Jaeger, Werner. *Paideia: The Ideals of Greek Culture*. Vol. 1. Oxford: Basil Blackwell, 1939. (See also vols. 2 and 3.)

John Paul II. *Pastores Dabo Vobis*. Rome: Libreria Editrice Vaticana, 1992.

Jones, M., et al. *Toward Human Flourishing*. Macon, GA: Mercer University Press, 2013.

Jung, J. *Character Formation in Online Education*. Grand Rapids: Zondervan, 2015.

Kekes, J. *Facing Evil*. Princeton: Princeton University Press, 1990.

Kelsey, D. *Between Athens and Berlin*. Eugene, OR: Wipf & Stock, 2011.

———. "Reflections on a Discussion of Theological Education as Character Formation." *Theological Education* 25, no. 1 (1988): 62–75.

Kierkegaard, S. *The Present Age*. New York: Harper Perennial Modern Classics, 2010.

Kikawada, I. "The Double Creation of Mankind in Enki and Ninmah." *Iraq* 45, no. 1 (1993): 43–45.

Kinnaman, D. *What's Next for Biblical Higher Education?* Barna Group, commissioned by the Association for Biblical Higher Education, 2017.

Kinnaman, D., and B. Hempell. "London School of Theology: Perceptions of Theological Higher Education among Key Stakeholders." Unpublished paper, Barna Global, 2015.

Kiss, E., and P. Euben. "Aim High: A Response to Stanley Fish." In *Debating Moral Education*, edited by E. Kiss and P. Euben, 57–75. Durham, MD/London: Duke University Press, 2010.

———. *Debating Moral Education*. Durham, MD/London: Duke University Press, 2010.

———. "Debating Moral Education: An Introduction." In *Debating Moral Education*, edited by E. Kiss and P. Euben, 3–26. Durham, MD/London: Duke University Press, 2010.

Kohlberg, L. *The Philosophy of Moral Development*. San Franciso: Harper & Row, 1981.

Kohls, P. "A Look at Church Leadership in Africa." *Africa Journal of Evangelical Theology* 17, no. 2 (1998): 107–126.

Koons, R. "The War of the Three Humanisms: Irving Babbitt and the Recovery of Classical Learning." *Modern Age* (Summer 2010): 198–207.
Kotzee, B., A. Carter, and H. Siegel. "Educating for Intellectual Virtue: A Critique from Action Guidance." Forthcoming in *Episteme*. Accessed 8 February 2019. https://www.academia.edu/38286274/Educating_for_Intellectual_Virtue_A_critique_from_action_guidance?source=swp_share.
Krabill, J., and S. Murray. *Forming Christian Habits in Post-Christendom: The Legacy of Alan and Eleanor Kreider*. Harrisonburg, VA: Herald, 2011.
Kreider, A. *The Patient Ferment of the Early Church*. Grand Rapids: Baker Academic, 2016.
Krekcir, R. (lead researcher). *Statistics on Pastors: 2016 Update*. Francis A. Shaeffer Institute of Church Leadership Development (FSICLD), 2016. Accessed 20 May 2018. http://files.stablerack.com/webfiles/71795/pastorsstatWP2016.pdf.
Kristjánsson, K. *Aristotelian Character Education*. New York: Routledge, 2015.
———. "Ten Myths about Character, Virtue and Virtue Education – Plus Three Well-Founded Misgivings." *British Journal of Educational Studies* 61, no. 3 (Sept 2013): 269–287.
———. "There Is Something about Aristotle: The Pros and Cons of Aristotelianism in Contemporary Moral Education." *Journal of Philosophy of Education* 48, no. 1 (2014): 48–68.
Kronman, A. *The Lost Lawyer*. Cambridge, MA: Harvard University Press, 1995.
Küng, H. *A Global Ethic for Global Politics and Economics*. New York: Oxford University Press, 1998.
Lagrange, R. *Reality, a Synthesis of Thomistic Thought*. Ex Fontibus Co, 2015.
Larson, C., and B. Martin. "An Examination of the Effectiveness of a Collegiate Character Education Program." *Journal of College and Character* 6, no. 6 (2005): 1–17.
Lausanne Movement. "The Cape Town Commitment." 2010. https://www.lausanne.org/content/ctc/ctcommitment.
Leclerc, J. *The Love of Learning and the Desire for God*. New York: Fordham University Press, 1961.
Lee, C., and M. Taylor. "Moral Education Trends over 40 Years." *Journal of Moral Education* 42, no. 4 (2013): 399–429.
Lee, C., et al. "E-character Education among Digital Natives: Focusing on Character Exemplars." *Computers and Education* 67 (2013): 58–68.
Lee, J. "Moral and Character Education in Korea." In *Handbook of Moral and Character Education*, edited by L. Nucci, 326–343. New York: Routledge, 2014.
Lewis, C. S. *The Abolition of Man*. San Francisco: HarperOne, 2001.
———. *Mere Christianity*. Samizdat, public domain, 2014. Accessed 13 March 2019. http://www.samizdat.qc.ca/vc/pdfs/MereChristianity_CSL.pdf.
———. *That Hideous Strength*. London: Pan Books, 1983.
Lewis, H. *Excellence without a Soul*. New York: Public Affairs, 2006.

Lickona, T. *Educating for Character: How Our Schools Can Teach Respect and Responsibility.* New York: Bantam, 1992.

———. "Religion and Character Education." *Phi Delta Kappan* (Sept 1999): 21–27.

Lickona, T. et al. "Character Education Partnership Eleven Principles." Character Education Partnership, 2007. Accessed 30 May 2019. https://www.character.org/character/.

Lindbeck, G. "Spiritual Formation and Theological Education." *Theological Education*, Supplement 1 (1988): 10–32.

Locke, J. *Some Thoughts Concerning Education*. 1693. Accessed 30 May 2019. https://books.google.it/books?id=OCUCAAAAQAAJ&pg=PA1&source=gbs_toc_r&cad=4#v=onepage&q=habit&f=false; also Spark Notes, accessed 3 July 2018. http://www.sparknotes.com/philosophy/lockethoughts/.

Looms, S. R., and D. P. Spears. *Education for Human Flourishing: A Christian Perspective.* Downers Grove, IL: InterVarsity Press, 2001.

Luo, S. "Confucius's Virtue Politics: Ren as Leadership Virtue." *Asian Philosophy* 22, no. 1 (Feb 2012): 15–35.

Mabey, C. et al. "Having Burned the Straw Man of Christian Spiritual Leadership, What Can We Learn from Jesus about Leading Ethically?" *Journal of Business Ethics* 145, no. 4 (Nov 2017): 757–769. Accessed 4 February 2019. Springerlink.com, https://link.springer.com/article/10.1007/s10551-016-3054-5.

MacDonald, D. "Luke's Antetextuality in Light of Ancient Rhetorical Education." In *Ancient Education and Early Christianity*, edited by M. Hauge and A. Pitts, 155–164. New York: T&T Clark, 2016.

MacIntyre, A. *After Virtue*. London: Duckworth, 2007.

Mahmood, S. *The Politics of Piety*. Princeton: Princeton University Press, 2011.

Mahn, J. "Kierkegaard after Hauerwas." *Theology Today* 64 (2007): 172–185.

Marcia, H. "Moral Character." In *The Stanford Encyclopedia of Philosophy*, edited by Edward N. Zalta. Fall 2016 ed. Accessed 31 January 2018. https://plato.stanford.edu/archives/fall2016/entries/moral-character/.

Marenbon, P. *The Philosophy of Peter Abelard*. Cambridge: Cambridge University Press, 1997.

Maskell, D., and I. Robinson. *The New Idea of the University*. Thorverton: Imprint Academic, 2002.

Matook, S., and B. Butler. "Social Media and Relationships." *The Encyclopedia of Digital Communication and* Society, First Edition, edited by R. Mansell and H. Peng, 1–12. Hoboken, NJ: Wiley-Blackwell, 2015. Accessed 11 April 2017. https://www.researchgate.net/publication/263325419_Social_Media_and_Relationships.

May, M., and W. Brown. *The Education of American Ministers*. New York: Institute of Social and Religious Research, 1934.

McClaren, B. *A New Kind of Christian*. New York: Harper Collins, 2019.

McClellan, E. *Moral Education in America: Schools and the Shaping of Character from Colonial Times to the Present*. New York: Teachers College Press, 1999.

McKnight, S. "Five Streams of the Emerging Church." *Christianity Today* 51, no. 2 (2007): 36–39.

———. "The Ironic Faith of Emergents." *Christianity Today* 52, no. 9 (2008): 62–63.

Meye, R. "Theological Education As Character Formation." *Theological Education*, Supplement 1 (1988): 96–126.

Moses, S. "Keeping the Heart: Natural Affection in Joseph Butler's Approach to Virtue." *Journal of Religious Ethics* 37, no. 4 (2009): 613–629.

Mouw, R. *The Challenges of Cultural Discipleship*. Grand Rapids: Eerdmans, 2011.

Mouw, R., and R. Lovin. "Public Character in Action: Patterns and Possibilities." *Theological Education* 38, no. 1 (2001): v–xi.

Nettleship, R. L. *The Theory of Education in the Republic of Plato*. Honolulu: University Press of the Pacific, 1906.

Neuhaus, R. J. *Theological Education and Moral Formation*. Grand Rapids: Eerdmans, 1992.

Newman, J. H. *The Idea of a University*. New York: Longman Green, 1899.

Nichols, R. "A Sense of Shame among the Virtues." *Journal of Moral Education* 45, no. 2 (2016): 166–178.

Niebuhr, R. *The Purpose of the Church and Its Ministry: Reflections on the Aims of Theological Education*. New York: Harper & Row, 1977.

Nmah, P. E. "Theological Education and Character Formation in Nigerian Christianity: A Reflection." *African Research Review* 7, no. 1, serial no. 28 (Jan 2013): 34–46.

Nucci, L., et al. *Handbook of Moral and Character Education*. New York: Routledge, 2014.

O'Brien, P. *The Epistle to the Philippians: A Commentary on the Greek Text*. New International Greek Testament Commentary. Grand Rapids: Eerdmans, 1991.

O'Connell, T. *Making Disciples: A Handbook of Christian Moral Formation*. New York: Crossroads, 1988.

Ogden, G. *Discipleship Essentials*. Downers Grove, IL: InterVarsity Press, 2007.

O'Sullivan, W. M. "Henry Nutcombe Oxenham: Enfant Terrible of the Liberal Catholic Movement in Mid-Victorian England." *Catholic Historical Review* 82, no. 4 (Oct 1996): 637–660.

Ott, B. "Transforming the Habitus: Insights from Martin Buber on Faith-Based Character Formation." *Mennonite Quarterly Review* (April 2019): 193–212.

———. *Understanding and Developing Theological Education*. Carlisle: Langham Global Library, 2016.

Oxenham, H. "Catholic Education." *The Rambler* 3. London: Burns & Lambert, 1860.

Oxenham, M. *Higher Education in Liquid Modernity*. New York: Routledge, 2012.

Pansters, K. *Franciscan Virtue*. Leiden: Brill Academic, 2012.

Pavela, G. "A Renewed Focus on Student Ethical Development." *Synthesis: Law and Policy in Higher Education* 10, no. 3 (Winter 1999): 733–752.

Pazdan, M. "Wisdom Communities: Models for Christian Formation and Pedagogy." *Theological Education* 34, no. 2 (Spring 1998): 25–30.

Peters, R. S. "Moral Education and the Psychology of Character." *Philosophy* 37, no. 139 (Jan 1962): 37–56.

Plato. *Meno*. Translated by B. Jowett. Project Gutenberg. Accessed 13 February 2018. http://www.gutenberg.org/files/1643/1643-h/1643-h.htm.

———. *The Republic*. In *The Works of Plato and Aristotle: 35 Works*. Edited by B. Jowett. C&C Web Press, 2009. Ebook.

Porter, J. *The Recovery of Virtue: The Relevance of Aquinas for Christian Ethics*. Louisville: Westminster/John Knox, 1990.

Pritchard, I. "Character Education: Research Prospects and Problems." *American Journal of Education* 96, no. 4 (Aug 1988): 469–495.

Proctor, R. E. *Defining the Humanities*. 2nd ed. Bloomington: Indiana University Press, 1998.

Racelis, A. "Developing a Virtue Ethics Scale: Exploratory Survey of Philippine Managers." *Asian Journal of Business and Accounting* 6, no. 1 (2013): 15–37.

Rawls, J. *A Theory of Justice*. Cambridge, MA: Harvard University Press, 1999.

Readings, B. *The University in Ruins*. Cambridge, MA: Harvard University Press, 1996.

Robinson, E., et al. "Humanistic Education to Character Education." *Journal of Humanistic Counselling, Education and Development* 39, no. 1 (2000): 21–26.

Roso, C. "Culture and Character Education in a Jewish Day School." *Journal of Research on Christian Education* 22 (2013): 30–51.

Rozko, J. R. "The Missiological Future of Theological Education: A Whitepaper." A Joint Venture of 3DM and The Order of Mission, 2102. Accessed 10 May 2018. https://www.academia.edu/4148055/The_Missiological_Future_of_Theological_Education.

Rüegg, Walter, ed. *A History of the University in Europe*. Vol. 1, *Universities in the Middle Ages*. Cambridge: Cambridge University Press, 1996.

The Sacred Congregation for Catholic Education. "The Gift of the Priestly Vocation (*Ratio Fundamentalis Institutionis Sacerdotalis*)." Osservatore Romano, Vatican City, 2016. Accessed 10 August 2018. http://www.clerus.va/content/dam/clerus/Ratio%20Fundamentalis/The%20Gift%20of%20the%20Priestly%20Vocation.pdf.

Sanderse, W. *Character Education*. Delft: Eburon, 2012.

Schuller, D., M. Strommen, and M. Brekke. *Ministry in America*. San Francisco: Harper & Row, 1980.

Seaman, B. *Binge: What Your College Student Won't Tell You*. Hoboken, NJ: John Wiley & Sons, 2005.

Seneca. *Moral Letters to Lucilius*. Wikisource. Accessed 12 March 2018. https://en.wikisource.org/wiki/Moral_letters_to_Lucilius.

Shaw, P. *Transforming Theological Education*. Carlisle: Langham Global Library, 2014.

Sheldrake, P. *A Brief History of Spirituality*. Oxford: Blackwell, 2007.

Slote, M. "Virtue Ethics." In *The Blackwell Guide to Ethical Theory*, edited by H. LaFollette and I. Persson, 325–347. Oxford: Blackwell, 2000.

Smilie, K. "Humanitarian and Humanistic Ideals." *Journal of Thought* (Summer 2012): 63–84.
Smith, M. *Tolkien's Ordinary Virtues*. Downers Grove: InterVarsity Press, 2002.
Soloveitchik, B. *The Lonely Man of Faith*. New York: Doubleday, 2006.
Sommers, C., and F. Sommers. *Vice and Virtue in Everyday Life*. Toronto: Nelson, 2004.
Spears, O., and S. Loomis. *Education for Human Flourishing*. Downers Grove: IVP Academic, 2009.
Stanislas, G. M. *The Education of Character*. [n.p.]: HardPress, 1914.
Steibel, S. "Christian Education and Spiritual Formation: One and the Same?" *Christian Education Journal* 7, no. 2, Series 3 (2010): 340–355.
Stern, A. "Becoming a Mensch: Timeless Talmudic Ethics for Everyone." *Psychiatric Times* 28, no. 8 (Aug 2011). Accessed 6 November 2018. http://www.psychiatrictimes.com/articles/becoming-mensch-timeless-talmudic-ethics-everyone.
Stückelberger, C. "Integrity: The Virtue of Virtues." In *Global Ethics for Leadership*, edited by C. Stückelberger, W. Fust, and O. Ike, 311–328. Geneva: Globalethics.net, 2016.
Stückelberger, C., W. Fust and O. Ike, eds. *Global Ethics for Leadership: Values and Virtues for Life*. Geneva: Globalethics.net, 2016.
Tarcov, N. *Locke's Education for Liberty*. Chicago: University of Chicago Press, 1984.
Taylor, B. *Leaving Church*. Norwich: Canterbury Press, 2006.
Taylor, C. "The Location of Theological Schools." *Theological Education* 1, no. 2 (Winter 1965): 104–109.
———. "Sources of Renewal." *Theological Education* (Winter 1967): 319–325.
Tenelshof, J. "Encouraging the Character Formation of Future Christian Leaders." *Journal of the Evangelical Theological Society* 42, no. 1 (1997): 77–90.
Timpe, K., and C. Boyd. *Virtues and Their Vices*. Oxford: Oxford University Press, 2014.
Tjeltveit, A. "Virtues (Natural and Theological) Moral Selfhood, Goodness and God." Review of A. Dell'Olio, "Foundations of Moral Selfhood: Aquinas on Divine Goodness and the Connection of the Virtues." *Journal of Psychology and Theology* 33, no. 1 (2005): 72–75.
To, S., S. Yang and C. Helwig. "Democratic Moral Education in China." In *Handbook of Moral and Character Education*, edited by L. Nucci. New York: Routledge, 2014.
de Tocqueville, A. *Democracy in America*. 1840. Translated by H. Reeve. Accessed 16 February 2019. http://seas3.elte.hu/coursematerial/LojkoMiklos/Alexis-de-Tocqueville-Democracy-in-America.pdf.
Tracy, D. "Can Virtue Be Taught? Education, Character and the Soul." *Theological Education*, Supplement 1 (1988): 33–52.
Treier, D. *Virtue and the Voice of God*. Grand Rapids: Eerdmans, 2006.
Trombino, Mario. *La Filosofia Greca Arcaica e Classica*. Bologna: Poseidonia, 1997.

Tuschling, A., and C. Engemann. "From Education to Lifelong Learning: The Emerging Regime of Learning in the European Union." *Educational Philosophy and Theory* 38, no. 4 (2006): 451–469.
Vasalou, S. "Educating Virtue As a Mastery of Language." *Journal of Ethics* 16, no. 1 (2012): 67–87.
Vauclair, C., M. Wilson and R. Fischer. "Cultural Conceptions of Morality: Examining Laypeople's Associations of Moral Character." *Journal of Moral Education* 43, no. 1 (2014): 54–74.
Volf, M., and M. Croasmun. *For the Life of the World: Theology That Makes a Difference*. Grand Rapids, MI: Brazos Press, 2019.
Walker, D., M. Roberts, and K. Kristjánsson. "Towards a New Era of Character Education in Theory and in Practice." *Educational Review* 67, no. 1 (2015): 79–96.
Walker, G., et al. *The Formation of Scholars*. San Francisco: Josey Bass for the Carnegie Foundation, 2008. Kindle.
Ward, B. *The Sayings of the Desert Fathers*. Kalamazoo: Cistercian Publications, 1975.
Warfield, B. "The Religious Life of Theological Students." *The Master's Seminary Journal* 6, no. 2 (Fall 1995): 181–195.
Warren, H. "The Shift from Character to Personality in Mainline Protestant through 1935–1945." *Church History* 67, no. 3 (Sept 1998): 537–555.
Wenar, Leif. "John Rawls." *The Stanford Encyclopedia of Philosophy*, Spring 2017 Edition. Edited by Edward N. Zalta. https://plato.stanford.edu/archives/spr2017/entries/rawls/.
West-Burnham, J. "Understanding Quality." In *The Principles and Practices of Educational Leadership*, edited by T. Bush and L. Bell, 313–324. London: Paul Chapman, 2002/2005.
Whitcomb, D., et al. "Intellectual Humility." *Philosophy and Phenomenological Research* 94, no. 3 (2017). Accessed 13 August 2018. http://digitalcommons.lmu.edu/cgi/viewcontent.cgi?article=1030&context=phil_fac.
White, M., and A. Murray, eds. *Evidence-Based Approaches in Positive Education*. Dordrecht: Springer, 2015.
Wolterstorff, N. *Educating for Life*. Grand Rapids: Baker Academic, 2002.
———. *Educating for Responsible Action*. Cambridge, MA: Eerdmans, 1980.
———. *Educating for Shalom: Essays on Christian Higher Education*. Cambridge, MA: Eerdmans, 2004. Kindle.
Wren, T. C. "Philosophical Moorings." In *Handbook of Moral and Character Education*, edited by L. Nucci, 11–29. New York: Routledge, 2014.
Wright, N. T. *After You Believe*. New York: Harper Collins, 2010.
Wright, P. H. "Self-Referent Motivation and the Intrinsic Quality of Friendship." *Journal of Social and Personal Relationships* 1, no. 1 (1985): 115–130.
Yaran, C. *Understanding Islam*. Edinburgh: Dunedin Academic Press, 2007.

Websites

The Character Project (Wake Forest University): http://www.thecharacterproject.com/about.php

Educating for Intellectual Virtues (Loyola Marymount University Los Angeles): http://intellectualvirtues.org/

Happiness and Well-Being (University of St Louis): http://www.happinessandwellbeing.org

Institute for the Study of Human Flourishing (University of Oklahoma): http://www.ou.edu/flourish

International Society for MacIntyrean Enquiry: http://www.macintyreanenquiry.org/

Jubilee Centre for Character and Virtues (University of Birmingham): http://www.birmingham.ac.uk/research/activity/education/jubilee-centre/index.aspx

Miroslav Volf's work on virtues can be seen in the Yale Center for Faith and Culture: https://faith.yale.edu

The Philosophy and Theology of Intellectual Humility (St Louis University): http://humility.slu.edu/

The Self, Motivation and Virtue Project (Marquette University): http://smvproject.com/

The Virtue Blog (University of Chicago): http://thevirtueblog.com/2015/10/29/the-generative-adult/

The Virtues Project™ (a global grassroots initiative to inspire the practice of virtues in everyday life, sparking a global revolution of kindness, justice, and integrity in more than 100 countries): https://virtuesproject.com

Blog

Participate in Marvin Oxenham's blog on this book, at www.charactereducation.blog.

Index

A

academic 9, 15, 21, 30, 36, 50, 59, 86, 95, 132–134, 228, 238, 247, 276, 299, 309, 323

accreditation xv, 9, 46, 49, 52, 91, 133, 137, 138, 141, 296, 357, 363–369, 372

Ambrose 114, 190, 222

andragogy 337

Aquinas 32, 54, 80, 118, 166, 169, 186, 217, 227, 228, 273, 274, 285, 338

arête 26, 63, 173, 188, 197, 199, 203–206, 210, 214, 227, 263, 270, 375

Aristotle 25, 32, 69, 70, 71, 78, 81, 102–111, 113–128, 142, 144, 146, 148, 152, 163, 185–188, 196, 199, 201, 205, 210–212, 214, 218, 224, 227, 241, 247, 248, 257, 262, 263, 266, 273, 274, 280, 289, 301, 302, 308, 338, 339, 341

art 50, 58, 68, 167, 189, 217–219, 274, 276, 297, 312, 323, 328, 368

assessment 351

C

Cassian 221, 284

Catholic 21, 23, 31, 46, 85, 133, 230, 246, 287

Certification 363, 369

change 10, 12, 19, 39, 43, 44, 47, 53, 87, 131, 132, 142, 145, 254, 256, 263, 284, 309, 310, 367, 369

church 10, 11, 18, 22, 45, 57, 58, 75, 83, 84, 87–89, 91– 99, 132–134, 138, 165, 190, 198, 200, 211, 222, 229, 314

Church of England 46

Cicero 71, 189–192, 205, 219, 223, 227, 241

civility 59, 72, 139, 197, 202, 204, 211, 272, 284, 291, 308

Comenius 242, 263–265

community 10, 11, 17, 50, 51, 54, 65, 68, 74, 84, 85, 93, 94, 97, 105, 110, 115, 117, 118, 124, 126, 133, 136, 138, 165, 178, 182, 188, 202, 225, 248, 249, 264, 267, 276, 281, 288, 297, 299, 301–304, 306–310, 315, 316, 321, 322, 355

compassion 25, 60, 62, 78, 96, 124, 126, 194–199, 211, 225, 274, 275, 280, 286, 287, 333

Confucius 123, 124, 170, 171, 175, 263

constancy 192, 255, 284, 285, 342

courage 62, 78, 107, 118, 126, 156, 172, 176, 181, 189, 194, 195, 197, 200, 204, 220, 238, 270, 271, 274, 275, 280, 282, 286, 298, 309, 335

curriculum 28, 40, 51, 124, 133, 136, 203, 266, 267, 297, 299, 317, 318, 321, 324, 331, 332

D

Democracy 74

design 15, 38, 45, 122, 133, 163, 201, 215, 252, 267, 268, 312, 317, 318, 325, 327, 329, 331–333, 367

Dewey 54, 116, 128, 153, 235, 248, 338

diligence 25, 120, 194, 195, 197, 202, 204, 211, 225, 265, 274, 289, 290, 314, 345

discipleship 11, 18, 28, 31–33, 45, 51, 75–81, 88, 92, 145, 200, 234, 270
discipline 80, 200, 219, 234, 237, 265, 275, 282, 297, 308, 310, 312, 322, 340

E
emotions 86, 115, 116, 127, 149, 153, 178, 219, 261, 273, 327, 330, 331, 333, 340, 353
evangelical 21
extra-curricular 13, 27, 29, 42, 45, 47, 51, 132, 245, 266, 296, 297, 299, 358, 365

F
faith 25, 63, 74, 78, 97, 181, 195, 197, 202, 205, 211, 226, 230, 231, 273, 274, 276, 287, 343, 372
faith communities 10
Farley 7, 45, 186, 338
friendship 31, 53, 97, 172, 225, 286–288, 301, 308, 312, 313, 334

G
global 3, 38, 42, 43, 93, 115, 121, 123, 128, 132, 135, 156, 170, 186, 233, 239, 366
goodness 13, 80, 118, 170, 181, 194, 196, 199, 215, 226, 228, 231, 243, 272, 289, 290, 308

H
habituation 109, 322–324, 338–340, 343
happiness 17, 60, 70, 103, 104, 113, 118, 119, 168, 189, 190, 196, 199, 210, 218, 224, 227, 237, 248, 289, 318, 320, 352, 355, 356
Hauerwas 44, 118, 145, 158, 161, 166, 244, 249

hope 25, 42, 53, 127, 162, 197, 210, 211, 215, 267, 273–275, 286, 288, 293
humility xv, 10, 25, 60, 62, 72, 78, 79, 97, 108, 113, 119, 126, 170, 172, 177, 181, 194, 195, 197, 198, 201, 202, 211, 220, 225, 270, 274, 275, 280, 283, 284, 290, 305, 306, 309, 335, 352, 354

I
intellectual virtues 25, 45, 72, 78, 106, 116, 145, 188, 245, 253, 263, 264, 274–276, 290, 309, 321, 323, 328, 335, 354, 357, 367
Islam 123, 125, 126

J
justice 25, 59, 60, 64, 68, 69, 72, 87, 107, 126, 156, 172, 189, 192, 194, 195, 197, 199, 211, 218, 265, 270, 273–275, 281, 282, 286, 291, 298, 310, 348

L
Lausanne 57
liberalism 71–73, 146
love 25, 59, 63, 72, 78, 96, 119, 124, 170, 171, 194, 195, 197, 198, 202, 204, 211, 218, 220, 224, 225, 265, 273–275, 282, 285, 286, 297, 312

M
MacIntyre 44, 101, 104, 157, 249
magnanimity 63, 78, 195, 197, 204, 211, 272, 290, 314
ministry 11, 12, 16, 18, 28, 49, 51, 92–94, 96, 97, 238
moral education 36, 41, 44, 54, 70, 71, 102, 111, 114, 125, 128, 132, 136, 143, 144, 146, 152, 181, 198, 211, 230, 234, 241, 242, 244, 245, 248, 265, 357

moral universalism 151, 154, 156
moral virtues 25, 72, 106, 116, 152, 188, 263, 273, 274, 275, 321

O
online 137, 172, 311, 312, 313, 334, 335
Orthodox 8, 21, 83, 87

P
paideia 45, 185, 186–189, 194, 257, 302
phronesis 104, 106–109, 117, 148, 149, 157, 173, 199, 200, 257, 261, 280, 281, 310, 323, 330, 340, 342, 346, 352, 355
Plato 59, 67, 81, 91, 116, 142, 185–188, 205, 211, 212, 263, 301, 302, 304, 310
Protestant 21, 47, 85, 133, 229, 234, 235, 237, 246
prudence 25, 87, 107, 189, 195–198, 200, 225, 270, 273–276, 280, 281, 283, 287, 290, 330, 348, 352
public virtues 45, 87, 205, 245, 320, 321

R
recapitulation 81, 214
rules 23, 24, 49, 52, 59, 80, 94, 106, 108, 115, 128, 182, 196, 281, 283, 297, 304, 307, 312

S
Scripture 10, 88, 151, 162, 163, 164, 176, 177, 223, 246, 272, 299, 321
Seneca 81, 189–192, 196, 204, 205, 285, 310
Situationism 152
society 11, 18, 39, 40, 48, 54, 58–60, 63, 64, 70, 71, 73, 97, 124, 125, 127, 132, 134, 136, 142, 147, 149, 158, 171, 241, 243, 245, 248, 253, 255, 284
spiritual formation 15, 27–34, 44, 47, 50, 132, 133, 135, 223, 228, 367

T
temperance 25, 62, 78, 87, 99, 189, 195, 197, 198, 204, 272–275, 283, 348
theological virtues 68, 69, 87, 178, 218, 226–228, 285, 286, 358
theology 10, 363
truthfulness 79, 126, 178, 192, 194, 195, 197, 198, 202, 248, 270, 280, 281, 286, 310

U
university 21, 35, 37–42, 47, 49, 53, 62, 131, 136, 228, 238, 241, 243, 245, 253, 266, 269, 276, 369, 372

W
Western 121, 122, 170, 183, 185, 194, 229, 230, 275

ICETE is a global community, sponsored by nine regional networks of theological schools, to enable international interaction and collaboration among all those engaged in strengthening and developing evangelical theological education and Christian leadership development worldwide.

The purpose of ICETE is:
1. To promote the enhancement of evangelical theological education worldwide.
2. To serve as a forum for interaction, partnership and collaboration among those involved in evangelical theological education and leadership development, for mutual assistance, stimulation and enrichment.
3. To provide networking and support services for regional associations of evangelical theological schools worldwide.
4. To facilitate among these bodies the advancement of their services to evangelical theological education within their regions.

Sponsoring associations include:

Africa: Association for Christian Theological Education in Africa (ACTEA)

Asia: Asia Theological Association (ATA)

Caribbean: Caribbean Evangelical Theological Association (CETA)

Europe: European Evangelical Accrediting Association (EEAA)

Euro-Asia: Euro-Asian Accrediting Association (E-AAA)

Latin America: Association for Evangelical Theological Education in Latin America (AETAL)

Middle East and North Africa: Middle East Association for Theological Education (MEATE)

North America: Association for Biblical Higher Education (ABHE)

South Pacific: South Pacific Association of Evangelical Colleges (SPAEC)

www.icete-edu.org

Langham Literature and its imprints are a ministry of Langham Partnership.

Langham Partnership is a global fellowship working in pursuit of the vision God entrusted to its founder John Stott –

> *to facilitate the growth of the church in maturity and Christ-likeness through raising the standards of biblical preaching and teaching.*

Our vision is to see churches in the majority world equipped for mission and growing to maturity in Christ through the ministry of pastors and leaders who believe, teach and live by the Word of God.

Our mission is to strengthen the ministry of the Word of God through:
- nurturing national movements for biblical preaching
- fostering the creation and distribution of evangelical literature
- enhancing evangelical theological education

especially in countries where churches are under-resourced.

Our ministry

Langham Preaching partners with national leaders to nurture indigenous biblical preaching movements for pastors and lay preachers all around the world. With the support of a team of trainers from many countries, a multi-level programme of seminars provides practical training, and is followed by a programme for training local facilitators. Local preachers' groups and national and regional networks ensure continuity and ongoing development, seeking to build vigorous movements committed to Bible exposition.

Langham Literature provides majority world preachers, scholars and seminary libraries with evangelical books and electronic resources through publishing and distribution, grants and discounts. The programme also fosters the creation of indigenous evangelical books in many languages, through writer's grants, strengthening local evangelical publishing houses, and investment in major regional literature projects, such as one volume Bible commentaries like *The Africa Bible Commentary* and *The South Asia Bible Commentary*.

Langham Scholars provides financial support for evangelical doctoral students from the majority world so that, when they return home, they may train pastors and other Christian leaders with sound, biblical and theological teaching. This programme equips those who equip others. Langham Scholars also works in partnership with majority world seminaries in strengthening evangelical theological education. A growing number of Langham Scholars study in high quality doctoral programmes in the majority world itself. As well as teaching the next generation of pastors, graduated Langham Scholars exercise significant influence through their writing and leadership.

To learn more about Langham Partnership and the work we do visit **langham.org**

www.ingramcontent.com/pod-product-compliance
Lightning Source LLC
Chambersburg PA
CBHW052042220426
43663CB00012B/2413